D1478520

GEOGRAPHIC PROFILING

GEOGRAPHIC PROFILING

D. Kim Rossmo

CRC Press

Boca Raton   London   New York   Washington, D.C.

Library of Congress Cataloging-in-Publication Data

Rossmo, D. Kim
    Geographic profiling/ D. Kim Rossmo
         p. cm.
    Includes bibliographical references and index.
    ISBN 0-8493-8129-0
    1. Criminal psychology. 2. Environmental psychology. 3. Criminal behavior, Prediction of. 4.
Behavioral assessment. 5. Applied human geography. 6. Crime analysis. I. Title.
    HV6080.R575 1999
    364.3--dc21

                                      99-051414
                                            CIP

Foreword

Criminology Comes of Age

Scientific criminology has its roots in crime mapping. The first great systematic studies of crime were cartographic exercises made possible by record-keeping systems created to track criminal convictions in France and England during the early part of the 19th century. Compared with maps of demographic, economic, and social data, crime maps established some of the great and enduring facts of the science: crime in general is associated with the distributions of youth, males, the poor, and of the poorly educated. Maps of crime patterns in major American cities during the early 20th century reconfirmed the 19th century findings, and added the observation that crimes and criminals' residences cluster in places predicted by urban form and transportation network geometry and that those places exhibited little local social organisation.

These broad criminological findings resulted in broad policy prescriptions for crime reduction. The observations on the correlation of youth and crime led to special handling for youthful criminals: juvenile courts, reduced punishments, and special school programs. The observed correlation between crime and males led to special programs aimed at males: organised sports programs, industrial job training, and counselling. Most importantly, the correlation between crime and poverty resulted in programs aimed at the elimination of poverty and in social interventions aimed at improving the organisation of impoverished neighbourhoods. Such programs were especially prominent and especially well funded in the 1960s and 1970s, led by the American "War on Poverty" programs which — although desirable in their own right — were funded on the promise that crime would be reduced.

Crime was *not* reduced. Both violent and property crime rates skyrocketed. Crime rates tripled between 1960 and 1980 in both the U.S. and Canada; violent crime rates quintupled over the same period in England and Wales. At the same time, criminology provided little that proved useful to law enforcement.

iii

What went wrong? Why was the early promise of crime mapping so misleading? Why is this book an important corrective?

Rules That Commute

Maps are important analytic tools. They can display enormous amounts of information in readily understandable form, but they can also be misleading: they are often used to show average areal tendencies at the cost of obscuring important variations within areal units. It becomes tempting to assume that the average areal description also describes all the individual locations within the area.

The mapping trap is but one part of the broader problem of ascribing aggregate average characteristics to individuals: the ecological fallacy. For instance, if a crime map shows that crime rates are high in a poor neighbourhood, two mistaken conclusions are sometimes drawn. The first is that most of the people in the neighbourhood are criminals. The second is that people are criminal because they are poor. In fact, studies of individuals demonstrate that most poor people are honest, even in high crime neighbourhoods. Studies of individual criminals show that adoption of a criminal lifestyle leads to poverty at least as often as poverty tempts people into crime.

Criminology as a science has provided little to the professional world of crime control because it has often been seduced by the ecological fallacy. Crime control, and especially law enforcement, requires prescriptions that can help resolve individual as well as aggregate situations. It needs rules that commute.

By that, I mean statements of relationships that can be used to predict both directions across a function. An elementary equation from beginning physics is an example: $F = mv$. Force equals mass times velocity. This means that the force with which a bullet hits a target can be calculated from its mass and its velocity. Because the relationship commutes, the equation could be algebraically manipulated to permit calculation of a bullet's velocity from its mass and the force with which it hit, or to calculate its mass from the force with which it hit and the velocity at which it was moving when it hit.

Many of the findings of criminology do not commute. For instance, while most criminals live in poor neighbourhoods, most poor people are not criminal. While most burglars are youthful, most youths do not commit burglaries. While most serious child abusers were themselves abused as children, most abused children do not become child abusers. As a result, criminology has historically provided little that is helpful to those charged with solving crimes, or predicting an offender's future dangerousness, or reducing fear in the community.

In this book, Kim Rossmo presents an elegant demonstration of a new set of criminological observations and rules that *do* commute.

Environmental Criminology and the Path to Crime Control

Environmental criminology studies criminal events as products of the convergence of potential offenders with potential targets at specific points in space-time under specific sets of limiting and facilitating conditions. Studies in this field have focused on spatial patterns in offender and target movement against the backdrop of broader social routines. They have generally demonstrated that offenders, like other people, move around in predictable and routine ways. The journey to crime is similar to and subject to the same constraints as the journey to work or the shopping trip. In this sense, at least, most criminals are like everybody else.

Environmental criminologists have largely been interested in crime prevention. Their work has focused on predicting those places that are likely to be vulnerable to crime because of the way they fit into people's routine activities and travel patterns. Situational prevention techniques prevent crimes by preventing the convergence of offenders and targets in vulnerable locations without simply displacing them to other places.

In this book, Kim Rossmo demonstrates that the models derived from environmental criminology, and now taken as commonplace in the crime prevention field, in fact commute. Models that predict where criminals are likely to commit their crimes, based on knowledge about their normal main activity nodes, can be usefully reversed to aid criminal investigations. The locations of criminal events constitute spatial traces of offenders' activity patterns. Analysed in light of journey to crime models, a set of linked crime locations can point investigators to the offender's main activity nodes and provide a useful tool for prioritising investigative leads. Criminology finally comes of age: it provides rules that are useful to all phases of crime control.

Paul J. Brantingham
Professor of Criminology
Simon Fraser University
Burnaby, British Columbia, Canada

Preface

My own interest in the area of geographic profiling stems from two sources. First, as a new police officer assigned to Vancouver's Skid Road, I could not help but notice the relevance of environmental criminology, particularly the ideas of Professors Paul and Patricia Brantingham from Simon Fraser University. The street has its hot spots, patterns, and rhythms — drug dealers handle their markets; prostitutes work their favourite corners; even fleeing criminals follow predictable patterns.

Second, as a police veteran of 20 years, I find the reasons for most crimes, if seen from the perspective of the offender, are not difficult to understand. Serial violent crime, however, is on the extreme fringe of human behaviour, a ritual of violence that defies simple explanation. Comprehending these individuals and their actions, even if only in some small measure, was a daunting challenge.

The research and development of geographic profiling was thus undertaken in an effort to integrate the academic with the practical, the scholastic with the professional. I hoped that by combining science and strategy, experiment and experience, something useful would be produced for the worlds of both the ivory tower and the street.

The Author

D. Kim Rossmo is the Detective Inspector in charge of the Vancouver Police Department's Geographic Profiling Section. Over the course of his 20-year policing career he has worked assignments in organised crime intelligence, emergency response, patrol, crime prevention, and community liaison. He holds a Ph.D. in criminology and has researched and published in the areas of policing, offender profiling, and environmental criminology. He is an Adjunct Professor at Simon Fraser University, sits on the editorial board for the international journal *Homicide Studies*, and is a member of the American Society of Criminology.

Dr. Rossmo is the Vice President of the Canadian Association of Violent Crime Analysts, a member of the International Association of Chiefs of Police Investigative Operations Advisory Committee, and a former Executive Vice President of the Canadian Police Association. In 1998 he was made a Fellow of the Western Society of Criminology, and in 1999 accredited as one of British Columbia's top innovators and granted an Outstanding Alumni of the Year Award from Simon Fraser University for his work in developing geographic profiling.

His present duties include assisting police agencies in Canada, the U.S., Britain, and Europe, including the Royal Canadian Mounted Police, the Federal Bureau of Investigation, and Scotland Yard, in cases of serial murder, rape, bombing, and arson. He has been recognized as an expert witness in the geography of crime and the hunting patterns of serial offenders. Dr. Rossmo is currently involved in several research, writing, and development projects.

Acknowledgments

Like much research, this book is the product of many people in addition to the author. I would like to thank the following for their support and guidance during the research that led to the development of geographic profiling: Professor Paul Brantingham, Professor Patricia Brantingham, Professor John Lowman, and Professor Tom Calvert, Simon Fraser University; Professor John Yuille, University of British Columbia; and Professor Ronald Clarke, Rutgers University.

I would also like to acknowledge the encouragement and assistance of the following researchers and authors: Professor Eric Hickey, California State University; Professor Steven Egger, Sangamon State University; Professor James LeBeau, Southern Illinois University; Professor George Rengert, Temple University; Jonathan Alston, Simon Fraser University; Anne Davies, London Metropolitan Police; and Doctor Janet Jackson, The Netherlands Institute for the Study of Criminality and Law Enforcement.

As an investigative technique, geographic profiling owes a debt to the following: Chief Constable Ray Canuel, Chief Constable Bruce Chambers, Deputy Chief Constable Brian McGuinness, Deputy Chief Constable Ken Higgins, Inspector Ken Doern, Inspector John Eldridge, and Cheryllynne Drabinsky, Vancouver Police Department; Staff Sergeant Doug MacKay-Dunn, Vancouver Integrated Intelligence Unit; Assistant Commissioner Joop Plomp, Inspector Ron MacKay, Inspector Glenn Woods, Staff Sergeant Keith Davidson, and Corporal Scot Filer, Royal Canadian Mounted Police; Detective Inspector Kate Lines and Detective Sergeant Brad Moore, Ontario Provincial Police; Detective Chief Inspector Adrian Hogg and Detective Sergeant Neil Trainor, National Crime Faculty; Supervisory Special Agent James A. Wright, Supervisory Special Agent Gregg O. McCrary, and Dr. Roland Reboussin, Federal Bureau of Investigation; Sergeant John House, Royal Newfoundland Constabulary; Corporal Guy Pollock, Coordinated Law Enforcement Unit Intelligence Section; Lieutenant Debra Davidoski, Milwaukee Police Department; Corporal Steve Hess, Justice Institute of British Columbia; Diane Bell, British Columbia Federation of Police Officers; and all the police investigators who were willing to try geographic profiling during its early days.

Supervisory Special Agent Judson Ray, Federal Bureau of Investigation, facilitated the initial data collection from the National Center for the Analysis of Violent Crime. Janice Campbell-Barnett, Kim Bufton, Rebecca Wall, Laurie Henderson, Rose Chow, Kevin Bonnycastle, Michelle Jenion, Dorothy Lott, and Kellie Smith all supplied invaluable research assistance. Jay Clarke, Michael Slade, Chief Superintendent Robert DeClercq, and Special X helped spread the word. And the students from both my *Phenomenon of Serial Murder* and *Forensic Behavioural Science* classes more than adequately demonstrated that learning occurs on both sides of the podium.

Rigel was made possible through the vision, business acumen, and programming expertise of Ian Laverty, David Demers, Barry Dalziel, Tim Lochner, Matt Naish, Brian Eng, and Lisa Shields, Environmental Criminology Research, Inc.; and Jennifer Thompson, Facet Decision Systems. Important development funding was provided by the National Research Council of Canada and the Simon Fraser University Industry Liaison Office.

I am indebted to Becky McEldowney and the professional team at CRC Press for making this book happen. Finally, a special thanks to my parents, family, and friends for their constant support and encouragement.

Dedication

Dedicated to those who hunt the predators.

Table of Contents

List of Tables

List of Figures

*From Rossmo, D.K. (1995b). Multivariate spatial profiles as a tool in crime investigation. In C.R. Block, M. Dabdoub, & S. Fregly (Eds.). *Crime analysis through computer mapping* (pp. 65-97). Washington, DC: Police Executive Research Forum. Used with permission.
**From Rossmo, D.K. (1997). Geographic Profiling. In J.L. Jackson, & D.A. Bekerian (Eds.). (1997b). *Offender profiling: Theory, research and practice* (pp. 159-175). Chichester: John Wiley & Sons. Used with permission.

Quotation

It is quite a three-pipe problem.

— Sherlock Holmes, in *The Red-Headed League*,

Sir Arthur Conan Doyle, 1891

Introduction

1

Interview the subjects, what they'll tell you is, the thing that was really appealing to them was the hunt, the hunt and trying to look for the vulnerable victim.

— FBI Special Agent John Douglas; Mind of a Serial Killer, 1992, p. 3

This book is about geographic profiling. It is also about serial crime and violent predators. Human hunters are not common, but when they do strike, the public and the criminal justice system are significantly affected. Beyond the violence and tragedy of the crimes, these offenders generate tremendous fear in the community and demand significant resources from police, courts, and prisons. Most homicides and rapes are solved because there is a connection between the offender and the victim. Such a nexus is lacking in cases of stranger crime, and its investigation involves sifting through hundreds of suspects and thousands of tips. Consequently, police suffer from the problem of information overload. If we wish to enhance the investigative response to this type of random violence, it is important to expand our knowledge of serial predators and their hunting behaviour.

Geographic profiling is an investigative methodology that uses the locations of a connected series of crime to determine the most probable area of offender residence. It is applied in cases of serial murder, rape, arson, robbery, and bombing, though it can be used in single crimes that involve multiple scenes or other significant geographic characteristics. Developed from research conducted at Simon Fraser University's School of Criminology, the methodology is based on a model that describes the criminal hunt. This book examines and discusses the spatial patterns produced by the hunting behaviour and target locations of serial violent criminals. Hunting behaviour refers to victim search and attack processes engaged in by an offender, and target locations are the various geographic sites connected to a crime series. Serial murder, for example, includes victim encounter, attack, murder, and body dump sites. The patterns and methods of offender hunting activity are analyzed from a geography of crime perspective. By establishing these patterns, it is possible to outline, through analyzing the locations of the crimes, the most probable area of offender residence.

The conceptual basis of this relationship is provided by the crime site selection model of Brantingham and Brantingham, who observe that individuals, including criminals, do not move randomly through their environment. The research led to an algorithm for predicting offender residence from crime site geography. The resulting computer system produces jeopardy surfaces — three-dimensional probability surfaces that indicate the most probable area of offender residence. These are displayed through the production of colour isopleth maps that provide a focus for investigative efforts.

Geographic profiling can be used as the basis for several investigative strategies, including suspect and tip prioritization, address-based searches of police record systems, patrol saturation and surveillance, neighbourhood canvasses and searches, DNA screening prioritization, Department of Motor Vehicle searches, postal or zip code prioritization, and information request mail-outs. It is important to stress that geographic profiling does not solve cases, but rather provides a method for managing the large volume of information typically generated in major crime investigations. It should be regarded as one of several tools available to detectives, and is best employed in conjunction with other police methods. Address information is an element of most record systems, and geographic profiling can be applied in a variety of contexts as a powerful decision support tool. Geographic crime patterns are clues that, when properly decoded, can be used to point in the direction of the offender.

For example, in the investigation of a series of over 20 rapes from 1988 to 1996 in St. Louis, Missouri, Detective Mark Kennedy employed both psychological and geographic profiling to prioritize a list of some 90 suspects for DNA testing. In addition to a residential focus, the geoprofile drew attention to the St. Louis State Hospital, and to what appeared to be likely commuting routes used by the offender. When the Southside Rapist was identified through DNA testing subsequent to a burglary arrest, it was found that he moved several times during the crime series. The geoprofile identified his residential area during his most active rape period — one home was in the top 2% (0.4 mi^2), and the other, across the street from the St. Louis State Hospital, in the top 5.6% (1.2 mi^2) of the hunting area.

The knowledge gained through research and experience of how and where criminal predators hunt for victims has both practical and theoretical implications. Geographic profiling is now an investigative support service offered to law enforcement agencies in cases of serious violent crime. It has been used by police departments in North America, Europe, and Australia. An ongoing study of the spatial patterns of criminal offenders is now occurring in several countries.

This book is designed to be a reference work on geographic profiling for both police practitioners and academic researchers. It covers investigative initiatives, crimes, and research studies in Canada, the U.S., and Britain. Its outline follows an order progressing from problem through to solution. Chapter 1 is an introduction. Chapter 2 discusses serial murder and the relevance of geography and distance for child murder and homicide investigation. Research on serial rape and arson is covered in Chapter 3. The general focus is on those aspects of serial crime related to offender hunting, crime location, movement, and geography. This discussion provides a context for the investigative problems and forensic behavioural science-based strategies brought up in Chapter 4. One of those strategies, criminal profiling, warrants its own examination in Chapter 5. Chapter 6 moves into the area of behavioural geography, and introduces concepts of importance for understanding the geography of crime research and theories presented in Chapter 7. Influences on criminal targets, including the hunt for victims, are discussed in Chapter 8.

Chapter 9 analyzes the spatial patterns of criminal predators, presenting original research findings from the study on the geography and targets of serial murderers conducted at Simon Fraser University. Chapter 10 focuses on the conceptual basis of geographic profiling, performance measures, relevant considerations, operational procedures, and the understudy training program. Chapter 11 presents several investigative strategies used with a geographic profile. Case examples illustrate these tactics, but it should be stressed that profiling only plays a support role. It does not solve crimes — that is the responsibility of the assigned investigator. There is also a discussion of a geographic profile based on the 19th-century murders of Jack the Ripper. Chapter 12, the conclusion, considers future research and where we need to go from here. The appendices contain research data and coding forms. A glossary explaining specialized terms and a comprehensive bibliography close the book.

One final note: depending upon the specification in the original source, both kilometres and miles are quoted in distance measures.[1]

---

[1] The relevant distance conversions are: 1 kilometre = 0.621 miles, 1 mile = 1.609 kilometres; 1 metre = 1.094 yards, 1 yard = 0.914 metres; 1 centimetre = 0.394 inches, 1 inch = 2.54 centimetres; 1 hectare = 2.471 acres, 1 acre = 0.405 hectares; 1 square kilometre = 0.39 square miles, 1 square mile = 2.59 square kilometres.

Serial Murder

2

2.1 Serial Murder

When the throat of Victorian prostitute Polly Nichols was slashed in Buck's Row on Bank Holiday, August 31, 1888, serial murder became part of our cultural lexicon (Rumbelow, 1988). Jack the Ripper was certainly not the first nor last of his type, but the unsolved mystery of the Whitechapel murders still symbolizes our inability to understand these dangerous predators. Serial murder is a frightening and perplexing phenomenon that has proven to be a difficult puzzle for both criminal investigators and criminological researchers. Despite being a rare event, this crime has a broad-based impact on the larger community (Jenkins, 1992a; Silverman & Kennedy, 1993). Fear, shock, repugnance, scientific curiosity, and morbid fascination are all common reactions to such cases (see Dietz, 1995). There are also growing concerns about the increase in the prevalence of these dangerous predators. It has even been suggested that serial killers are the quintessential criminal of a violent, postmodern society (Carputi, 1990; Richter, 1989; see Ellis, 1991; Kerr, 1992).

Adequate definitions and typologies are necessary for the study of any phenomenon. Serial murder means different things to different people, and the label risks lumping a diverse group of offenders into a single synthetic category. As Clifford Robert Olson, Canada's most infamous serial murderer, aptly states (uncorrected quotation): "We cant look into other serial killers minds as to what they do unless they allow to give there thoughts and views, You dont find many that have done this any place" (personal communication, September 10, 1991). The thoughts of interviewed serial killers show just as many differences as they do commonalities.

Murder, abhorrent as it may be, is still possible to understand. Feelings of anger, betrayal, and frustration; motives of revenge, money, and expediency;

5

assaults that cross the line between injury and death — all these are within the scope of our imagination. Indeed, it has been said that almost anyone is a potential killer. Serial murder, however, is beyond our normal range of experience. It is what the ghost of Hamlet's father describes as "foul and most unnatural murder." Unfortunately, this strangeness does not facilitate efforts to explain, predict, and prevent.

2.1.1 Definitions and Typologies

> Patterns of murders committed by one person, in large numbers with no apparent rhyme, reason, or motivation.
>
> — Title of hearings before the U.S. Senate, 98th Congress, on the issue of serial murder; *Patterns of Murders*, 1983

Defining serial murder is less than straightforward and attempts to distinguish and classify the phenomenon are often inconsistent. The label multiple murder[2] is generally used to refer to mass, spree, and serial murders. Time interval between separate offences is the most common variable used to distinguish these groupings (Holmes & De Burger, 1988). Mass murder involves those incidents where several victims are killed simultaneously, or within a relatively brief time period — a "sustained burst" (Leyton, 1986). Holmes and De Burger (1988) define mass murder as "the slaying of several people, in the same general area, at roughly the same time, by a lone assailant" (p. 18).

Spree killings, an intermediate classification between mass and serial murder, involve those incidents where several victims, usually selected randomly, are killed over a relatively short period (hours to weeks) by a reckless, impulsive assailant (Holmes & De Burger, 1988). The Federal Bureau of Investigation (FBI) defines spree murders as those characterized by "killing at two or more locations with no emotional cooling-off period between murders. The killings are all the result of a single event, which can be of short or long duration" (Ressler et al., 1988, p. 139).

Definitions of serial murder are more problematic as the time periods involved are greater. Brooks, Devine, Green, Hart, and Moore (1987) provide the following definition of serial murder:

> Serial murder is defined as a series of two or more murders, committed as separate events, usually, but not always, by one offender acting alone. The crimes may occur over a period of time ranging from hours to years. Quite

---

[2] The term multicide has also been used to refer to instances where an offender kills more than one victim (Dickson, 1958).

often the motive is psychological, and the offender's behavior and the physical evidence observed at the crime scenes will reflect sadistic, sexual overtones. (p. vii)

Keeney and Heide (1994a) review and criticize ten different definitions for serial murder from the literature, and then suggest an eleventh, more inclusive, description. Perhaps the simplest and most functional definition is the one used by the FBI:

Serial murderers are involved in three or more separate events with an emotional cooling-off period between homicides. This type of killer usually premeditates his crimes, often fantasizing and planning the murder in every aspect, with the possible exception of the specific victim. Then, when the time is right for him and he has cooled off from his last homicide, he selects his next victim and proceeds with his plan. The cool-off period can be days, weeks, or months and is the main element that separates the serial killer from other multiple killers. (Ressler et al., 1988, p. 139)

Other researchers have proposed replacing counts of crime with an assessment of propensity to re-offend (Kocsis & Irwin, 1998; see below). Holmes and De Burger (1988) suggest the following elements as central to serial murder: (1) a pattern of repetitive homicide; (2) one victim and one assailant per murder event; (3) victim and perpetrator are strangers or slight acquaintances; (4) murders are psychogenic in origin; and (5) a lack of an obvious motive (though intrinsic motives, nonrational to an outsider, may exist).

The condition of one victim and one assailant per murder event are not central elements of serial murder. There is no shortage of cases involving incidents of more than one victim per attack (Kenneth Bianchi, Edmund Kemper III, and Richard Ramirez, for example). And four separate studies have determined multiple offenders are involved in a significant percentage of serial murder cases: (1) 14% (Hickey, 1997); (2) 21% (Jenkins, 1990); (3) 11.9% (Rossmo, 1995a); and (4) 25% (Simonetti, 1984). These estimates suggest that over one quarter of serial killers operate as teams or in groups (e.g., 28% in Hickey's study), though Newton (1992) found 87% of the American serial killers in his sample were "lone wolves."

Holmes and De Burger (1988) divide serial murderers into four categories (one of which is broken down into three subcategories) according to motive, pattern of homicidal behaviour, and decision-making process. This grouping is based on such variables as victim selection, choice of murder location, and method of killing. They derived their classification from an analysis of the crime behaviour patterns of 110 serial murderers, using interview and biographical data, court transcripts, case studies, and clinical reports as information sources. Their schema is as follows.

1. Visionary motive serial murderers hear messages and see visions that create a "rationale" for the killings.
2. Mission-oriented motive serial murderers believe that they have a task to accomplish, involving the elimination of some "sinful" group such as prostitutes from society.
3. Hedonistic motive serial murderers derive pleasure from the homicidal act. This type is subdivided into: (1) lust killers, who typically indulge in sexual sadism, anthropophagy, piquerism, or necrophilia; (2) thrill killers, who enjoy the "high" of murder; and (3) comfort killers, who are oriented towards enjoying life, a goal facilitated through the use of someone else's money (e.g., "black widow" murderers).
4. Power/control-oriented motive serial murderers seek dominance over others. Control of a person's life and death is seen as the ultimate act of power.

Barrett (1990) proposes a five-category scheme for classifying serial murderers by motive, based on a cross between the Holmes and De Burger typology, and the FBI system for classifying serial rapists (Hazelwood, 1995): (1) the visionary serial killer; (2) the revenge serial killer; (3) the anger excitation serial killer; (4) the power assertive serial killer; and (5) the opportunist serial killer. Fox and Levin (1992) also propose a modified Holmes and De Burger typology, with three categories, each with two subtypes: (1) thrill serial killers — (a) sexual sadism, (b) dominance; (2) mission serial killers — (a) reformist, (b) visionary; and (3) expedience serial killers — (a) profit, (b) protection. They note thrill killings are the most common, and expedience killings the least common types. Rappaport (1988) divides serial killers into functionaries of organized crime groups, custodial poisoners and asphyxiators, psychotics, and sexual sadists. This grouping is somewhat confusing, however, as it is based on a mixture of method and cause.

Serial murder definitions and taxonomies are problematic because of ambiguities concerning victim number and temporal spacing.[3] Some types of multiple murder — the Nazi concentration camp massacres, ethnic cleansing, political terrorism killings, and organized crime contract executions — cannot be accurately classified within these parameters (Levin & Fox, 1985; Leyton, 1986; see Dillon, 1989). In Pennsylvania, there is a town square monument to Tom Quick, the celebrated Delaware "Indian Slayer," who was responsible for 99 kills (Randall, 1988). Yet many of these deaths were legally murders, occurring after the signing of peace treaties. By some definitions,

---

[3] See Ball and Curry (1995) for a discussion of the logic, methods, and errors of definition within criminology.

Tom Quick was a Colonial frontier hero; by others, he was one of America's earliest serial killers.

A nurse who poisons a number of patients within the same hospital over several months would likely be classified as a serial killer, even though the crimes all occurred in one location (Leyton, 1986). Cases of random mass poisonings, such as the 1982 Chicago Tylenol tamperings, are even more complicated to categorize (Levin & Fox, 1985). If several people die over an extended period of time and in different geographic locations as the result of a single episode of tampering, are they the victims of a mass or serial killer? Most typologies of human behaviour lack inclusiveness and category mutual exclusivity. Despite their grey areas, they can be helpful for understanding variations in offender behaviour.

The *Crime Classification Manual* (CCM) is the first attempt to develop a comprehensive diagnostic system, using standardized terminology, to classify offence and offender characteristics for the crimes of murder, sexual assault, and arson (Douglas, Burgess, Burgess, & Ressler, 1992a). The result of a research project conducted by the National Center for the Analysis of Violent Crime at the FBI Academy, the CCM was designed to assist police investigations, facilitate research, and improve communication between criminal justice and mental health experts. It is modeled on the American Psychiatric Association's *Diagnostic and Statistical Manual of Mental Disorders*, and uses subcategories of Uniform Crime Reports (UCR) definitions based on four types of primary criminal intent: (1) criminal enterprise; (2) personal cause; (3) sexual intent; and (4) group cause. Classification variables include modus operandi, weapon use, victimology, physical evidence, autopsy results, and similar factors. The CCM provides investigative questions and considerations for each crime subtype. While it is a useful step, the CCM has been criticized for being atheoretical and lacking empirical verification of its category structure.

2.1.1.1 Characteristics

From a study of 42 mass and serial killers and FBI data on simultaneous homicides, Levin and Fox (1985) constructed profiles of the typical multiple murderer. Such killers are most often white males in their late twenties to early thirties. Rarely psychotic, they are more ordinary in background, appearance, and personality than anything else. The murderous act is usually precipitated by a period of frustration and then triggered by some particular event.

Levin and Fox (1985) note that while half of the single victim homicides in America involve black offenders, only 20% of the multiple murders in their study (U.S. cases from 1974 to 1979) had a black perpetrator — considerably closer to the 11.7% actual racial composition of blacks in the U.S.

(Cleveland, 1985). Hickey (1997) observed that 20% of the serial killers in his research (U.S. cases from 1800 to 1995) were black, and that they were more likely to be involved in recent cases. Newton (1992) found 16% of the U.S. serial killers in his study were black.

Levin and Fox's (1985) sample included only one female and they note that, according to FBI statistics, fewer than 7% of all simultaneous homicides involved female offenders. All 36 sexual murderers in the study by Ressler et al. (1988) were male, and at least one of the authors believes there has never been a true female serial killer (Ressler, 1993; Ressler & Shachtman, 1992; but see also Epstein, 1992). Hickey (1997), however, found 16% of the serial murderers who operated in the U.S. between 1800 and 1995 to be female, proportional to the involvement of females in murder generally (Holmes & De Burger, 1988; Levin & Fox). He also notes that females were involved in 36% of the team killer cases. Females comprised 10% of the serial murderers in Newton's (1992) sample.

Segrave (1992) discusses 83 female serial and mass killers from around the world who murdered from 1580 to 1990. She describes the typical female serial killer as having murdered 17 people over a five-year period, most often by poison. These crimes usually take place within the home of the offender or (less often) the victim. The murders almost never occur on the street or in a public place. Many of the victims are from powerless groups, and most are related or closely tied to the killer (see also Hickey, 1986; Scott, 1992).

In their study of solo female serial murderers, Keeney and Heide (1994c) found a similar lack of mobility; 13 of 14 offenders were place-specific killers, their victims typically in custodial care (43%) or family members (37%). They observed differences between these females and their male counterparts in terms of behaviour patterns, methods of victim search and attack, use of torture, crime scene organization, motive, and psychiatric disorders (histrionic or manic-depressive diagnoses are more likely). They suggest that unique as well as common aetiological factors are involved in cases of female serial murder (see also Pearson, 1997; Scott, 1992).

Hinch and Scott (1995) observe that female serial killers who act alone generally wish to avoid attention, employing more subtle methods of murder than their male counterparts through concealing bodies or explaining victims' deaths by accident or illness. Perhaps this is an example of how sex roles influence even the most extreme forms of criminality. Or maybe these women just wish to avoid suspicion as they typically kill relatives or acquaintances.

2.1.2   Incidence, Population, and Growth

Though statistically rare,[4] serial murder has a disproportionate impact on communities that extends far beyond the range of the immediate victims and their families. Changes in single indices of crime seriousness (weighted measures designed to assess the relative seriousness of criminal offences) can be almost completely accounted for by shifts in homicide rates, despite the fact that over 90% of all major crime is property related (Epperlein & Nienstedt, 1989). Also, risk of victimization and fear of crime are not spread uniformly throughout society, but are influenced by such factors as sex, age, race, income level, and geography (Coburn, 1988; Fattah, 1987; Kposowa, 1999; Langan & Innes, 1985; Lea & Young, 1984; Rose & McClain, 1990). Certain groups seem to be particularly vulnerable to serial murder — prostitutes, young women alone, hitchhikers, children, homosexuals, skid road derelicts, elderly women, and hospital patients (Hickey, 1990, 1997; Levin & Fox, 1985).

Statistical analyses of the incidence and increase of serial murder must deal with definitional difficulties and linkage problems, in addition to variations in social and historical context, police response, and official record-keeping practices. By definition, a serial murder must be committed by a serial murderer, but determining just exactly who is a serial murderer is problematic. Estimates of the incidence of serial murder and the size of the serial killer population are often inflated, inaccurate, and varied, based on inadequate data sources and unarticulated or haphazard methodologies (see Jenkins, 1994). By its very nature serial murder is a major news item, and therefore often used as a political rallying point.[5] Both Kiger (1990) and Jenkins (1992a) insightfully discuss the role of hysteria, inflated research claims, and media impact in the construction of social problems surrounding serial murder.

Assume for the sake of argument that the unapprehended Seattle-area Green River Killer has gone into retirement, never to kill again (see Smith & Guillen, 1991). Would he still be counted in an estimate of the serial murderer population? And should a potential serial killer, apprehended and incarcerated after his first homicide, be included in such estimates (Bishop, 1946; Boyd, 1988)? Aleksandr Koryakov stabbed three children and their teacher in a single act of murder before being apprehended by Latvian police, qualifying as a mass but not a serial killer (Latvian kindergarten killer, 1999). But he later confessed this was only the start of a homicide spree intended to rival that of Andrei Chikatilo, the Rostov Ripper, who was convicted of 53 murders in Russia. It is assumed that "serial killer" is a status theoretically capable of capture in a count done at a single point in time. This is a problematic assumption.

---

[4] All forms of homicide are uncommon and most killings involve intimates, as opposed to strangers (Boyd, 1988; Fattah, 1991; Silverman & Kennedy, 1993; Skogan & Antunes, 1979). Reed and Gaucher (1976) note "the amount of repetitive killing in Canada is miniscule and certainly far less than appears to be generally believed" (p. 1).

[5] This is nothing new. See Rumbelow (1988) for the response of the lower class to the Whitechapel murders of Jack the Ripper in 1888.

Linkage problems prevent many incidents of serial homicide from being recognized as such (Holmes & De Burger, 1988; Norris, 1988). Murders committed in different locations and separate police jurisdictions may not be seen to be part of a single series. Even those killings that occur in the same city might not be connected if there is a high murder rate, an overworked homicide squad, or if the crimes are spread out over time.

The only official records in some cases may be missing person reports. Without a body, it is doubtful that a homicide statistic will ever be recorded. Many serial killers, including Jeffrey Dahmer, John Wayne Gacy, Jr., and Juan Vallejo Corona, buried or hid the bodies of their victims. Several of the groups at high risk — prostitutes, the itinerant, the destitute — may go missing without anyone noticing. With no complaint, there is no official missing person report.

Despite these difficulties, several researchers have attempted to estimate the prevalence and extent of serial homicide. Leyton (1986) states that there may be up to 100 of these murderers operating in the U.S., responsible for the deaths of thousands of people. He expresses some surprise at this relatively low number considering the present violent state of society. Holmes and De Burger (1988), however, estimate that there are currently 350 serial killers in the U.S. alone, responsible for between 3500 and 5000 deaths annually. Norris (1988) states he has researched 260 serial murderers, responsible for 10,360 victims (for a comparatively high average of 40 victims per murderer), though he does not provide a list of who these killers are.

Jenkins (1989) found several hundred serial murder cases, 49 of which involved 10 or more victims, recorded in newspaper archives since 1971. The U.S. Justice Department conservatively estimates there are 35 active serial killers operating within the U.S. (Levin & Fox, 1985), though their methodology has never been published. Jenkins suggests that there are approximately 400 victims of serial murder per year, while Fox and Levin (1992) have calculated that fewer than 240 people fall prey to serial killers annually in the U.S. Hickey (1997) found, for the peak period of 1975 to 1995, only 7.7 reported new cases (49 to 70 victims) per year.[6] The Federal Bureau of Investigation Behavioral Science Unit (BSU) has stated they receive approximately 30 requests annually for assistance in serial murder cases (Hagmaier, 1990).

Kiger (1990) has critically evaluated the various methods used to estimate the incidence of serial murder, and points out problems with unexplained

---

[6] The U.S. Justice Department's estimates are for active murderers, while Hickey's are for new cases. These figures do not appear so dissimilar when it is realized that the median number of years of homicidal activity for the serial killers in Hickey's sample was 4.3 years (1991). Jenkins (1988b) estimates a career length of just under 4 years for serial murderers in England.

methodologies and calculation procedures. In the U.S., the current UCR system does not allow the tracking of single offenders, and Supplemental Homicide Report (SHR) incident-based data, which often suffer from missing information, only allow counts of mass, not serial, murder. Some researchers have used the sharp rise in the number of stranger and unknown motive homicide categories in the SHR as the basis for evaluating serial murder increases. This is an unsound extrapolation; increases in felony murders (particularly those that are drug related and difficult to solve), urbanization levels, and demands upon police departments all affect uncleared murder rates (see Cardarelli & Cavanagh, 1992). Some estimates have conflated unknown and stranger relationship homicide categories, leading to high estimates of the latter. Advocacy numbers claim 50% of all murders are stranger offences, but 18 to 25% is a more accurate estimate (Riedel, 1998). Jenkins (1988a, 1994) and Kiger (1990) have criticized the manner in which these data have been used to estimate the occurrence of serial murder.

Mortality data from the National Center for Health Statistics (NCHS) Division of Health Statistics have been used to check UCR homicide data. This information is not particularly useful for estimates of serial murder, but Kiger (1990) notes that coroner data on the number of unidentified bodies found each year, while not completely congruent, could be relevant. The FBI National Crime Information Center (NCIC) keeps a computerized record of such bodies. It also lists missing persons as does the Canadian Police Information Centre (CPIC) operated by the Royal Canadian Mounted Police (RCMP). While calculations of the number of serial murder victims, particularly children, have been based on this data, there is a problem estimating the percentage of cases involving hidden bodies.

The number of children who go missing for reasons not related to parental abductions is relatively small. In contrast to inflammatory statements made by certain special interest organizations, Kiger (1990) estimates somewhere between 20 to 300 children in the U.S. are murdered annually by strangers (see also Allen-Hagen, 1989; Finkelhor, Hotaling, & Sedlak, 1990). Between 1984 and 1988, only 3% of the 16,511 cases of missing and murdered children reported to the U.S. National Center for Missing and Exploited Children were abducted by strangers (Hickey, 1990). Of these 495 children, 15% (75) were found dead, and 47% (235) are still missing. Presumably, some unknown fraction of these murders were committed by serial offenders.

Cavanagh (1993) presents a method for estimating the number of serial murder victims from official sources. For the period from 1976 to 1989, he aggregated SHR data from census subregions into 45 records (9 subregions by 5 time periods). The different types of homicide that might reasonably be related to serial murder were totaled for each record, and the combination that best predicted serial murder determined through regression analysis.

The homicide categories included stranger or unknown, bodily contact, fel- ony, and sexual murders. The model was calibrated against recorded counts of serial murder victims collected by Newton (1990a, 1990b). Cavanagh cautions his model is a preliminary exploration, and notes weaknesses in Newton's enumeration that could bias the results. Nevertheless, he has devel- oped a feasible approach, with an articulated methodology, for estimating rates of serial murder from SHR and census data. This is a significant improvement over inflated estimates and impressionistic guesswork.

While serial murder is not a problem unique to the latter half of the 20th century, most researchers agree the number of such killings is increas- ing (Hickey, 1997; Holmes & De Burger, 1988; Levin & Fox, 1985; Leyton, 1986; Newton, 1992; Norris, 1988; Ressler, Burgess, & Douglas, 1988; see also Boyd, 1988). Based on a comprehensive study of 399 serial murderers, Hickey (1997) found a ten-fold increase in active offenders per year for the period 1970 to 1995, compared to 1800 to 1969.[7] He notes the number of victims per case has dropped, likely due to increased police efficiency (see also James, 1991). Since 1925, this figure has been in the range of 7 to 13 total murders per case. Jenkins (1988b) estimates that five to six is a likely annual total of victims for recent American serial murderers, and four for English serial killers. Fox and Levin (1992) suggest that while six victims per year is typical, the figure should actually be doubled (to 12) to account for unknown victims.

Jenkins (1988a, 1989, 1992b) has analyzed cases of "extreme" serial mur- der (involving ten or more victims) in the U.S. for the period from 1900 to 1990, and concludes that "serial homicide was a common experience in the early years of this century, little less frequent than in recent years" (1989, p. 378). He does find evidence, however, of a "serial murder wave," particu- larly involving lust killings, in the U.S. from 1940 to 1990. He documented 11 cases of lust murder from 1950 to 1964, 11 cases from 1965 to 1969, and 12 cases in 1973. While recognizing the actual scale of the problem may have been blown out of proportion to benefit certain ideologies or interest groups, he still concludes that "there simply were more serial killers, more of whom could be categorized as lust murderers. A new problem was identified because a new problem had come into being" (1992b, p. 13). Jenkins lists 49 mur- derers active in an 18-year period, a four-fold increase from the first part of the century (not adjusted for population growth). There is also historical evidence of this type of crime in both England (1988b) and Germany (1988a).

---

[7] These figures are not adjusted for population growth; per capita serial murder rates have only doubled over the last few decades. This estimate may also be temporally biased as the more recent a case, the greater the probability it will be located by a researcher in newspaper files or other written works.

Several problems exist with historical research into the incidence of serial murder. In addition to the hurdles encountered in attempts to locate old data sources and the problem of less than rigorous practices in past record keeping, many cases of serial killings probably went officially undetected. Itinerant murderers would have travelled and killed more freely in pre-telecommunication days. Early mass and serial murderers may have been characterized as demons, witches, or werewolves rather than as criminal offenders (Hickey, 1997). Violence and murder were much more common in Europe during the medieval period than today (Brantingham, 1987; Brantingham & Brantingham, 1984; Wilson, 1984; see also Goodman & Waddell, 1987; Gurr, 1989a; Johnson, 1988). Conversely, offenders were likely apprehended much sooner in rural or village settings than large urban areas. Many potential serial murderers would thus have been caught and executed after their first victim.

Jenkins (1993b) also points out that a growth in the number of potential offenders does not necessarily follow from an increase in reported cases of serial murder. He argues that the construction of official records of serial killing is influenced as much by victimological and bureaucratic factors as by the population of actual murderers:

> Rather, the vital elements [in the production of "crime waves" of serial murder] may be the increasing opportunities to find vulnerable people to victimize, and the chance to escape apprehension after committing a murder. The opportunities might increase as a consequence of economic developments, or as a result of changes in mores, while bureaucratic and political factors might well affect the likelihood of detection. In either case, though, a murder "wave" could occur independently of the changing characteristics of the offender population. (p. 471)

These definitional and measurement issues make assessments of serial murder levels difficult, and it is not easy to predict the development of future trends. The FBI has suggested the following factors may have had influences: mobility, "easy" victims (in terms of target selection), urbanization, social anonymity, violence in the mass media, pornography, and illicit drug use (Mathers, 1989; Ressler & Shachtman, 1992).

It is important to understand the level and seriousness of this crime without succumbing to unreasonable fear and unwarranted panics. Kiger (1990) puts the problem in perspective when she refers to the dark figure of serial homicide and warns that "the incidence of serial murder in the United States is currently unknown, as is the prevalence of active offenders" (p. 47). The magnitude and exact growth of serial homicide is not yet measurable with any degree of accuracy, and inflated estimates and unfounded theories may create more problems than they solve.

2.1.3   Theories

A mind full of fire, and a fist full of steel.

— **Graffiti, Vancouver, British Columbia, April 1995**

Explanations for serial murder run the gamut from the biological to the psychological to the sociological. While this crime is currently not fully understood, there have been some efforts to explore its aetiology. Lunde (1976) states that almost all multiple killers are clinically insane white males, and their psychoses typically take the form of paranoid schizophrenia or sexual sadism. He suggests childhood experiences may play a role in shaping the distorted world views commonly held by such offenders. Bartol and Bartol (1986) caution that it would be a mistake to "assume with Lunde that almost all mass murderers are mentally disordered in the clinical sense of that term .... they tend to be extremely introverted persons who perceive and think about the world in ways much different from our own" (p. 185). Criminal courts have demonstrated a pattern of decreeing most serial killers legally sane (see also Ogle, Maier-Katkin, & Bernard, 1995), and some commentators have cautioned that insanity is a label lacking demonstrable reliability and validity (Boyd, 1988; Szasz, 1971).

Brittain (1970) observes that sexual sadists may repeatedly kill when provoked by actions that cause a perceived loss of self-esteem. But by replacing the term "serial murderer" with the labels "paranoid schizophrenic" and "sexual sadist" in their explanations, neither Lunde nor Brittain make real progress towards the understanding of the causes of this form of destructive behaviour. They also ignore the fact that most people in these groups never become murderers, let alone repetitive killers.

Adopting a biosocial approach, Norris (1988) suggests that serial murderers suffer from a medical pathology and their violent actions are caused by organic brain malfunctions that lead to episodic and uncontrollable acts of violence. He views serial killers as having lost their free will, as victims of a form of contagious disease.

> Serial murderers share a significant number of common medical/psychological patterns that include evidence of possible genetic defect, soft and hard signs of brain damage resulting from injuries or other physical trauma, severe chemical imbalances brought about by chronic malnutrition and substance abuse, an absence of a sense of self which is the result of consistently negative parenting or nonparenting, and an almost hair-trigger violent response to external stimuli with no regard for the physical or social consequences. (p. 40)

The violent upbringing and negative parenting experienced by these offenders as children may have led to the reversal of the traditional dichotomies of reward and punishment, love and hate, resulting in the development of a "nonpersonality type," incapable of controlling harmful impulses and functioning within the context of a normal social framework. Norris (1988) proposes that serial killers go through a ritual of murder comprising seven key phases:

1. Aura phase — the killer withdraws from reality;
2. Trolling phase — the compulsive search and hunt for the next victim;
3. Wooing phase — the victim is conned into the killer's trap;
4. Capture phase — the offender's penultimate moment;
5. Murder phase — the killer's fantasies are ritually enacted;
6. Totem phase — the reliving of the crime through souvenirs in order to sustain the "high"; and
7. Depression phase — the killer loses the power he realized through the murder, setting off the whole process once again.

Lange and DeWitt, Jr. (1990b) state there is evidence that many serial killers suffer from head injuries or physical brain pathology. Their research examined 165 motiveless murderers, from 1600 to the present, representing all parts of the world. Neurological malfunctions, caused by head injuries, epilepsy, or other forms of subtle deep temporal lobe spiking, generates interictal or post-ictal seizures that can lead to irresistibly compulsive autonomic or "automatic" behaviour. Their hypothesis is that serial murderers become victims of uncontrollable brain activity that leads to "fits" or "dazes" within which the killings occur.

Biological and genetic theories of crime are not currently popular in criminology and it is often difficult to obtain the data necessary to test offender hypotheses at the biological level (Vold & Bernard, 1986). Still, several new research initiatives have been developed in the biosocial area over the last decade (see, for example, Fishbein, Lozovsky, & Jaffe, 1989). On one hand, the temptation to explain complicated patterns of human behaviour in a simple manner is strong, especially when that behaviour is violent, frightening, and alien (Boyanowsky, 1990). Such theories are comforting as they physically and congenitally separate the rest of us from the "monsters" in our society. Our culture, and therefore we as individuals, can then avoid all responsibility for these savage crimes. But on the other hand, serial murder is a rare phenomenon and individual-level explanations undoubtedly play a part.

Biological theories must be integrated with sociopsychological or sociological theories to address the cultural dissimilarities found in crime, murder, and multiple murder (Ressler et al., 1988). On their own they lack the ability to explain historical and geographic differences in criminal activity. In summarizing the evidence connecting neurochemical dysfunctions with impulsivity, negative affect, sensation-seeking, and other cognitive correlates of antisocial behaviour, Fishbein (1998) notes that any biological predisposition will be influenced by triggering socio-environmental factors. "Put simply, abnormalities in certain neurobiological mechanisms heighten sensitivity to adverse environmental circumstances, increasing the risk for an antisocial outcome" (p. 3).

Levin and Fox (1985) criticize the narrow theoretical focus on the offender in studies of multiple murder, stressing that while the role of biology and the effects of early experience cannot be ignored, "situational factors — experiences and learning beyond the fifth year of life ... are at least as critical in encouraging a murderous response from someone who may or may not be predisposed to violence" (p. 39). Cater (1997) also argues that serial murderers learn to become such, and therefore are products of society. He suggests that social profiles may help in early identification of warning signs.

Holmes and De Burger (1988) employ a sociopsychological approach to understanding serial murder, suggesting repetitive homicidal behaviour patterns are generated from a mind-set with the following critical features:

1. An intrinsic and persistent motivation to kill;
2. An expressive orientation to murder reinforced by the ability to psychologically "gain" from such violent acts (often linked to consistent fantasies); and
3. Central sociopathic features (e.g., absence of guilt, warped notions of love, capacity for extreme but casual and emotionless aggression, impulsivity, uncontrolled desires, asocial perspectives).

Holmes and De Burger (1988) warn that serial killers are not a homogeneous group, either in their actions or biographies. They therefore eschew a single causative theory, suggesting instead that if the dominant motives develop in conjunction with a certain mind-set under the right conditions, repetitive homicidal behaviour can result. Such a structure is seen to be necessary, but not in itself sufficient. They do not explain what such conditions and motives might be, or how such a mind-set comes about.

The sources of the repetitive homicide pattern are thus seen as psychogenic — the killer's psyche is characterized by values, norms, beliefs, perceptions, and propensities that facilitate and legitimate multiple acts of murder. But while the motivations are aberrant and their locus intrinsic, they are not the result of psychopathology or organic brain disease. Sociogenic factors, while not a direct cause, are important for understanding the context within which propensities for murder develop. Holmes and De Burger's comments should be seen as more of a set of descriptive propositions rather than as a comprehensive theory.

Noting the frequency with which examples of dissociative processes can be found in the literature on serial murderers, Vetter (1990) suggests that systematically administering Bernstein and Putnam's Dissociative Experiences Scale (DES) to known serial killers might prove to be a fruitful avenue for new research. In his view, the behaviour of many such killers shows evidence of what he terms the Mephisto Syndrome, a combination of dissociation and psychopathy (see also Carlisle, 1993).

Dissociative disorders feature "a disruption in the usually integrated functions of consciousness, memory, identity, or perception of the environment" (American Psychiatric Association, 1994, p. 477). Dissociation ranges from common daydreaming to the controversial multiple personality disorder. The disorders, as presently defined in the *Diagnostic and Statistical Manual of Mental Disorders* (4th Edition) (DSM-IV), include dissociative amnesia, dissociative fugue (formerly psychogenic fugue), dissociative identity disorder (formerly multiple personality disorder), depersonalization disorder, and dissociative disorder not otherwise specified.

Thrill-seeking, pathological glibness, antisocial pursuit of power, and lack of guilt characterize the extreme "true" psychopath (Vetter, 1990). The DSM-IV employs the term antisocial personality disorder (ASPD), rather than sociopath or psychopath. The ASPD diagnostic criteria in the DSM-IV have been significantly revised from those in the previous edition, DSM-III-R, as they had come under attack for being too broad and behaviourally oriented (Hare, Hart, & Harpur, 1991).

These critiques led to the development of the Psychopathy Checklist — Revised (PCL-R) by Robert Hare of the University of British Columbia. Based on the work of Cleckley (1982) and others, this instrument is a more accurate measure of psychopathy as a personality disorder (Hare, 1993; Hare, Harpur, Hakstian, Forth, Hart, & Newman, 1990; Hare, McPherson, & Forth, 1988; Hart, Hare, & Harpur, 1991, 1992). Research on psychopathy with the PCL-R helped inform the development of the modified ASPD diagnostic criteria now used in the DSM-IV.

Hare (1993) developed key diagnostic symptoms to assess psychopathy based on the traits outlined in Hervey Cleckley's *Mask of Sanity*. These can be grouped into two factors, one describing personality, and the other behavioural, characteristics:

- Emotional/interpersonal: (1) glib and superficial; (2) egocentric and grandiose; (3) lack of remorse or guilt; (4) lack of empathy; (5) deceitful and manipulative; and (6) shallow emotions.

- Social deviance: (1) impulsive; (2) poor behaviour controls; (3) need for excitement; (4) lack of responsibility; (5) early behaviour problems; and (6) adult antisocial behaviour.

Psychopathy is well summed up by the "dead conscience" self-diagnosis of Richard Ramirez, the Night Stalker. But while many serial murderers appear to possess psychopathic personalities, the disorder is not in itself a sufficient condition for repetitive violence and most psychopaths are not criminals, let alone serial killers (Andrews & Bonta, 1994; Hare, 1993; Siegel, 1992).

Ressler et al. (1988) analyzed motives and patterns of violent criminal behaviour through interviews of 36 convicted and incarcerated male sexual murderers, 29 of whom had killed more than one person. They also reviewed various psychiatric, police, court, and prison archival data sources. They construct a motivational model for sexual homicide that integrates social environment, childhood and adolescent formative events, subsequent patterned responses, resultant actions towards others, and offender reaction via a mental "feedback filter" to violent acts.[8]

Stage one of their motivational model describes the existence of an ineffective social environment for the murderer during childhood (Ressler et al., 1988). His caretakers tend to ignore his behaviour, support his distortions of events, and generally act in a nonintervening and nonprotective manner. Life attachments and bonding forces are thus inadequately developed. Stage two of the model explains the critical importance of such formative events as sexual and physical abuse, developmental failure through negative social attachment, a diminished emotional response, and interpersonal failure caused by inconsistent parenting and deviant role models.

Stage three involves the patterned responses to these early influences. Rather than learning positive critical personal traits, the interviewed murderers in this study developed fetishes, preferences for autoerotic activities, feelings of entitlement, and characteristics of social isolation, rebelliousness, aggression, and deceit. The resultant cognitive mapping and processing is structured through daydreams, fantasies, visual thoughts, and nightmares. Their internal dialogues involve absolutes, generalizations, and strong, limiting presuppositions. Their fantasy themes include dominance, power, control, violence, sadism, masochism, revenge, torture, mutilation, rape, and death (see Dietz, Hazelwood, & Warren, 1990). They require high levels of kinesthetic stimulation and aggressive experience for sexual arousal.

---

[8] Ressler et al. (1988) note their motivational model only focuses on cognitive and psychosocial factors, and does not address neurobiological or genetic influences that "may be present under certain conditions" (p. 69). They do not state what those conditions are.

The cognitive structure of the murderer during childhood eventually influences his or her behaviour. Stage four describes the external actions demonstrated by the offender during periods of childhood, adolescence, and adulthood. Typical behaviour patterns of the sexual murderer as a child involve cruelty to both animals and children, disregard for others, firesetting, theft, mischief, and joyless, hostile, aggressive, repetitive play patterns. Adolescent and adult criminal actions may include assaults, break and enters, arsons, abductions, rape, nonsexual murder, and sex-oriented murder, often involving rape, torture, mutilation, or necrophilia. It is significant to note that many serial killers commit their first murder during their early or mid-adolescent years. Henry Lee Lucas claims to have committed his first murder at either the age of 8 (Peters, 1990) or 14 (Egger, 1990).[9]

There are similarities between some of these actions and the "Macdonald triad," a set of childhood characteristics associated with future violent behaviour: torture of small animals, firesetting, and enuresis (Macdonald, 1961, 1963; see also Beirne, 1999; Levin & Fox, 1985). David Berkowitz (the "Son of Sam") was responsible for numerous arsons and suspected of several dog killings prior to, and during, his murder spree. He kept yearly journals with detailed records of 1411 fires — locations, dates, times, and fireboxes (Ressler & Shachtman, 1992; Terry, 1989; Time-Life, 1992b).

Stage five is a feedback filter process that serves as a justification system for the violent acts of such offenders. By reacting to and evaluating earlier antisocial behaviours the sexual murderer in effect learns more "efficient" patterns of operation. Errors are eliminated; methods of avoiding detection and punishment improved; new means to increase control, dominance, and power discovered; and enhanced states of arousal learned. Fantasies become more sophisticated and refined during this period; the potential for increased violence and repetitive homicide lies at this stage of the model.

This is one of the few research projects directly examining the sexual murder population. The study has some methodological problems, however, and Ressler et al. (1988) caution their offender group is not a representative random sample. The model has yet to be empirically tested, though a study of 62 serial murderers by Cleary and Luxenburg (1993) found similar background characteristics of abuse and broken homes. Ressler et al. do not supply tests of statistical significance and some of the reported relationships may be the result of chance (Homant & Kennedy, 1998). Also, a lack of comparative background data for the general population prevents their findings from being contextualized. For example, 61% of the sexual murderers they interviewed admitted to having rape fantasies during childhood or adolescence.

---

[9] This inconsistency is not due to source materials as both Peters and Egger personally interviewed Lucas (for a dissenting view on Lucas's other claims to homicidal fame, see Jenkins, 1988a; Rosenbaum, 1990b).

For this figure to have real meaning it must be placed in some sort of context — what are the comparative responses to this same question from samples of the overall populations of noncriminal males, criminal offenders, sexual offenders, and nonsexual murderers? The lack of control groups limits the interpretation of their research (see Robertson & Vignaux, 1995).

Lange and DeWitt, Jr. (1990b) state that the 36 sexual murderer sample used in this research was inadequate for extrapolation purposes, and the database flawed to the extent that the U.S. Department of Justice cut off the project's funding after an external review (see Nobile, 1989). They also express concern regarding the uncritical acceptance by the FBI of the statements of the interviewed killers (but see Ressler et al., 1988, for a partial discussion of this problem). They underline their indictment with a quote from sex murderer Colin Pitchfork: "Probation officers and psychiatrists, these people are quite happy if you tell them what they want to hear .... I can't believe how easy it is to spin yarns to these people." Others, while somewhat skeptical of the methodology, view the FBI's research from a more balanced perspective (Copson, 1993).

Hickey (1997) has assessed possible applications of various criminological theories for the explanation of serial murder. These include a form of social structure theory (the relationship between urbanism and murder), social process theory (the learning of aggression), neutralization theory (the dehumanization of murder victims), Hirschi's (1969) control theory (weakened social bonds), and labelling theory (the formation of the killer's self-image). Hickey concludes that "Because research into serial murder is in its infancy, the haste to draw quick conclusions about its etiology is not only speculative but dangerous" (p. 85). He particularly questions beliefs concerning the influence of alcohol and pornography on the cause of serial murder.

Hickey (1997) proposes a tentative multiple-factor model for the purposes of future research and discussion. This trauma-control model describes processes and factors that may influence early stages in the development of a serial killer. A series of traumatic events (such as parental rejection, an unstable family life, or sexual abuse) lead to feelings of inadequacy and low self-esteem. As more trauma is suffered, increasingly violent fantasies start to develop. "The most critical factor common to serial killers is violent fantasy" (p. 91). States of dissociation may also result as a means of psychological protection.

In the cases of some serial murderers, background factors and facilitators may be precursors to violence. These factors can be biological, psychological, or sociological, and facilitators involve alcohol, drugs, or pornography. On their own, however, these background factors and facilitators are insufficient, as millions of people are constantly exposed to similar conditions without becoming killers. Instead, such factors can act as catalysts for aggressive behaviour on the part of those who experience increasingly violent fantasies. If this process of trauma and fantasy continues it may eventually lead to the acting out of violent and murderous thoughts. When this develops into a cycle where the killing feeds back into the trauma and the fantasy life, repeated murders result unless the offender is caught. The validity of this theory for serial killer development remains to be empirically tested.

Mitchell (1997) notes that most human behavior cannot be adequately accounted for by any single explanation. He proposes an integrated approach linking the background of the offender to triggers that prompt violent action. His model of serial murder comprises three interactive elements: (1) the foundation of the pathology (biological predisposition combined with environmental trauma and stressors); (2) a path of stressors resulting in the first murder (maladaptive coping skills, retreat into fantasy, and dissociation); and (3) an obsessive-compulsive ritualistic cycle (refractory period followed by a renewal of the homicidal urge).

Cameron and Frazer (1987) see social and political context as critically important in the understanding of repetitive sexual and lust murderers. They note that feminists "locate male violence against women in the realm of the *political* ... a collective, culturally sanctioned misogyny which is important in maintaining the collective power of men" (p. 164). Caputi (1990) states that serial and sexual murder "are crimes of sexually political import ... a product of the dominant culture. It is the ultimate expression of a sexuality that defines sex as a form of dominion/power" (p. 2).

They suggest that male violence is facilitated through the depersonalization of women and their objectified social representation. Sex murder, an extreme form of this violence, can be viewed as a form of sexual terrorism, though Cameron and Frazer (1987) caution that this account of sex murder is not adequate by itself. However, they fail to address the central question why some males — and females — repeatedly torture and kill innocent victims (both female and male, human and animal) while the vast majority of the members of society, subject to the same cultural images, never murder anyone. Feminist scholarship in this area has been criticized for its sensationalistic preoccupation with the male sexual murder of females, while ignoring those incidents involving male victims and female serial killers (Cluff, Hunter, & Hinch, 1997; Pearson, 1997). Misogyny may play an important role in understanding certain types of serial and mass murder, and probably influences victim selection,[10] but it is not in itself a sufficient explanation.

---

[10] The victims of serial killers are more likely to be female than male. Hickey (1997) found 35% of serial murderers targeted only females, 22% only males, and 42% both sexes. By comparison, only about one-quarter of all murder victims in the United States are female (Holmes & De Burger, 1988).

Leyton (1986) characterizes serial murder from an historical sociological perspective, describing it as a form of "sub-political and conservative protest which nets the killer a substantial social profit of revenge, celebrity, identity, and sexual relief .... a primitive rebellion against the social order" (p. 14). Seeking to achieve personal status and revenge for past denial, the repetitive killer strikes back at society. Consequently, different social orders produce different types of serial killers. He describes several explanatory factors for the modern American phenomenon of serial murder, observing the abnormal number of serial murders there compared to other parts of the world.[11] Other historical periods would possess distinct aetiologies dependent primarily upon class structure and relations. The increased experience of family breakdown, within the context of a stratified and class hierarchical society, has led to a growth in the number of people who lack a feel of social "place." These individuals may not ever develop a coherent socially constructed identity.

This lack of identity is agitated by the internal social crises created when middle-class positions close and cultural ambitions are stifled. Many tensions exist within modern North American society: urbanization, mobility, anonymity, loss of community, family disintegration, failure, alienation, and despair. These are most acute in the lower classes and their members the most threatened. Leyton suggests such factors can lead the upper working and lower middle classes to attack those they perceive as excluding or oppressing them in an effort to "level" society. These attacks occur in a social context significantly marked by the impact of a culture of violence. Modern American society condones revenge and links violence to lust and sex. Consequently, such revenge or grudge murders engendered by failed ambitions are a path to "success," to attention and celebrity.

While this seminal theory helped lay the groundwork for future research, it was based on limited data, and the conjectures were not empirically tested. All serial killers are grouped together, an approach that appears unjustified. Also, the preponderance of data on serial murder victimology indicates that members of powerless groups are most at risk (see below). Leyton's ideas are intriguing and informative, but on their own, historical and sociological explanations are insufficient explanations for rare behaviours.

---

[11] The United States may have more than its share of serial killers, but there are many documented cases from other countries. Jenkins (1988b, 1994) lists 12 English serial murder cases, involving at least 4 victims, from 1940 to 1985, and 7 German cases, involving at least 10 victims, from 1910 to 1950. The total for England represents 1.7% of all known murders in that country, a similar percentage to that found for serial killing within the U.S. (Fox & Levin, 1992; Jenkins, 1988b, 1994). Pinto and Wilson (1990) list 17 cases of serial murder in Australia from 1900 to 1990, 14 of which occurred since 1959. Currently, South Africa and the former Soviet republics appear to be plagued with a disproportionate number of such killers.

Other researchers have presented a potpourri of theories to explain the genesis of serial, sexual, and sadistic murder: sexual repression and conflict (Heilbroner, 1993); maternal seductiveness and rejection coupled with unavailability of the father (Revitch, 1965); borderline personality organization and gender identity conflict (Rappaport, 1988); learning theory (Hale, 1993); antisocial personality disorder (Spore, 1994); dissociation and obsession (Carlisle, 1993); obsessive-compulsive disorder, organicity, and multiple personality disorder (Brown, 1991b; see also Reese, 1979); paraphilic sexual sadism (Drukteinis, 1992); the "Right Man" syndrome, defined as a violent incapacity to be wrong (Wilson & Seaman, 1990); ego-inflating self-conception and the exercise of dark desires through adventurous risk and sexual recreation (Green, 1993); Münchausen syndrome by proxy (Keeney & Heide, 1994c); and classical necrophilia and vampirism (Brown, 1991a).

While explanations for the origins of such extreme violent behaviour are many and varied, ranging from the biogenetic to the socio-historical, very few of them are based on sound empirical research. Limited case studies, unrepresentative samples, problematic interviews, unspecified methodologies, untested classifications, and pure speculation characterize many of the discussions of serial murder. The lack of an empirically-based taxonomy also hinders attempts at explanation. The very term "serial killer" acts as a single label, yet work in the area of criminal profiling suggests several different personality types are involved, each with distinctive antecedents and violent behaviour triggers.

Single factor theories are dangerous, and it is likely several critical factors on multiple levels — biological, psychological, and sociological — must be present to produce the necessary conditions for the creation of a serial murderer. Such a process requires the overlapping causal influences to be positioned just so; if anything is out of line then the path of development is blocked. Thus, serial and multiple murderers are still rare. Available research suggests that an abusive childhood, inconsistent parenting, and violent sexual fantasies are likely to be important causative factors.

The lack of a theoretical explanation for the motivations of serial murderers is not an impediment to understanding other elements of their crimes. The requirements of daily life occupy so much time that it is hard to differentiate offenders from nonoffenders simply because the former typically behave like the latter (Brantingham & Brantingham, 1998). Searching for underlying patterns in the "randomness" of such crime series can lead to analyses that may be informative and telling. This is the effort to find the "logic" in the pathologic.

2.1.4   Victimology

> In cases a lot are just encountered by the serial killer who is hunting for the
> victim he needs: As for how are they stalked, approached, attacked, and
> trapped, each serial killers has his own personal mode and manner or form
> of current style and fashion ... the serial killer kills strangers 95 percent of
> the time because as the safest target in terms of avoiding detection ....
> Children: young boys and girls are frequently desirable victims by the serial
> killer for sex .... Most serial killers have selected there murder scenes by the
> place they take there victims to: as for the relevant geographice areas selected
> by the offender (serial killer) this dependes on the seasons, and were the
> serial killer is killing.
>
> — **Clifford Olson's description of how serial murderers select their
> victims and crime sites; Olson, 1992b, pp. 6–8, uncorrected quote**

One of the purposes of victimology is to help explain the role of the victim
in the occurrence of crime. It stresses the importance of dynamic behaviours,
and environmental, situational, and triggering factors for an understanding
of crime patterns. "In the victimological perspective, violent behavior is
viewed not as a unilateral action but as the outcome of dynamic process of
interaction" (Fattah, 1991, p. xiv).

The chances of any given individual becoming a victim of serial murder
is extremely low, on par with the odds of being struck by lightning. Most
homicide victims are killed by intimates or associates and stranger murder
is rare (Silverman & Kennedy, 1993). Only 6% of homicides in the U.S.
involve sexual assault. Serial killers are believed to be responsible for 1 to 2%
of all murders in the U.S. and England; such murder would then account for
only 1 out of every 10,000 U.S. deaths (Fox & Levin, 1992; Jenkins, 1988b,
1994). Hickey's estimates are even lower (1997); he collected a total of 2526
to 3860 recorded serial killings in the U.S. from 1800 to 1995. Even for the
peak period of his study (1975 to 1995, 974 to 1398 victims), the annual risk
rate was only about 1 in 5 million. Cavanagh (1993) calculated a significantly
higher total of 1424 U.S. serial murder victims for the period from 1976 to
1989. His figures are based on Newton's (1990a, 1990b) collection of cases
which, he cautions, includes incidents that might not be considered as true
serial murders by all researchers.

It is essential to recognize, however, that risk of crime is not spread
uniformly throughout the population. Particular types of people, by virtue
of their sex, age, race, occupation, or location, are at much higher risks of
victimization (Block, Felson, & Block, 1985). "Just as lions look for deer near
their watering hole, criminal offenders disproportionately find victims in
certain settings or high-risk occupations" (Felson, 1987, p. 914). Keppel

(1989) lists six activities commonly engaged in by serial murder victims at the point of approach: (1) sleeping at home; (2) looking for a job; (3) going to a tavern; (4) prostitution; (5) walking on a college campus; and (6) hitch-hiking. Hickey assessed victim facilitation as high in 16%, low in 72% to 75%, and mixed in 9 to 12% of serial murders. Godwin and Canter (1997) found in a study of 54 male U.S. serial killers, convicted of a minimum of 10 murders, that 92% of their victims were strangers, 4% were acquaintances, 3% were friends, and 1% were family members. Prostitutes accounted for 28% of this sample.

Sexual and physical assaults against prostitutes are disturbingly common. Between 1991 and 1995, 63 known prostitutes were murdered in Canada, almost all female (Duchesne, 1997). This represents 5% of all reported female homicides (n = 1118) during the same time period. The prostitute murder risk in British Columbia has been estimated at ranging between 60 to 120 times that of the general adult female population (Lowman & Fraser, 1995). Clients are responsible for the bulk of these homicides (n = 50), most of which occur in the offender's vehicle. Stranger relationships and the private nature of the street sex trade make the identification of the killer difficult, and the majority of prostitute murders go unsolved (54% vs. 20% for murder generally).

Godwin (1998) states that the ecology of victim target networks can help police identify previously unknown victims and possible future victims. He proposes that the decision-making process of serial murderers is based on an assessment of gain (potential victims) and risk factors (surveillance, police, escape routes). Victim social networks also help define the areas of highest risk for victimization by serial murderers. Such places include urban subculture domains (e.g., bars, red-light districts), isolated landscapes (e.g., parking lots, jogging paths), neighbourhoods of the elderly or poor, skid rows, and university campuses. Hickey (1997) found that some serial murderers attacked only females or males, but many targeted either sex. Most victims are strangers but family members and acquaintances are not immune. Two-thirds of serial murder victims are preyed upon by someone from their own (usually urban) community. Death is usually from strangulation or beating.

Victim choice may provide insights to the nature of the offender, and detailed victimology is one of the key information requirements in the criminal profiling process (Douglas, Ressler, Burgess, & Hartman, 1986; Holmes & Holmes, 1996). The victim is often symbolic and may remind the killer of someone from their past.[12] Particular victim appearances, specific actions, or the elicitation of certain responses may trigger a murderous reaction from the offender. "The plan or fantasy constructed earlier [by the killer] may call

---

[12] One study of sexually sadistic criminals, however, found only 17% (5) of the 30 cases involved a victim that resembled someone of psychological significance to the offender (Dietz et al., 1990).

for a victim who meets certain criteria, and many murderers have been known to seek out a victim who is exactly right for the fantasy" (Ressler et al., 1988, p. 50). Several of the sexual murderers in the FBI study admitted they hunted nightly for victims,[13] though the proper circumstances for an attack only arose occasionally.

Some serial murderers have specific and articulated victim criteria. Joel Rifkin, who strangled 17 street prostitutes in New York, confessed to driving around for hours, circling the red-light strolls of Lower Manhattan in a search for just the right type of woman — petite, with straight dark hair and sexy jewelry (Pulitzer & Swirsky, 1994a). He only killed those who accepted money for sex and then did something to anger him. Robert Hansen, Alaska's worst serial killer, had three triggering requirements. Victims had to approach him for sex, refuse to do a requested sexual act, and then try to escape (Du Clos, 1993; Gilmour & Hale, 1991; Pulitzer & Swirsky, 1994b).

By comparison, Clifford Olson varied both the age and sex of his victims (Ferry & Inwood, 1982; Mulgrew, 1990). He picked up potential victims at bus stops, offered them jobs, and enticed them into his car through beguilement and seduction (Worthington, 1993). Some he drove home, others he sexually assaulted or even murdered. Olson himself does not seem to know why he killed those he did; on one occasion he stated he murdered so the victim would not report the sex assault to the police, and on another he blamed his use of alcohol and pills.

Victim selection may depend upon serial murder type because of variations in offender motivation (Holmes & Holmes, 1996). Nonspecific victim selection is associated with the visionary serial murder type, known victims with visionary and comfort killers, and relational victims with comfort serial murderers. Barrett (1990) observes that over time serial killers become less selective as they become constrained by victim availability.

In an excerpt from an interview with a convicted serial murderer, Holmes and Holmes (1996) presents an offender's perspective on the issue of victim selection:

> The traditional school of thought has it that serial murderers, on the whole, select their victims on the basis of certain physical and/or personal characteristics ... male or female, black or white, young or old, short or tall, large-busted or small, shy or forward, and so on. ... [W]hen a typical serial killer begins an active search for human prey, he will go to great lengths to capture and victimize only those individuals who closely fit the mold of his preferred "ideal."

[13] See the discussion in Ressler and Shachtman (1992) on the hunting behaviour of David Berkowitz, the Son of Sam.

I am personally convinced that every serial killer does indeed nurture a rather clear mental picture of his own ideal victim ... Notwithstanding this point, however, I strongly believe that in the case of most serial killers, the physical and personal characteristics of those on their respective list of victims only infrequently coincide with the desired traits of their imagined "ideal"...

There are two basic, interrelated reasons for this disparity. The first centers upon the extreme caution exercised by a serial killer in his predatory search for a victim; the second, upon the nature of the compulsion that drives him to violence .... This unremitting sense of caution has direct ramification on victim selection in that, during the course of his search for human prey, a serial killer is seldom apt to find his preferred ideal victim in a position of safe and easy capture. In truth, it is a difficult and time-consuming task to locate any potential victim who can be readily seized without risk of detection.... A serial killer could, of course, bide his time. He could reject all other easy prey until, at last, his ideal victim appeared in circumstances perfectly suited to his caution. In actual practice, however, he rarely will choose to wait very long.

Why is this so? Because as the second reason given earlier, the nature of a serial murderer's compulsion for violence is such that it precludes any prolonged or self-imposed delay in acting out his brutal urges. Initially, he may have set out fully determined to succeed at capturing his ideal victim ... But, as time passes without his promptly accomplishing this specific end — a common occurrence within his many hunts ... his intense and mounting hunger for real life violence against a real life captive inevitably compels him to settle for any soonest-available victim of opportunity. (pp. 69–70)

As suggested by this offender, target choice is not just determined by fantasy and psychological pathology; it is also influenced by such factors as victim availability and attack opportunity (Jenkins, 1993b). By definition, a serial killer must have been responsible for at least three separate acts of homicide, and to achieve this status a criminal needs to escape apprehension. Consequently, murderers who prey on "easy victims" whose actions make them easy targets and whose lifestyle socially marginalizes them, are more likely to be repeatedly successful (Cleary, Klein, & Luxenburg, 1994). Egger (1998) refers to these victims as the "less-dead" — the prostitutes, street people, runaways, homosexuals, and elderly who are society's throwaways. Opportunity is thus important in understanding and explaining patterns of victimization. "Fashions in multiple homicide appear to change over time in ways that reflect changes in potential victim populations .... Victimological factors can ... [also] go far toward accounting for distribution by place and region" (Jenkins, pp. 471–472).

Beyond the actual murder victims, there are a host of secondary victims who suffer from the crimes of serial killers (Fox & Levin, 1996b; Holmes & De Burger, 1988; Ressler et al., 1988). Family and friends experience the grief, loss, and financial strain associated with the death of a loved one, and they are often subjected to "repeat victimization" by the press, police, and courts. Treatment programs are available for offenders, but usually there is no provision for psychological counselling for victims' families. In response to these issues, self-help groups and advocacy agencies such as Parents of Murdered Children, the Adam Walsh Child Resource Center, and Victims of Violence International have been formed (Sullivan, 1995).

Society is also victimized by these predators through the resulting fear and suspicion they cause (Fowler, 1990). Increased mistrust of strangers, fear of public spaces, and reluctance to help others all contribute towards the breakdown of community. Additionally, the economic losses associated with cases of serial murder are high; investigation expenditures, court costs and legal fees, and long-term incarceration expenses add up to millions of dollars (Victims of Violence Society, 1990). The psychological and fiscal impact of serial murder spreads far beyond the small number of actual homicide victims.

2.2   Child Murder

Child murder is a matter of great concern to society. Most murders of children are committed by family members and stranger child homicide is rare. Still, when this type of crime does occur, the impact on a community is tremendous. It has been suggested that some serial murderers target children because they represent the future. These offenders are extracting revenge from a society they feel has wronged them. Adults, however, are the most common victims of serial killers (Hickey, 1997). The U.S. Office of Juvenile Justice and Delinquency Prevention (OJJDP) estimates that annually there are one to two stranger abductions per million population, with teenagers (14 to 17 years of age) at highest risk (Allen-Hagen, 1989; see also Lau, 1989); this figure does not seem to be increasing. Serial murder cases with child victims are more likely to involve a family member or acquaintance as the offender.

Child molesters may be either situational or preferential (Lanning, 1995). Situational offenders do not prefer children, but will victimize them — and any other group — that opportunity presents. Preferential offenders, often referred to as pedophiles, do possess a sexual preference for children, and will typically develop skills in identifying and targeting vulnerable victims. Some pedophiles can watch a group of children and often know which ones are from dysfunctional families (Lanning, 1995). Child molesters tend to be nomadic as they often have to move when their presence is found out. Many pedophiles are predators who repeatedly commit crimes, but only a few are killers.

Extensive study of child murder and its geography has been done in both Great Britain and the U.S. The CATCHEM database contains information since January 1, 1960, on all child sexual homicides in the U.K. (Burton, 1998; Copson, 1993). With over 3000 cases, the system analyzes murder and offender data for investigative prediction purposes (see below). It is maintained by the Derbyshire Constabulary, and administered by Detective Inspector Chuck Burton who has discovered several interesting findings in the data. The clearance rate for child sexual homicides where the victim was transported was less than half that for crimes with no transportation. The offender's vehicle is often the murder scene in cases of victim transportation. The more locations used in the murder (i.e., separate encounter, attack, murder, or body dump sites), the more geographically complex the crime, and the lower the clearance rate.

In cases where the victim was not transported by vehicle (n = 190), 98% of the victim's bodies were deposited within 50 yards of a footpath, and all were found within 100 yards. While concealment appeared to be intended in 46% of these cases, only 5% of the time was the body buried, as opposed to 17% of the cases where it was placed in water. The body was found within a half mile of where the victim was last seen in 91% of the cases, and within one mile 97% of the time.

In child homicides involving victim transportation by vehicle (n = 89), 88% of the victim's bodies were deposited within 50 yards, 97% within 100 yards, and all within 150 yards of a road or track affording vehicular access. The body was left outdoors 94% of the time. While concealment appeared to be intended in 57% of the cases, only 12% of the time was the body buried, as opposed to 20% of the cases where it was placed in water.

Hanfland, Keppel, and Weis (1997) conducted a study of child abduction murders in the U.S. There are approximately 100 such incidents annually, comprising only 0.5% of all murders. The project analyzed 777 case investigations, representing 562 child victims and 419 killers. Of these, 138 cases were part of 55 series. The typical victim was female, mean age of 11 years, and sexual assault was the primary motivation. Stranger offenders were involved in 53%, friend or acquaintance in 39%, and family member or intimate in 9% of the cases. The older the victim, the greater the likelihood the murderer was a stranger.

The typical offender was 27 years of age, male, and unmarried, though only 17% lived alone. About 50% were unemployed and 16% were transient. The majority had criminal records, 60% with previous violent crimes. More than half of the murderers had committed prior offences against children; this increased to 76% for serial offenders. A similar modus operandi was present in two-thirds of the offenders' prior crimes. Police had contact with the killer before he became a prime suspect in about one third of the murders, usually within 24 hours of the crime. Investigative red herrings are not uncommon in child homicides, and the study found they were encountered in 38% of the cases. Despite perceptions to the contrary, the media helped more often than it hindered an investigation.

In child abduction murder cases, the victim was killed in less than 1 hour in 44%, 3 hours in 74%, and 24 hours in 91% of the cases. Only 42% of the victims were still alive at the time they were reported missing. The majority were opportunistic (57%), and only a few were specifically targeted (13%). Serial offenders selected male victims more often than nonserial offenders (38 vs. 22%). Most of the serial crimes involved stranger offenders (80%).

Hanfland et al. (1997) geographically analyzed child murder, dissecting the incidents into victim encounter, murder, and body recovery sites. The typical child abduction murder scenario involves a victim encountered in an urban area near their home, transported to a rural area, killed, and then dumped near the murder site. Confirming the CATCHEM research, this study found murders involving multiple locations are difficult to solve; the more sites, the lower the clearance rate.

The encounter site is usually close to both the victim's residence (less than 200 feet in 33%, and less than 0.25 miles in 58% of the cases) and last known location (less than 200 feet in 65% of the cases). If the encounter site was unknown in a murder investigation (17% of the time), the clearance rate dropped to 40% below the mean; if known, it rose to 13% above the mean. This indicates the importance of thorough neighbourhood canvasses and area searches. The killer was in the area of the encounter site because he belonged there two thirds of the time, underlining the need for police to not only ask what was unusual, but also what was normal during their canvasses. In 29% of the cases, the offender lived in the neighbourhood, within 200 feet of the victim encounter site in 18%, and within 0.25 miles in 35% of the crimes.

Next to the body recovery site, the murder scene possesses the most physical evidence (see also Lowman & Fraser, 1995); unfortunately, in multiple location crimes, it is the site most often unknown (23%). Distance from murder site to body recovery site was less than 200 feet 72% of the time. Distance from the murder site to the encounter site was less than 200 feet in 31%, and less than 0.25 miles in 47% of the cases.

The body recovery site contains the most physical evidence; fortunately, it is almost always located, at least in those cases known to police. Concealment of the corpse was more likely in child abduction murders (52%) than in murder generally (14%). A child's body can be very difficult to find because of its small size. For example, the body of a child 4 feet in height requires only about one-third the volume of a 6-foot-tall adult. Consequently, search-ers have to be especially diligent when looking for young children.

Some offenders returned to the body dump site (22%), and some left town following the murder (21%). The killer occasionally kept the victim longer than necessary (15%), but this was usually for less than a day. In these situations, the body was stored in the offender's residence (50%), vehicle (28%), or other easily accessible location (22%). Rarely (5%) was the victim's body actually recovered from the killer's home. The choice of the body dump site was specific in 37%, random in 37%, and forced by circumstances in 14% of the murders. The victim was found in his or her own home in 4% of the cases; younger victims were more likely to be dumped closer to their home. Approximately 63% of the time, the body was located more than 1.5 miles from the victim's residence. Evidence discarded by the murderer was recovered in 21% of the cases. More often than not (59%), it was recovered within 1 mile of the body dump site, and half the time it was found along the roadway travelled by the killer.

2.4   Murder and Distance

In a Washington State study of single-victim single-offender murders from 1981 to 1986 (n = 967, 74% cleared), Keppel and Weis (1994) found the more information known regarding times and locations of the crimes, the greater the likelihood the case will be solved. Crime locations provide evi-dence and witnesses; time of offence allows suspect alibis to be verified or refuted. Together, they permit investigators to establish if the victim and a suspect were in the same area at the same time.

Their study broke murder down into five potential different locations: (1) victim last seen site; (2) initial contact site; (3) initial assault site; (4) murder site; and (5) body recovery site. Police investigators are most likely to know the location of body recovery, followed in order by the murder, victim last seen, initial assault, and initial contact sites. This information influences case clearance in two ways. First, the more crime sites known, the greater the chance the case will be solved. If at least four of the five potential locations are known to police, the clearance rate is 85%; otherwise, it is only 14%. Second, the study found higher clearances associated with those murders characterized by shorter distances between crime sites, particularly from where the victim was last seen to body recovery. The clearance rate is 86% if this distance is less than 200 feet, dropping to 50% if it is greater. Longer distances impede and delay finding all crime locations, and therefore all available evidence.

Keppel and Weiss note that 24 hours appears to be a critical time thresh-old. As time elapses, evidence deteriorates and witnesses' memories fade.

While a murder suspect was in custody within 24 hours in 66% of the cases, the chances of the crime being solved dropped significantly if no one was arrested by 48 hours. The study found more cases cleared where the time between locations was less than 24 hours, with an average decrease of 30% in the solution rate otherwise. If the time between when a victim was last seen and when their body was recovered was less than 24 hours, the clearance rate was 82%; otherwise, it dropped to 42%.

Dramatic differences are found by combining time and distance effects. If there are 24 hours or less between the time a victim is last seen and when their body is recovered, and if the distance between these sites is less than 200 feet, the clearance rate rises to 86%. If the time is greater than one month, and the distance more than 1.5 miles, the clearance rate drops to 4%. Offenders may intentionally separate the locations associated to a murder to delay body recovery, facilitate evidence destruction, involve different police jurisdictions, and complicate the investigation.

Serial Rape and Arson

Serial murder is rare, but serial crime is not. While this book is primarily concerned with serial killers, rapists, and arsonists, many bank robbers, burglars, auto thieves, shoplifters, and con artists are also serial offenders. Several studies have shown that the distribution of offending frequency rates, lambda (λ), is highly skewed with some criminals possessing λ values in the range of 10 to 50 times that of others (Canela-Cacho, Blumstein, & Cohen, 1997; Marvell & Moody, 1998). This implies a high degree of serial criminality. For example, if we make the modest assumption that 10% of offenders demonstrate a λ value 10 times that of the other 90%, then this results in over 50% of all crimes being the responsibility of only 10% of offenders. One study of paraphiliacs (n = 411, mean duration of deviant arousal = 12 years) found, on average, 581 attempted and 533 completed sex offences, and 336 victims per offender (Abel, Mittelman, & Becker, 1985). But these averages are misleading because 70% of the offences were actually committed by only 5% of the offenders.

The very nature of a skewed λ distribution means that, while most criminals are not serial in nature, most crime is. Similarly, Hare (1993) notes that approximately 20% of prison inmates are psychopaths — versus only about 1% of the general population — and these individuals are responsible for more than half of all serious crime. In a study of fugitive migration, for example, Rossmo (1987) found that Canadian criminal fugitives had a mean of 15 previous charges and 10 previous convictions.

It has been suggested the difficulty in determining who is a serial predator could be addressed by replacing crime count with a psychodynamic assessment of a criminal's propensity to re-offend (Kocsis & Irwin, 1998). Compulsive criminal fantasies appear to be fed by a distinctive internal drive mechanism, involving the elements of psychopathy, narcissism, sadism, paraphilia, fantasy, compulsiveness, and dissociation. For example, Prentky, Burgess, Rokous, Lee, Hartman, Ressler, & Douglas (1989) found that serial sexual murderers were much more likely than single sexual murderers to have acted out conscious fantasies (86 versus 23%).

A stranger victim is one mark of a serial offender. Kocsis and Irwin (1998) suggest the following additional indicators of serial crime:

- Murder: postmortem mutilation or cannibalism, stylized or "dramatic" positioning of the corpse, sexual assault, necrophilia, overkill, torture, and souvenir collection.
- Rape: stylized verbal scripts demanded from the victim, sadistic or violent behaviour, paraphilic activities, offender's inability to penetrate the victim or to climax, and souvenir collection.
- Arson: destruction of property in addition to fire damage, sexual activity at the crime scene, the presence of signature (e.g., graffiti, fecal matter or urine, token object), and stylized behaviour in the fire setting.

Alston (1994) differentiated between series types and classified them into five different patterns. A class I series (the most common) is the traditional case of a single offender with multiple victims. A class II series involves two offenders and multiple victims. Class III, IV, and V series comprise several offenders attacking multiple victims in different partnership combinations (e.g., Smith commits some of his crimes with Jones, others with Anderson, and still others alone). Alston notes that higher order types are unstable and often break down into class I or class II series.

Serial murder, rape, and arson cases comprise the bulk of the demand for geographic profiling services. How similar, at least geographically, are these different types of crime? Warren et al. (1995) observed variations in the spatial patterns of serial rapists and arsonists, noting that the latter were more likely to reside within the perimeters of their hunting areas. They suggest "geographical patterns of serial offenses may be crime specific, and that patterns that are characteristic of some types of serial crime may not be characteristic of others" (p. 219).

While this observation is likely correct to a point, it also appears that the similarities are stronger than the differences. Research on the geography of serial predators has demonstrated many commonalities,[14] and operational experience has helped confirm these findings. Parallels in spatial behaviour appear to be the product of common underlying human processes. Taylor (1977) makes the argument that "there are no patterns; there are only processes" (p. 134).

---

[14] This research has studied serial murder (Hickey, 1997; Holmes & DeBurger, 1988; Rossmo, 1995a), serial rape (Alston, 1994; Canter & Larkin, 1993; LeBeau, 1987a, 1987b, 1992; Warren, Reboussin, & Hazelwood, 1995), and serial arson (Icove & Crisman, 1975; Sapp, Huff, Gary, Icove, & Horbert, 1994).

3.1 Serial Rape

Serial rapists exhibit several patterns of similarity to serial killers, which is hardly surprising considering many of the latter began as rapists and often intersperse murders with non-lethal sex assaults. James LeBeau (1985, 1987c, 1991, 1992), one of the first researchers to distinguish between patterns of serial and nonserial rape, observed differences between offender groups in the type of area targeted. The relationship between victim and offender in serial rape is also different from rape generally. While the majority (84%) of serial rapists are strangers, about half of overall rape victims know their attacker, and only a minority of child abductions and sexual assaults involve strangers (5 to 30%). Miethe and McCorkle (1998) report that multiple offenders are present in less than 10% of all rapes, though they do not provide the comparable percentage for serial rape.

Neighbourhoods with high overall rape rates are characterized by ethnic diversity, population turnover, and multiple unit rental dwellings. They tend to be in large metropolitan areas, and their populations have disproportionate levels of unemployed and low income inhabitants (Miethe & McCorkle, 1998). The incidence of sexual assault is greatest in summer (July, August), and lowest in winter (December, January, February). These crimes disproportionately occur on the weekend and during the evening (37% between 6:00 pm and midnight).

Many sexual attacks take place near the home of either the victim or offender (37%), and only a minority (14%) occur in public areas, parking lots, or alleys (Miethe & McCorkle, 1998). If the offender is a stranger, however, about half of the assaults happen in open public areas or parking lots. Low density cities have less surveillance and higher rates of rape (Felson, 1998). Neighbourhoods characterized by a mix of residential, industrial, and commercial land use put people on streets containing parking lots, abandoned buildings, and deserted blocks, making them more vulnerable to attack. These areas are typically in low income districts.

While rape is often seen as a crime of power and anger, several researchers have noticed the importance of sex as a primary motive for certain rapists (Felson, 1993; Prentky et al., 1989; Soley, 1998). The principal components of the human sex drive include the biological, physiological, and psychosexual (Hazelwood & Warren, 1995a). The psychosexual component is the most important to the police investigator for an understanding of sex crime. Fantasy thus plays a key role in criminal sexuality. Generally, the more complex the crime, the greater the fantasy, and the more intelligent the offender (Hazelwood & Warren, 1995a). Because reality is imperfect and never lives up to fantasy, criminal offenders feel the need to try again, creating a process that results in serial sex crime.

A child molester and rapist, who burglarized homes to attack his victims, described the excitement of crime with a sexual component. His deviant fantasies intertwined with the thrill in knowing he might be caught.

> It was good for me and I didn't really care about anyone else. Once I did break into the houses the rush was incredible. I knew that I had control, there was nothing anyone could do to stop me. And once I got away with it, I went to more dangerous things, more daring. ... I preferred that rush over anything else. (Wood, Gove, Wilson, & Cochran, 1997, p. 358)

Collateral materials may be found by investigators during the search of a sex offender's residence (Hazelwood & Lanning, 1995). These are articles not directly associated with the offender's crimes but rather provide evidence or information regarding sexual preferences, interests, or activities. They often show the nature of the criminal fantasy. Types of collateral material include:

- Erotica — Material with a direct sexual purpose;
- Educational — Material that provides knowledge on how to commit a crime, avoid arrest, or manipulate the court system;
- Introspective — Material that provides an understanding of deviant sexual behaviour and paraphilias; and
- Intelligence — Material that assists in the planning and execution of future crimes.

The FBI employs a rapist typology based on categories developed by Groth, Burgess, and Holmstrom (1977). Using power, anger, and sexual motives as its framework, the FBI/Groth typology includes: (1) power-reassurance; (2) power assertive; (3) anger-retaliatory; and (4) anger-excitation rapists. An FBI study found that categorization accuracy rates for profilers following this typology ranged from 80 to 95% (Warren, Reboussin, Hazelwood, & Wright, 1991). Hazelwood (1995) outlines the FBI/Groth typology and describes the associated offender and offence characteristics.

The power-reassurance rapist bolsters his masculinity through the exercise of power over women. He is often referred to as the "gentleman rapist." This type of rapist normally preselects victims through surveillance or peeping activities, and may have several potential victims lined up. Therefore, if one assault is unsuccessful, he will often seek another victim nearby on the same night. The power-reassurance rapist will typically use a surprise approach and attack in the late evening or early morning hours. His assaults exhibit a consistent pattern, occurring within the same locale in neighbourhoods of similar socioeconomic status. He will be a chronic offender who may take souvenirs from his victims and keep a record of his crimes. This is the most common type of rapist.

The power-assertive rapist uses his attacks to express what he believes is his "natural" dominance over women. He is a selfish offender, unconcerned over the welfare of his victim. This type of rapist will normally employ a con approach, and then force the victim to engage in repeated sexual assaults. The victim will often be left in a state of partial nudity at the assault location, which will be a place of convenience and safety for the offender. The timing of these attacks is typically intermittent. This is the second most common type of rapist.

The anger-retaliatory rapist is motivated by feelings of rage and retaliation; he wants to "get even" with women. The victims are symbols of someone else, often exhibiting certain appearance, dress, or occupational similarities. Sex is used to punish and degrade, and the attacks are typically frenzied with excessive levels of force. They occur as the result of an emotional outburst and therefore lack premeditation. This impulsivity means there is little planning or advance victim selection; usually only a short time is spent with the victim. This offender's attacks are sporadic and can occur anytime during the day or night. This is the third most common type of rapist.

The anger-excitation rapist achieves sexual excitement from observing the victim's reaction to physical or psychological pain. The rapes may involve torture and are characterized by fear and brutality. These crimes are fantasy based, and such details as weapons, tools, transportation, and travel routes are thoroughly preplanned. The offender typically uses a con approach, then attacks and binds the victim, taking her to a preselected location that offers privacy. He will usually keep her for a period of time, and may tape or video record his sexually sadistic activities. Normally the victim is a stranger, and no pattern to the timing of the attacks is evident. This is the least common type of rapist.

Soley, Knight, Cerce, and Holmes (forthcoming) point out that rape typologies lack empirical verification and remain, for the most part, untested. The Groth rapist typology, for example, provides global classification criteria only, assessments of its validity are limited, and there are no estimates of interrater reliability. Weaknesses in offender typologies hinder the progress of criminal investigative analysis, and result in the absence of adequate, standardized measurements of crime-scene indicators and a lack of consensus on offender classification. Soley et al. suggest that the MTC: R3 (Massachusetts Treatment Center Rapist Typology, Version 3) is the most reliable and valid of rapist typologies, the result of a rational and empirical development of a taxonomic system. There are four major motivational themes in the MTC: R3: (1) opportunity; (2) pervasive anger; (3) sexual gratification (sadistic and non-sadistic); and (4) vindictiveness.

Building upon previous research using FBI data (Knight, Warren, Reboussin, & Soley, 1998), Soley et al. examined the ability of crime scene

variables to predict MTC: R3 rapist type. They found interesting results with
the predictive domains of expressive aggression (e.g., injuries requiring medical treatment, cuts, bruises, abrasions, biting, weapon use), and adult antisocial behaviour (e.g., alcohol use, drug use, presence of weapon). Those
domains with larger numbers of variables had better prediction power.

Evidence of the ability to predict rapist type from crime-scene variables
provides an empirical framework for profiling. Soley et al. suggest that "geographic profiling technology ... could be joined with crime-scene personality
profiling (CIA) to provide law enforcement with immediate, empirically-
based information not only on rapist type, but also on where the rapist may
be operating from" (p. 18). To some extent the Royal Newfoundland Constabulary (RNC) Criminal Suspect Prioritization System (CSPS) does this
through the use of offence themes to determine the likely criminal background
of a rapist or armed robber, and then applying this information in conjunction
with geographic proximity to identify potential offenders from existing police
records (House, 1997). Valid and reliable offender classification schemes amenable to quantification and capture in a computer database are first necessary
for this approach to become standard police investigative practice.

Promising research in Britain by Davies, Wittebrood, and Jackson (1997,
1998) demonstrates that certain crime scene behaviours exhibited by stranger
rapists are useful for predicting elements of the offender's criminal record.
Variables such as concealment of identity, familiarity with the criminal justice
system, control of the victim, method of approach, criminal behaviour, and
alcohol involvement, were used in a logistic regression to determine criminal
record characteristics. Their model best predicted prior convictions for burglary (69% accurate), violent crime (59% accurate), and one-off crimes (i.e.,
no other sexual offences) (71% accurate). These models are potentially valuable
tools in the generation and prioritization of suspects in sexual assault cases.

An FBI study of 41 incarcerated serial rapists responsible for a minimum
of 10 victims begins to provide a more detailed description of this type of
sex offender (Hazelwood & Warren, 1995b). The rapists in the sample
attacked a total of 837 victims, an average of 20.4 victims per offender. The
majority of the victims were strangers (84%), and half were attacked in their
own homes, usually while alone (79%). In contrast to popular perception,
only 12% of these rapes occurred outside (6% in streets or alleys, and 6% in
parking lots or on highways). Warr (1988) estimates that 50 to 60% of all
rapes are residential. These findings challenge the assumption of rape as a
street crime, and the perception of safety within the home.

In many ways these sexual offenders appeared normal. The majority had
stable employment, lived with someone (78%), and had been married at least
once (71%). Most resided in single-family dwellings, but a significant minority lived in apartments. They tested at above average intelligence. But a

significant number had problems as juveniles. The study noted the presence of enuresis (32%), cruelty to animals (19%), and fire setting (24%) — the Macdonald triad — in the sample. Also common were stealing and shoplifting (71%), youthful alcohol abuse (63%), and assaults against adults (55%). The majority began their careers as voyeurs (68%). For example, the Ski Mask Rapist, Jon Berry Simonis, began peeping when he was 15 years of age, before progressing to exposing, obscene telephone calls, and finally rape (Michaud & Hazelwood, 1998).

There was evidence of abuse in the backgrounds of most of these offenders; 76% claimed to have been sexually victimized as youngsters, 73% psychological abuse, and 38% physical abuse. Most of the time it was a parent or caretaker responsible for the abuse. In those instances of sexual molestation originating from a family member, the person responsible was just as likely to be female as male, but if the abuse came from a stranger, the victimizer was almost always male.

The mean age at first rape was 21.8 years, at middle rape, 25.8 years, and at last rape, 29 years. Almost all of this group had prior arrests and 58% had been institutionalized (46% in correctional centres and 12% in mental health facilities). Previous crimes commonly included residential burglaries close to the offender's home. Although they had been convicted of a mean of 7.6 previous sexual assaults, they reported actually being responsible for a mean of 27.8 such crimes. In other words, they were convicted of only one sex crime out of every 3.7 they committed.

Grubin and Gunn (1990) found that 86% of the English and Welsh serial and single rapists (n = 142) they studied had a criminal history, typically involving some type of theft. Half had four or more previous convictions, and 29% received their first sentence before 20 years of age. There was a greater percentage of serial rapists with previous sex crimes, usually indecent exposure or indecent assault, than single rapists (46 versus 25%). The research noted a pattern of increasing criminality amongst rapists.

The FBI research observed premeditated rape to be more prevalent than opportunistic or impulsive rape, and it is not uncommon for victims to be selected through offenders window peeping or following women home. Prior to the attack, several rapists entered the victim's home during her absence to gain familiarity with the premises. Despite this, Hazelwood and Warren (1995b) caution that most serial rapists do not hunt or stalk particular individual victims. Rather, their hunt appears to be, like that of most offenders, haphazard and only roughly preplanned; about one-third of the offenders had consumed alcohol prior to their crimes, and disguises were only worn in 7 to 12% of the cases.

Hazelwood and Warren (1995b) conclude that target selection in serial rape is typically not symbolic. Instead, victims are chosen because of general proximity, availability, and premise access. Victim selection criteria reported by the offenders in this study include availability (98%), gender (95%), location (66%), age (66%), race (63%), physical characteristics (39%), clothing (15%), and no specific traits (25%).[15] The average victim was in her twenties, but 19% were children. The research found that white serial rapists, unlike black rapists, do not cross race lines. White European males were observed to be the most sexually deviant offenders.

Vehicles were commonly used during the rapes; of these, 62% were the offender's, 7% were borrowed, and 8% were the victim's. No stolen vehicles were involved in the crimes associated with this study. Some rapists drove their victims to cemeteries to commit the assault because they believed that police rarely patrol graveyards (Michaud & Hazelwood, 1998).

The surprise attack was the most commonly used approach, followed by the con and then the blitz. Rapists stay twice as long on average with victims who resist. Following an attack, 12 to 15% revisited the crime scene, 8 to 13% communicated with the victim, and 28% followed the investigation in the media. About half (44 to 51%) of the offenders felt guilty afterwards.

Other research conducted by the FBI suggests that five crime scene behaviours can be used to predict "increasers," rapists who increase their use of violence in future rapes (Hazelwood, Reboussin, & Warren, 1989; Warren et al., 1991): (1) no negotiation with the victim; (2) lack of victim reassurance; (3) use of bindings; (4) transportation of the victim from the encounter site; and (5) macho offender image. This scale correctly predicted violence escalation in 89% of the research cases. Increasers comprised 25% of the studied rapist population. On average, they had twice as many victims (40 versus 22), and their attacks were three times as frequent as non-increasers (a mean of 19 days versus 55 days between crimes).

These findings were not replicated by either Grubin and Gunn (1990) or by Warren et al. (1995). The former analysis of serial rapists from England and Wales (n = 11) found that increasers tended to be younger and suffer from premature ejaculation. The latter study of U.S. serial rapists (n = 108) observed that white rapists were more likely to increase their level of violence. The inconsistencies between the studies may be attributable to sample differences in level of criminal activity.

In another FBI study of serial rape, the concept of the convex hull polygon (CHP) was used to characterize and examine spatial patterns of serial rapists. The CHP is the area enclosed by the convex polygon that connects the outer locations of a crime series, containing by definition all the offender's crime sites. The residence of the rapist was located within the CHP in 24%, and outside the CHP in 76% of the cases. Warren et al. (1995) created four

---

[15] Percentages do not add to 100 as multiple responses were allowed.

geographical models based on two dichotomized parameters — offender residence (within or outside the CHP), and mean distance to crime sites (near or far). The frequencies for these groupings in their data were as follows: (1) model 1 (inside near), 13%; (2) model 2 (inside far), 11%; (3) model 3 (outside near), 37%; and (4) model 4 (outside far), 39%.

The typical crime in this research involved a stranger victim (92%), attacked by surprise (78%), inside their home (60.2%), during the early morning hours (32% between 18:00 and midnight, 52% between midnight and 06:00) (Warren et al., 1995). Anger excitation rapists showed a somewhat different pattern. They were more likely to exhibit specific victim selection criteria (55% versus 16%), and almost all (91%) committed their crimes in the victim's home.

Certain crime scene aspects help identify components of offender spatial behaviour. For example, the FBI serial rape study looked at differences between marauders and commuters. The former commit their crimes around home, while the latter commute to a different region to offend (these concepts are discussed later in more detail). Nighttime offending by serial rapists was found to be a modal characteristic for 90% of the marauders, compared to 70% of the commuters (Warren et al., 1995). This result could stem from marauders wishing to protect their identities, or simply from commuter travel logistics. Commuters also demonstrated more ritualized behaviour than marauders. Minimum crime trip distances (i.e., smaller "nonoffending areas") were shorter for marauders than for commuters (0.74 versus 2.51 miles), nonwhites than whites (1.23 versus 2.70 miles), younger than older offenders (0.59 versus 2.58 miles), and nighttime than daytime rapists (1.44 versus 3.12 miles). Not surprisingly, minimum and mean crime trip distances were correlated.

Other findings of geographic interest include:

- 61% of the rapes occurred indoors;
- The most common initial contact site was the victim's home (60.2%), followed by a public street (20.4%);
- 51% of the rapists were commuters; and
- A vehicle was used in only 15% of the assaults.

Hazelwood and Warren (forthcoming) found ritual to be a determinant of sex offender spatial behaviour. They classify serial sexual criminals into the impulsive offender, who commits unsophisticated, reactive, and unplanned crimes, and the less common ritualistic offender, who commits planned, rehearsed, and generally more sophisticated crimes. Impulsive sex offenders, characterized by diverse criminal histories and generic sexual interests, are usually less specific in victim selection and not as careful regarding identification than ritualistic offenders, who have pervasive fantasies and diverse paraphilic interests. Consequently, the former tend to travel shorter distances to offend (2.30 versus 3.64 miles), and commit their crimes over smaller areas (4.57 versus 20.39 mi^2).

Experienced rapists prefer to attack women in their homes than on the street, because once they are inside they are relatively safe from observation or interference (see Warr, 1988). Hazelwood recounts the case of an educated power reassurance rapist who preselected up to six potential victims. If the first rape attempt failed, he assaulted a backup victim, her home serving as his "safe house" while police responded to the first attack. It is not surprising the most common nonsexual offence in a rapist's background is breaking and entering. Some of their crimes are actually "bonus rapes," the result of an offender opportunistically encountering a woman during a burglary (Warr, 1988).[16] Also, many attempted sexual assaults involving forcible entry are demoted to burglary; if police cannot prove the former, they will charge the offender with what the available evidence supports (Michaud & Hazelwood, 1998). Conversely, fetish and voyeuristic burglaries may be precursors to sexual assaults and homicides. Schlesinger and Revitch (1999) observed that 42.3% of the sexual murderers (n = 52) they studied possessed a history of burglary.

In his study of 30 serial rapists in British Columbia, responsible for 183 incidents, Alston (1994) determined rape locations were spatially patterned. Kolmogorov-Smirnov tests for goodness of fit revealed significant clustering and the presence of distance decay in the data. Serial rapists used a narrow search space that closely followed their activity paths. Using curvilinear distance[17] measures, Alston found that 94% of the offences were within 2.5 kilometres of the offender's activity space, and most were within 0.30 kilometres. Activity space was defined as the offender's activity nodes (past and present homes, current and previous work sites, and residences of partners, friends, and family members) and connecting routine pathways. When activity nodes alone were considered, 72% of the offences were within 5 kilometres, and most were within 2 kilometres. The mean curvimetre distance from rape site to nearest offender activity node was 0.91 kilometres (median = 0.72 km, standard deviation = 0.89). The mean curvimetre distance from rape site to nearest offender routine pathway was 0.53 kilometres (median = 0.41 km, standard deviation = 0.93).

For those crimes where the geographical milieu was known, prostitution strolls and hitchhiking regions appeared to be favoured target regions for

[16] Felson and Clarke (1998) note that one type of crime can generate opportunities for another type of crime. Some rapes are byproducts of burglary, robbery, or other property offences.

[17] Curvilinear (curvimetre) distance is the "wheel distance," or the length measured following a street network. Such distances are usually longer (they can be equal to, but never shorter) than straight-line crow-flight measures.

offenders. Almost all of the offences involved the use of a vehicle by the rapist. Approximately 43% of the serial rapists used a con approach, 28% a blitz/surprise approach, and 11% a quasi-acquaintance approach (method of approach was unknown in 18% of the cases).

3.2 Serial Arson

Arson is a tremendously expensive and dangerous crime; sometimes it is also an antecedent to serial and sexual murder. Arson resulted in over a billion dollars in property loss (mean of $11,980 U.S. per fire) in the U.S. during 1991, and was the second cause of death in residential fires (Sapp, Huff, Gary, & Icove, 1994). The material cost of arson in New South Wales was assessed at $65 million (Australian) during 1986, with a total economic value, including incidental costs such as loss of business and productivity, and rises in insurance premiums, of $260 million (Kocsis, Irwin, & Hayes, 1998). As with murder, there are serial, spree, and mass arsons.

A comprehensive study of serial arson was conducted by the U.S. Bureau of Alcohol, Tobacco and Firearms (BATF, or more commonly, ATF) and the FBI (Sapp et al., 1994; Sapp, Huff, Gary, Icove, & Horbert, 1994; Wright & Gary, 1995). They examined 83 convicted serial arsonists, responsible for 2611 arsons (an average of 31.5 fires per arsonist), and 7 deaths by fire. The ATF and FBI use a serial arson typology containing the following categories: (1) vandalism; (2) revenge; (3) excitement; (4) crime concealment; (5) profit; (6) mixed; and (7) mentally disordered. The Crime Classification Manual (CCM) includes the extremist and excludes the mentally disordered category.

The vandalism arsonist sets fires for mischief, with the intent to destroy property. These crimes often involve juvenile, prank, or gang activity, and common targets include school property, abandoned structures, and vegetation. Their fires are set in familiar areas within 0.5 to 1 mile of their home. They usually walk, but may drive to the crime scene.

The revenge arsonist seeks retribution for some perceived wrong that may have occurred months or years in the past. This category includes the subtypes of personal, group, institutional, and societal retaliation. Personal revenge arson is usually directed against an individual's home or vehicle. Group revenge arson often targets churches, agency headquarters, meeting places, and symbolic targets. Institutional revenge arson attacks government, medical, religious, educational, and military structures. Society revenge arson involves random targets, escalation, and serial offences. Sapp et al. (1994) note that offenders harbouring a grudge against an institution or society may feel the need for multiple acts of retribution because of the amorphous nature of their target, resulting in a higher number of serial arsons. Revenge arsonists typically select targets from inside their comfort zone, within 1 to 2 miles of their home, and walk to the crime scene.

The excitement arsonist desires thrills, recognition, or attention. Thrill arsonists plan their crimes and crave the excitement surrounding fire and its emergency response. This is the most dangerous type of arsonist. The excitement can be sexual in nature, though this is rare. Recognition arsonists include the "hero" type who reports the fire, warns or saves others, or helps in the fire fighting. Attention arsonists feel the need to be important. Excitement arsonists usually target familiar areas, within 1 to 2 miles of their home, and walk to the crime scene. They need to set increasingly larger fires over time.

The crime concealment arsonist lights fires as a secondary act to hide another crime, such as embezzlement, burglary, or murder (crime concealment is a major factor in arson homicide). This type of offender selects targets in familiar areas. They typically walk to the fire scene, which is close by, within 1 to 2 miles of their home. Accomplices are often involved.

The profit arsonist sets fires for monetary reasons. This category includes individuals who set fires for insurance fraud or business reasons, and professional "torches" for hire. Their targets are preselected and often involve travel, usually by vehicle or public transportation. Accomplices are usually involved.

The mentally disordered arsonist suffers from emotional or psychological problems. The mixed motive arsonist displays a range of motivations for the crimes. The extremist arsonist uses fire to further political, social, or religious purposes. Typical targets include abortion clinics and animal laboratories. Multiple offenders are common, and incendiary devices are often used, sometimes in an "overkill" manner. Sapp et al. (1994) state that power and revenge appear to be important and general causal factors for the crime of arson that cut across all types.

The serial arsonists in the ATF/FBI study were classified as follows: (1) vandalism, 7.3%; (2) revenge, 41.4%; (3) excitement, 30.5%; (4) crime concealment, 4.8%; (5) profit, 4.8%; (6) mentally disordered, 6.1%; and (7) mixed motives, 6.1%. Revenge arsonists were broken down into personal retaliation (14.7%), group retaliation (5.9%), institutional retaliation (20.6%), and societal retaliation (58.8%) subtypes. Excitement arsonists were broken down into thrill (64%), recognition (16.0%), and attention (16.0%) seekers.

The most common reported reasons for fire setting were revenge (63.9%), excitement (26.5%), emotional problems (22.9%), profit (12%), vandalism (9.6%), and to hide another crime (4.8%).[18] Stress, including interpersonal conflicts and financial difficulties, was reported as a precipitating factor by 44.6% of the serial arsonists. The typical emotion felt by these offenders during the arson was anger (33.3%).

---

[18] Percentages do not add to 100 as multiple responses were allowed.

The typical serial arsonist was male (94%), white (81.9%), young (most fires are set by juveniles), single (65.9%), nocturnal, and of average to above average intelligence. Over half were labourers. Two-thirds described themselves as middle class and one-third as lower class. About half indicated they came from dysfunctional families. Only 16.3 % of this groups lived alone, but most lacked stability in their interpersonal relationships. A single family house was the most common type of residence (42.9%), followed by apartment (23.8%), and rooming house (18.1%). Tattoos (43.4%) and physical disfigurements (22.9%) were relatively common. Approximately 25% reported they were homosexual or bisexual. Accomplices to the arsons were involved in 20.3% of the cases, most typically with crime concealment and profit motivated offender types.

Most of this group had prior felony arrests (86.6%, 23.9% involving arson), many with multiple felony arrests (63.4%). The first arson for this group occurred at the mean age of 15 years; the arson recidivism rate is 28%. The majority spent time in juvenile institutions (54.2%), often several times, and most had been in county jails (67.5%). Half of these offenders had psychological histories, over one third with multiple psychological problems. One-quarter had attempted suicide.

Differing levels of planning were reported by the arsonists in this study. Many responded that their fires were premeditated and planned (46.2%), others said impulsive (35%), and a few opportunistic (12.8%). There was no discernable pattern of target selection exhibited by these offenders. Reported reasons included random selection (17.6%), prior knowledge (14.6%), convenience (11.8%), within walking distance (5.9%), and multiple reasons (32.4%).

The serial arsonists in this sample were not particularly mobile; 95.1% of the fires were set in areas familiar to the offender. Their crime trip distances demonstrate both distance decay and the presence of a buffer zone (see below): 20.3% set fires within 0.5 miles of their residence, 50% within 1 mile, 70% within 2 miles, and 86.3% within 60 miles; 6.8% travelled varying distances, and 6.8% set fires in their home or institution. Most of them walked to their crimes (60.8%), a few rode a bicycle (5.1%), and some drove a vehicle (20.3%), though most did not own one. Also present in the sample were mixed travel modes (6.3%), and cases where the offender was already at the scene (7.6%). Fires were often set after work or school (42.5%), and occasionally on the way to or from work or school (7.5%).

The most common targets in this study were residences (10.5%), often porches or garages (26.5% of all residential arsons), businesses (18.1%), other structures (14.6%), vehicles (16.3%), vegetation (16.5%), and other (e.g., dumpsters, trash cans, rags, etc.) (24%); structural fires accounted for 43.2% of all the arsons. These results differ from UCR statistics, primarily because nuisance fires are often set for excitement by serial arsonists. The comparable

UCR figures are residences (34.1%), businesses (13.3%), other structures (8.6%), vehicles (26.1%), vegetation and other (18%); structural fires accounted for 55.1% of all UCR recorded arsons.

The majority of the fires were unsophisticated, set with material available from the crime (58.9%) and ignited by matches, lighters, or cigarettes (92.1%). Prior to the crime, almost half of these arsonists reported using alcohol, and one third drugs. Several arsonists remained at the scene (31.4%); others left but went to a place from which they could watch the fire (28.6%); and many left the area completely (40%). Of those who left, over half (52.9%) returned to the crime scene later, the majority within one hour (54%) and almost all (97.3%) within 24 hours.

These offenders were often identified as suspects in the arsons prior to their arrest. There was an 11% clearance rate for the arsons committed by this group, and they were suspected but not charged in another 11% of their fires. According to UCR data, the national arson clearance rate from 1982 to 1991 was 18.3%, suggesting that serial arson is a more difficult crime to solve.

When asked about their actions following an arson, 18.1% reported they followed the case in the media, 20.4% communicated with either the police, victim, or media, 13.3% set additional fires in the same location, 6% moved, and 4.8% left town. Only a few (4.8%) stated they felt remorse or guilt. Many (43.5%) did not consider the possibility of getting caught, and would not have been deterred even if they had known arrest would be the outcome. Serial arson appears to be a compulsive crime, and while the research did not find an increase in frequency, it noted an increase in fire severity for most (64.9%) offenders. Adults set more fires than did juveniles.

Pyromania is a rare disorder involving multiple episodes of purposeful fire setting. The diagnostic criteria listed in the DSM-IV include: (1) multiple deliberate fire setting; (2) tension or emotional arousal prior to the fire; (3) fascination with and interest in fire and its contexts; (4) pleasure, gratification, or relief when setting or witnessing fires; (5) the arsons were not set for instrumental, revenge, or mentally disordered reasons; and (6) the behaviour is not better explained by conduct disorder, manic episode, or ASPD diagnoses (American Psychiatric Association, 1994).

Pyromaniacs are usually adult males with learning difficulties and poor social skills. They are not psychotic and tend to plan their crimes and be indifferent to the consequences of the fire, both in terms of property and of life. They often watch fires, set off false alarms, and become involved to varying degrees with local fire departments. Pyromania is episodic and the fire setting may vary in frequency (American Psychiatric Association, 1994). Sapp et al. (1994) question whether true pyromania actually exists, noting that if it does, its occurrence must be very infrequent.

Forensic Behavioural Science

4

Criminal investigation has direct comparisons to scientific research: both processes involve data collection, observation, research (investigation), the effort to establish truth, and the search for proof. Occam's Razor, a basic principle of science, states when multiple explanations for a phenomenon exist, the simplest one should be chosen — a truism also in police investigation. The physical sciences have provided a variety of criminalistic techniques for police investigators, including DNA comparisons, ballistics, fiber analysis, and fingerprinting. It is only logical that the behavioural sciences be exploited as well. This chapter analyzes the investigative difficulties associated with criminal predators and introduces the forensic behavioural science approach. Techniques of linkage analysis and other investigative techniques are discussed. Criminal and geographic profiling are examined in separate chapters.

4.1 Investigative Difficulties

Here's one clue/That you shall be given/Whoever I take./They all will be women? ....

Blood is red/You pigs are blue/Start counting victims?/There'll be a few

Grass in green/The branches are dead/If you ever find her?/She'll surely be dead.

Like the rest/She shall be killed/Because her use/has been fulfilled

— Trial transcript of poem seized from Terrence Burlingham, convicted of murdering two women in Cranbrook, British Columbia, during 1984

The nature of criminal predators causes unique problems for law enforcement, requiring special police responses and investigative strategies. It has been suggested there are only three ways to solve a crime: (1) confession; (2) witness; or (3) physical evidence (Klockars & Mastrofski, 1991; Simon, 1991). Traditionally, the search for witnesses, suspects, and evidence has followed a path outwards from the victim and crime scene. Most homicides are cleared for the simple reason that they involve people who know each other, and the process of offender identification may only require suspect elimination. Boyd (1988) found that 80% of convicted murderers in Canada had killed either family members or acquaintances, while Silverman and Kennedy (1993) determined that 8% of Canadian murders from 1961 to 1990 involved strangers, and 14% occurred during the commission of another crime. Such obvious connections rarely exist in cases of serial murder, rape, or arson. The lack of relationship between victim and offender makes these crimes difficult to solve (Skogan & Antunes, 1979). Working outwards from the victim during the investigation of a stranger attack is a difficult task. The alternative, then, is to work inwards, trying to establish some type of link between potential suspects and the victim or crime scene.

This process requires the determination and delineation of a likely group of potential suspects, a process referred to by Kind (1987b) as "framing," and by Skogan and Antunes (1979) as establishing the "circle of investigation." This effort typically involves the inspection of individuals with relevant criminal or psychiatric records, the accumulation of intelligence, and the collection of suspect tips from members of the public. The Rand study of the criminal investigation process found the information that led to solved crimes most likely came from the public, then from patrol officers, and third, from detectives (Chaiken, Greenwood, & Petersilia, 1991). This underlines the importance of effective channels of communication between the police and the community, and within the police organization.

Canadian and British police officials believe the performance of their information management systems have much to do with their ability to utilize large amounts of data collected during major inquiries (Green & Whitmore, 1993). In 1990, a typical year, the U.K. had a 90% homicide clearance rate, Canada, 78%, but the U.S., only 67%. The application of information theory concepts to the policing process has significant potential (see Krippendorff, 1986). But while information is an important determinant of the likelihood that police will solve a crime, it must be of a useful nature (Kind, 1987b; Lyman, 1993; Skogan & Antunes, 1979). The determination of what is helpful, and what is not, is a less than straightforward task.

The investigative process is based upon the proper collection, analysis, and sharing of information. But not all information has the same value, and investigators must be wary of "static" or "noise" — useless or misleading information. And because investigative efforts can produce hundreds and even thousands of potential suspects, problems with information overload often develop. This is the classic needle in the haystack problem (see the discussion on the Gainesville Slayings investigation in Fox & Levin, 1994).

In the still unsolved Green River Killer case, for example, 18,000 suspect names have been collected, but as of February 1992, the police have only had time and resources to investigate fewer than 12,000 of these (Montgomery, 1993). Police have gathered 8000 tangible items of evidence from the crime scenes, and a single television special on the case generated 3500 tips. In Britain, the nationwide search for Robert Black, the Staffordshire serial murderer, amassed details on 185,000 people and tens of thousands of vehicles over the course of 11 years before the child killer was finally caught (Wyre & Tate, 1995).

The Narborough Murder Enquiry, a massive four-year manhunt in Leicestershire, England, obtained close to 4000 blood samples for DNA testing prior to charging Colin Pitchfork with the deaths of two teenage girls (Wambaugh, 1989). The Yorkshire Ripper case amassed 268,000 names before it was over; police initiated 115,000 actions, visited 27,000 houses, and took 31,000 statements. Up to 1000 letters were received daily from the public, and a total of 5.4 million vehicle registration numbers were recorded by investigators (Doney, 1990; Nicholson, 1979).

A corollary to the problem of information overload is the high cost associated with any extensive, long-term investigation. The final price of the Atlanta Child Murders investigation was more than $9 million (Dettlinger & Prugh, 1983), while the Yorkshire Ripper Inquiry involved a total of 5 million hours of police time (Doney, 1990). By early 1992, the still unsuccessful Green River Task Force had accumulated expenses of approximately $20 million (Montgomery, 1993).

It is important for police detectives to know which offences are connected, and which ones are not, so information between related cases can be collated and compared. Confusion over which crimes are part of the series has developed in several investigations involving serial killers, including Henry Lee Lucas, Peter Sutcliffe, and Clifford Olson. In other cases, particularly those involving high risk victims, authorities may not be aware a predator is operating within their jurisdiction.

The problem of series identification becomes much worse with mobile offenders who commit crimes in different areas. When a criminal investigation has to cross jurisdictional boundaries, issues of coordination, cooperation, and competition arise. This "lack of sharing or coordination of investigative information relating to unsolved murders and to the lack of adequate networking among law enforcement agencies" has been termed linkage blindness (Egger, 1984). The problem can also occur within a single large police organization, as happened in New York City when the Son of

Sam killed his early victims in different precincts (Ressler & Shachtman, 1992). Serial rape is just as susceptible to linkage blindness, but serial arson is less so due to the limited geographic range of the typical arsonist.

Several other investigative difficulties exist that complicate efforts to link crimes and apprehend serial killers and violent sex offenders (Egger, 1990, 1998; Holmes & De Burger, 1988; James, 1991; O'Reilly-Fleming, 1992). These problems include:

- The intense public fear, media interest, and political pressure surrounding these cases;
- Police inexperience[19] with serial murder cases, including an unwillingness to acknowledge the situation and commit sufficient resources, ignorance of appropriate investigative strategies, and overlooking victimological information;
- The complexity of personnel and coordination logistics, especially when multiple jurisdictions and agencies are involved. In the Yorkshire Ripper case, for example, 250 full-time detectives were assigned for over a three-year period (Doney, 1990);
- Offender learning and improvement from "practice;"
- Copy cat crimes; and
- False confessions from unbalanced people attracted by the notorious publicity.

In a comparison of solved (n = 399) and unsolved (n = 75) serial murder cases, Mott (1999) correctly hypothesized the former group would be characterized by higher killing rates, lower victim vulnerability, and indoor body disposals. Contrary to her expectations, however, offender mobility and multiple crime sites were also related positively to crime solution, though she cautions these results may be data artifacts. Discriminant analysis correctly classified 75.2% of the cases.

4.2 Police Strategies

For heaven's sake catch me Before I kill more. I cannot control myself.

—Message written in lipstick on the living room wall of Frances Brown, victim of serial murderer William Heirens; Kennedy, 1991, p. 38

---

[19] Many countries, including Britain, Canada, and the U.S., are now attempting to pool investigative expertise in "low volume crimes." Perhaps the current record is held by Captain Piet Byleveld of the South African Police Service in Johannesburg, who has investigated six serial murder cases during his career.

In an attempt to overcome the obstacles facing serial violent crime cases, a variety of law enforcement strategies have been developed over the past few years (Egger, 1990). One of the cornerstones of this effort has been the creation and use of behavioural science-based methods in the police investigative process. The application of scientific studies of human behaviour to analyze criminal actions has led to linkage analysis systems, criminal profiling, geographic profiling, and crime-specific statistical databases. This field is sometimes referred to as forensic behavioural science to distinguish it from the more academic pursuits of traditional psychology and sociology (though one could argue that "forensic," which means "belonging to courts of law," is not the most appropriate term for a set of methods primarily investigative in nature).

Connected to the behavioural science approach has been the design of information management systems and suspect prioritization methods to enhance investigative effectiveness and efficiency (Jackson, van den Eshof, & de Kleuver, 1994; Ressler & Shachtman, 1992). Scrutiny of people of interest, in the effort to work backwards from them to the victim, is a difficult and time consuming process. Thorough interrogations of suspects, detailed interviews of their associates (who may be witnesses, whether they know it or not), and extensive searches for, and analyses of, physical evidence consume valuable and limited resources. By using a methodology to prioritize the police approach, investigative efforts can be tailored to the priority rating of the individual suspect. By focusing on the most probable suspects, all else being equal, the offender will more likely be identified sooner.

Kind (1987b, 1990) suggests the use of "frames" and "forms" to help prioritize suspects during the course of a police investigation. Frames are flexible and fuzzy enclosures employed to delineate potential suspects, while forms are tendencies for groups of people to behave in like fashion. Utilized in conjunction with each other, these concepts produce combined (i.e., intersecting) frames that outline the most productive lines of inquiry. While all criminal investigations can employ this form of information management, the approach is particularly useful in large-scale major inquiries.

4.2.1 Linkage Analysis

When FBI Special Agent Clarice Starling finds a Black Witch Moth (*Erebus odora*) chrysalis lodged in the throat of serial killer Buffalo Bill's latest victim, a connection is soon made to another murder. But real crimes, unlike those in Thomas Harris' popular novel *Silence of the Lambs* (1988), are often much more difficult to link. "Prostitute strangled, dumped at the side of the road, no physical evidence," is a depressingly familiar crime scene description.

Establishing which offences are part of a series is an important and essential task in the investigation of serial crime (see Gottlieb, Arenberg, & Singh, 1998). This process is known as linkage analysis[20] or comparative case analysis (CCA). Realizing the extent of the crime pattern helps determine the appropriate level of police response, facilitates information sharing between investigators and jurisdictions, outlines case similarities, and identifies common suspects. If and when the case is solved, additional crimes are cleared and the court delivers a more appropriate sentence (including dangerous offender or habitual felon designations). Knowing all the pieces of the puzzle allows a more comprehensive picture of the offender to be formed and prevents linkage blindness from occurring.

For example, during 1993 and 1994 the Tag Team Rapists broke into several ground floor suites in Surrey, British Columbia, and attacked single women, many of whom had children. The crimes were occurring close together, but within two separate neighbourhoods (Newton and Bear Creek) that were a significant distance apart. One of the questions concerning investigators was the offender's method of travel — on foot or by vehicle? Project Escalate's first step was to examine all possible related crimes, including sexual assaults, attempts, burglaries, and prowlings. Eventually 14 different incidents were identified as being part of the series. Weather conditions on the dates and times of these events were then checked with the Environment Canada Vancouver Weather Information office. It was determined that every one of these incidents occurred on a dry night. The probability of this many fall and winter nights in the rainy Pacific Northwest without precipitation is very low. This suggested that the offenders intentionally refrained from hunting during inclement weather, an indicator they usually walked. The two offenders have now been apprehended and convicted, and this prediction turned out to be accurate. But the question of offender transportation could not be answered with any degree of confidence until after the linkage analysis had been completed and as many of the pieces of the puzzle as possible assembled.

There are three main methods used by police investigators to link crimes prior to an offender's apprehension. They are: (1) physical evidence; (2) offender description; and (3) crime scene behaviour. Each method has its strengths and weaknesses. It is not uncommon for a series of crimes to be connected through a combination of these means.

4.2.1.1   Physical Evidence

Physical evidence provides the most certain means of linking crimes, though evidence of a type suitable for doing so may not be present in every case. One of the more powerful forensic methods, DNA profiling, has been heralded as the most revolutionary technology in the field of criminal

---

[20] This is not to be confused with the similar but distinct function of "link analysis," performed on such systems as the i2 *Analyst's Notebook*. Link analysis examines inter- and intra-crime associations between names, telephone numbers, vehicles and the like. Linkage analysis considers likelihood of crime similarity.

investigation since the development of the Henry System for fingerprinting (Bigbee, Tanton, & Ferrara, 1989; Burke & Rowe, 1989; Eisner, 1989; Gaudette, 1990; Kelly, Rankin, & Wink, 1987; Lowrie & Wells, 1991; Wambaugh, 1989). As both semen and blood contain DNA, the potential for ascertaining and verifying links in cases of violent and sexual crimes is significant. One of the necessary steps to realize the potential of DNA analysis is the establishment of centralized indices to facilitate computerized searches and comparisons (Adams, 1989; Miller, 1991).

In 1990, the FBI began development of a national DNA identification index, completing the combined federal, state, and local police agency pilot project in 1993 (Brown, 1994; see also Weedn & Hicks, 1998). Designed for the compatible storage and comparison of DNA records, the Combined DNA Index System (CODIS) consists of two investigative indices — the forensic index for unsolved crimes, and the convicted offender index for known felons. A missing persons and unidentified bodies index will also be part of the system.

One of the important functions of such a system is the establishment of series crimes (Brown, 1994). For example, DNA pattern matching linked 18 unknown suspect serial cases together in Minnesota, eventually helping to solve them by matching specimens of two offenders to the crime scenes. Such results are more common in Britain where a DNA database has been in existence for some time (Davies & Dale, 1995b; "DNA profiling," 1995). As of May 1997, it has been responsible for over 5000 hits — defined as a match between crime scenes or between crime scene and offender — in the U.K. Canada has also enacted legislation for the establishment of a national DNA data bank.

Automated fingerprint identification systems (AFIS) — the method that identified Richard Ramirez as the Night Stalker — are becoming increasingly common in police agencies, allowing comparisons and matches that sheer volume would have previously precluded (Sparrow, 1994). Programs such as the *Integrated Ballistics Identification System* (*IBIS*), networked into the joint ATF/FBI National Integrated Ballistic Information Network (NIBIN), link crimes committed with firearms through computerized comparisons of microscopic bullet striation patterns and shell casing marks (Dees, 1994; Strandberg, 1994; see also Davis, 1958; Di Maio, 1985). And the British Shoeprint Image Capture and Retrieval System (SICAR) is a national database that connects crime scenes through the geometrical shapes associated with stored images of footprint evidence.

4.2.1.2 Offender Description
Descriptions of offenders have provided a common and long used method of linking crimes. Mug shot books, while still in existence, are being replaced by computerized photographic databases that allow for certain physical description parameters to be used to narrow the search.

This is all predicated upon the assumption that there was a witness to the crime. There may not be one in the case of murder or arson. Even in a sexual assault, the victim must see, remember, and accurately recall (acquire, retain, and retrieve) the offender's description. The ability for investigators to obtain an accurate physical description depends upon such factors as lighting conditions; whether the offender was masked; if the attack was from the rear; and the level of victim trauma, stress, fright, alcohol use, forgetfulness, and cooperation.

Individual physical appearance is also subject to modification. Weight changes slowly, hair more quickly, and clothing daily. Even more stable descriptors such as age, race, height, and build will be viewed subjectively by different victims. Ted Bundy, for example, was able to tremendously vary his description as can be seen from photographs and police "wanted" posters (Michaud & Aynesworth, 1983; Winn & Merrill, 1979).

The prevalence of video cameras has enhanced the ability of police to use offender descriptions. Most banks and financial institutions, and many businesses, transportation centres, and building lobby areas have been outfitted with video cameras. CCTV (closed circuit television) coverage of city centres, parking lots, and other public places is now common in Britain. Police agencies make routine use of the photographs and videotape from these cameras to assist in their investigations.

Automated recognition systems for digital facial images now exist and are used for both comparison and identification purposes (Mardia, Coombes, Kirkbride, Linney, & Bowie, 1996). Distance and angle measurements are taken between certain facial points (e.g., from lower point of the ear to nose tip, the tangent to chin tip and nose tip, etc.) for both anterior (front) and profile (side) views. Horizontal and vertical landmarks are calculated to produce a mathematical "profile" of the face. This landmark-based data then provides the means of determining correlations between facial images.

These systems can be connected to video cameras placed within airport terminals and used to scan custom and immigration lines. A match with an image in the facial database alerts officials to the possible presence of a person of interest, such as a criminal, missing person, fugitive, abducted child, or terrorist. Police investigators have also used computerized facial recognition systems to assess the probability that two robbers captured on bank cameras are, in fact, the same person. These methods increase the value of offender image data, and echo the early work of Alphonse Bertillon in criminal identification through body measurement.[21]

---

[21] Ear patterns are also unique and have been used successfully to identify both criminals and victims.

4.2.1.3   Crime Scene Behaviour

The behavioural analysis of crime scenes provides a third, and rapidly developing, methodology for offence comparison. Linking crimes behaviourally requires comparing similarities versus differences for both related and unrelated crimes (see Robertson & Vignaux, 1995). Like crimes should show more similarities than differences, and unlike crimes, more differences than similarities. These comparisons are usually assessed in terms of proximity in time and space between offences, comparable modus operandi (method of operation), and the presence of signature.

Crimes that take place close together in space and time are obviously more likely to be connected than those separated by significant distance and occurring years apart. This is not to say that some offenders do not travel great distances, change residences, or interrupt their criminal activity for personal, employment, or institutional reasons. It only means that geographic and temporal factors affect the probability of offence linkage, with those more proximate more likely to be connected.

Modus operandi (M.O.) involves the mechanics of the crime, and can be broken down into three chronologically-ordered stages comprising the methods used by an offender to: (1) hunt (find and attack the victim); (2) protect identity; and (3) escape from the scene. Modus operandi has also been defined as those actions used by the offender to: (1) commit the crime; (2) protect identity; and (3) escape from the scene. It has been our experience, however, that significant offender behaviour exists in the search and hunt for a victim, and therefore M.O. should include these activities. Protection of identity can also occur at any and all stages of the offence.

The matrix in Table 4.1 helps categorize modus operandi behaviour and can serve as a framework for comparative case analysis. It is based on the above three stages divided into aggressive (what is done to accomplish the crime) and defensive (what is done to protect the offender) actions:

Table 4.1   Modus Operandi Matrix

Action/Stage	Hunt	Crime	Escape
Defensive			
Offensive			

Modus operandi is not constant, but rather varies and changes for a variety of reasons. Like all human behaviour, it is subject to individual deviation and random fluctuations. M.O. is responsive to environmental influences, such as victim reaction, the physical conditions of a crime setting, and ongoing police activities and media attention. Displacement may result from police activities, and can take the form of changes in the spatial, temporal, target, tactical, or functional characteristics of the crimes (Gabor, 1978; Reppetto, 1976). Over time, an offender's method of operation often evolves as the result of education, maturity and experience; fantasy progression and development can also occur.

Unlike M.O., "signature" is constant, though certain aspects of its expression may evolve and improve over time (Keppel, 1995; Keppel & Birnes, 1997). Signature is defined as behaviour that goes beyond the actions needed to commit the crime; it is a fantasy-based ritual or combinations of rituals that represent a unique and personal expression of the offender (Douglas & Munn, 1992). When present, it provides a useful method for establishing links between crimes and can indicate certain underlying needs of the offender (Homant, 1998).

Staging is another consideration when examining behaviour (Douglas & Munn, 1992). Staging occurs when the crime scene is purposely altered. This is usually done by the offender in an attempt to mislead the police and typically involves a criminal who knew the victim and hopes to create a convincing alternative scenario. Crime scenes have also been changed by family members to protect the victim from embarrassment (in cases of auto-erotic fatalities, for example).

One of the functions of criminal profiling is the assessment of the like-lihood that one or more crimes were committed by the same offender. In Projects Eclipse and Kayo, a team of profilers assessed several unsolved murders of prostitutes and young women in Vancouver and Edmonton, respectively, in the effort to establish possible connections between the crimes (MacKay, 1994). Geographical analysis can also help disentangle different series of crimes (see the discussion on parsing and crime sets in Chapter 9).

The reality, however, is that the ability of the police to link serial crimes is limited. Establishing offence connections is often a difficult exercise, especially so in busy urban environments characterized by high levels of crime. The backdrop of other, similar offences can interfere with the process, and such "background noise" can make it difficult to know who is responsible for what. Consistency and constancy are not characteristics of many criminal offenders, and when an analysis does indicate that certain crimes are connected, the links are usually referred to in terms of probabilities rather than certainties. This is made all the more difficult when multiple offenders are involved.

A further complication is that the links might be between different incident types. For example, in the case of a serial rapist who breaks into apartments to attack women, police must review not just other rapes and attempts, but also sexual assaults, residential burglaries, and prowlings. Correctly establishing a serial criminal's pattern can involve analyzing hundreds or even thousands of crimes.

The major response to these problems has been the establishment of computer systems containing centralized investigative information networks.

The idea of a national computer database to link murders originated with Pierce Brooks, a retired captain of detectives in the Los Angeles Police Department (LAPD) homicide unit (Brooks, 1984; Howlett, Hanfland, & Ressler, 1986). During his investigation of California serial killer Harvey Glatman in the late 1950s, Brooks found he had to resort to combing various newspaper files in order to locate murders that might fit the pattern from outside LAPD's jurisdiction (Newton, 1998; Ressler & Shachtman, 1992). With input from the National Serial Murder Advisory Group, the Violent Criminal Apprehension Program (VICAP) Program was formed in the early 1980s (Keppel & Weis, 1994).

Under the auspices of the National Center for the Analysis of Violent Crime (NCAVC), VICAP went operational in 1985. It uses a standardized form containing a series of behaviourally-oriented questions concerning the crime, victim, and offender that allows for computerized matching of similar cases from a national database. As part of its protocol, VICAP identifies critical time and location factors, including the different types of scenes associated with a murder: (1) victim's last known location; (2) site of offender's initial contact with victim; (3) murder or major assault site; and (4) body recovery site (Ressler et al., 1988). This allows for the calculation of time and distance relationships, the importance of which was stressed by the National Serial Murder Advisory Group (Keppel & Weis, 1994).

Britain and Europe have had modus operandi-based crime notification systems for series detection — the matching of crime with crime, and offence with offender — since 1907 (Brooks et al., 1987, 1988; Green & Whitmore, 1993; Rebscher & Rohrer, 1991). The British police developed a Crime Pattern Analysis (CPA) computerized database within the National Criminal Intelligence Service (NCIS) following the Yorkshire Ripper case. Currently, the Serious Crime Analysis Section (SCAS), National Crime Faculty, is mandated to conduct comparative case analysis for murders, rapes, and abductions.

Several states have also developed their own computerized crime linkage systems, some of which feed into VICAP. Examples of these programs include the Washington Homicide Investigation Tracking System (HITS) (also used in Oregon and Idaho); the New York Homicide Assessment and Lead Tracking (HALT) system; the Florida Violent Crime Investigation System (ViCIS); the Indiana Criminal Apprehension Assistance Program (ICAAP); the Iowa Sex Crimes Analysis System; the Michigan Sex Motivated Crime File; the Minnesota Sex Crimes Analysis Program (MN/SCAP); the New Jersey Homicide Evaluation and Assessment Tracking (HEAT) System; the North Carolina State Homicide and Assault Reporting (SHARE) system; the Oklahoma Sex Crime Analysis and Reporting System (SCARS); and the Pennsylvania ATAC Program (Cryan, 1988; Geberth, 1994; Keppel & Weis, 1993a, 1993b; Collins, Johnson, Choy, Davidson, & MacKay, 1998). Also, six Regional Information Sharing Systems

(RISS) Programs now exist across the U.S. to provide multi-jurisdictional intelligence and investigative analysis networks (U.S. Department of Justice, 1998).

Sex offences are much more common than murder, and when these programs began to collect data on rapes and sexual assaults the power and usefulness of computerized crime linkage systems became readily apparent. Pattern recognition models for linking and predicting serial arsons, based on cluster analysis of variables related to location, time of day, day of week, and modus operandi, have also been developed (Icove, 1981; Icove & Crisman, 1975).

The Canadian Violent Crime Linkage Analysis System (ViCLAS), developed by the RCMP, went national in 1995 (Johnson, 1994). Since then, ViCLAS has achieved international recognition and has now been adopted for use by Austria, The Netherlands, Australia, Belgium, Germany, and Britain, along with certain American states including Indiana, New Jersey, and Tennessee (Collins et al., 1998; Kocsis & Davies, 1997). Several other countries are considering its introduction. Significant new versions of both VICAP and ViCLAS were introduced in 1999.

ViCLAS uses a relational database within a Windows environment. Terminals across the country communicate over a national wide-area network (WAN) to a central database in Ottawa, Ontario. Data transmission is encrypted on dedicated lines. There is also continual case tracking and auditing. In Ontario, ViCLAS reporting is mandatory as the result of one of the recommendations of the Campbell report, a judicial review into the investigation of the Paul Bernardo murder case. As of mid-1999, there are over 70,000 cases on ViCLAS.

A major difficulty with computerized linkage systems is low reporting rates. This causes a serious data shortage problem because case matches are an exponential function of reporting level.[22] For example, if only 50% of the crimes are entered, then only 25% of the potential linkages can be identified; with a 20% reporting rate, the linkage ability drops to 4%. It is paradoxical that some police officers, who typically possess little faith in offender rehabilitation, fail to see the value in a comprehensive criminal tracking system.

One of the common reasons quoted for failure to report cases is the time it takes an investigator to complete the input forms, which can involve over 150 questions. Therefore, the choice of behaviours used in the analysis is critical. Both discrimination and utility are important. Certain offender

---

[22] Generally, if x represents the reporting rate, and y the linkage rate (expressed as proportions of their potential totals), then: $y = x^{1/2}$. This equation is an approximation because the exact relationship depends on the mean number of crimes in a series, and on how a series connection is defined (e.g., if 3 crimes out of a possible 10 are connected, does this qualify as a successful series identification?).

actions are so common (e.g., vaginal intercourse) as to be poor discriminators. Other behaviours are so rare (e.g., the offender writes on the victim's body) that they are unlikely to be encountered.[23] Crime linkage is a holistic process and the questions must also provide a full understanding of events. System designers need to balance the requirement for parsimony with the necessity for a comprehensive assessment of crime scene behaviour.

An underlying assumption of linkage systems is that the analyzed behaviours are more or less consistent across offences. An examination of child abduction murders in the U.S. showed that victim gender and use of bindings were the most important and consistent linkage variables (Hanfland, Keppel, & Weis, 1997). Offender speech forms have been found consistent and useful in connecting rape cases (Dale & Davies, 1994a), and the London Metropolitan Police Sexual Assault Index analyses verbal themes as part of the process of linking crimes (Copson, 1993). However, FBI research on 108 serial rapists determined that 58% of the 119 behavioural variables they examined reflected zero or minimal consistency across crimes (Warren et al., 1995). Alone, such questions make a poor basis for a case linkage system; together, they may point to common underlying fantasies or behavioural themes.

The true strength of these systems therefore lies in their ability to make concurrent comparisons between multiple variables. A study of British serial rapists found that 28% of the offenders took steps to prevent their face from being seen by the victim (Davies & Dale, 1995b). In the FBI research, it was noted that 70% of the attacks took place indoors, and 60% within the victim's home (Warren et al., 1995). These are not powerful discriminators separately, but assuming independence between questions, they can be combined in powerful ways. A burglary rapist who covers his face might only represent 17% of the offender population. Additional variables can help increase the focus. To facilitate this analytic process, the latest version of ViCLAS produces multivariate statistics upon demand.

The process of recognition — whether it be of faces, scenes, automobiles, voices, architecture — is based less on individual elements than on the relationships between them. Humans are much better than serial-processing computers at image and complex pattern recognition (Marshall & Zohar, 1997). As of today, most computerized case linkage systems are only designed to manage and search through large volumes of information, leaving the ultimate determination of case association to the analyst. As the volume of information collected by these databases increases, the need for expert system support becomes more crucial.

---

[23] A question can be reversed and phrased in the negative (e.g., "Was the victim transported?" becomes "Did the crime take place at a single location?"); an inversion makes a common behaviour uncommon.

Grubin, Kelly, and Ayis (1996) caution that because of "the softer and more fluid substance of behavioural 'evidence' ... [the process of linking crimes] must be based on scientific principles rather than on a combination of intuition, experience and theory" (pp. 12, 20). They summarize the practical problems in using offender behaviour to link crimes as follows: (1) consistent but common behaviours; (2) consistent but uncommon behaviours; (3) preciseness of behaviour description; (4) behaviour influenced by victim response; (5) weighting and relative importance of behaviours; (6) variation in behaviour consistency; (7) evolution of behaviour; and (8) interpretation of behaviours.

Grubin et al. (1996, 1997) examined how offender behaviours at crime scenes group and interact in an effort to link serious stranger sexual offences. Four domains — control, sex, escape, and style — were used to identify 30 dichotomous variables for cluster analysis. The research assessed consistency within a domain over a series of offences (vertical consistency), and the degree to which similar domain patterns occur within an offence (horizontal consistency). Behavioural consistency across offences was found, lending support to the efficacy of this approach. This method of looking for the emergence of constant patterns is similar to the process of DNA matching where genetic alleles are compared.

The concept that linked crimes should be interconnected provides one simple method for pattern determination. In other words, if crime A shows similarities to crime B, and crime B shows similarities to crime C, then crime C should also show similarities to crime A. If this is the case, then the probability of these crimes being connected increases.

Consider an example involving the investigation of five prostitute murders in which police want to establish which crimes are connected. The victims are Smith, Jones, Baker, Anderson, and Williams. Analysts have determined there are seven crime scene behaviours of interest. These are:

Variable 1 — victim strangled;
Variable 2 — victim found nude;
Variable 3 — bindings used;
Variable 4 — skid row prostitute;
Variable 5 — victim's body concealed;
Variable 6 — victim decapitated; and
Variable 7 — victim stabbed.

Table 4.2 shows the case variable matrix for this example. Vn refers to the variable number, and Cn to the victim (crime) number. An X indicates the presence of that variable in a given murder. The results from the case variable matrix are then plotted in a case linkage chart. This diagram depicts

Table 4.2 Case Variable Matrix

Victim/Variable	V1	V2	V3	V4	V5	V6	V7
C1 (Smith)	X	X	X	X			
C2 (Jones)	X	X	X	X	X		
C3 (Baker)		X		X			X
C4 (Anderson)	X					X	
C5 (Williams)	X		X	X	X		

the strength of association, in terms of the behaviour variables of interest, between the different crimes. The proper selection and phrasing of crime behaviours are important parts of this analysis. Figure 4.1 shows the case linkage chart for this example.

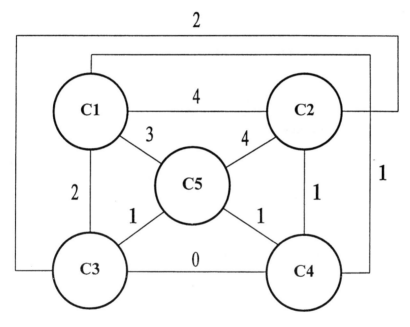

Figure 4.1 Case linkage chart.

In this example, crimes 1, 2, and 5 (Smith, Jones, and Williams) show an interconnected pattern, suggesting that they were all committed by the same offender. This approach can be refined by weighting the importance of the variables under consideration. Variables that are less common (e.g., victim was decapitated) establish a stronger probability of connection than those more common (e.g., victim was strangled). This method is particularly useful when physical evidence exists establishing definitive links between some cases but not others. Behavioural interconnections can help determine the probable extent of the crime series. Such an approach was used in Lübeck,

Germany, to help link offences in a series of arsons that lacked comparative physical evidence between crime scenes.

In summary, the crime linkage methods discussed in this section can be outlined as follows:

1. Physical evidence
2. Offender description
3. Crime scene behaviour
    a) Proximity in time and place
    b) Modus operandi
       • Find and attack the victim
       • Commit the crime
       • Escape from the scene
    c) Signature

4.2.2 Other Investigative Tactics

Egger (1990, 1998) identifies additional responses that have been used or are being developed and experimented with by police agencies to assist in solving cases of serial murder (see also U.S. Department of Justice, 1991b). These investigative approaches include:

• Task forces set up at the local level, or in cases of multi-jurisdictional crimes, at the regional level. It is also possible to implement centralized coordination in the absence of a formalized task force;
• Computerized analysis systems. These major case management systems store, collate, and analyze large volumes of investigative data. For example, Scotland Yard detectives use the British Home Office Large Major Enquiry System (HOLMES), and FBI agents use the Rapid Start Information Management System (Doney, 1990; Federal Bureau of Investigation, 1996);
• Law enforcement conferences focused on a specific series of solved or unsolved murders (see Green & Whitmore, 1993). The RCMP have sponsored two such conferences in Canada to examine homicides of prostitutes and young women. In 1991, Project Eclipse assessed 25 unsolved murders in Vancouver, and in 1993, Project Kayo examined 14 such crimes in Edmonton (MacKay, 1994; see also Lowman & Fraser, 1995);
• Geographical pattern analysis (geographic profiling or geoforensics);
• Clearinghouses that provide information on an ongoing basis to police agencies involved in investigating serial murder;
• Investigative consultant teams, composed of investigators with experience in similar cases, that provide advice and assistance to the agency

responsible for a serial murder investigation (see Brooks, 1982; Brooks et al., 1988); and

- Payment of money to a serial murderer for evidence. To date, this has only occurred in the Clifford Olson case in British Columbia (Bayless, 1982; Mulgrew, 1990).

Police departments may also use psychics to help search out clues (see Dettlinger & Prugh, 1983; Lyons & Truzzi, 1991), and have been involved in the production of special television programs designed to elicit tips, witnesses, and bring about designed responses in the offender. And normal investigative techniques, routine police patrol work, unsolicited suspect confessions, and sheer luck have all played significant roles in the solving of serial murder cases (Keppel, 1989; Levin & Fox, 1985).

Criminal Profiling  5

'Now, I have here a watch which has recently come into my possession. Would you have the kindness to let me have an opinion upon the character of the late owner?'

'He was a man of untidy habits — very untidy and careless. He was left with good prospects, but he threw away his chances, lived for some time in poverty with occasional short intervals of prosperity, and, finally, taking to drink, he died. That is all I can gather.'

'How in the name of all that is wonderful did you get these facts? They are absolutely correct in every particular.'

'Ah, that is good luck. I could only say what was the balance of probability. I did not at all expect to be accurate.'

'But it was not mere guesswork?'

'No, no: I never guess. It is a shocking habit — destructive to the logical faculty. What seems strange to you is only so because you do not follow my train of thought or observe the small facts upon which large inferences may depend.'

— *The Sign of the Four,* Sir Arthur Conan Doyle, 1888

Sherlock Holmes' inductive construction for Doctor Watson of the personal characteristics of the owner of a pocket watch was part of the craft of profiling. Criminal or psychological profiling[24] is one of the primary investigative

[24] The terms offender profiling, criminal personality assessment, and crime scene profiling are also used.

tools used to prioritize suspects and assist in cases of sexual violent crime. It can be defined as the identification of "the major personality and behavioral characteristics of an individual based upon an analysis of the crimes he or she has committed" (Douglas et al., 1986, p. 405). Or, more simply and generally, as the inference of offender characteristics from offence characteristics (Copson, 1995).

The construction of such a behavioural composite — a social and psychological assessment — is based on the premise that the proper interpretation of crime scene evidence can indicate the personality type of the individual(s) who committed the offence. Human action is "the expression of an individual personality structure within a concrete framework of space and time" (Rebscher & Rohrer, 1991, p. 243). Certain personality types exhibit similar behavioural patterns, and knowledge of these patterns or "clue texts" can assist in the investigation of the crime and the assessment of potential suspects.

Profiling is therefore an attempt to generate a consistent personality pattern, and is based on the principle that character traits can be inferred from crime scene behaviour and then used to predict other behaviour (Homant & Kennedy, 1998). Trait theory assumes that human behaviour is consistent and predictable, though some social psychologists hold that personality is not a good predictor of action in a specific situation. The fundamental attribution error results when behaviour is seen only as the product of internal dispositions and situational influences are ignored (Homant, forthcoming). Profilers counter they deal with cases involving extreme pathology, and serious adult antisocial behaviour appears to be particularly stable. In any case, traits are best measured through multiple tests.

Offender dangerous prediction is related to profiling. But as difficult and contentious as future behaviour assessment is, the inferential burden is even greater in crime scene profiling because the latter must go from behaviour to individual to behaviour. Criminal profiling structures its analysis through answers to three primary questions:

1. What happened at the crime scene?
2. Why did these events happen?
3. What type of person would have done this?

Responses to these questions are "based on a mixture of operational experience with similar crimes, statistical knowledge gleaned from the analyses of sets of similar cases and knowledge gathered from clinical research and practice" (Jackson et al., 1994, p. 22). Unlike the "just the facts" nature of most investigative methodologies, profiles are composed of probabilistic knowledge concerning the criminal offender. There is a hierarchy of investigative methods in terms of quality of information content: (1) physical evidence; (2) witnesses; and (3) profiling. It is therefore important to realize that profile information should be considered subservient to physical evidence.

5.1   Development of Profiling

While research on "criminal anthropology" dates back to 1820 (Teten, 1989), the first known offender profile was prepared for the investigation of the murders of Jack the Ripper (Rumbelow, 1988). Dr. Thomas Bond, a surgeon with the Great Western Railway and a lecturer in forensic medicine, conducted the postmortem examination of Mary Kelly, generally acknowledged as the last of the Ripper victims. In a report written November 10, 1888, and sent to Robert Anderson, the Head of CID (Criminal Investigation Department) for the London Metropolitan Police, Bond made inferences regarding the Ripper's physical appearance and condition, occupation, income, habits, motives, sexual paraphilias, and mental health. He concluded that the murderer was subject to periodical attacks of "homicidal and erotic mania."

The modern use of psychological profiling in the criminal investigation process can be traced to the work of psychiatrist Dr. James A. Brussel, who profiled New York City's Mad Bomber in 1956 (Brussel, 1968). By combining criminal statistics, psychiatry, and crime scene investigative insights, Brussel made several accurate predications concerning the description and background of the bomber, George Metesky (Teten, 1989). Another early profiling effort came from the Medical-Psychiatric Committee formed in 1964 to analyze the Boston Strangler; it was unsuccessful as its members could not agree on which of the murders were linked (Frank, 1966).

Since 1978, investigative support, research, and training in this area has been provided within the U.S. by the Behavioral Science Unit — now known as the National Center for the Analysis of Violent Crime (NCAVC) — located within the Critical Incident Response Group (CIRG) at the FBI Academy in Quantico, Virginia. Training for criminal profiling in North America is provided by the NCAVC and the International Criminal Investigative Analysis Fellowship (ICIAF) (Lines, 1999). The NCAVC was established in 1984 by the FBI in response to concerns over the rapid increase in violent crime throughout the U.S. during the previous decade (Depue, 1986). In addition to providing profiling services, referred to as criminal investigative analysis (CIA), the NCAVC is responsible for VICAP, research, and instruction components (Ressler et al., 1988; Van Zandt & Ether, 1994).

The Police Fellowship, initiated by the FBI but now an independent professional body, provides a structured and mentored two-year intensive understudy program for qualified law enforcement candidates (see Teten, 1989). Criminal profiling in Canada has followed the FBI/ICIAF model, and the RCMP Behavioural Sciences and Special Services Branch and the Ontario Provincial Police (OPP) Behavioural Sciences Section now provide this service nationally (Cavanagh & MacKay, 1991; Lines, 1999; MacKay, 1994).

In Britain, the more general terms of offender profiling and behavioural analysis are used in recognition of contributions from psychology, psychiatry, geography, mathematics, statistics, and detective expertise. Offender profiling consists of the prediction of offender characteristics, crime scene assessment, establishment of crime series, and provision of investigative advice. It is based on three distinct approaches: (1) practical detective expertise; (2) behavioural science theory; and (3) statistical analyses of solved case information. The behavioural science research has two contrasting threads — one in the area of clinical psychology, and the other in environmental psychology (Copson, 1993). The latter field has been concerned with drawing geographical as well as behavioural inferences concerning the offender.

The statistical analysis approach to criminal profiling has its genesis in the development of the CATCHEM database, a collation of all sexually motivated child murders and abductions in Great Britain since 1960 (Aitken, Connolly, Gammerman, & Zhang, 1994; Burton, 1998; Copson, 1993). Containing 3310 cases (as of end 1997), the system also has a refined database of 470 victims and 417 offenders that is used for prediction purposes. Statistical profiles for unsolved crimes are produced through comparisons to solved cases in the refined database[25] (see above). These are empirical and make no assumptions regarding offender motivation or personality. Amongst other predictions, the statistical profiles estimate journey-to-crime ranges, and distance between crime scene and dump site in cases of missing bodies (Copson, 1993). Analyses to date of the CATCHEM data suggest that Bayesian belief networks, a graphical method for depicting probabilistic relationships (e.g., between offender, victim, and crime characteristics), shows promise for statistical modeling (Aitken et al., 1994; Aitken, Connolly, Gammerman, Zhang, Bailey, Gordon, & Oldfield, 1995; see also Iversen, 1984).

The National Crime Faculty (NCF) at the Police Staff College in Bramshill coordinates offender profiling and related services for the British police. They provide operational support, investigative training, crime analysis, data collection, and research on serious crime issues. The NCF maintains a list of accredited offender profilers, and a register of contacts for expert support in the areas of prosecution, forensic science, intelligence, investigation, and behavioural science. They are also engaged in Operation Enigma, an exam-

[25] The detection rate is 94% for the entire database, and 88.7% for the refined database.

ination of possible connections between unsolved and solved murders of females within the U.K.

The Policing and Reducing Crime Unit (PRC) of the British Home Office assists the NCF in several areas, including research (e.g., theory validation, profiling utility, rape geography, etc.), building violent criminal databases, and determining the optimal manner of delivery for profiling services (Aitken et al., 1995; Copson, 1993; Dale & Davies, 1994a, 1994b; Davies & Dale, 1995b; Farrington & Lambert, 1993). They are currently involved in an assessment of all operational offender profiles within the U.K.

5.2   Organized and Disorganized Crime Scenes

The FBI profiling approach is based upon a systematic process that follows a four-stage sequence: (1) data assimilation; (2) crime classification; (3) crime reconstruction; and (4) profile generation (Jackson & Bekerian, 1997a). The criminal profile generating process involves the use of decision models, based on data inputs, to develop crime assessments and criminal profiles (Ressler et al., 1988). Further investigation may provide feedback to the system. Depending upon offence type, different criminal personality typologies are employed in the profiling process. For murder cases, psychological profilers use the categories of organized and disorganized, as determined from crime scene behaviour and offender lifestyle. While this is an ideal dichotomy, most real killers are mixed to some degree.

Organized offenders typically plan their crimes, likely have access to a vehicle, and travel further from home to offend. They are usually intelligent and sane, but may be psychopathic. Characteristics include superior intelligence, social and sexual competence, skilled occupation, high birth order status, father with stable work history, inconsistent childhood discipline, controlled mood during crime, alcohol use, precipitating situational stress, living with a partner, mobile, car in good condition, investigation followed in the news, and possible change of jobs or move from town after the crime (Ressler et al., 1988). Organized crime scene characteristics include a planned crime, stranger victim, victim personalized, demand for submissive victim, use of restraints, conversation controlled, crime scene controlled, aggression prior to death, weapon and evidence absent, victim's body transported, and body hidden.

Disorganized offenders typically act spontaneously and do not plan their crimes. They tend to live or work near the crime sites. Many suffer from some form of psychosis such as paranoid schizophrenia. Characteristics include average to below average intelligence, social and sexual immaturity, poor work record, low birth order status, father with unstable work history, harsh childhood discipline, anxious mood during crime, minimal use of alcohol, living alone, crime scene near residence or work, does not follow the investigation in the news, and minimal change in lifestyle after the crime (Ressler et al., 1988). Disorganized crime scene characteristics include a spontaneous crime, knowledge of victim or location, sudden violence to victim (blitz attack), minimal use of restraints, depersonalization of victim, minimal conversation, random and sloppy crime scene, postmortem sex, weapon and evidence present and body left in view and not removed from crime scene.

There is supporting evidence that crime scenes can be reliably categorized as organized or disorganized, and that this typology is correlated with offender characteristics (Homant & Kennedy, 1998). An FBI study of crime scene classification (n = 220) found an interrater agreement level of 74.1% (Ressler & Burgess, 1985). Kocsis et al. (1998) examined arson cases in New South Wales, Australia, to determine whether the organized/disorganized dichotomy was a subjective categorization or actually intrinsic to the crime itself. The study found support for the latter hypothesis. A cluster analysis of crime scene variables produced two basic groupings that matched *a priori* organized/disorganized categories and offender characteristics. But the need still exists for further research into this offender profiling dichotomy and the development of objectively quantifiable scales for categorizing crime scenes (Homant & Kennedy, 1998).

The most commonly used profiling methodology appears to be crime scene analysis (the FBI approach), followed by diagnostic evaluation (Wilson, Lincoln, & Kocsis, 1997). Investigative psychology, another profiling method primarily used in England, is based upon a five-factor model constructed from facet theory and smallest space analysis (SSA): (1) attempted intimacy; (2) sexual gratification; (3) aggression; (4) impersonal interaction; and (5) criminality (Canter & Heritage, 1990). The Australian national police Criminal Profiling Research Unit developed a profiling model from the statistical analysis of 86 sexual murders from 1960 to 1998 (Kocsis, 1999). After elimination of actions common to most crimes, four distinct behaviour patterns emerged: (1) the predator pattern, characterized by torture, sadism and a high level of planning; (2) the perversion pattern, typified by organized behaviour and bizarre sexual perversions; (3) the fury pattern, distinguished by hatred, hostility, and excessively brutal attacks; and (4) the rape pattern, in which sexual assault is the primary purpose and the murder is accidental or committed to avoid apprehension (the offender is often vaguely acquainted with the victim). Predator and perversion patterns are methodical (organized), and fury and rape patterns haphazard (disorganized).

5.3 Applications of Profiling

Profiling requirements are information intensive, perhaps because of the method's probabilistic nature. In turn, a profile can provide a variety of suggestions concerning offender characteristics including likely age, race, sex, socioeconomic status, residence description, method of transportation, education level, marital status, employment background, criminal record particulars, psychiatric history, social and sexual development, military history, physical characteristics, habits, degree of organization, pre-offence behaviour, post-offence behaviour, and the possibility of accomplices (Geberth, 1996; Ressler et al., 1988).

Profiles also attempt to give a general estimate of the criminal's residence proximity to the crime scenes (e.g., "the offender likely lives or works in the neighbourhood of the murders"). Background information necessary for a profile includes, amongst other details, the addresses of the victim's residence and employment, where he or she was last seen, the locations of the crime sites, and a map of the victim's travels prior to death (Geberth, 1996).

In addition to the criminal profiling of unknown suspects and the establishment of investigative priorities, profiling techniques have been used for a variety of other purposes. These include indirect personality assessments (to assist in developing interviewing, undercover, or cross-examination approaches), equivocal death analyses, development of investigative and trial strategies, establishing grounds for search and seizure, threat assessments, and informing linkage analyses (Ault & Hazelwood, 1995; Cavanagh & MacKay, 1991; Jackson et al., 1994).

Offences suitable for profiling involve those incidents where the suspect has demonstrated some form of psychopathology or the offence is of an unusual, bizarre, violent, sexual or repetitive nature (Geberth, 1981). Profiles have been prepared in cases of mutilation, torture, and lust murders; serial killings; homicides involving postmortem cutting, slashing, evisceration, or body exploration; ritualistic and Satanic or cult crimes; rapes and sadistic sexual assaults; random arsons; child molestings; bombings; bank robberies; and false rape allegations (Cavanagh & MacKay, 1991). It has even been suggested that the personality traits of a murderer may be profiled based on the characteristics of the handgun (type, model, image, calibre, and ammunition) used (Bensimon, 1997).

Howard Teten (1989), a former FBI member and one of the fathers of criminal profiling, however, cautions that the technique should only be applied to specific types of crimes, typically those involving overt sexual activity or loss of contact with reality by the offender. Profiling property or drug-related crimes is also problematic; there is usually little contact with the victim or time spent at the scene in property offences, and drug use alters the basic personality of the offender. Rape crimes where the victim was unconscious or cannot remember the incident, or the offender was under the influence of drugs, did not speak, used minimal force, or did not engage in atypical sexual activity, are difficult to profile (Hazelwood, Ressler, Depue, & Douglas, 1995). Generally, cases lacking offender behaviour or other relevant information will prove difficult to profile. And because of its probabilistic nature, profiling is more powerful in multiple than single crime cases. Kennedy and Homant (1997) suggest that "modern profiling in general is a viable and intriguing investigative tool that can be useful within limits.... [but] refinement efforts should first be directed to improving the study of serial rape and murder before reaching too far out into other crime categories" (pp. 226, 228).

Detective John Baeza (1999) of the New York Police Department outlines criteria for what a police task force should expect from a psychological or geographic profile. Profilers need to operate within their area of expertise, integrate physical with behavioural evidence, and be prepared to visit the crime sites. The report itself should be written, comprehensive, and provide investigative suggestions. Profilers have to be able to explain their logic, and investigators must be willing to ask questions about methods and conclusions. He observes that while profiles are only a tool and their results are not set in stone, they can play a useful role in task force management through suspect and tip prioritization. FBI and Fellowship profilers often follow a case consultation model where investigators present the details of their crimes to a panel of profilers using photographs, maps, charts, and reports. After questions and answers, a brainstorming session leads to a collaborative profile and specific case strategies, all documented by the investigator.

5.4   Critiques

Profiling has generated its share of interest, controversy, and censure (Jeffers, 1991; Jackson et al., 1994; Jenkins, 1994; Levin & Fox, 1985; Masters, 1994; Poythress, Otto, Darkes, & Starr, 1993; Rosenbaum, 1993; Turco, 1990). It has been suggested that profiles provide information that is general and ambiguous at best, and misleading at worst. In particular, profiling has been criticized as wanting programmatic validity and reliability research, and for lacking a proper theoretical basis. Bartol (1996) surveyed 152 full and part-time police psychologists and found that 70% were uncomfortable with the validity and usefulness of profiling; many thought more research was needed. The investigative psychology approach has been questioned in Britain because of a lack of empirical verification and the mysterious methodology underlying smallest space analysis (Copson & Holloway, 1996). Meanwhile, an analysis of profiling results from a small number of cases in Australia produced mixed results (Wilson & Soothill, 1996).

Perhaps the most serious censure to date of profiling, at least within North America, originated from a U.S. Congressional review (Jeffers, 1991). The U.S. House of Representatives Armed Services Committee (HASC), while reviewing the Navy investigation of the 1989 explosion on the USS *Iowa*, became concerned over the manner in which a conclusion of "intentional action" had been reached (Poythress et al., 1993). Gunners Mate Clayton Hartwig was singly blamed for the tragic incident that resulted in the deaths of 47 sailors. He was alleged to have set off an explosion of a 16-inch turret gun in order to commit suicide (Nelson, 1990).

The Naval Investigative Service (NIS) had requested that the National Center for the Analysis of Violent Crime conduct a reconstructive psychological evaluation. This procedure, part of the FBI's profiling service, is termed equivocal death analysis (EDA), and is conceptually similar to a psychological autopsy (Ebert, 1987; Poythress et al., 1993; see Fowler, 1986, for example). In suspect cases, EDA attempts to determine manner of death — accidental, suicidal, homicidal, or indeterminate — through the use of retrospective psychological techniques.

The HASC was concerned over the validity and reliability of EDA, and these worries were only exacerbated by the disinterest displayed by NCAVC profilers for issues of validity and data integrity (Poythress et al., 1993). They asked for assistance from the American Psychological Association (APA), whose officials responded by forming a review panel comprising 12 psychologists and 2 psychiatrists. The majority of the APA experts subsequently found the FBI's analysis invalid, and the panel was unanimous in its criticism of EDA procedures, methodology, and unarticulated limitations (*U.S.S. Iowa Tragedy*, 1990). The lack of concern expressed by BSU profilers over validity and reliability was found to be unacceptable (*Review of Navy investigation*, 1990). In short, the FBI did not pass the APA peer review.

Calling the process an investigative failure, the HASC noted that: "The major problem with the Navy investigation is that it fell into the trap of an excess of certitude. Thin gruel became red meat. Valid theories and hypotheses were converted into hard fact" (Poythress et al., 1993, p. 10). The APA expert panel cautioned: "The conclusions and inferences drawn in psychological reconstructions are, at best, informed speculations or theoretical formulations and should be labeled as such ... The kinds of unequivocal, bottom-line statements offered by the FBI in its EDA report, regarding Clayton Hartwig, are not defensible within the technical limitations of our science" (Poythress et al., p. 12). In 1990, Sandia National Laboratories in New Mexico was able to replicate the turret gun explosion through accidental means, further undermining the Navy's investigative conclusions (Jeffers, 1991; Nelson, 1990).

During the hearings, FBI personnel pointed out in rebuttal that the *U.S.S. Iowa* equivocal death analysis was focused on answering the single question as to whether the explosion was suicide, homicide, or suicide/homicide; accidental death was not an option. And while psychologists on the APA panel criticized the FBI's methodology, not all disagreed with their conclusions (Michaud & Hazelwood, 1998).

Homant and Kennedy (1998) help explain the police perspective on profiling validity. "From a law enforcement point of view, there is no need to wait for assurances that profiling in general is a valid process, as long as there are not any more promising alternatives and as long as the process is used cautiously" (p. 323). While suspects and lines of inquiry should not be excluded just because they fail to fit the profile, investigators sometimes must make hard decisions quickly; under such conditions, profiling information — even of the "informed guess" type — may be of value.

Still, the APA review contains important warnings regarding the use, limitations, and dangers of psychological profiling. "Profiles should be viewed as supportive and not substantive" (Jackson et al., 1993a, p. 31). The FBI itself cautions that profiling is still more of an art than a science, and should never be considered a replacement for traditional investigative methodologies (Ault & Reese, 1980; Hazelwood & Douglas, 1980; Porter, 1983, 52; Ressler & Shachtman, 1992). Discussion has taken place in regards to developing automated crime profiling through the use of artificial intelligence and computer-assisted expert systems, but to date this goal has not been realized (Icove, 1986; Reboussin & Cameron, 1989; see also Benfer, Brent, & Furbee, 1991; Bunge, 1991). Dietz (1985) suggests that "it may be more accurate to regard profiling as a process of logical reasoning that draws on experience, insight, and judgment at each step of the process. In this sense profiling may resemble the process of clinical reasoning in medicine" (pp. 217–218).

5.5   Evaluation Studies

These concerns, critiques, and suggestions have led to a variety of evaluation studies designed to examine the investigative merits of criminal profiling. Evaluative research has occurred in the U.S., Britain, The Netherlands, Canada, and Australia. These studies often approach the assessment task by addressing three key issues: (1) how accurate is profiling; (2) how reliable is the process; and (3) how useful are the results? For a profile to be useful, it must assist in the investigative decision making process. Suggestions that are vague, general, unworkable, or of low probability are not likely to produce helpful leads. These questions and requirements provide an important framework for the development of any new investigative methodology, psychological and geographic profiling included.

One of the first criminal profiling evaluation projects was an FBI in-house survey of 192 users of BSU-prepared profiles, comprising 209 cases (65% involving homicide, 35% rape, and 27% other offences)[26] (Institutional Research and Development Unit, 1981). The study determined that only 46% of these crimes had been subsequently solved. Of these 88 investigations, the profile was found to have helped: (1) focus the investigation (72% of the cases); (2) locate possible suspects (20%); (3) directly identify the suspect (17%); (4) assist in the prosecution of the suspect (6%); or (5) was of no assistance (17%).[27] Of the 104 unsolved investigations, the profile was still seen as helpful in terms of generating leads, suggesting motives, and confirming other findings. The BSU typically receives only the most difficult of cases, those that have defied traditional investigative efforts, and these findings need to be placed within that context (Fox & Levin, 1992; see also Jackson et al., 1994).

Pinizzotto and Finkel (1990; see also Jackson et al., 1994; Pinizzotto, 1984) examined criminal profiling outcomes and processes through the expert/novice approach, a technique used in cognitive psychology to explore expertise in specific domains. Between-group differences were analyzed in a study that included profilers, police detectives, psychologists, and students. The researchers found that the group of profilers wrote more detailed and valid reports than did the other groups, but they observed mixed results concerning ability to correctly predict offender characteristics. No between-group qualitative differences in information processing were noted.

Kocsis, Irwin, Hayes, and Nunn (forthcoming) conducted a similar study to test the influence of investigative experience, knowledge of criminal psychology, objective and logical analysis, and intuition on the psychological profiling process. Predictions for a murder case were compared between groups of profilers, police officers, psychologists, students, and psychics. Profilers were slightly more accurate than nonprofilers in the identification of offender cognitive processes, physical characteristics, social history and habits, and offence behaviours. Psychologists did better in some areas such as determining the offender's personality characteristics. Psychics appeared to rely upon nothing more than social stereotypes of murders.

The Netherlands Institute for the Study of Criminality and Law Enforcement (NISCALE) conducted several evaluation studies of specific profile analysis and investigative advice as provided by the Scientific Advisory Unit of the Dutch National Criminal Intelligence Division (CRI) (Jackson et al., 1994; Jackson, van Koppen, & Herbrink, 1993a, 1993b). They first explored

---

[26] Percentages do not add to 100 as a single case may involve more than one type of offence.
[27] Percentages do not add to 100 as multiple responses were allowed.

differences between the operational mental schemata of experienced police investigators and offender profilers (Jackson et al., 1994). Models for structuring knowledge consist of domain, inference, task, and strategic layers (Adhami & Browne, 1996), and expert knowledge is derived from a series of "if-then" rules (some areas of expertise contain heuristics numbering in the tens of thousands). To be useful, an expert's knowledge must be applicable, have the potential to be generalized to other situations, contain structure and organization, and possess depth.

The cognitive representations and strategies employed by detectives were found to be qualitatively different from those used by profilers. Specifically, the if-then production rules of the police detectives were either too global (general) or too specific (idiosyncratic) to be of much investigative value. Another component of the study found process differences between an experienced sexual offence detective and an FBI-trained Dutch profiler. The former was observed to work in a bottom-up fashion, concerned with the "what," while the latter had a top-down approach, and focused on the "who."

The research revealed interesting differences in how profilers and detectives assimilated data (Jackson, 1994). On average, profilers devoted substantially more time per case on police tip reports than did detectives (12 hours, 29 minutes vs. 2 hours, 33 minutes), and about the same amount of time on the autopsy reports (14 minutes vs. 16 minutes). Profilers spent less time per case on the main police reports (4 hours, 54 minutes vs. 6 hours, 28 minutes), the geographical locations (18 minutes vs. 31 minutes), and the crime scene photographs (26 minutes vs. 1 hour, 9 minutes). Overall, profilers spent considerably more time than did detectives on data assimilation (18 hours, 21 minutes vs. 10 hours, 57 minutes). The observation that, on average, detectives spent more of their time on the geographic locations than did profilers (4.72% of total time vs. 1.6%, a factor of 1.7 in terms of absolute time), is interesting in light of the findings of Pinizzotto and Finkel (1990): "It was the detective group that scored higher in the homicide questions dealing with the offender's employment and the offender's residence in relation to the crime scene" (p. 224).

The NISCALE study also looked at "consumer satisfaction" and found the great majority of detective-customers were satisfied with the criminal investigative analysis service (Jackson et al., 1994). While the profiles themselves received mixed reviews, it was observed that several other, perhaps more important, functions were also provided (Jackson et al., 1993a). Investigative suggestions, personality assessments, profile writing, crime assessments, interviewing techniques, and threat assessments were all part of the profiler's repertoire. Detectives noted additional benefits resulting from the profilers' expertise with bizarre crimes and the fresh perspective they brought to an investigation. "By taking an independent stance, not bogged down with the inconsequential details that a detective actively working on a case has to contend with, the professional profiler can offer directions and advice that can result in the team achieving success in apprehending the culprit" (Jackson et al., 1993a, p. 32).

The NISCALE evaluation discovered that "no criminal was actually caught as a direct result of the profiles made" (Jackson et al., 1993a, p. 24), but this appears to have resulted from problems with customers as well as profilers. While the reports of the profilers were sometimes criticized as being too vague and general, inflexibility on the part of detectives stemming from lack of acceptance, differences in opinion, financial restraints, time delays, and organizational considerations, all contributed to instances where the profiles were not acted upon (Jackson et al., 1993a). The CRI now first confirms that sufficient investigative resources exist to follow up any profiling suggestions that might result (Jackson et al., 1994).

The NISCALE study concluded that profiling is not an end in itself, but only a management instrument for helping direct certain types of criminal investigations (Jackson et al., 1994). The importance of ongoing criminological and evaluative research was also stressed. For example, while an independent study validated some of the derivation principles used in profiling rape cases, other rules were not substantiated within the Dutch context. Collaboration within the scientific forum is therefore regarded as an integral component of the CRI's ongoing policies.

The Offender Profiling Research Programme is a comprehensive evaluation of profiling use within the U.K. being conducted by the PRC and the National Crime Faculty (Copson, 1993; Davies & Dale, 1995b). Interim study results suggest that the perceived usefulness of profiling advice is more associated with a strategic understanding of the crime and its investigation rather than with the profile's inferential aspects (Oldfield, 1995). Such a finding is consistent with the conclusions of the Dutch research (Jackson et al., 1994).

As part of this research program, Copson (1995) surveyed detectives who had used profiling services in Britain (n = 184); the majority of cases involved either murder or sex crimes. Profiling was defined as "any predictions, recommendations and observations based on the inference of offender characteristics from behaviour exhibited in a crime or a series of crimes, and offered to investigators as the product of statistical or clinical expertise" (p. v). Detectives were not always clear on what they expected from a profile, but the following information was most commonly mentioned: (1) offender characteristics; (2) understanding of the offender and the future threat level; (3) interview strategies; and (4) linkages between crimes. When asked if they would seek profiling advice again, 68.5% of the respondents stated they definitely would, and 23.9% that they probably would.

A previous study by Britton in the U.K. suggested that profiles were not particularly helpful in directly leading to the arrest of a suspect, but the process appears viable and shows promise and potential. A review by Goldblatt of profiling advice in solved cases determined that 72% of predicted offender characteristics (n = 114) were correct, 19% were incorrect, and 9% lacked sufficient information to be classified. Copson found that only 14.1% of the profiles helped solve a case and a slim 2.7% actually identified the offender. But profiling advice did open up new lines of inquiry in 16.3% of the cases; 82.6% of the respondents stated the profile provided operationally useful information, and 53.8% that it added value to their investigation.

In addition to the accuracy of a profile, detectives were further concerned over the timeliness and clarity of the response. Verbal profiles, in particular, were not helpful; written reports are less likely to be misunderstood or forgotten. But it is also incumbent upon the investigators to ask questions and seek explanations regarding things they do not understand. Unfortunately, profiling advice was not always acted upon, limiting its potential utility. It would be interesting to compare the results of this study with research on such established investigative techniques as crime scene fingerprinting and eyewitness interviews.

Copson suggests that profiles are most useful indirectly, assisting detectives in understanding the crime and developing an "investigative philosophy." He also notes they help ensure that a complete and proper investigation has been done. The Association of Chief Police Officers (ACPO) Crime Committee on Behavioural Science and Investigative Support has now developed policy regarding research, operational use, and media disclosure for the British police service in an effort to improve the quality of profiling advice in criminal investigations.

5.6   Profiling and Probability

To many police investigators, profiling is an arcane art, its predictions originating from a black box. For offender profiling to realize its potential, two things must happen. First, profilers must better understand the requirements and needs of police investigations; and second, investigators must better understand the nature and use of profiles. Profiles do not solve crimes as that can only be done by way of a confession, witness, or physical evidence (Klockars & Mastrofski, 1991). Instead, they are best used to guide strategy development, support information management, and improve case understanding.

There is a symbiosis between the investigation and the profile; the more complete and thorough the former, the more accurate the latter (Teten, 1989). For example, if a careful linkage analysis has not been done, then the investigation suffers from an incomplete pattern and the profile is missing important data. Proper information collection — from the crime scene, during the follow-up investigation, and as part of routine police practice — is particularly important (Bekerian & Jackson, 1997); also, the value of a profile is significantly enhanced when it is combined with other investigative tools, both behavioural and traditional.

Profiling is not independent of other forms of investigative analysis. A framework for crime analysis methods has been developed by Mario de Cocq (1997), head of Interpol's Analytical Criminal Intelligence Unit (ACIU). Analytic techniques are first classified as either strategic or operational, and then grouped by focus on criminal incident, offender, or crime control method. Within this framework, "specific profile analysis [unknown offender(s)]" — psychological and geographic profiling — is categorized as operational/offender. Comparative case (linkage) analysis is categorized as operational/criminal incident. This approach allows for both similarities and differences between analytic methods to be readily identified.

Part of the difficulty with profiling has been its probabilistic nature. Police investigators are uncomfortable with such methods of inquiry, preferring instead to rely upon "certainties." This often leads to problems in the understanding, use, and evaluation of profiling services. The following example clarifies the point. A man consults a statistician before gambling on a game of dice. He is advised that the number most likely to turn up is 7, and he bets accordingly. But when he rolls a 5, the bet is lost.

Was the advice inaccurate? Well, any student of probability knows that 7 is the most likely number to result from the roll of a pair of dice, with 2 and 12 being the least likely. Still, the probability of 7 occurring in any *single* roll is only 1 in 6. The statistician's advice was not a prediction — in fact, a better forecast (with a 5/6 chance of being correct) would have been a number other than 7. Rather, the advice was a statement regarding the most likely single outcome. While the prediction was wrong, it was also accurate, and any future prediction would still be 7. This information is thus of greater value when used over the course of a series of games. In other words, while no one can predict a given spin of the roulette wheel, there is little doubt the house will make money at the end of the day. Similarly, profiling is optimally employed by an investigation when it assists in the direction of repetitive efforts and the prioritization of volume work.

5.7 Expert Testimony

Expert testimony from profilers has been introduced now in both American and Canadian courts. Subject matter has included future dangerousness, threat level, similar fact evidence, case linkage, crime scene signature, staging, and insanity (see Keppel, 1989, 1995; Keppel & Birnes, 1997). Profiling has also played a role in premises liability litigation where the court must establish if the proximate cause of damages was a breach of duty to provide proper security (Kennedy & Homant, 1997). Opinion evidence regarding likely criminal response to security measures influences establishment of a cause-in-fact relationship between the alleged negligence and plaintiff injury. In these circumstances, most of the profile is an attempt to predict the behaviour of the typical offender — persistence, desistance, or displacement — under certain security conditions. While such information may assist juries in appropriate cases, prediction of specific individual behaviours with any degree of confidence is difficult, even for experts (Homant, forthcoming).

This is particularly so when the offender is unknown (i.e., not identified and apprehended). Homant (forthcoming) proposes a typology for offender deterrence based on factors of criminal motivation and desire to avoid capture: (1) calculating — motivated and cautious; (2) opportunistic — unmotivated and cautious; (3) determined — motivated and incautious; and (4) impulsive — unmotivated and incautious. Adjustments are made based on offender intelligence, target significance, and evidence of irrationality (e.g., use of drugs or alcohol). Profiling can play a role in premises security litigation through interpreting signature, reconstructing crime scenes, and assessing motivation.

To be so designated, an expert witness must meet three requirements: (1) their testimony must be relevant; (2) their field must require scientific, technical, or specialized knowledge; and (3) they must have the necessary background to qualify as an expert in the field (e.g., skill, specialized training, formal education, experience) (Garland & Stuckey, 2000). Relevance has been defined as evidence that affects the probability of existence for facts of consequence to the trial (Robertson & Vignaux, 1995). Until 1993, determination of "scientific knowledge" used to follow the Frye test (*Frye v. United States*), which asked if the knowledge was generally accepted as reliable within the relevant scientific community. That year the U.S. Supreme Court decided that U.S. Federal Rules of Evidence superseded Frye (*Daubert v. Merrell*, 1993). The Daubert test is now used to determine if a subject matter has reached the stature of "scientific knowledge." It is a more flexible and less stringent test than Frye, and is based on the following factors: (1) falsifiability (the testability of the technique); (2) peer review and publication; (3) the actual or potential error rate and the maintenance of operational standards; and (4) general acceptance of the methodology within the relevant scientific community. These are currently the principles guiding admissibility of scientific evidence in American courts.

The Canadian test is not as strict as the U.S. one. In *R. v. Mohan* (1994), the Supreme Court of Canada outlined the requirements for admissibility of expert evidence: (1) relevance to a fact in issue; (2) necessity in assisting the trier of fact; (3) absence of an exclusionary rule; and (4) a properly qualified expert. Novel scientific theories or concepts are subject to special scrutiny concerning their validity and reliability. This scrutiny is a flexible test that considers acceptance within the scientific community; suggested criteria include testability, peer review, and publication. Canadian courts have stated that expert opinion evidence can be rendered to assist the trier's understanding of psychology, behaviour, and human conduct; but they have also cautioned that the confirmation methods used in profiling "should be considerably sharpened and disciplined" (*R. v. Clark*, 1998, p. 21). Profiles are not generally introduced as evidence in British courts.

Profiling is based on inductive, probabilistic methods. What is the proper role of such evidence in the courtroom? All science is inductive and scientific "laws" are only predictions based upon repeated observations. By contrast, deductive systems are derived from axioms or established rules. The only true deductive system is mathematics, though many scientific theories are so well accepted they are often treated as established facts in normal life for all intents and purposes. It has been said that science is quantitative and law is qualitative (Forst, 1996a). For example, "beyond a reasonable doubt," the standard for criminal conviction, is a subjective determination and has not been translated by either statute or case law into a specific number.[28] Generally, probabilistic information is valid, especially in cases involving circumstantial evidence, though experts are ill advised to go beyond the established boundaries of their discipline. They must also be prepared to articulate the logic and specify the data upon which their conclusions are based (Homant, forthcoming).

The most appropriate manner of introducing and weighing profiling expertise in court is through the use of Bayesian probability methods. Bayes' rule is a logical theorem that provides the means of updating probabilities given new information of relevance (Iversen, 1984). It can be expressed as follows:

$$\text{(prior odds)(likelihood ratio)} = \text{posterior odds.} \qquad (5.1)$$

The prior odds are those that existed before the new information, and the posterior odds, those after. Probability always ranges between 0 and 1; odds are the ratio of the probability that something is true to the probability that it is not: $p / (1 - p)$. The likelihood ratio is the quotient of the probability

[28] In a survey of 1200 U.S. judges, two-thirds thought "beyond a reasonable doubt" represented a probability of guilt of at least 95%.

of the evidence given that an assertion is true (i.e., the accused individual is guilty), divided by the probability of the evidence given that the assertion is false (i.e., an accused individual is innocent). This can be expressed as follows:

$$\text{likelihood ratio} = P(E|G)/P(E|I). \qquad (5.2)$$

The probability of guilt given the evidence ($P(G|E)$) can be determined from the probability of the evidence given guilt ($P(E|G)$). According to Bayes' rule:

$$P(G|E) = P(G)\ P(E|G)\ /\ [P(G)\ P(E|G) + P(I)\ P(E|I)]. \qquad (5.3)$$

If the probabilities of guilt and innocence are equal (i.e., $P(G) = P(I) = 0.5$), then the above equation simplifies to: $P(G|E) = P(E|G)$. The higher the prior probability of guilt, the more attenuated the impact of the evidence (likelihood ratio) on the posterior probability of guilt.

Expert testimony, however, should be limited to providing the likelihood ratio resulting from the observation, profile, or test result. Behaviour science evidence, whether it be similar fact, signature, psychological, or geographic in nature, can only be justified on this basis. Estimating probability of guilt or innocence assumes knowledge of the prior odds, and this determination is the responsibility of the judge or jury — not the expert witness (Robertson & Vignaux, 1995).

Errors in the use of probability within the court context unfortunately are not uncommon. The prosecutor's fallacy results from transposing the conditional in either the numerator or denominator of the likelihood ratio (see also Martin, 1992). This occurs, for example, when the probability of the evidence given guilt, $P(E|G)$, is equated with the probability of guilt given the evidence, $P(G|E)$. In other words, while all cows are four-legged animals, not all four-legged animals are cows. This type of error within a behavioural science context results if: (1) a crime scene indicates a certain personality profile with a 90% level of confidence, and the assumption is made that a person who matches the profile is 90% likely to be guilty (transposing the conditional in the numerator); or (2) only 10 murders out of a database of 50,000 exhibit a specific crime scene behaviour, and the conclusion is reached that the probability of such a similarity occurring by chance is one in 5,000 (transposing the conditional in the denominator, also referred to as the coincidence fallacy). The former type of error occurred in the aftermath of the 1996 Atlanta Olympics pipe bombing. Security guard Richard Jewell became a major suspect in the investigation simply because he fit the FBI profile for a certain type of bomber. Effectively branded guilty, it took several weeks before he was eventually cleared (Reid, 1996).

The defence attorney's fallacy occurs when evidence is considered in isolation, rather than as a totality. It is the combined impact of different, and independent, evidential elements that is important.[29] This type of error within the behavioural science context results if a profile is ignored because it lacks dramatic discriminatory power, instead of the findings considered in conjunction with other existing evidence, and used to increase the posterior odds appropriately.

5.8   Future of Profiling

Notwithstanding his claim to be a consulting detective, Sherlock Holmes employed inductive methods almost as often as deductive ones (Teten, 1989). Despite his renowned successes, such procedures by their very nature carry a certain failure rate. Wrong predictions are part of any probabilistic-based methodology, including profiling (Homant & Kennedy, 1998). It is important that profiles be used by both providers and consumers in a careful and ethical manner, with an awareness of their limitations and an understanding of the proper application of stereotypes and prioritization methods. Grubin (1999) also cautions that profiling is not about "getting into the mind" of the criminal, and we should be concerned when the profiler becomes more newsworthy than the profile.

"In summary, there is enough research to suggest that crime scene profiling may have sufficient reliability and validity to be useful for some purposes. The literature suggests that the concept of behavioral traits and consistency across situations is respectable, if measured in broad contexts" (Homant & Kennedy, 1998, p. 338). The development of profiling and other forensic behavioural science techniques is in its early days. While this may sometimes result in frustration, it is also an exciting time with much potential for future evolvement. For example, offender profiling may benefit significantly from the application of fuzzy logic (Kosko & Isaka, 1993; Yager & Zadeh, 1994). Traditional Boolean logic is dichotomous and follows the law of the excluded middle — answers are either yes or no. Fuzzy logic allows for subjectivity and "maybes." These shades of meaning can be given intermediate values between 0 and 1. Verma (1997) discusses how imprecise features and characteristics may be fuzzy variables. A sufficient number of such parameters can form a fuzzy prototype pattern class (e.g., young, tall, heavy, violent). This is similar to the concept of frames, flexible and fuzzy enclosures used to prioritize suspects during an investigation (Kind, 1987b, 1990). Estimating min-max values can help define the limits of the pattern

---

[29] These errors in logic can also occur within a profile. Use of spurious, intervening, and non-independent variables is problematic and their use will skew an analysis.

set. This approach can be of assistance in many ways, including the reconciliation of varying descriptions in a series of connected crimes. Austin (1996) used a fuzzy logic expert system for offender profiling that analyzed crime, victim, and event details to connect rapes to rapes, and offenders to rapes.

Profiling is a useful and promising investigative methodology. It is also a novel technique, the maturation of which requires a commitment to not only data collection, analysis, and research, but also to operational feedback and integration. Inductive systems require systematic methods for developing and expanding their knowledge base. It is thus critical for scientific and investigative methodologies to be concerned with issues of validity and reliability (see Oldfield, 1995). Profiling knowledge originates from experience, research, and statistical databases. While experience is important, if not vital, it can also be idiosyncratic, containing limitations and unrealized biases, upon which profiles may be based. Experience should therefore be triangulated with research findings. Specification of the limitations inherent in a method's underlying assumptions is also important. Finally, a technique must possess utility if it is to have value in the real world of police investigation. Such considerations are what distinguish profiling predictions from psychic guesses.

Behavioural Geography

Human geography studies people and their activities, and physical geography studies the natural environment (Goodall, 1987). While these two areas are not unconnected, human geography is specifically concerned with three integrated themes: (1) spatial analysis; (2) interrelationships between people and the environment; and (3) regional syntheses of the first two themes. Its major fields of study include behavioural, economic, historical, political, regional, rural, social, transport, and urban geography.

Behavioural geography examines how people come to terms with their physical and social environments, and uses behaviourism as a means of understanding patterns of human spatial action. How people codify, respond to, and react with their environments is explained in terms of cognitive processes such as learning and stimulus-response. Those areas of behavioural geography and the related quantitative techniques relevant for an understanding of crime patterns and offender spatial behaviour are discussed below.

6.1   Movement and Distance

Perhaps the most basic heuristic in geography is the nearness principle, also known in psychology as the least-effort principle (Zipf, 1950). A person who is "given various possibilities for action ... will select the one requiring the least expenditure of effort" (Reber, 1985, p. 400). This maxim describes a great deal about the movement of people but many other factors come into play in the psychology and behaviour of choice (Cornish & Clarke, 1986b; Luce, 1959; Tversky & Kahneman, 1981). Least effort is an important principle in the study of crime journeys.

When multiple destinations of equal desirability are available, the least-effort principle suggests the closest one will be chosen. The determination of "closest," however, can be a problematic assessment. Isotropic surfaces, spaces exhibiting equal physical properties in all directions, are rarely found within the human geographical experience. Instead, individuals are confronted with anisotropic surfaces where movement is easier in some directions or along certain routes, and harder along others. People travel through networks of roads and highways by "wheel distance" (Rhodes & Conly, 1981)- rather than by Euclidean distance.

Other factors can be just as important as physical space. Macrolevel travel choices are influenced by time and money expenditures — distance is not as important as connections, time, and costs to an air traveller. Income and socioeconomic status thus have important influences on spatial behaviour, as a shortage of financial resources constrains choices and determines which options are seen as viable.

Microlevel movement within cities is similarly affected; urban areas are primarily anisotropic, often conforming to some variation of a grid or Manhattan layout[30] (Lowe & Moryadas, 1975), with dissimilar traffic flows along different routes. As it is not just a question of minimizing distance, but of reducing time, effort, and costs, the layout of a city, an offender's mode of transportation, and any significant mental or physical barriers must also be considered in the spatial analysis of crime patterns.

The subjective psychological perception of distance is just as critical as the objective physical space involved. An individual's perception of distance is influenced by several factors, including (Stea, 1969):

1. Relative attractiveness of origins and destinations;
2. Number and types of barriers separating points;
3. Familiarity with routes;
4. Actual physical distance; and
5. Attractiveness of routes.

While the nearness principle appears to be a simple one, its actual implementation is complicated, requiring an awareness of both objective (physical) and subjective (cognitive) factors. In understanding human movement it is just as important to take into account mental or cognitive maps and their creation as it is to consider physical maps.

---

[30] Studies of movement within different city structures require different metrics. The grid (Manhattan) pattern describes most North American cities, but crow-flight measures are more useful for studies of British cities. Both Manhattan and crow-flight distances are specific forms of the more general Minkowski metric (Waters, 1995b). An individual's mental map and internal representation of the spatial environment, however, may influence movement more than the external world does.

6.2   Mental Maps

Mental maps[31] are cognitive images of familiar areas such as neighbourhoods or cities, formed from a distillation of the particular transactions a person has with his or her surroundings. Unlike hummingbirds and other animals that retain detailed images of their spatial experiences, humans generalize this knowledge within their memories. Mental maps have an influence on crime site selection because a target cannot be victimized unless an offender is first aware of it.

> A mental map is a representation of the spatial form of the phenomenal environment which an individual carries in his or her mind. The representation is of the individual's subjective image of place (not a conventional map) and not only includes knowledge of features and spatial relationships but also reflects the individual's preferences for and attitudes towards places .... The product of this process, at any point in time, is a mental or cognitive map and can be shown cartographically as a perception surface. (Goodall, 1987, p. 299)

These images are the result of the reception, coding, storage, recall, decoding, and interpretation of information; cognitive maps also involve nonspatial dimensions such as colour, sound, feeling, sentiment, and symbolization (Brantingham & Brantingham, 1984; Clark, 1990).

Geographic information is an important determinant of movement and therefore of one's social, employment, educational, and economic position (Gould, 1975); but this information is incomplete, and ignorance barriers based on linguistic, political, natural, religious, and cultural differences may form (Brantingham & Brantingham, 1984; Gould & White, 1986). Spatial interaction is thus influenced by an individual's location, both geographic and social, and the knowledge and perception held of viable movement options.[32]

While cognitive images vary in relation to a person's biography, social class, location, and environment, most people's mental maps have much in common. This results from the fact that humans perceive things in like fashion. Lynch (1960) states image composition is based on five elements:

1. Paths — routes of travel that tend to dominate most people's images of cities (e.g., highways, railways);

---

[31] Individuals spatially interact with many different areas and therefore require several maps, resulting in mental atlases (Lowe & Moryadas, 1975).

[32] See Rengert and Wasilchick (1985) for a discussion of the influence of geographic information on burglary target selection.

2. Edges — boundaries of lines that help to organize cognitive maps (e.g., rivers, railroads);

3. Districts — subareas with recognizable unifying characteristics, possessing well-established cores but fuzzy borders (e.g., financial districts, skid roads);

4. Nodes — intense foci of activity (e.g., major intersections, railroad stations, corner stores); and

5. Landmarks — symbols used for orientation but which typically are not physically entered (e.g., signs, tall buildings, trees).

6.3   Awareness and Activity Spaces

Mental maps are developed from individuals' experiences within their awareness space. An awareness space is defined as:

> all the locations about which a person has knowledge above a minimum level even without visiting some of them ... Awareness space includes activity space (the area within which most of a person's activities are carried out, within which the individual comes most frequently into contact with others and with the features of the environment), and its area enlarges as new locations are discovered and/or new information is gathered. (Clark, 1990, pp. 24–25)

An activity space[33] contains those areas that comprise a person's habitual geography, made up of routinely (daily or weekly) visited places and their connecting routes (Jakle, Brunn, & Roseman, 1976). Activity space plays a central role in the Brantingham and Brantingham model of crime site selection, and therefore is an integral part of the theory underlying geographic profiling. "Where we go depends upon what we know ... What we know depends on where we go" (Canter, 1994, p. 111).

> Mental maps provide the outer limits of potential action space, which may be defined as the area containing the majority of destinations of a particular individual. It is a subspace within the mental map and frequently tends to be discontinuous in the sense that stretches of unknown, possibly undesirable, territory lie between preferred areas. The configuration of action space is frequently linear, especially in automobile-oriented societies. Moreover, movement patterns defining action space may have well-marked directional biases from an individual's home base, so elongation in one direction is offset by attenuation in other directions. (Lowe & Moryadas, 1975, p. 139)

---

[33] Some writers use the term action space for both activity space and awareness space.

6.3.1 Anchor Points

Within an activity space are anchor points or bases, the most important places in one's spatial life (Coucelis, Golledge, Gale, & Tobler, 1987). The main anchor point for the vast majority of people is their residence, but other bases may exist such as a work site or close friend's home. Some street criminals do not have a fixed address, basing their activities out of a bar, pool hall, or some other social activity location (Rengert, 1990). They can also be transient, homeless, living on the street, or mobile to such a degree that their anchor point constantly shifts. Offender anchor points are important in the understanding of crime patterns.

> Especially significant are the "anchor points" which focus the routine activities of criminals on specific sites in our urban environments .... If a criminal routinely visits the same location nearly every day, this location may serve as an "anchor point" about which other activities may cluster. This proposition is implicitly recognized when we document that most crime occurs near the home of the criminal (Brantingham and Brantingham, 1984). The home is the dominant anchor point in the lives of most individuals. However, other anchor points also are important influences on the spatial behavior of criminals. (Rengert, 1990, pp. 4–5)

Criminals, to the extent that they live in everyday society, are bound by the normal limitations on human activity, shaped by the dictates of work, families, sleep, food, finances, transportation, and so forth. Canter (1994) suggests that environmental psychology and an understanding of offenders' mental maps ("criminal maps") can assist in the investigation of violent crime. Offenders operate within the confines of their experience, habits, awareness, and knowledge. "Like a person going shopping, a criminal will also go to locations that are convenient" (p. 187).

Criminal predators may be stable or nomadic. Stable offenders possess a permanent anchor point during their period of criminal activity. Nomadic offenders are transient, lacking a fixed address or anchor point. Albert DeSalvo, for example, resided in the same dwelling throughout his killing period, while Ottis Toole lived on the road, travelling from city to city, and state to state. Other offenders fall somewhere between these two positions. David Berkowitz resided in two different locations in New York City during his crimes, while Ted Bundy, though not nomadic, moved several times during his murder spree (Terry, 1987; U.S. Department of Justice, 1992).

6.4 Centrography

The spatial mean (sometimes referred to as the centroid or mean centre) is a univariate measure of the central tendency of a point pattern (Taylor, 1977), and has been used to analyze crime site patterns. This geographic "centre of gravity" minimizes the sum of the squared distances to the various points in a pattern. It provides a single summary location for a series of points and has a variety of geostatistical uses collectively referred to as centrography.

The spatial mean is defined as:

$$(SM_x, SM_y) \tag{6.1}$$

where:

$$SM_x = \left(\sum_{n=1}^{C} x_n \right) \Big/ C \tag{6.2}$$

$$SM_y = \left(\sum_{n=1}^{C} y_n \right) \Big/ C \tag{6.3}$$

and:

SM_x is the x coordinate of the spatial mean;
SM_y is the y coordinate of the spatial mean;
C is the total number of crime sites; and
x_n, y_n are the coordinates of the nth crime site.

It is possible to determine a weighted mean centre if certain points are more important in a centrality analysis than others. The median centre – also known as the centre of minimum travel – is another measure of central tendency in point patterns and is found by locating the position from which travel to all points in a spatial distribution (i.e., the sum of the distances) is minimized. There is no general method for its calculation and the median centre must be calculated through an iterative process.

Changes over time in the location of the spatial mean allow for the calculation of the geographic equivalents of concepts of velocity (rate of spatial change), acceleration (rate of change in velocity), and momentum (velocity multiplied by number of points) (LeBeau, 1987b). The spatial mean is the basis for calculating the standard distance of a point pattern, a measure of spatial dispersion analogous to the standard deviation (Taylor, 1977). When used with the mean centre it can help describe two-dimensional distributions, and through the concept of relative dispersion (the ratio of two standard distances), allow for comparisons of spread between different sets of points. Similarly, the median distance is the radius which encompasses one half of the points in a spatial distribution.

The standard distance is defined as:

$$Sd = \sqrt{\left(\sum r_{ns}^2\right)\big/C} \tag{6.4}$$

where:

Sd is the standard distance;
C is the total number of crime sites; and
r_{ns} is the distance between the spatial centre and the nth crime site.

Centrography has been used in a variety of criminological studies and investigative contexts. The spatial mean and changes in its location over time were calculated for rape incidents in San Diego (LeBeau, 1987b). An investigative review team helped locate the hometown of the Yorkshire Ripper from the geographic centre of the murder sites (Kind, 1987a). A similar approach in a blackmailing case used cash withdrawal points from automated teller machines (ATMs) to determine the offender's residence area east of London (Britton, 1997). Such techniques were also employed in a retrospective analysis of the Hillside Stranglers (Newton & Swoope, 1987). The FBI and ATF analyze serial arson cases by determining the spatial mean of fire sites (Icove & Crisman, 1975). Traditionally, centrography has been the primary form of geographic analysis used to support criminal investigations.

As helpful as centrographic analysis may be in certain cases, the spatial mean suffers from three serious methodological difficulties: (1) it generally provides only a single piece of information; (2) it is distorted by spatial outliers; and (3) theory suggests the intersection between offender activity space and target backcloth (the distribution of crime targets across the physical landscape) may produce crime locations unrelated to measures of central tendency. If the activity space of an offender is not centred around his or her home, or if the target backcloth is highly variable, then the spatial mean of the crime sites and offender residence are not correlated.

A study of the spatial patterns in a sample of British serial rapists revealed the limitations in centrographic analysis (Canter & Larkin, 1993). The study plotted maximum distance from residence to crime site against maximum distance between crime sites, producing the following regression equation:

$$y = 0.84\,x + 0.61 \tag{6.5}$$

where:

y is the maximum distance in miles from residence to crime site; and
x is the maximum distance in miles between crime sites.

The gradient of 0.84 in Equation 6.5 indicates an eccentric placement of the residence vis-à-vis the crime sites (a perfect centric placement would yield a gradient of 0.5). Similar regressions for U.S. and British serial murder crime location data yield values of 0.81 and 0.79, respectively (Canter & Hodge,

1997), and an Australian study found gradients of 0.77 for rape, 0.60 for arson, and 0.65 for burglary (Kocsis & Irwin, 1997). This eccentricity suggests the spatial mean is limited in its ability to predict offender residence location.

Additionally, the spatial mean lacks real world significance. The geographic centre of Canada is in the Northwest Territories which tells one little about the demographic, economic, or political patterns of that country. LeBeau (1987b) notes "an important property about the mean center to remember is that it is a synthetic point or location representing the average location of a phenomenon, and not the average of the characteristics of the phenomenon at that location" (pp. 126–127; see also Taylor, 1977).

Studies of journey-to-crime trips, particularly those that are offence specific, help determine the most likely radius within which offenders search for victims. For example, research has consistently shown targets are typically located within one or two miles of offender residence (see McIver, 1981). When utilized in conjunction with the spatial mean, such information may be of investigative value.

6.5 Nearest Neighbour Analysis

While the spatial mean provides a way to measure central tendency in a point pattern, nearest neighbour analysis, first developed by plant ecologists, supplies a way to quantify spacing between points (Taylor, 1977; see Boots & Getis, 1988; Garson & Biggs, 1992). Distances between points and their closest neighbours provides important information concerning a pattern's degree of randomness and underlying evolution. It is also possible to calculate other proximity pattern measures including centroid, k-nearest neighbour, mean interpoint, and furthest neighbour distances (Garson & Biggs).

The random allocation of points to a map can be described by the Poisson process (Taylor, 1977). The Poisson probability function is defined as:

$$p(x) = e^{-\lambda} \lambda^x / x! \tag{6.6}$$

where:

$p(x)$ is the probability that a given small area will contain x points; and

λ is the expected probability of finding a point within that area.

Connecting nearest neighbour analysis to the Poisson probability function allows the degree of clustering, dispersion, or randomness in a given independent point pattern to be calculated. The R scale, the ratio between the actual average nearest neighbour distance and that expected under an

assumption of randomness, provides a simple index for measuring divergence from randomness. It is calculated as follows:

$$R = r_a/r_e \qquad (6.7)$$

where:

$$r_e = 1/2\sqrt{(n/A)} \qquad (6.8)$$

and:

R is the R scale value;
r_a is the actual average nearest neighbour distance;
r_e is the expected average nearest neighbour distance;
n is the number of points; and
A is the area size.

Theoretically the R scale can fall between the limits of 0 to 2.149, though
real world patterns tend to range between 0.33 and 1.67 (Taylor, 1977). A
value of 1 (meaning that $r_a = r_e$) indicates a random pattern, values smaller
than 1, a clustered pattern, and values larger than 1, a dispersed pattern.
Problems result in the interpretation of the R scale if boundary placement is
distorted (Garson & Biggs, 1992).

It is possible by chance for a randomly produced pattern to appear
aggregated or dispersed, therefore it is necessary to determine the significance of the R scale value (Taylor, 1977). This can be accomplished through
the Z-score calculated from the standard error of the expected average
nearest neighbour distance. The associated two-tailed probability may then
be determined from a table of normal distribution values (e.g., Blalock,
1972). The standard error (SE) is estimated as follows:

$$SE\,r_e = 0.26136/\sqrt{n^2/A} \qquad (6.9)$$

where:

$SE\ r_e$ is the standard error of the expected average nearest neighbour
            distance (r_e);
n is the number of points; and
A is the area size.

While the R scale provides a measure of spatial randomness, it says
nothing about the actual evolution of the point pattern. More than one
distinct process can be operating as might be found with a series of chaotic
binary points (Boots & Getis, 1988). Statistical tests are only inferential, and

it may be necessary to corroborate results over time or examine higher-order or k-nearest (e.g., second-nearest) neighbour distances.

Geography Of Crime

"Murder Alley" was the name given to an unpaved lane near downtown Kenosha, Wisconsin, where seven bizarre homicides took place between 1967 and 1981 (Newton, 1990a). The frequency and unusual nature of the crimes — including a corpse found in a hearse, another buried beneath a rose garden, and a triple homicide — prompted investigators to publicly comment that something strange was happening in this "Bermuda Triangle of murder."

During its early years, Los Angeles was a violent frontier town. In 1850, the year California joined the Union, "Los Diablos" experienced a murder a day; with a population of 4000, this translates into a homicide rate of 1 murder per 11 residents (Blanche & Schreiber, 1998). Most of these murders took place close to the central plaza in a narrow alley slum named Calle de los Negros ("Nigger Alley"), a collection of shabby buildings, housing saloons, brothels, and gambling dens. Shootings, riots, lootings, and lynchings were common activities.

"What surfaces in terrible places... is a rapport between persons and places such that the techniques of the habitat and forms of personation become indistinguishable" (Seltzer, 1998, p. 233). Routine activity and ecology of place theories provide an explanation for the phenomena of dangerous places or "dreadful enclosures." The related concepts of "fishing holes" and "trap lines" — used by serial killers and rapists in the hunt for victims — also help explain the clustering of predatory murders and rapes. The geography of crime encompasses the study of the spatial and temporal distribution of criminal offences.

The methodological and theoretical approaches developed in a variety of disciplines are often adopted to the study of crime and criminals, and the fields of geography and urban analysis provide several analytical tools for criminologists. Perspectives that make particular use of geographic techniques include the social ecology of crime, environmental criminology, geography of crime, routine activity approach, situational crime prevention, and problem-oriented policing (Brantingham & Brantingham, 1981b; Brantingham & Jeffery, 1981; R. V. Clarke, 1992, 1997; Felson, 1986; Goldstein, 1990; Lowman, 1986; Smith, 1986). Work in such areas has provided the conceptual foundations for geographic profiling.

7.1   Geography and Crime Studies

Geographical patterns in crime have been noted since the mid-19th century pioneering work of Andre-Michel Guerry and Lambert-Adolphe Quetelet who mapped, on a national basis, violent and property offences and examined their spatial relationship to poverty (Brantingham & Brantingham, 1981c; Vold & Bernard, 1986). The most famous spatial crime studies were conducted in the early 20th century, when the city of Chicago served as an inspiration source and a field of experimentation for University of Chicago sociologists (Warren, 1972; Williams & McShane, 1988). The geographical focus of criminology had shifted from regional areas to city neighbourhoods.

The Chicago School's human ecology and theories of urban growth, developed by Robert Park and Ernest Burgess, served as guides for former probation officer Clifford R. Shaw and his colleague Henry D. McKay (Brantingham & Brantingham, 1984; Vold & Bernard, 1986). While working for the Illinois Institute for Juvenile Research, Shaw and McKay examined a plethora of urban social ills, including the politically important issue of crime (Williams & McShane, 1988; Wilson, 1984). Much of this study was done along the margins of society; researchers observed, talked to, and examined criminals, gang members, hoboes, immigrants, and slum dwellers. Most importantly, they did this within the "natural" urban contexts associated with the people they were studying. This attempt to triangulate the subjective human perspective with more objective demographic statistics exemplified the work of the Chicago School (Smith, 1986).

While there is a long tradition of spatial crime analysis, the ultimate units of concern are individual human beings and their day-to-day social interactions, not census statistics or demographic data. This point seems to have been forgotten during the unfruitful positivistic geographic research of the 1960s, when complicated but theoretically weak factor analytic methods were used to correlate a spectrum of spatially distributed variables (Smith, 1986).

Recent developments in the spatial study of crime have been more promising. The integration of geographical perspectives, urban planning tactics, environmental criminology, and ecological approaches based on econometric studies has led to a series of interesting studies (Brantingham & Brantingham, 1981a; Lowman, 1986; Smith, 1986). While the field has been primarily instrumentalist in nature, writers such as Lowman and Smith have commenced the development of a critical geography of crime, and left realists are now concerned with the situational and spatial nature of crime (Kinsey, Lea, & Young, 1986; Lea & Young, 1984).

Geographic concepts and terms are important in understanding criminal target patterns and constructing crime site selection models. They also provide the elements necessary to develop methods of offender residence prediction. Some of these ideas are presented below.

7.1.1   Journey-to-Crime Research

The journey-to-crime literature includes numerous studies of crime trips for a variety of offence types in several North American and European cities. This research has often explored the influence of such offender and offence characteristics as sex, race, age, prior criminal experience, nature of home area, crime type, target area attributes, and perceived level of gain (Baldwin & Bottoms, 1976; Capone & Nichols, 1975; LeBeau, 1987a; Nichols, 1980; Reppetto, 1974; Rhodes & Conly, 1981).

These studies have produced several common findings, including the following observations:

- Crimes often occur in relatively close proximity to the home of the offender. "While criminals are mobile, they don't seem to go very far in committing a crime. A majority of crimes appear to take place within a mile of the criminal's residence" (McIver, 1981, p. 22). Time is a commodity and almost all people act in a manner to conserve its use (Brantingham & Brantingham, 1984; LeBeau, 1992; Rebscher & Rohrer, 1991; Rengert & Wasilchick, 1985; Rhodes & Conly, 1981). This pattern is consistent with the nearness and least-effort principles. Table 7.1 presents a summary of the findings from journey-to-crime research.
- Crime trips follow a distance-decay function with the number of crime occurrences decreasing with distance from the offender's residence (Brantingham & Brantingham, 1984; Capone & Nichols, 1975; Rhodes & Conly, 1981). This pattern is similar to that exhibited in other forms of human movement (Jakle, Brunn, & Roseman, 1976).
- Juvenile offenders are most likely to commit their crimes within their home area, and are less mobile than adult offenders (Baldwin & Bottoms, 1976; Gabor & Gottheil, 1984; Warren et al., 1995).
- Differences in crime trip distances between offence types have been consistently found. Violent crimes, for example, usually occur closer to the offender's residence than do property offences (Baldwin & Bottoms, 1976; Gabor & Gottheil, 1984; LeBeau, 1987a; Rhodes & Conly, 1981).

- Most cities contain high crime rate neighbourhoods, the arrangement and location of which influence the patterning of crime trips (Gabor & Gottheil, 1984; Rhodes & Conly, 1981).

A crime trip, or the journey to crime, is usually defined by some direct or surrogate measure of distance between offender residence and location of offence. This may or may not have been the actual journey taken by the offender who could have originated his or her travel from work, the house of a friend, or the local bar. For example, in Pettiway's (1995) study of Philadelphia crack cocaine users, 25.7% originated their drug buying trip from home, with street corners and outside hangouts (22.9%), friends and relatives (10.7%), shopping and business (10.8%), recreation (7.4%), and other places (22.4%) comprising the remaining origins. Of significance, however, is the finding that, regardless of origin, most destinations were in the offender's neighbourhood (61%). Almost all trips (93%) began and ended within the city limits of Philadelphia. These results "suggest that even when individuals engage in activities away from their places of residence, they tend to return to locations near those places" (p. 515).

In a study of robbery in northern California, Feeney (1986, 1996) found 70% of offenders robbed in their home towns, and over one third in their own neighbourhoods. Of the 30% who offended in a different town, only half went there to commit a robbery; the rest were there for some other reason. Those who commute to rob almost always choose a contiguous town. Robbery is a casually planned crime, and the study found fewer than 5% of offenders make detailed plans such as observing the layouts of prospective targets, establishing contingencies, or predetermining escape routes (Feeney, 1986). Victims are chosen because of convenience, appearance of money, low risk, and the possibility of a fast getaway. Or, in the words of one robber, "'Just where we happened to be, I guess'" (p. 92).

Canter and Gregory (1994) analyzed crime trip patterns for 45 serial rapists responsible for 251 offences committed during the 1980s in Greater London and Southeast England. The mean number of rapes per offender in this sample was 5.6 (standard deviation = 3.6), with a minimum of 2 and a maximum of 14. It was theorized that offenders with greater access to resources will exhibit longer journeys to crime. Therefore, rapists with more geographic knowledge, money, and time have the capability of travelling further distances to commit their crimes. Canter and Gregory (1994) propose that criminals with greater resources (geographic knowledge, financial, time) travel further to offend. They analyzed crime trip distances for a sample of serial rapists using dichotomized parameters of race, venue, weekday, and offender age. It was suggested an expert system for determining area of criminal residence could be based upon this approach. The basic viability of the system remains unknown, however, as the study negated its results by using the same data set for both learning and testing.

White rapists were found to travel further to commit their crimes than black rapists, the latter having an 80% chance of living within a half mile of one of their offences. Rapists who chose outside venues typically journeyed 2.7 times as far as those who chose inside or mixed venues. Weekend rapists averaged minimum crime trip distances 2.5 times as great as weekday offenders, though this difference was not statistically significant. Older rapists (over 25 years of age) appeared to travel further than younger rapists, but this finding also was not statistically significant. The percentages for each group found to have travelled under a half mile from their home base to their first known offence were: blacks, 74%; whites, 18%; inside/mixed, 70%; outside, 28%; weekday, 41%; weekend, 50%; mixed, 60%; under 25 years of age, 54%; over 25 years of age, 38%; and total, 47%.

Results from journey-to-crime studies are usually reported in one of four manners: (1) mean crime trip distances; (2) medial circles; (3) mobility triangles; and (4) distance-decay functions. Studies using mean crime trips compute the arithmetic average for the distance travelled by offenders from home to offence location. Some researchers employ the geometric mean to avoid the distortion of extreme values (LeBeau, 1987a), while others use additional descriptive statistics such as the mode (Rhodes & Conly, 1981), maximum crime trip distance (Canter & Larkin, 1993), minimum crime trip distance (Warren et al., 1995), range (Turner, 1969), and directional information (Rengert & Wasilchick, 1985).

The major problem with the use of the mean or mode is the limited information a univariate statistic provides. The mean is also susceptible to the influence of spatial outliers and may say little about the typical journey. And as an average distance is produced from an aggregation of trips involving several offenders, it might not accurately describe any one type of offender.

Studies using medial circles define a radius containing a certain percentage of offences.[34] In a study of robbery within Boston, Reppetto (1976) found 90% of the offences occurred within 1.5 miles of the offender's residence. As with mean crime trips, medial circles supply only a single measure of crime journeys, says little of the typical crime trip, and expresses almost nothing about cases that fall outside of the set radius.

Mobility triangles were first used by Burgess (1925) to describe situations where offence location and offender residence were in different neighbourhoods; this was in contrast to neighbourhood triangles where the crime takes place in the offender's home area. Subsequent developments of the mobility triangle concept adopted various combinations of crime scene, offender res-

---

[34] If the circle contains one-half of the offences, the radius is equivalent to the median crime trip distance.

idence, and victim residence spatial conjunction (Amir, 1971; Normandeau, 1968). Crime journey research findings are often presented in the form of the percentage of offences that fit into the neighbourhood triangle (Plough-man & Ould, 1990; Rand, 1986).

Research using neighbourhood or mobility triangles raises the question of how to define the concept of "neighbourhood." Census tract delineations are often used, but this is a problematic assumption. Census tracts are only rough approximations of neighbourhoods and more sophisticated concepts of mobility, routine activities, and target selection are available (e.g., Brant-ingham & Brantingham, 1981; Felson, 1986). Other studies do not define the concept of neighbourhood, but rather use the subjective interpretations of respondents (see, for example, DeFrances & Smith, 1994).

The most useful presentation of crime trip data is the distance-decay approach, a graphical curve that shows the number of trips for several different radii (e.g., half-mile increments) from the offender's residence (see, for example, Capone & Nichols, 1976; Rhodes & Conly, 1981; also Baldwin & Bottoms, 1976). Such formats allow for an inspection of the distance-decay function, providing more information for further analysis and a fuller understanding of the nature of crime journeys.

Van Koppen and de Keijser (1997) have questioned the accuracy of distance decay findings in the journey-to-crime literature. Using randomly generated data that lacked distance decay, they were able to show the aggregation of individual crime trips led to a distance-decay result. Their main point is correct. Individual behaviour cannot be safely inferred from aggregate data, an error referred to as the ecological fallacy.

Research at a certain spatial level of analysis may produce conclusions that, while valid at that scale, are invalid at different levels (Goodall, 1987). When research arguments are made by relating results derived from one geographic level of analysis to another, an ecological fallacy occurs. This usually involves the application of correlates derived from areal data to individuals, though an ecological fallacy can occur by moving in either direction through the spatial analytic framework (Brantingham & Brantingham, 1984). The scale problem, as geographers refer to it, can be a serious difficulty for attempts to generalize from geographical areal research as changes in focus may mask the true nature of relationships (Langbein & Lichtman, 1978; Taylor, 1977).

For example, combining individual crime trip distances without first standardizing the data[35] often obscures the existence of the buffer zone. The method of van Koppen and de Keijser, however, actually created non-random distances with a bias towards shorter crime trips, therefore introducing

---

[35] One method of standardization is to divide every individual crime trip distance by the offender's mean crime trip distance.

distance decay (Rengert, Piquero, & Jones, 1999). True random data would show a uniform distribution. They also did not distinguish between studies of destination and origin distance decay. Finally, they ignored research that properly established distance decay in serial criminals (e.g., Davies & Dale, 1995b; Rossmo, 1995b; Sapp et al., 1994; Warren, Reboussin, Hazelwood, Cummings, Gibbs, & Trumbetta, 1998).

It has been suggested that as an offender's criminal career matures, journey-to-crime distances lengthen and size of hunting area increases (Brantingham & Brantingham, 1981; Canter & Larkin, 1993). After the arrest of David Berkowitz, police searching his apartment "found maps of Connecticut, New York, and New Jersey, marked and annotated in such a way that investigators took them as evidence that Berkowitz was planning to extend his killing grounds" (Time-Life Books, 1992b, p. 179). Hungarian Sylvestre Matuschka killed 22 people and injured 75 more in engineered train wrecks (Nash, 1992). Upon his apprehension in 1932, authorities seized railway schedules and maps for France, Italy, and The Netherlands – all part of his plan to cause future wrecks monthly (Seltzer, 1998).

The FBI believes that the first attack in a serial murder series is the one most likely to be closest to the offender's home (Warren et al., 1995). Both Barrett (1990) and Canter (1994) note that the first crime of a serial offender may be spontaneous and impulsive, and victim selectivity tends to decrease over time (see, for example, the discussion on changes in Jeffrey Dahmer's murder pattern, in Ressler & Shachtman, 1992). These observations indicate the importance of a temporal dimension in the analysis of spatial crime patterns (see Kind, 1987a; LeBeau, 1992; Newton & Newton, 1985; Newton & Swoope, 1987).

In an FBI study of travel distances and offence patterns for 108 U.S. serial rapists responsible for a total of 565 offences, Warren et al. (1995) observed that the rape closest to the offender's residence was the first in 18%, but the fifth in 24% of the cases. A British study of 79 rapists and 299 sexual offences (Davies & Dale, 1995a) found no significant difference in distance between first and last crime trip for prolific offenders (those with five or more rapes). Noting that habitual burglars and robbers travelled longer distances, Davies and Dale (1995a) suggest that for those rapists with a history of break and entry, the first rape in a series might well be their fiftieth housebreaking. Any maturation in crime pattern would therefore have occurred long ago. This problem is compounded by the fact that sexual assaults are notoriously underreported, and the first known rape might actually be the offender's second or third (Davies & Dale; Leyton, O'Grady, & Overton, 1992). Such a misinterpretation happened in the Vampire Killer case where Sacramento County police believed the second murder was actually the first (Ressler & Shachtman, 1992).

The journey-to-crime concept implies a home base from which the trip commenced, yet some offenders may not have a residence. Convicted criminals also tend to be less residentially stable than noncriminals, and psychopaths in particular are nomadic. Rossmo found that a significant number of criminal fugitives in Canada are willing to travel thousands of miles to avoid prison (1987; Rossmo & Routledge, 1990). Marvell and Moody (1998) observed that a small but highly active group of major criminals were extremely mobile, for reasons that included fear of the police, conflicts with other criminals, or general wanderlust. These offenders engaged in a succession of road trips involving temporary stays in different regions, or permanent moves of residence every few months or years from one state to another. It is therefore important not to confuse transiency with crime trips.

Travelling offenders are in the minority, and fewer than 10% of the criminals Canter (1994) studied were of "no fixed abode" at the time of their arrest. Davies and Dale (1995b) determined that 22% of those rapists for whom they had such information were itinerant. Victims were confronted at their homes in 41% of the cases,[36] and within public areas (including apartment building common areas) in 58% of the cases. They observed that "some rapists were obviously drawn to areas where potential victims were accessible, such as red-light districts ... The distance the offenders travelled was clearly related to the proximity of their own residence to these locations" (Davies & Dale, 1995a, p. 13).

These places of victim accessibility include both nodes (e.g., entrances to train stations or apartment blocks), and routes used by females commuting to work, school, shopping, and entertainment areas. Because the value of these "victim hunting grounds" depended upon female activity level, their desirability is influenced by time of day. Distinct clusters of contact sites were noted, some associated with victim availability, others with residences of people significant to the offender (Davies & Dale, 1995a). Ted Bundy's FBI wanted poster alerted people to his preferred target areas — beaches, ski resorts, discotheques, and college campuses (Ressler & Shachtman, 1992). Such finding are consistent with Brantingham and Brantingham's (1981, 1993b) pattern theory and model of crime site selection, discussed in the next section.

---

[36] House (1993) examined offence venue for 61 Canadian cases of stranger sexual assault committed by 30 offenders (40% of whom were serial rapists, each responsible for an average of 2.8 crimes). He found 61% of the crimes occurred outdoors and 39% inside (38% of which were in the victim's residence).

Table 7.1 Journey–to–Crime Research[3]

Source	Crime	Location	Year	Crime Trip Distance	Comments
Aitken et al. (1994)	sex motivated child murders	Great Britain	1960–1991	91.6% < 5 mi	> 5 mi if offender travel or victim abduction indicated
Alston (1994)	stranger serial sexual assault	British Columbia	1977–1993	31.1% < 0.5 km; 44.4% < 1 km; 55.6% < 1.5 km; 60.0% < 2 km; 75.6% < 3 km	distance to nearest offender activity node
Amir (1971)	rape	Philadelphia	1958–1960	72% within home area (5 blocks)	mobility triangles
Baldwin & Bottoms (1976)	property crime	Sheffield	1966	47% < 1 mi; 69% < 2 mi	
Baldwin & Bottoms (1976)	breaking offence	Sheffield	1966	54.4% < 1 mi; 74.8% < 2 mi	
Baldwin & Bottoms (1976)	larceny offence	Sheffield	1966	51.9% < 1 mi; 74.3% < 2 mi	
Baldwin & Bottoms (1976)	taking & driving offence	Sheffield	1966	45% < 1 mi; 63.3% < 2 mi	
Boggs (1965)	homicide & assault	St. Louis		most likely within residential area	
Boggs (1965)	rape & robbery	St. Louis		most likely within nonresidential area	
Bullock (1955)	homicide	Houston	1945–1949	40% < 1 block; 57% < 0.4 mi; 74% < 2 mi	
Canter & Hodge (1997)	serial murder	U.S.		40 km; body dump site: 9 km/90 km mean min./max. (25% < 5 km; 50% < 15 km)	89% marauders; 11% commuters
Canter & Hodge (1997)	serial murder	Britain		24 km; body dump site: 6 km/36 km mean min./max.	86% marauders; 14% commuters

Table 7.1 Journey-to-Crime Research (Continued)

Source	Crime	Location	Year	Crime Trip Distance	Comments
Canter & Larkin (1993)	serial rape	Greater London & SE England	1980s	1.53 mi mean min. crime trip distance	87% marauders; 13% commuters
Capone & Nichols (1976)	robbery	Miami	1971	1/3 < 1 mi; 1/2 < 2 mi; 2/3 < 3 mi	
Capone & Nichols (1976)	armed robbery	Miami	1971	26% < 1 mi; 45% < 2 mi; 59% < 3 mi	
Capone & Nichols (1976)	unarmed robbery	Miami	1971	36% < 1 mi; 60% < 2 mi; 75% < 3 mi	
Chappell (1965)	burglary	England	1965	50%/85% < 1 mi (< 21/14 years)	
Davies & Dale (1995b)	stranger rape	England	1965–1993	17% < 0.5 mi; 29% < 1 mi; 52% < 2 mi; 60% < 3 mi; 69% < 4 mi; 76% < 5 mi	approach site; 72%/24% < 1.8 mi (</> 26 years)
DeFrances & Smith (1994)	all offences	U.S.	1991	43% in own neighbourhood (violent crime 44.7%; murder 44.5%; rape 59.6%)	sample survey of state prison inmates
Erlanson (1946)	rape	Chicago	1938–1946	87% within home neighbourhood	home neighbourhood = police precinct
Farrington&Lambert (1993)	burglary & violent offences	Nottinghamshire	1991	69.2%/55.3% < 1 mi; 80.7%/67.8% < 2 mi (burglars/violent offenders)	younger & smaller offenders lived closer
Gabor & Gottheil (1984)	total of 10 crimes	Ottawa	1981	1.22 mi (70.5% in-towners)	out-of-towners, NFAs, & n/k excluded
Gabor & Gottheil (1984)	homicide	Ottawa	1981	0.54 mi (71% in-towners)	out-of-towners, NFAs, & n/k excluded
Gabor & Gottheil (1984)	rape & indecent assault	Ottawa	1981	1.43 mi (90% in-towners)	out-of-towners, NFAs, & n/k excluded

Geography Of Crime — 107

Study	Crime	City	Years	Distance	Notes
Gabor & Gottheil (1984)	armed robbery	Ottawa	1981	1.22 mi (80% in-towners)	out-of-towners, NFAs, & n/k excluded
Gabor & Gottheil (1984)	unarmed robbery	Ottawa	1981	0.62 mi (55% in-towners)	out-of-towners, NFAs, & n/k excluded
Gabor & Gottheil (1984)	assault	Ottawa	1981	1.33 mi (90% in-towners)	out-of-towners, NFAs, & n/k excluded
Gabor & Gottheil (1984)	break & enter	Ottawa	1981	0.35 mi (65% in-towners)	out-of-towners, NFAs, & n/k excluded
Gabor & Gottheil (1984)	auto theft	Ottawa	1981	1.24 mi (70% in-towners)	out-of-towners, NFAs, & n/k excluded
Gabor & Gottheil (1984)	theft over $200	Ottawa	1981	1.74 mi (90% in-towners)	out-of-towners, NFAs, & n/k excluded
Gabor & Gottheil (1984)	theft under $200	Ottawa	1981	1.19 mi (60% in-towners)	out-of-towners, NFAs, & n/k excluded
Gabor & Gottheil (1984)	cheque fraud	Ottawa	1981	1.74 mi (35% in-towners)	out-of-towners, NFAs, & n/k excluded
Hanfland (1982)	public indecency	Eugene, Oregon	1978–1981	2.60 mi	older offenders travelled further
Hanfland (1982)	burglary	Eugene, Oregon	1978–1981	1.79 mi	older offenders generally travelled further
Hanfland (1982)	rape/sodomy	Eugene, Oregon	1978–1981	2.66 mi	older offenders generally travelled further
Hanfland (1982)	robbery	Eugene, Oregon	1978–1981	2.67 mi	no age relationship
LeBeau (1987a)	rape	San Diego	1971–1975	2.5 mi	geometric mean; Manhattan geometry
LeBeau (1987a)	serial rape	San Diego	1971–1975	1.77 mi	geometric mean; Manhattan geometry
LeBeau (1987a)	nonserial rape	San Diego	1971–1975	3.5 mi	geometric mean
LeBeau (1992)	serial rape & related crime	San Diego	1971–1975	25.88/1.89/0.52/3.33 km (4 serial rapists)	attempts, sex-related crimes, & burglaries

Table 7.1 Journey-to-Crime Research (Continued)

Source	Crime	Location	Year	Crime Trip Distance	Comments
Normandeau (1968)	robbery	Philadelphia		1.57 mi; 33% within home census tract	mobility triangles
Pettiway (1995)	crack cocaine drug buys	Philadelphia		45%/64% < 0.5 mi (white/black); 55%/77% < 0.5 mi (male/female)	1.0/0.73 mi white/black; 0.9/0.46 mi male/female
Pope (1980)	burglary	6 California urban areas		52% < 1 mi	
Pyle (1974)	rape	Akron	1972	1.34 mi	
Pyle (1976)	crime against the person	Cleveland		61% within home census tract	
Pyle (1976)	property crime	Cleveland		48% within home census tract	
Rand (1986)	total of 8 crimes	Philadelphia	1968–1975	30.77% within home census tract	juvenile offenders; mobility triangles
Rand (1986)	criminal homicide	Philadelphia	1968–1975	53.13% within home census tract	juvenile offenders; mobility triangles
Rand (1986)	rape	Philadelphia	1968–1975	53.13% within home census tract	juvenile offenders; mobility triangles
Rand (1986)	robbery	Philadelphia	1968–1975	31.87% within home census tract	juvenile offenders; mobility triangles
Rand (1986)	aggravated assault	Philadelphia	1968–1975	38.60% within home census tract	juvenile offenders; mobility triangles
Rand (1986)	burglary	Philadelphia	1968–1975	42.02% within home census tract	juvenile offenders; mobility triangles
Rand (1986)	larceny	Philadelphia	1968–1975	14.77% within home census tract	juvenile offenders; mobility triangles
Rand (1986)	vehicle theft	Philadelphia	1968–1975	23.05% within home census tract	juvenile offenders; mobility triangles

Study	Offence	Location	Year	Distance findings	Notes
Rand (1986)	simple assault	Philadelphia	1968–1975	39.41% within home census tract	juvenile offenders; mobility triangles
Reiss (1967)	Part I & Part II offences	Seattle	1965	not likely to be in home census tract	
Rengert & Wasilchick (1985)	suburban burglary	Delaware Co.		52% < 5 mi; 71% unemployed; 40% employed	work & recreation site directional biases
Reppetto (1976)	robbery	Boston		0.6 mi; 90% < 1.5 mi	
Reppetto (1976)	residential burglary	Boston		0.5 mi; 93% < 1.5 mi	
Rhodes & Conly (1981)	rape	Washington, D.C.	1974	1.15 mi; 0.73 mi median; 62% < 1 mi	wheel distance
Rhodes & Conly (1981)	robbery	Washington, D.C.	1974	2.10 mi; 1.62 mi median; 37% < 1 mi	wheel distance
Rhodes & Conly (1981)	burglary	Washington, D.C.	1974	1.62 mi; 1.20 mi median; 47% < 1 mi	wheel distance
Rossmo & Baeza (1998)	serial rape	New York City	1984–1992	2.5 mi (residence); 1.0 mi (anchor point)	
Sapp et al. (1994)	serial arson	U.S.		27.1% < 0.5 mi; 56.8% < 1 mi; 77.1% < 2 mi; 81.2% < 5 mi; 86.6% < 10 mi	95.1% acquainted with crime area; 60.8% walked
Shaw (1998)	sex murder	U.K.		2.4 mi / 1.0 mi median (encounter site) 2.2 mi / 1.0 mi median (body dump site) 65% within home area	25% in offender's home 85% < 9.5 km
Suttles (1968)		Chicago			
Topalin (1992)	serial rape	London area	1980s	2.81 mi; 20% in or close to home	juvenile offenders 0–27 mi range; first convicted offence
Turner (1969)	assault & vandalism	Philadelphia	1960	0.4 mi; 75% < 1 mi; 87% < 2 mi	0–23 mi range; juvenile offenders
Waller & Okihiro (1978)	burglary	Toronto		50% < 0.5 mi	

Table 7.1 Journey-to-Crime Research (Continued)

Source	Crime	Location	Year	Crime Trip Distance	Comments
Warren et al. (1995)	serial rape	U.S.		3.14 mi; 1.66/4.93 mi average closest/furthest (local offenders, travel < 20 mi)	rituals, restraints, burglary, all indicate further travel
White (1932)	violent crime	Indianapolis	1930	0.85 mi	
White (1932)	property crime	Indianapolis	1930	1.72 mi	
White (1932)	manslaughter	Indianapolis	1930	0.11 mi	
White (1932)	rape	Indianapolis	1930	1.52 mi	
White (1932)	robbery	Indianapolis	1930	2.14 mi	
White (1932)	assault	Indianapolis	1930	0.91 mi	
White (1932)	burglary	Indianapolis	1930	1.76 mi	
White (1932)	embezzlement	Indianapolis	1930	2.79 mi	
White (1932)	auto theft	Indianapolis	1930	3.43 mi	
White (1932)	larceny	Indianapolis	1930	1.53/1.42 mi (grand/petty larceny)	
Wolfgang (1958)	homicide	Philadelphia		50%+ within home of offender or victim	

[37]NFA means no fixed address, and n/k, not known. Unless otherwise specified, the figures in the *Crime Trip Distance* column refer to mean journey-to-crime distance.

From Rossmo, D.K. (1995b). Multivariate spatial profiles as a tool in crime investigation. In C.R. Block, M. Dabdoub, & S. Fregly (Eds.). *Crime analysis through computer mapping* (pp. 65-97). Washington, DC: Police Executive Research Forum. Used with permission.

3.
37

7.2   Environmental Criminology

Environmental criminology is interested in the interactions between people and what surrounds them (Brantingham & Brantingham, 1998). Crime is viewed as the product of potential offenders and their immediate and distal setting. "Environmental criminologists set out to use the geographic imagination in concert with the sociological imagination to describe, understand, and control criminal events" (Brantingham & Brantingham, 1981c, p. 21). Their research is distinguished from the earlier ecological work of the Chicago School by this concern with the environment and by a change in focus from offender to criminal event. The field is multidisciplinary, its threads derived from human ecology, environmental psychology, behavioural geography, and the cognitive sciences.

Traditionally, the main interest of criminological positivism has been the offender, and much effort has gone into studying their backgrounds, peer influences, criminal careers, and the effects of deterrence. This focus has ignored the other components of crime — the victim, the criminal law, and the crime setting (Jeffery, 1977). Crime setting or place, the "where and when" of the criminal act, makes up what Brantingham and Brantingham call the fourth dimension of crime, the primary concern of environmental criminology.

Research in this area has taken a broad approach by including operational, perceptual, behavioural, social, psychological, legal, cultural, and geographic settings in its analyses. Micro, meso, and macrolevels have all been examined, and future research efforts will likely attempt a theoretical synthesis (Brantingham & Brantingham, 1981c, 1984, 1998). One of environmental criminology's major interests, the study of the dimensions of crime at the microspatial level, has led to useful findings in the area of crime prevention (see, for example, R. V. Clarke, 1992, 1997). Other projects include the analyses of crime trips (Rhodes & Conly, 1981), efforts to understand target and victim selections through opportunities for crime (Brantingham & Brantingham, 1981c), crime prevention initiatives, notably crime prevention through environmental design (CPTED) (Jeffery, 1977; Taylor, Gottfredson, & Brower, 1980; Wood, 1981), studies of shopping mall crime (Brantingham, Brantingham, & Wong, 1990), proposals for rapid transit security (Brantingham, Brantingham, & Wong, 1991; Buckley, 1996; Felson, 1989), and the analysis of patterns of fugitive migration (Rossmo, 1987; Rossmo & Routledge, 1990).

Various theoretical approaches have been identified within the environmental criminology field, including the consequence model, contextual theory, event mobility model, human ecology, pattern theory, rational choice theory, routine activity theory, and strategic analysis (Brantingham & Brantingham, 1998). Despite their differences, these approaches all share a common concern for context. Felson and Clarke (1998) suggest that individual behaviour is a product of a person's interaction with their physical setting, and that setting provides varying levels of opportunity for crime. Routine activity, rational choice, and pattern theories have different emphases — society, local area, and the individual, respectively. But all three perspectives converge at the nexus of setting and opportunity. Crime opportunities depend on everyday movements and activities. Society and locality can change and structure crime opportunity, but it is the individual who chooses to offend.

Geographic profiling is based on the ideas and theoretical principles of environmental criminology. Pattern, routine activity, and rational choice theories all provide relevant perspectives, as does the geography of crime research within the event mobility model. [37]Any research into the target patterns and hunting behaviour of criminal predators must be aware of the microlevel dimensions of offender, victim, crime, and environment.

7.2.1   Routine Activity Theory

For a direct-contact predatory crime to occur, the paths of the offender and victim must intersect in time and space, within an environment appropriate for criminal activity. The routine activity perspective studies the processes and patterns associated with these requirements by examining how illegal acts depend upon regular legal activities. "Structural changes in routine activity patterns can influence crime rates by affecting the convergence in space and time of the three minimal elements of direct-contact predatory violation: 1) motivated offenders, 2) suitable targets, and 3) the absence of capable guardians against a violation" (Cohen & Felson, 1979, p. 589). The opportunity structure for crime can therefore be summarized as follows:

$$\text{crime} = (\text{offender} + \text{target} - \text{guardian})(\text{place} + \text{time}).$$

The potential criminal must be motivated at the time of the encounter. The target needs to be seen as suitable or desirable from the perspective of the offender. Capable guardians include police, security, place managers, and ordinary citizens going about their daily activities. John Eck expanded routine activity theory by also considering the role of offender handlers (e.g., parents, work colleagues, etc.) who control the criminal, and place managers (e.g., shopkeepers, building superintendents, etc.) who supervise the environment, in addition to victim/target guardians.

---

[37] The event mobility model, pioneered by James LeBeau and George Rengert, sees crime as a dynamic byproduct of spatial mobility influenced by nodes, paths, and movement.

Felson (1998) suggests that to learn about a crime's "chemistry," one must first find who and what must be present, and who or what must be absent, for the crime to occur. Determine the setting (time and place) where these conditions are likely to happen, and then establish the access to and escape from this location. The acronym VIVA — the value or desirability of the target, the inertia of the target, the visibility of the target, and the access to and escape from the target — describes the salient risk factors associated with crime.

Rhythms are important for understanding the ebb and flow of people through an environment (Felson, 1998). A given location may range from crowded to deserted, depending upon the time, day of week, or month. There are rhythms associated with work, entertainment, shopping, bars, transit, traffic, parking, temperature, weather, lighting, police, victims, guardianship, and sleep. Rhythms make it difficult to think about geography independently of time. In order to understand the rational order of crime we need to consider, in Marcus Felson's words, "map, clock, and calendar" (1986, p. 128).

Serial rape patterns are shaped by both offender activity space and victim routine activities and a useful investigative perspective may be gained by considering how the spatial and temporal patterns (time, weekday, season, weather, date, place) of each bring them into contact. Current and past routine daily activities of the rapist are important, as is the influence of prior crime "successes." A sexual predator will "pass by the same bus stop every morning of his way to work for a month, seeing the same person or same type of person, nursing his fantasy, building up his confidence, until finally he assaults him or her" (Pearson, 1997, p. 160). Ouimet and Proulx (1994) found pedophiles had a higher chance of recidivism if their routine activities put them in contact with places frequented by children (e.g., schools, playgrounds, parks, daycare centres, etc.).

A framework for analyzing factors of importance in geographic profiling may be built from routine activity theory. A given crime can be dissected into components of offender, target, and environment. Productive lines of inquiry are then developed by considering the individual components and their respective overlaps. The Venn diagram in Figure 7.1 shows the interrelationship between different crime components.

This breakdown results in seven different areas for consideration. These areas, along with associated issues, are outlined as follows:

1. Offender — typology;
2. Victim — victimology;
3. Environment — neighbourhood, landscape, situation;
4. Offender/target — victim preference and specificity, hunting style;

Figure 7.1 Offender/target/environment Venn diagram.

5. Offender/environment — transportation, offender's mental map and activity space, hunting ground;
6. Target/environment — target backcloth, neighbourhood rhythms, encounter site; and
7. Offender/victim/environment — crime and crime scene.

This framework suggests other questions of interest to a geographic profile, some of which are presented in Chapter 10.

7.2.2   Rational Choice Theory

The rational choice perspective takes a decision-making approach to explaining crime (Clarke & Felson, 1993b; Cornish & Clarke, 1986b). It is a "voluntaristic, utilitarian action theory in which crime and criminal behavior are viewed as the outcomes of choices. These, in turn, are influenced by a rational consideration of the efforts, rewards, and costs involved in alternative courses of action" (Cornish, 1993, p. 362).

> [Rational choice theory assumes] that offenders seek to benefit themselves by their criminal behavior; that this involves the making of decisions and of choices, however rudimentary on occasion these processes might be; and that these processes exhibit a measure of rationality, albeit constrained by limits of time and ability and the availability of relevant information. (Cornish & Clarke, 1986a, p. 1)

This theoretical perspective can trace its roots to the economic model of "rational man" and the classical school of Cesare Beccaria and Jeremy Bentham (Jeffery & Zahm, 1993; see also Jacoby, 1979). The original psychological and economic models had a utilitarian philosophy that analyzed cost vs. expected utility, but their lack of concern with motive and preference limited their application to an understanding of criminal behaviour.

The rational choice perspective as presented by Cornish and Clarke (1986a) is based on three concepts: (1) criminal offenders are rational and make choices and decisions that benefit themselves; (2) a crime-specific focus is required; and (3) there is a distinction between choices related to criminal involvement and decisions related to criminal events. This framework results in a significant degree of importance being laid on situational variables such as scene and victim characteristics, and their choice-structuring properties. Offender perceptions are also meaningful for an understanding of the crime-related calculus.

Experience changes an individual's information processing, and a criminal may improve his or her decision making over time. Learning is an integral part of rational choice theory which sees behaviour as interactional and adaptive (Cornish, 1993), but rational does not equal intelligent or sophisticated. The cleverness of the average offenders is exaggerated in what Felson calls the "ingenuity fallacy." Most crime is quick, easy, and unskilled. It is typically spontaneous or, at best, only casually planned; it is rarely well thought out. Many rapes, for example, occur by accident, the result of a burglar encountering a woman during a break in. The choices of offenders are often based on standing decisions that exhibit bounded rationality, limited by constraints of time, effort, and information. This is best understood through the concept of akratic behaviour, or temporal rationality, in which temptations override long-term decisions, especially if the former are visceral or emotional and the latter are rational (Trasler, 1993).

Pathological crimes involve non-pathological behaviour, and contrary to some beliefs, violent criminals including sex offenders exhibit a substantial degree of rationality (Miethe & McCorkle, 1998). Even psychotic individuals with unfathomable motives commit their crimes in manners that contain rational elements (Homant, forthcoming). "It may be that our reluctance to construe aggressive or violent behaviour as instrumental rather than expressive (or normal rather than pathological) sometimes has more to do with our own fears than with the facts of the matter" (Cornish & Clarke, 1986a, p. 14).

Former Florida deputy sheriff Gerard Schaefer, Jr., convicted in 1973 of two homicides and suspected of 11 others, wrote out the following murder plan, showing rationality in choice of crime location:

In order to remain unapprehended, the perpetrator of an execution-style murder such as I have planned must take precautions. One must think out well in advance a crime of this nature, in order for it to work.

We will need an isolated area, accessible by a short hike, away from any police patrols or parking lovers. The execution site must be carefully arranged for a speedy execution, once the victim has arrived... A grave must be prepared in advance away from the place of execution. (King, 1996, p. 219)

Rational choice and routine activity theory together provide powerful tools for understanding predatory criminal behaviour. In Felson's view, "rational choice theory deals mainly with the content of decisions; routine activity approaches, in contrast, are seen to deal with the ecological contexts that supply the range of options from which choices are made" (Cornish & Clarke, 1986a, p. 10; see also Clarke & Felson, 1993a, 1993b; Felson, 1986). This is a useful convergence, and pattern theory, situational crime prevention, and problem-oriented policing (POP) all draw from their juxtaposition. Offender foraging space is determined by routine activities and rational choice (Canter & Hodge, 1997), and the perspectives have much to offer for both the theoretical and practical components of geographic profiling.

7.2.3 Crime Pattern Theory

As chaotic as crime appears to be, there is often a rationality influencing the geography of its occurrence and some semblance of structure underlying its spatial distribution. Using an environmental criminology perspective, Brantingham and Brantingham (1981, 1984) present a series of propositions that provide insight to the processes underlying the geometry of crime. Their model of offence site selection, called crime pattern theory, suggests that criminal acts are most likely to occur in areas where the awareness space of the offender intersects with perceived suitable targets (i.e., desirable targets with an acceptable risk level attached to them).

These ideas suggest that most offenders do not choose their crime sites randomly. While any given victim may be selected by chance, the process of such random selection is spatially structured whether the offender realizes it or not. The psychological profile prepared by the FBI in the case of the Atlanta Child Murders proposed the following:

Your offender is familiar with the crime-scene areas he is in, or has resided in this area. In addition, his past or present occupation caused him to drive through these areas on different occasions ... the sites of the deceased are not random or "chance" disposal areas. He realizes these areas are remote and not frequently traveled by others. (Linedecker, 1991, p. 70)

After the arrest of Wayne Williams, police were able to determine that he had, in the past, done freelance photography assignments near several of the victim's burial sites. "Very few criminals appear to blaze trails into new, unknown territories or situations in search of criminal opportunities" (Brantingham & Brantingham, 1998, p. 4). This spatial selection process is consistent with the routine activity approach with its emphasis on the relevance of regular and routine victim behaviours for an understanding of crime patterns (Clarke & Felson, 1993a). Ford (1990) stresses the investigative importance of identifying "routine victim activities and expected behaviors related to contact with and risk of victimization by a serial predator" (p. 116).

Crime pattern theory combines rational choice, routine activity theory, and environmental principles to explain the distribution of crimes. Target choice is affected by the interactions of offenders with their physical and social environments (Brantingham & Brantingham, 1993b). Potential victims are not considered in isolation from their surrounding environment; the entire "target situation" must be seen as acceptable by the offender before a crime will occur (Brantingham & Brantingham, 1993b).

"*Pattern* is a term used to describe recognizable interconnectiveness [physical or conceptual] of objects, processes, or ideas" (Brantingham & Brantingham, 1993b, p. 264). This is a multidisciplinary approach that explores patterns of crime and criminal behaviour through an analysis of the processes associated with crime, site, situation, activity space, templates, triggering events, and motivational potential.

"Each criminal event is an opportune cross-product of law, offender motivation, and target characteristic arrayed on an environmental backcloth at a particular point in space-time. Each element in the criminal event has some historical trajectory shaped by past experience and future intention, by the routine activities and rhythms of life, and by the constraints of the environment" (Brantingham & Brantingham, 1993b, p. 259). Environment in this context involves sociocultural, economic, institutional, and physical structures, at micro, meso, and macrolevels.

Brantingham and Brantingham used the concepts of opportunity, motivation, mobility, and perception in the development of their model of crime site geography. The model is based upon the following propositions:

(1) Individuals exist who are motivated to commit specific offenses.

(a) The sources of motivation are diverse. Different etiological models or theories may appropriately be invoked to explain the motivation of different individuals or groups.

(b) The strength of such motivation varies.

(c)The character of such motivation varies from affective to instrumental.

(2)Given the motivation of an individual to commit an offense, the actual commission of an offense is the end result of a multistaged decision process which seeks out and identifies, within the general environment, a target or victim positioned in time and space.

(a)In the case of high affect motivation, the decision process will probably involve a minimal number of stages.

(b)In the case of high instrumental motivation, the decision process locating a target or victim may include many stages and much careful searching.

(3)The environment emits many signals, or cues, about its physical, spatial, cultural, legal, and psychological characteristics.

(a)These cues can vary from generalized to detailed.

(4)An individual who is motivated to commit a crime uses cues (either learned through experience or learned through social transmission) from the environment to locate and identify targets or victims.

(5)As experiential knowledge grows, an individual who is motivated to commit a crime learns which individual cues, clusters of cues, and sequences of cues are associated with "good" victims or targets. These cues, cue clusters, and cue sequences can be considered a template which is used in victim or target selection. Potential victims or targets are compared to the template and either rejected or accepted depending on the congruence.

(a)The process of template construction and the search process may be consciously conducted, or these processes may occur in an unconscious, cybernetic fashion so that the individual cannot articulate how they are done.

(6)Once the template is established, it becomes relatively fixed and influences future search behavior, thereby becoming self-reinforcing.

(7)Because of the multiplicity of targets and victims, many potential crime selection templates could be constructed. However, because the spatial and temporal distribution of offenders, targets, and victims is not regular, but clustered or patterned, and because human environmental perception has some universal properties, individual templates have similarities which can be identified. (1981, pp. 28–29).

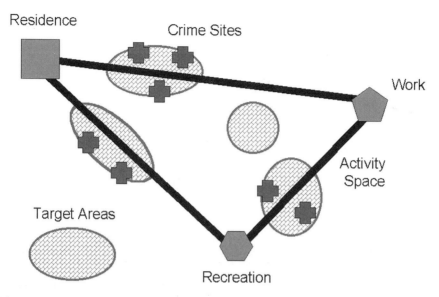

Figure 7.2   Crime site search geography.

Targets are selected from an offender's awareness space and assessed against the criteria of suitability (gain or profit) and risk (probability of being observed or apprehended). These targets are scanned for certain cues (visibility, unusualness, symbolism) that are evaluated in terms of fit to the individual's template. From the perspective of the offender, rational choices are then made and specific targets chosen for victimization. Such a selection-process is consistent with the concept of an offender operating within his or her "comfort zone" (Keppel, 1989).

A person's awareness space forms part of his or her mental map and is constructed primarily, but not exclusively, from the spatial experiences of the individual. An awareness space is derived from, amongst other sources, an activity space, the latter being composed of various activity sites (residence, workplace, social activity locations, etc.) and the connecting network of travel and commuting routes. Well-known locations (landmarks, tourist sites, important buildings) may also become part of a person's awareness space without actually being a component of their activity space.

Brantingham and Brantingham propose a dynamic process of target selection, with crimes occurring in those areas where suitable targets overlap the offender's awareness space (Figure 7.2). Offenders then search outward from these areas, the search behaviour following some form of distance-decay function (Brantingham & Brantingham, 1981, 1984; Rhodes & Conly, 1981). Search pattern probabilities can be modeled by a Pareto function, starting from the sites and routes that compose the activity space and then decreasing as distance away from the activity space increases. The Pareto function,

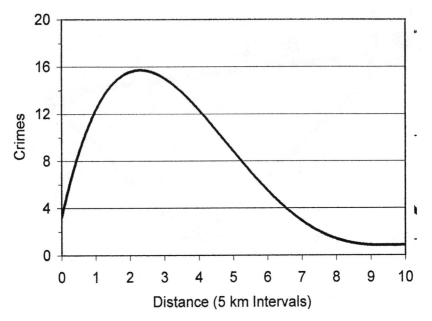

Figure 7.3   Distance-decay function.

named after the Italian economist, is suitable for fitting data that have a disproportionate number of cases close to the origin, making it appropriate for modeling distance-decay processes (Brantingham & Brantingham, 1984). It takes the general form: $y = k/x^b$.

There is usually a "buffer zone," however, centred around the criminal's residence, comparable to what Newton and Swoope (1987) call the coal-sack. effect. Within this zone, targets are viewed as less desirable because of the perceived level of risk associated with operating too close to home. For the offender, this area represents an optimized balance between the maximization of opportunity and the minimization of risk. The buffer zone is most applicable to predatory crimes; for affective-motivated offences it takes on less importance, as can be seen by the fact that domestic homicides usually occur within the residence. Figure 7.3 shows an example, derived from a serial rape case, [38] of a typical buffered distance-decay function. The radius of the buffer zone is equivalent to the modal crime trip distance.

When Canter and Larkin (1993) regressed maximum distance from crime site to home against maximum distance between crime sites for a group of serial rapists in England, they found a regression equation constant equivalent to 0.98 kilometres (see Equation 6.5, above). This was the "safety zone"

[38] Figure 7.3 displays the fourth-order polynomial trend line fitted ($R^2 = 0.730$) to 79 crime trip distances for John Horace Oughton, the Vancouver Paperbag Rapist (Alston, 1994; see also Eastham, 1989).

within which sexual offenders are less likely to strike. Employing a similar analysis, Canter and Hodge (1997) found such zones for both U.S. and British serial killers (3.44 km and 0.53 km, respectively). But the idea of a "safety" is misleading, and some studies have misinterpreted the buffer zone as representing an area of no criminal activity. This is incorrect; a decrease in probability is not the same as zero probability. Much depends on whether an offender believes he or she can get away with the crime. Under the right circumstances, rapists have been known to attack women who live in their same apartment building.

There may be another explanation for the existence of the buffer zone. As the distance from an offender's residence increases, so do the number of potential targets. The increase in criminal opportunity is linear; for example, there are twice as many possible targets at a distance of two kilometres than there are at one kilometre from an offender's home. More generally, the target ratio between two distances is:

$$t_2/t_1 = d_2/d_1 \qquad\qquad (7.1)$$

where:

t_2 is the number of potential targets at d_2;
t_1 is the number of potential targets at d_1;
d_2 is the second distance; and
d_1 is the first distance.

Combining the linear increase in opportunity with the exponential decrease in travel inclination creates a buffered distance-decay function. This process is equivalent to a spiral search that may be a more accurate means of describing what offenders really do. The search may be physical, or it may be mental as various possible targets are considered and assessed (see Wright & Decker, 1996). Modeling this process produces theoretical distributions that closely match empirical ones. Mean and modal journey-to-crime distances can be varied through a parameter describing the probability of target selection. Greater distances result from either specific limited targets or discerning offenders (i.e., lower target selection probabilities). This may explain many of the empirical results found in the journey-to-crime literature.

The journey-to-crime function, comprised of least effort, spiral searches, and detection avoidance, could be the result of something known as the principle of least action. First suggested in 1744 by Pierre-Louis Maupertuis, a Berlin scientist, and later developed by the famous French mathematician Joseph-Louis Lagrange, least action refers to the minimization of quantities within dynamic systems (e.g., energy, distance, time, change, effort, cost, etc.). Most aspects of nature seem to follow the rule of economy suggested by the least action principle. It appears in theoretical physics, linguistics, finance, and many other areas (Casti, 1998). Apparently, the world is lazy. Refracted light bends at angles that create a path of minimal travel time. Word frequency studies show languages attempt to communicate as much information as possible in the fewest number of symbols. The coding regions in DNA molecules appear to do the same, and least action governs human movement patterns.

Studies of trail systems, for example, show that people do not just follow the shortest path. Instead, they do something more complicated by minimizing their discomfort. Existing routes may not be the most direct but creating new paths takes effort, so walkers compromise between convenience and distance. Trail growth (caused by people walking) and decay (brought on by weather and overgrowth) has been shown to follow processes of natural competition and selection (Casti, 1998).

Target and Hunt

8

8.1 Target Patterns

From the bodily outline drawn on the surface of the scene of the crime...
what progressively emerges is the outlined shape of the killer.

– Seltzer, 1998, p. 48

The geography of crime literature indicates the importance of various factors
in determining the locations of a serial offender's crimes. The major influences on criminal target patterns are discussed below.

8.1.1 Place and Space

Crime event theory involves the study of locations (Eck & Weisburd, 1995b).
Ecological psychology tries to understand how places "work." Behaviour
settings (places) are free-standing, natural units of the everyday environment
with a recurring pattern of behaviours (standing patterns of behaviour), and
a surrounding and supporting physical milieu. These units organize community life. Examples include bus stops, taverns, billiard parlours, parking
lots, parks, playgrounds, street fairs, variety stores, welfare offices, and so on.
This is a place-based process of interest.

Weisburd has argued that more effective crime prevention and control
would occur with a shift of focus from individual offenders to specific places
(Taylor, 1997). The development of a complementary focus on the context
of crime, while a small scale concern, is perhaps more manageable. That
context can be seen through a cone of resolution, from macro to meso to
micro. Such studies so far have looked at CPTED, defensible space, territorial
functioning, situational crime prevention, and crime pattern theory.

There is an hierarchy of space that influences criminal action: (1) public space (e.g., street); (2) semi-public space (e.g., open front yard); (3) semi-private space (e.g., fenced backyard); and (4) private space (e.g., house) (Newman, 1972, 1996). As an offender moves from the street to an apartment building parking lot, to inside the building itself, and to the interior of an individual apartment, he is progressively entering more private space and concomitantly increasing his risk. Most crimes happen quickly and are over in a matter of a few minutes (Felson, 1998). Shorter times translate into lower risk. Consequently, offenders prefer to remain close to escape routes and avoid targets that are situated too far into private space. For example, auto theft from personal garages is a fraction of what it is from public lots.

Offenders "consistently commit crime in neighbourhoods they personally know well or that are very similar in physical, social and economic characteristics to their home neighbourhoods" (Brantingham & Brantingham, 1995, p. 13). Familiarity with, access to, and departure from a scene affect an offender's target choices (Beavon, Brantingham, & Brantingham, 1994). People congregate and interact at nodes. They also travel between such places via different modes of transportation. Nodes generate movement, and movement influences nodes.

Road network complexity and traffic flow are important crime determinants, and accessible or high-use areas experience more criminal problems. Beavon et al. (1994) found "that the design of street networks influences how people move about within a city and, consequently, their familiarity with specific areas" (p. 115). The permeability of a neighbourhood can be determined by the access from arterial routes, and a given block by the number of connecting streets. The beta index is a connectivity measure used for determining area permeability. For a given graph network the beta index is defined as follows:

$$\beta = e/v \qquad\qquad (8.1)$$

where:

β is the beta index;
e is the number of edges in the network; and
v is the number of vertices in the network.

Urban crime is more common along those streets arranged in a grid layout, and many burglars prefer corner houses because the intersecting roads offer two escape options[40] (Brantingham & Brantingham, 1975; Walsh, 1986).

---

[40] Cromwell, Olson, and Avary (1990, 1991) found that 39% of burglarized houses were located on corners. Offender preference for corner premises has been alternatively explained by the greater likelihood they will be noticed as potential targets, and by their lower surveillability (Reppetto, 1974).

Risk of crime is higher in counties crossed by interstate highways, and neighbourhoods close to freeway exits (Felson, 1998), and Rengert found 21% of the burglaries he studied in Connecticut were located within 0.25 miles of a freeway exit. These are all examples of "porous" areas.

By contrast, offenders dislike organic street layouts with their winding streets, crescents, and cul-de-sacs. Both entrance and escape is limited, and criminals run a greater risk of becoming trapped. Neighbourhoods with few access paths, particularly those that are bounded and contained by edges, primarily experience crimes committed by insiders. Edges can be either physical or perceptual, and often exist at the juxtaposition of different neighbourhoods or land uses. Strangers are common in such areas and people travel along edges unnoticed. Higher crime rates result from the anonymity associated with these zones of transition (Brantingham & Brantingham, 1975, 1993a). Generally, a crime in a remote or "out of the way" location is more likely than one near a well-travelled route to be the responsibility of an offender with local area knowledge.

Routine activity theory suggests that because offenders need to intersect with victims in the absence of guardians, dangerous places are busy but not too busy. Hunters will seek out such places. Crime is patterned by an area's permeability, and by the presence and location of edges, generators, and attractors. The concepts of crime generators and attractors were first introduced by Brantingham and Brantingham (1995). A crime generator is a high-traffic location (e.g., shopping mall, entertainment centre, transportation hub, etc.) that experiences crime as a by-product of the large number of people — potential victims and offenders — who regularly visit there. On the other hand, a crime attractor is a place that attracts offenders through its reputation for crime opportunities (e.g., bar districts, red-light zones, drug markets, etc.). A person may commit an offence while visiting a crime generator, but that was not his or her reason for going there in the first place. Crime attractors, however, pull in offenders intent on criminal activity. Crime attractors and generators are usually nodes.

Crime hot spots are small geographic areas that contain a disproportionate number of offences (Block, 1990; Block & Block, 1995; Sherman, Gartin, & Buerger, 1989). Generally, many different offenders and victims frequent these concentrated zones of generalized criminal activity. Hot spots can be calculated from various algorithms, and depicted by circles, ellipses, irregular polygons, and street blocks. Are they dangerous places? Not necessarily.[41] Dangerousness is usually associated with the risk, or odds, of being victimized. A location may experience much crime simply by virtue of the fact that

---

[41] Similarly, fear and criminality of place are often incongruent. The former is influenced by isolation, darkness, emptiness, niches, and alleys. The latter is affected by activity, access, and the presence of people. Both are time dependent, but in different ways.

many people visit it. So while the numerator (number of offences) may be high, so is the denominator (population), resulting in a moderate victimization rate and risk level.

"Fishing holes" or "trap lines" (target-rich locations) act as crime attractors for violent predators. These places are seen as possessing high probabilities of containing potential victims, who may then be followed to a different location before being attacked. A trap line is a linear fishing hole, typically stretched along a street or commercial strip. Such locations can be dangerous places during active periods of criminal predators.

8.1.2 Hunting Grounds

Fishing holes and trap lines are attractive to offenders because of their potential for containing desirable targets. Norris (1988) observes that certain serial killers stake out territories where vulnerable victims are likely to be found, preferring such locations as parking lots, dark city streets, university campuses, school playgrounds, rural roads leading from schools, and so forth.

> A hunter goes where there is game ... Selection of a hunting territory is the first prerequisite for a successful kill. A slayer's choice of stalking grounds may be determined by a private fantasy of vision, but it must include the basic elements of reasonable access, a supply of ready victims, and a decent prospect for evading capture ... In short, the ideal hunting ground depends upon a given killer's personality and needs. (Newton, 1992, p. 64)

Victim selection often follows a multistaged or hierarchical process as a criminal makes step-by-step decisions regarding choice of neighbourhood, street, and building (Van Soomeren, 1989). Target preference first delineates the offender's hunting ground, then specific victims are selected from within that area.

> Attacks outdoors seem often to involve the preselection of an area by the offender with which he is familiar, rather than the preselection or targeting of particular victims. These offenders attack where they are comfortable and in surroundings which are known to them and where they may be confident of effecting escape. The victim is then selected by the circumstances in which she becomes available to the attacker and vulnerable to the attack. (Canter, 1994, p. 188)

LeBeau (1985) suggests type of hunting ground and differences in spatial behaviour are important for discriminating between serial and nonserial rapists. He found serial rapists overwhelmingly struck in areas characterized as small household, single and multiple family dwelling units, and inhabited by elderly and young renters. Canter (1994) noted consistency in offence venue (inside vs. outside) for serial rapists. Inside rapes indicate planning and suggest an offender with a previous criminal history, most probably involving break and entry (see also Jackson et al., 1994). Outside rapes are more likely to be spontaneous and opportunistic.

8.1.3   Target Backcloth

Target or victim backcloth is important for an understanding of the geometric arrangement of crime sites; it is the equivalent of a spatial opportunity structure (Brantingham & Brantingham, 1993b). It is configured by both geographic and temporal distributions of "suitable" (as seen from the offender's perspective) crime targets or victims across the physical landscape. The availability of particular targets may vary significantly according to neighbourhood, area, or even city, and is influenced by time, day of week, and season; hence, the term structural backcloth is also used.

Because victim location and availability play key roles in the determination of where offences occur, nonuniform or "patchy" target distributions distort the spatial pattern of crime sites. "A creature such as a field mouse, whose food is randomly distributed, needn't evolve complex foraging strategies, whereas one such as a lion, whose food sources are indicated by clues in the environment, will have an advantage if it can use sophisticated mental abilities such as planning" (Douglas, 1999, p. 33). Victim selections that are nonrandom, or based on specific and rare traits, require more searching on the part of the offender than those that are random, nonspecific, and common (Davies & Dale, 1995a; Holmes & De Burger, 1988). For example, if an arsonist prefers to select warehouses as targets, their availability and distribution as determined by city zoning bylaws, has a strong influence on where the crimes occur. If an arsonist has no such preferences, then the target backcloth is more uniform as houses and buildings abound, at least in urban areas. The target sites of a predator who seeks out prostitutes is determined primarily by the locations of red-light districts, while the attack sites of a less specific offender might be found anywhere.

A uniform victim spatial distribution means crime locations are primarily influenced by the offender's activity space; otherwise, crime geography is more closely related to target backcloth. In the extreme cases of an arsonist for hire or a contract killer, victim location totally determines crime site. A consideration of victim characteristics thus plays an important role in the development of an accurate geographic profile.

The target backcloth is influenced by both natural and built physical environments as these affect where people live. Housing development is determined by such factors as physical topography, highway networks, national boundaries, city limits, land use, and zoning regulations. The Werewolf Rapist, Jose Rodrigues, lived in Bexhill on the south coast of Britain during his series of 16 sexual assaults. With no potential victims situated in the English Channel to the south, he was forced to confine his attacks to locations north of his residence, which resulted in a distorted target pattern. It is sometimes possible to compensate for such problems through the appropriate topological transformation of the physical space within and surrounding an offender's hunting area.

8.1.4   Crime Sites

There may be various sites involved in a serial murder, each with a slightly different geographic meaning. These include: (1) victim encounter location; (2) point of first attack; (3) murder scene; (4) body dump site; and (5) vehicle or property drop sites. In some cases, these locations are the same (e.g., the body dump site is the murder scene). The fact that a crime can involve several different sites has been recognized in studies on rape. Amir (1971) conceptualized a rape incident as comprising the initial meeting place, the crime scene, and the after scene. LeBeau (1987c) proposed a five-category classification based on a combination of Amir's original scene types, the offender's residence, and the victim's residence.

For the purposes of geographic profiling, the locations of primary interest in a murder are the encounter, attack, murder, and body dump sites (EAMD). Other location types may or may not be present (and are of interest if so), but the EAMD classification covers all the necessary elements of the crime. Similarly, a rape case involves the encounter, attack, rape, and victim release sites. Arson entails only a single location as the targets are typically buildings, structures, or other stationary objects.

The number of different crime scene types is a surrogate measure of mobility. In a San Diego study, LeBeau (1987c) found travel by the offender with the victim to average 1.50 miles (n = 218), and the two-scene rape to be the most common. An examination of 11 cases of chronic serial rapists, responsible for a total of 89 offences (mean = 8.1) from 1971 to 1975, showed a journey-to-crime range of 0.30 miles to 30.0 miles (mean = 6.9 miles), and a range of mean distance between crime sites of 0.12 miles to 0.85 miles, with an unweighted average of 0.37 miles.

While all of the crime scene types are important in the construction of a geographic profile of an offender, their locations, particularly in homicide cases, are not always known to investigating police officers.[42] Prior to the apprehension of the offender, these places can be determined only through evidence recovery or witness statements. In a typical unsolved homicide, the

---

[42] Rape cases are more likely to be solved in those instances where the offender's M.O. provides an opportunity for the victim to obtain more information about the offender (LeBeau, 1987c). Method of approach and use of multiple crime scenes affect the amount of time the victim spends with the rapist, influencing the likelihood of offender arrest.

police know the body dump site (which may or may not be the murder scene), and the place where the victim was last seen. In some circumstances, they may only know one of these locations.

A given type of crime site does not have the same degree of relevance in all cases. If target selection is specific, as in a series of prostitute killings, then encounter locations are restricted, influenced more by the victim backcloth (e.g., where the red-light district is located) than by the offender's regular activity space. And sometimes the actual murder scene is unknown (Ressler & Shachtman, 1992). But police should be aware of the location of the dump site, providing, at least, that the victim's remains have been discovered.[43] In such a case, the body dump locations will likely provide the most information about the murderer (see Newton & Swoope, 1987; Rossmo, 1998). Details of these sites may also provide insight to the offender's psychology.

8.1.5   Body Disposal

While all the elements in a crime are important for an understanding of the offender's psychology, the manner and location of the victim's body disposal, which influences if and when the corpse is found, may be of particular significance.

> The method of handling and leaving the victim's body will also offer insight into the victim's relationship to the killer. A victim left clothed or in an area allowing easy discovery suggest that she was "loved" by the killer. A well-treated, and easily found victim may also signify a killer who has a religious upbringing and who does not feel a rage directed at the victim or at society.
>
> A victim who is left in a remote area with no care taken to bury the body suggests that the killer had little regard for her. Once she served his needs he only sought to dispose of her to avoid detection. It also suggests that the killer admits that he will continue to kill and that he hopes to deter police recognition of his activity. Victims left in a public location, dismembered or mutilated are intended to shock both the community and the intended target. (Barrett, 1990, p. 167)

The method of body disposal can also be a function of criminal experience and offender concerns regarding scientific evidence. The forensic-conscious murderer may perceive several benefits in transporting the victim's body from the murder scene because that is the site where the most physical evidence is found (Ressler & Shachtman, 1992).

---

[43] Keppel (1989) suggests that "the discovery of a multiple body recovery site where victims have been deposited at different times should alert authorities that they are probably faced with a serial murder investigation" (p. 66).

The more successful serial killers transport their victims from the scene of
the murder to a remote site or makeshift grave. The police may never locate
the body and thus never determine that a homicide has occurred. Even if
the bodies of the victims do eventually turn up at a dump site, most of the
potentially revealing forensic evidence remains in the killer's house or car,
where the victim was slain — but without a suspect, the police cannot find
these places to search. Moreover any trace evidence ... left on the discarded
body tends to erode as the corpse is exposed to rain, wind, heat, and snow.
(Fox & Levin, 1994, pp. 30-31)

Homicide detectives consider such a case the hardest type of murder to
solve, stripped as it is of chronology and physical evidence. "A dump job, in
... [a] park or in an alley, in a vacant house or a car trunk, offers nothing. It
stands mute to the relationship between the killer, the victim and the scene
itself" (Simon, 1991, p. 78). The crime scenes of prolific killer Ted Bundy
were rarely discovered because of his practice of transporting victims, but in
Tallahassee he attacked and left victims inside a sorority house that made it
possible for Florida authorities to recover incriminating physical evidence
(Cleary & Rettig, 1994; Flowers, 1993).

Ressler et al. (1988) report that 27% of the time (32 out of 118 cases) the
sexual murderers in their study admitted returning to the crime scene,[44] though
they did not specify which of the various different types of crime sites the
offenders returned to. Some killers moved their victims' remains. And some
just kept the bodies (or parts thereof) with them, in their homes. Location and
method of body disposal appear to be important components of many criminal
fantasies, perhaps originating from what Seltzer (1998) terms "the derivation
of identity from a hyperidentification with place" (p. 213).

Experience and research has shown that a victim's body is unlikely to be
carried more than 150 feet from the murder site to the dump site, or more
than 150 feet from a vehicle (Keppel & Birnes, 1995). An adult body dumped
in a remote area will usually be found within 50 feet of a road or trail (Keppel
& Birnes, 1995), and a child's body within 200 feet (Burton, 1998). A search
following the road network will therefore be more effective and efficient than
a standard grid search.

A murderer carrying a dead victim is subject to time, distance, speed,
and effort constraints that can be used to determine potential body dump
site locations. Naismith's rule is a travel time estimation technique based on
distance, degree of travel difficulty, elevation, and load. Some of the rules
regarding travel speed over terrain type include:

[44] David Berkowitz found returning to the scenes of his former shootings an erotic experience; Ted Bundy revisited the sites of his victims' remains to sexually assault their body
parts (Ressler & Shachtman, 1992).

- Easy going — 5 kilometres per hour;
- Easy scrambling — 3 kilometres per hour;
- Rough land, deep sand, soft snow, or thick bush — 1 kilometre per hour;
- Add 1 hour for every 500 metres elevation;
- Add 1 hour for every 1000 metres depression; and
- For every 5 hours of travel time, add 1 hour for fatigue.

These rules can be combined to provide total travel time estimates. For example:

$$T = d/x + h/y \qquad\qquad (8.2)$$

where:

T is the total travel time;
d is the horizontal distance;
h is the vertical distance;
x is the horizontal walking speed; and
y is the vertical climbing speed.

Naismith cautions these are only approximate guidelines, and individual performances vary depending upon stamina and fitness levels.

Offenders typically take the path of least resistance, and indicators such as tire tracks, footprints, discarded objects, scuff marks, broken branches, bent grass blades, and crushed plants can help determine their trail (Robbins, 1977; Sacks, 1999). Ground disturbances, changes in soil colour, and retarded, advanced, or altered vegetation cover may mark a body burial site, as can bird and scavenger activity (Skinner & Lazenby, 1983). France et al. (1997) list varies methods for the detection of clandestine grave locations, including the use of aerial photography, geology, botany, entomology, electromagnetics, metal detectors, infrared/thermal imagery, decomposition (cadaver) dogs, archaeology, anthropology, and ground penetrating radar (see also Kubik, 1996).

Human remains left in the wilderness will quickly become disarticulated and scattered as the result of animal — particularly canid — scavenging, complicating the process of evidence recovery. Research findings in the fields of forensic taphonomy (the study of death assemblages) and anthropology are of relevance for the problem of finding skeletal evidence and body dump sites (Haglund & Sorg, 1997). Coyotes in the Pacific Northwest have been known to skeletonize a body in 28 days, and disarticulate and scatter most of the skeleton in 2 months; after a year, the bones are dispersed over a large area (Haglund, 1997a).

The degree of animal movement of human remains is a function of corpse size and decomposition, position, degree of burial, presence of clothing or wrapping, relative size and strength of the scavenger, season, terrain, topography, and vegetation (Haglund, 1997a). Body movement, often indicated by drag marks or disturbed ground cover, occurs in stages between rest places or food caches; these locations may be marked by discoloration from body fluid seepage. Larger animals, able to drag an entire human corpse, often move it some distance before covering it with debris or burying it in a shallow grave. Heavily gnawed or chewed bones are likely to have been first carried off from the original body location.

Skeletal remains are usually found within 100 metres of the primary deposition site, but some pieces may be dragged as far away as 300 metres (Haglund, 1997a). Evidence is most likely located along animal trails and paths between primary body deposition and other recovery sites, but these trajectories might not be straight because of interim rest sites (Keppel & Birnes, 1995). Terrain, inclines, and sedimentation also influence the scatter pattern (Haglund, 1997b).

Teeth and bone fragments are often found in animal scats; their analysis can assist in species identification and determination of animal territory and movement patterns. Coyote ranges vary from an average of 3.2 kilometres in forested areas to 16.1 kilometres in open landscapes (Haglund, 1997a). Understanding faunal activity is an important step in establishing the evidence search area (Murad, 1997).

8.1.6 Learning and Displacement

The criminal hunt is influenced by both internal and external factors. Serial offenders gain knowledge with each new crime and they often learn from their experiences, successes, and failures, avoiding mistakes and repeating successful tactics (Cusson, 1993; Warren et al., 1995). Criminal development also results from education, changes in lifestyle, increased "professionalism," new associates, and disorder progression. Media disclosures and certain investigative strategies, particularly patrol saturation tactics, may create spatial and temporal displacement, altering the geographic behaviour of the offender to the point that apprehension is hindered or delayed.

After the media reported fibre evidence had been recovered from victims' bodies during the investigation of the Atlanta Child Murders, Wayne Williams changed his dumping grounds from remote roads and wooded areas to local rivers (Douglas & Olshaker, 1995; Glover & Witham, 1989). By disposing of unclothed bodies in this fashion he hoped that any physical evidence would be washed off by the water. The geography of Atlanta's rivers is markedly different from that of its roads and woods, therefore this change in M.O. led to a shift in the geographic pattern of the crime sites (see Dettlinger & Prugh,

1983). After the publication by the *Victoria Times-Colonist* of an unofficial profile on a dangerous serial arsonist in which a psychologist stated the offender was operating in his own neighbourhood, Manley Eng targeted a building on the other side of Saanich, British Columbia, removed from all his previous fires. And when New York papers wondered if the Son of Sam would continue his pattern and strike in each of the City's boroughs, David Berkowitz responded accordingly (Ressler & Shachtman, 1992).

Displacement is a change in an offender's pattern of behaviour as the result of crime prevention efforts, community wariness, or police investigative strategies. While displacement is by no means a certain result, it is more likely to occur with strongly motivated criminals such as sex offenders. There are five possible outcomes of displacement typically discussed in the literature: (1) spatial (geographic or territorial); (2) temporal; (3) target; (4) tactical; and (5) functional (activity) (Reppetto, 1976). Spatial displacement is the main concern for geographic profiling, but the other forms of displacement can also alter target patterns because of victim backcloth influences. Davies & Dale (1995b) found evidence for spatial, temporal, and tactical displacement in their study of British serial rapists.

Geographic or spatial displacement results when an offender relocates his or her criminal activity in response to a perceived increase in the risk of apprehension or reduction in opportunity (Gabor, 1978; Lowman, 1986). This geographic shift can be on a neighbourhood, metropolitan, or regional scale. Spatial displacement also involves a change in the type of place targeted within the same general area (e.g., from a downtown prostitution stroll to a downtown nightclub district). Some offenders move of their own accord and commit crimes in a new neighbourhood, but this is not characterized as displacement because the change resulted from something other than police or community action.

Temporal displacement results when an offender shifts his or her criminal activity to a different time period in response to a perceived modification in risk or opportunity environments. The shift is to a period (e.g., time of day, day of week, etc.) when acceptable risk and target availability levels exist. This may involve an extended period of offender inactivity, ranging from weeks to years, known as remission. Remission can also result from episodic behaviour on the part of the offender; in such cases, the temporal patterning of the crimes is the result of internal psychological factors, and not external influences. It is not uncommon for a criminal to appear to have gone into remission, when in reality he or she has only moved to another area — perhaps as the result of spatial displacement. Communication difficulties and linkage blindness then prevent the crimes in the new jurisdiction from being linked to the previous ones.

Target displacement occurs when an offender modifies the selection of premises, objects, or subjects as targets for his or her criminal activities. This may result from such activities as target hardening or community awareness. A child molester who selects older teenagers after increased vigilance around elementary schools has engaged in target displacement. Tactical displacement occurs when an offender uses alternative strategies or changes his or her M.O. to achieve the same criminal goals. This is usually the result of learning. Functional or activity displacement results when a different form or type of criminal behaviour is engaged in by the offender (e.g., a shift to bank robbing from safe cracking), often resulting from changes in opportunity due to technology. A rapist who begins to kill his victims strictly to prevent identification has engaged in functional displacement.

8.1.7 Offender Type

Criminal profiling can assist in determining the relationship between an offender's routine activities and his or her target patterns. The FBI dichotomizes repetitive sexual killers into organized and disorganized categories, based on offender personality and type of crime scene[45] (Ressler et al., 1988). These groups are alternatively labelled organized nonsocial and disorganized asocial offenders. FBI research suggests that organized offenders comprise 48% of the murderer population (both sexual and nonsexual), disorganized offenders 33%, mixed offenders 14%, and unknown cases 5% (Classifying sexual homicide crime scenes, 1985).[46]

Organized offenders usually plan their crimes, employ restraints, and attack strangers (Barrett, 1990). Most of the time, they have access to a serviceable vehicle and are willing to travel great distances. Organized offenders are more likely to expand the boundaries of their awareness space and hunt in areas located further from home. They are typically mobile murderers, often transporting victims to the murder site and then hiding their bodies (Ressler & Shachtman, 1992). In research of British child sexual murderers, Aitken et al. (1994) found that evidence of travel or victim abduction was

[45] A profile will indirectly infer organized or disorganized personality types from evidence and signs left by the offender at the crime scene (Crime scene and profile characteristics of organized and disorganized murderers, 1985). "Profilers pay particular attention to the manner in which a person was killed, the kind of weapon that was used ... If the killer brought along his own weapon, it points to a stalker, someone fairly well organized, even cunning, who came from another part of town and probably drove a car. If the killer used whatever weapon was available — a knife from the kitchen or a lamp cord — it points to a more impulsive act, a more disorganized personality. It also means that the person probably came on foot and lives nearby" (Porter, 1983, p. 47).
[46] By comparison, the FBI study of 36 sexual murderers classified 62% as organized, 25% as disorganized, and 13% as mixed; or, alternatively, 44% very organized, 19% organized, 6% mixed, 14% disorganized, and 17% very disorganized (Ressler, 1989).

indicative of journey-to-crime distances greater than 5 miles. Organized murderers follow their crimes in the news and may move or change jobs to avoid apprehension (Ressler et al., 1988).

Disorganized offenders may know their victims. They act spontaneously, and tend to live or work within walking distance of the crime sites, usually with their parents or in a small apartment. Disorganized killers murder their victims at or near the encounter site, and often leave the body in plain view at the murder scene. They often choose crime sites from familiar areas and strike close to the nodes and routes of their activity space. The awareness space of the disorganized criminal is likely to be smaller and less complex than that of the organized offender. Disorganized offenders are not concerned about the media, and are unlikely to significantly change their lifestyle to avoid apprehension.

8.2   Hunting Methods

Throughout accounts of serial murders run themes of adventurous risk in the stalking of human prey by stealth or deception, the excitement of the kill ... The egoism of the hunter permits the degradation of potential victims to the level of wild game. The planning, excitement, and thrill of the hunt overrides all other considerations except eluding capture.

– Green, 1993, pp. 143, 147

Serial violent criminals are predators — they search for human victims in manners similar to carnivores hunting for animal prey. And like wildlife, they employ various hunting styles in their efforts to seek out and attack victims. Target patterns are determined by offender activity, victim location, environment, and situational cues. Any analysis of the criminal hunt must consider these factors.

8.2.1   Target Cues

In a study of active urban burglars in Texas, Cromwell, Olson, and Avary (1990, 1991) found environmental and target cues played key roles in offender assessment of risk, effort, and gain. The burglars first determined if a premise was occupied using various external visual indicators. If the place appeared uninhabited, they assessed its surveillability (from neighbouring homes), and then its accessibility (usually from the side or rear). These burglars were looking for satisfactory, not optimal target choices. Offenders influenced by drugs or alcohol viewed targets as more vulnerable and crime as less risky.

Burglars search for their targets along obvious routes (Cusson, 1993), and Cromwell et al. (1990, 1991) found routine activity variables to be useful predictors of break-ins. Corner location, average traffic speed, proximity to schools, businesses, parks, churches, stop signs, traffic lights, four-lane streets, and the presence of a carport or absence of a garage were all significantly related to burglary risk. Corner homes, premises situated along streets with slower traffic, and places close to stop signs or traffic lights are more likely to be noticed by scouting burglars. Homes with carports or without garages allow occupancy to easily be assessed from vehicle presence. The time patterns of these criminals were determined by the time patterns of their victims. "The typical burglar is much more aware of our use of time than we are" (p. 59).

In a study of active burglars in St. Louis, Missouri, Wright and Decker (1996) observed that offenders found burglary sites in one of three ways: (1) through prior knowledge of the victim; (2) by obtainment of inside information; or (3) most commonly, by observation of potential targets. The third method provides insight to how certain violent criminal predators behave.

Typically, the choice of a house to break into is not spontaneous; instead, the groundwork has been done, possible targets lined up, and preliminary information collected. Offenders wish to determine potential risks and rewards before committing a break and enter. "'I look at a house two or three times before I go in it'" (Wright & Decker, 1996, pp. 41–42). Burglars are attracted by certain external "reward and risk" cues that allow them to make inferences regarding the occupants and contents of the house (a process that also leads some offenders to transfer responsibility for the crime to the target, claiming that the house was "just asking for it"). They had some knowledge of the occupants' routines, and noted such things as the number, presence, and absence of vehicles.

Wright and Decker (1996) considered how burglars locate their residential targets:

> But how do offenders come to be watching those places to begin with? Do they purposely seek them out? Or do they simply stumble on them in the course of their daily rounds? For most of the offenders in our sample who typically watched dwellings before breaking in to them, the answer seemed to fall somewhere between these two extremes. The subjects usually did not go out with the specific intention of looking for potential targets. Nor did they generally just happen upon places when locating prospective burglary sites was the last thing on their minds. Rather they were continually "half looking" for targets ... "I might go to the neighborhood park or something and then I might say, 'Well, I'm a go home this way today.' Then while I'm walkin' up the street I just be lookin', checkin' it out." (pp. 42–43)

Targets were usually found by offenders attuned to their surroundings during the course of their daily routine activities, and then intermittently watched (see also Cromwell et al., 1990, 1991). While this search process is more casual than determined, it is surprisingly effective, allowing offenders to build up a mental "card file" of potential targets. When a burglar wants to commit a break in, the various possibilities are reviewed and a decision made. If it turns out that a particular selection is unsuitable at the time, then the next target in the "card file" is chosen. This search process provides insight to the target selection of those serial rapists who break into homes, many of whom have previous burglary experience (see Schlesinger & Revitch, 1999).

In a study using routine activity and lifestyle/exposure perspectives, Warr (1988) found that homes — and women — at greater risk for burglary are also at greater risk for inside rape. A comparison of 1980 UCR Index offences for 155 Standard Metropolitan Statistical Areas (SMSA) revealed rape and burglary to be strongly correlated ($r = 0.79$). Both crimes also showed close and consistent similarities in their coefficients with a set of opportunity variables. These variables were grouped into three categories: (1) housing (e.g., low income, newer areas, rental premises, multiunit structures, etc.); (2) female occupancy (e.g., divorced, living alone or without other adults, etc.); and (3) combinations of the first two groups. For example, one of the strongest combination variables was "female householders, no husband present, aged 25–34, in a renter-occupied structure with more than 50 units" (rape, $r = 0.59$; burglary, $r = 0.54,$). A summary index of similarity was also very high ($r^2 = 0.99$). Warr concluded that home-intrusion rape (rape following an unlawful entry of the home) is a hybrid offence — it is a violent crime with the opportunity structure of a property crime (see also Felson & Clarke, 1998).

Police interviews with serial rapists have revealed a high awareness of environmental cues. One offender stated he selected homes by looking for driveways with oil spots, suggesting the absence of a vehicle. If he then saw a woman inside the house he presumed the man was absent. Another rapist said he avoided homes with boats parked outside as that indicated the presence of a male. A surprising number of victims leave their curtains open at night, even after being attacked. Even a cursory look inside a home can reveal much about who lives there, be they female, male, a couple, the elderly, or children. Some offenders demonstrate prior knowledge of their victims, probably gained through past surveillance, although others have been known to search through a victim's purse during the attack and then pretend to have possessed such information beforehand.

The search process described by Wright and Decker can also explain the clustering of rape sites and the occurrence of two or more attacks in a single evening. It is not surprising that targets with suitable offence characteristics are often situated close together. If an attack fails, a criminal simply has to go to the next location in their mental "card file" and try again, as in the case of the rapist with multiple preselected victims, described earlier. Because the contents of this file are strongly determined by the offender's activity space, the crime locations may provide a "road map" with significant investigative implications.

8.2.2 Hunting Humans

Anatoly Onupriyenko, convicted of murdering 52 people including families with children in Zhitomir, Ukraine, referred to himself as a hunter and his victims as the game. " 'I look at it very simply. As an animal. I watched all this as an animal would stare at a sheep' " (Shargorodsky, 1998).

The hunt for humans is much like the search for other criminal targets. But there are two complicating factors for the offender: first, people move about, and second, they have to be controlled. Criminal predators must employ search and attack methods that address these issues. Most previous classifications of serial murder and rape geometry have been limited to description, ignoring the processes that underlie the outcomes. One of the few exceptions is Petrucci's (1997b, 1998) empirical typology of victim-acquisition techniques used by serial sexual killers. Offenders from the U.S. (n = 146) were selected from Hickey's comprehensive serial murder database and coded on the basis of a six-item protocol. Petrucci found the following distinct groupings:

1. Abduction — The victim was attacked by surprise, and then transported to a different location where the murder occurred. This was the most common victim-acquisition technique (36%), and is suggestive of a fantasy-motivated offender. Of all serial murderers using this method, 67% were local, 94% were Caucasian, and 31% were disorganized.
2. Attacking — The victim was surprise attacked and then killed, with no transportation. This was the least common technique (16%), and is suggestive of an offender who is less concerned with apprehension. Of all serial murderers using this method, 71% were local and 43% were a minority.
3. Luring — The victim was first attracted or lured by deception, then attacked by surprise and killed. Voluntary or involuntary transportation may be involved. This was the second most common victim acquisition technique (25%), and is suggestive of a fantasy-motivated offender. Of all serial murderers using this method, 41% were local and 41% were travellers.
4. Combination — Victims were acquired through the use of multiple tactics. This was the third most common victim acquisition technique (23%), and is suggestive of an instrumental rather than a fantasy-

driven offender. Of all serial murderers using a combination of methods, 52% were travellers and 72% were organized.

Foraging theory has been applied to the understanding of criminal predators (Canter & Hodge, 1997). While it may suggest useful insights to the basics of hunting behaviour (Daly & Wilson, 1995), this perspective does not provide an adequate theoretical basis. Animals must eat to survive, and every hunt expends limited energy. Optimal foraging theory is based on a balance between opportunity maximization and effort minimization. But none of this is applicable to the criminal hunt.

Hunting method affects the spatial distribution of offence sites and any effort to predict offender residence from crime locations must consider this influence. It is therefore necessary to employ a hunting typology relevant to the production of spatial patterns of serial predators. The construction of the scheme now used as the standard in geographic profiling was informed by geography of crime theory, empirical data, and investigative experience.

While murder or rape can potentially involve several different types of crime locations, experience has shown that not all sites may be known to police. Victim encounter or last known location (usually a close proxy of encounter site) are often known in murder cases and always known in rape cases. Body dump sites are known in most murder cases and victim release sites in all rape cases, but if the murder act itself occurred in a different location, this site will likely be known only to the offender. A rape site may or may not be known to the victim, and hence the police. The hunting typology is therefore concerned with offender behaviour *vis-à-vis* the crime locations most probably known to police. Arson is simpler, involving stationary known targets and therefore only a single crime location. Consequently, only the first three search techniques, and none of the attack methods in the hunting typology discussed below, apply to serial arson.

8.2.3   Search and Attack

The hunting process can be broken down into two components: (1) the search for a suitable victim; and (2) the method of attack. The former influences selection of victim encounter sites, and the latter, body dump or victim release sites. The hunting typology results from a combination of the search and attack elements.

The following four victim search methods were isolated:

1. Hunter — An offender who sets out specifically to search for a victim, basing the search from his or her residence.
2. Poacher — An offender who sets out specifically to search for a victim, basing the search from an activity site other than his or her residence,

or who commutes or travels to another city during the victim search process.

3. Troller — An offender who, while involved in other, nonpredatory activities, opportunistically encounters a victim.
4. Trapper — An offender who has an occupation or position where potential victims come to him or her (e.g., nursing) or by means of subterfuge, entices victims into a home or other location they control (e.g., by placing want ads).

The following three victim attack methods were isolated:

1. Raptor — An offender who attacks a victim upon encounter.
2. Stalker — An offender who first follows a victim upon encounter, and then attacks.
3. Ambusher — An offender who attacks a victim after he or she has been enticed to a location, such as a residence or workplace, controlled by the offender.

Hunters are those killers who specifically set out from their residence to look for victims, searching through areas in their awareness space they believe contain suitable targets. This is the most commonly used method of criminal predators. Westley Allan Dodd, a serial killer executed for the murder of three children in the state of Washington, wrote in his diary, "Now ready for my second day of the hunt ... Will start at about 10 a.m. and take a lunch so I don't have to return home." He was worried, however, that if he murdered a child in the park through which he was searching, he would lose his "hunting ground for up to two to three months" (Westfall, 1992, p. 59). The crimes of a hunter are generally confined to the offender's city of residence. Conversely, poachers travel outside of their home city, or operate from an activity site other than their residence, in the search for targets. The differentiation between these two types is sometimes an intricate task, requiring a subjective interpretation of crime location familiarity. The hunter and poacher categories are similar, though not identical, to the "marauder" and "commuter" designations (Canter & Larkin, 1993), described and discussed later.

Trollers are opportunistic killers who do not specifically search for victims, but rather encounter them during the course of other, usually routine activities (see Eck & Weisburd, 1995b). Their crimes are often spontaneous, but many serial killers have fantasized and planned their crimes in advance so that they are ready and prepared when an opportunity presents itself. This has been termed premeditated opportunism, and is related to the concept of pattern planning (Cornish & Clarke, 1986a). In an interview, Eric Hickey

(1996), an incarcerated serial murderer responsible for 12 victims, discussed the details of one of his crimes. While it was an opportunistic attack, his assessment of the environment, victim approach, and con to move them to a more secluded area illustrate the killer's rationality and adaptation.

> It was the first time I ever abducted two at once, not the first time that I murdered two in the same day. I saw them out walking across a field. I was wandering. I was kind of in a controlled frenzy. I was certainly aware of what I was doing, in control, but inside I was desperate, and I would not have taken them had I not been there, anywhere else but there, I would have let them go. There was no reason. It was a cold day, no one was around. There was a secluded area nearby. In other words, it was a killing site, and I was in a very remote part of town. There were houses there but there was also fields off to one side. I had no vehicle there. (pp. 124–125)

Trappers have an occupation or position, such as a nurse or orderly in a hospital, where potential victims come to them. They also entice victims into their home or other location they control by means of subterfuge. This may be done through entertaining suitors, placing want ads, or taking in boarders. Black widows, "angels of death," and custodial killers are all forms of trappers, and most female serial murderers fall into this category (Hickey, 1986; Pearson, 1994, 1997; Scott, 1992; Segrave, 1992).

Raptors, upon encountering a victim, attack almost immediately. This is the most common method used by criminal predators. Stalkers follow and watch their targets, moving into the victim's activity space, waiting for an opportune moment to strike. The attack, murder, and body dump sites of stalkers are thus strongly influenced by the victims' activity spaces. Jon Berry Simonis, the Ski Mask Rapist, attacked women in Florida, Georgia, North Carolina, Ohio, Michigan, Wisconsin, Mississippi, Louisiana, Texas, Oklahoma, and California from 1978 to 1981, becoming progressively more violent before he was arrested by the Louisiana State Police. Simon sometimes stalked his victims, and through his work at a hospital had access to victims' medical records including their address, marital, and work details (Michaud & Hazelwood, 1998).

Ambushers attack victims they have brought or drawn into their "web" — someplace where the killer has a great deal of control, most often their home or workplace. The bodies are usually hidden somewhere on the offender's property.[47] While victim encounter sites in such cases may provide sufficient spatial information for analysis, many ambushers select marginal-

---

[47] Theoretically this does not have to always be so, but empirically it appears to be the rule. This probably results from the fact that ambushers are often also trappers, and the latter rarely exhibit significant mobility.

ized individuals whose disappearances are rarely linked, even when missing person reports are made to the police.

This hunting typology resembles that for burglars proposed by Bennett and Wright (1984), which includes planners, searchers, and opportunists. Surprisingly, it is also remarkably similar to Schaller's (1972) description of hunting methods used by lions in the Serengeti where he observed ambushing,

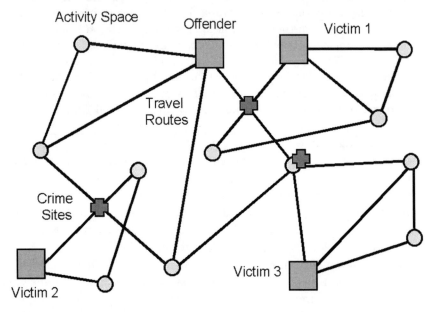

Figure 8.1   Raptor target pattern.

stalking, driving (direct attack), and unexpected (opportunistic) kills. Offenders may employ different hunting methods, but they usually adopt and stay with one, or at the most two approaches. For example, while trolling is not a primary criminal search technique, it is part of many offenders' repertoires.

8.2.4 Predator Hunting Typology

Target patterns are determined by offender activity space, hunting method, and victim backcloth. Hunting style is therefore helpful in determining which crime locations are the best predictors of an offender's anchor point under different circumstances. Another purpose of this typology is the identification of those situations where an analysis of the relationship between offender activity space and crime location geography is appropriate. This allows for the elimination of those cases where such an analysis is either impossible or redundant. Poachers, for example, who live in one city and commit their crimes in another, may not reside within their hunting area. Stalkers, whose crime locations are driven more by the activity spaces of their victims than by their own, produce more complex target patterns requiring different analytic methods. Figures 8.1 and 8.2 show, respectively, hypothetical target patterns for raptors and stalkers.

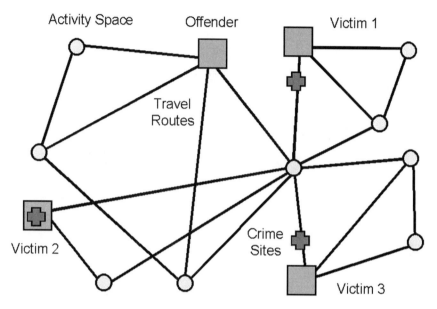

Figure 8.2   Stalker target pattern.

Table 8.1 presents the 12-cell matrix produced by a crosstabulation of the 4 search and 3 attack methods. The suitability for geographic profiling (from encounter and body dump sites) is indicated for each cell. The matrix uses a sliding scale of designations (*yes, possibly,* or *doubtful*) to refer to suitability likelihood. A designation of *redundant* refers to a situation where such an analysis is possible, but trivial. For example, while body dump locations can accurately determine the address of a trapper serial killer (e.g., one who entices victims into his or her home, murders them, and then buries their bodies in the basement), there is no need to do so. The cases of Belle Gunness, who poisoned her suitors, and Dorothea Puente, who murdered elderly tenants, are such examples. As search and attack methods are correlated, some hunting styles are more common than others. For example, hunter/raptors and trapper/ambushers are more frequent than hunter/ambushers or trapper/raptors. Also, the suitability ratings in Table 8.1 are only suggestive as individual cases may vary significantly from each other in terms of their spatial details.

Table 8.1   Criminal Predator Hunting Typology*

Encounter Sites	Search Method			
Attack Method	Hunter	Poacher	Troller	Trapper
Raptor	yes	possibly	yes	redundant
Stalker	yes	possibly	yes	redundant
Ambusher	yes	possibly	yes	redundant

Body Dump Sites	Search Method			
Attack Method	Hunter	Poacher	Troller	Trapper
Raptor	yes	possibly	yes	redundant
Stalker	possibly	doubtful	possibly	possibly
Ambusher	redundant	redundant	redundant	redundant

*From Rossmo, D.K. (1997). Geographic Profiling. In J.L. Jackson, & D.A. Bekerian (Eds.). (1997b). *Offender profiling: Theory, research and practice* (pp. 159-175). Chichester: John Wiley & Sons. Used with permission.

Predator Patterns

My only concerns was being prepared ... Some Saturdays and Sundays I drove along the Coast, not looking for hitch-hikers, just searching out places. On back-waters of the Pee-Dee River, near where I had worked with the cypress cutting and hauling crews, I found old logging roads that went for miles into the swamps — and more trails into marshes south of Georgetown ... I decided on spots I could get to quick from main Highways, but far enough away so I wouldn't have to worry about anybody seeing or hearing, and I always picked spots that had a nice burying place close by.

—Donald "Pee Wee" Gaskins, planning his South Carolina coastal kills;
Gaskins & Earle, 1993, p. 123

9.1 Spatial Typologies

Most research and commentary on the geography of serial murder and violent crime has been descriptive, aimed primarily at the classification of spatial patterns of crime scenes. This is an important prerequisite for understanding the methods used by predatory criminals during their hunt and the resulting geography of their crimes. It is from this basis that efforts to geographically profile violent offenders can begin. These typologies typically analyze such factors as victim selection, offender hunt, crime pattern, mobility, distance, and method of body disposal.

Holmes and De Burger (1988; see also Falk, 1990) categorize serial murder location patterns as: (1) concentrated (characteristic of the visionary, mission-oriented, hedonistic lust, and hedonistic comfort serial murderer types); or (2) dispersed (characteristic of the hedonistic thrill, and power/control-oriented serial murderer types). Thus serial killers are: (1) geographically stable (concentrated target patterns); (2) geographically transient (dispersed target

145

patterns); or (3) mixed (a combination of stable and transient). The motives of geographically stable serial killers are often sexual in nature, and their victims specifically selected. Transportation of the victim's body is a crime scene characteristic associated with the lust, thrill, and power/control-oriented serial murderer types (Holmes & Holmes, 1996).

Robbins (1991) researched differences in the methods and motives of geographically stable and geographically transient serial murderers. In a study of 20 well-known recent (1970 to 1991) convicted and incarcerated male serial killers, she found geographically stable serial murderers typically operate in areas occupied by members of their own race, seek specific victim traits, are organized, and plan their crimes in advance. They tend to be thrill oriented and young, and often commit their crimes under the influence of alcohol or drugs. These killers have been known to engage in necrophilia and decapitate their victims for the purposes of delaying identification. Body dump sites are different from murder scenes, necessitating transportation of the victim's body; both locations are chosen by the killer ahead of time.[48] Usually victims are left clothed and their remains are discovered.

Geographically transient serial murderers, by comparison, are more likely to have a history of sexual abuse in their backgrounds, tend to be less organized, and have shorter attention spans (Robbins, 1991). This typically results in a lower level of formal education, more marital breakdowns, and a record of working odd jobs. These killers often travel extensively and have a propensity for not staying long in one place. They are less victim specific and ritualistic in their crimes, often changing choice of weapon and method of operation. They are older, oriented towards power and control, and more frequently engage in biting and cannibalism (see Wilson, 1988). Usually victims are left unclothed and their remains are less likely to be discovered.

Table 9.1 summarizes the target pattern characteristics associated with various categories in the Holmes and De Burger serial murderer typology (including Barrett's opportunist serial killer type) (Barrett, 1990; Holmes & De Burger, 1988; Holmes & Holmes, 1996; Robbins, 1991).

In a study of 28 convicted serial sex murderers who targeted female victims, James (1991) noted various offender characteristics related to hunting behaviour and crime site geography. He recorded the following data on victim selection, hunting behaviour, offender transportation, attack, body disposal, and apprehension:

---

[48] Dietz et al. (1990) found 93.3% (28) of the sexually sadistic criminals they studied carefully planned their offences, 76.7% (23) took victims to a preselected location, and 60% (18) kept at least one victim captive for 24 hours or more (see, for example, Gaskins & Earle, 1993). Cases of extended captivity indicate an offender with access to a safe and secure place in which to hold the victim (Ressler & Shachtman, 1992).

Table 9.1 Holmes and De Burger Serial Murderer Typology

Serial Murderer Type	Victim Selection	Method	Crime Locations
Visionary	known & stranger nonspecific random	spontaneous disorganized	concentrated
Mission-Oriented	stranger specific nonrandom	planned organized	concentrated
Hedonistic Lust	stranger specific random	planned organized	concentrated body movement
Hedonistic Thrill	stranger specific random	spontaneous disorganized	dispersed body movement geographically stable
Hedonistic Comfort	known & relational specific nonrandom	planned organized	concentrated
Power/Control-Oriented	stranger specific nonrandom	planned organized	dispersed body movement geographically transient
Opportunist	stranger nonspecific random	spontaneous disorganized	dispersed

1. Victim Selection
   - 89% did not know their victims before the crime, and 29% had met or previously seen at least one of their victims (some killers attacked both strangers and acquaintances);
   - 50% offered their victims rides, 11% met them in bars, and 7% contacted them through newspaper advertisements;
   - 86% randomly selected their victims; and
   - 25% murdered prostitutes, and 21% were attracted to children (girls under the age of 12 years).
2. Hunting Behaviour
   - 32% planned their murders in advance, and 61% were familiar with the area where the crime was committed;
   - 18% followed and 18% hunted their victims; and
   - 46% operated with an accomplice, 32% with a male and 14% with a female.

3. Transportation
   - 78% used vehicles, either directly or indirectly, in the commission of their crimes;
   - 50% of those who directly used vehicles in their crimes offered their victims rides;
   - 54% drove their own vehicle, 9% a relative's, and 18% used a stolen automobile; and
   - 7% used public transportation, and 4% flew an aircraft.
4. Attack
   - 75% of the serial murderers conned their victims to gain control, and 68% used a ruse to get them to the attack location;
   - 21% employed immediate force to gain control; and
   - 32% attacked on their own property, 29% on the property of a relative or friend, and 29% in the victim's residence.
5. Body Disposal
   - 64% tried to conceal their victims' bodies in remote areas;
   - 29% buried their victims underground, and 21% dumped them in water; and
   - 68% moved the bodies of their victims after the murder.
6. Apprehension
   - 61% had a previous criminal record;
   - 11% had been observed within the crime area by police, and 18% were connected to the crime area by patrol officers;
   - 29% had been questioned and then released;
   - 14% were arrested through surveillance methods, and 8% through patrol work;
   - 31% were caught as the direct result of police investigation activities, and 61% from witness information; and
   - 32% kept incriminating evidence at their home or workplace, and 29% on their person or in their vehicle (some murderers did both).

Wingo classifies serial killers as "megastat," those who kill over time in a single static urban environment, or "megamobile," those who are mobile and travel over great stretches of geography (Egger, 1990). In their study of sexually sadistic criminals, Dietz et al. (1990) note that 40% of their subjects (n = 12) engaged in "excessive driving" (travelling long distances or with no clear direction). Davies and Dale (1995b) observe many British rapists are incessant prowlers, cruising by vehicle, public transportation, or foot. This finding has been confirmed in both U.S. and Canadian studies, underlining the investigative importance of recording information on prowlers, trespassers, and suspicious persons. Viable sexual assault suspects can often be found through such records when queried by geographic area.

Mobility, however, does not necessarily translate into range. Keppel (1989) notes "serial killers are highly mobile, frequently cruising and drawn to those victim contact areas where they feel they are in their 'comfort zone' " (p. 65). Such offenders typically have ready access to vehicles which they use to become familiar with their preferred victim encounter and body disposal areas. Keppel cites the examples of Wayne Williams and John Wayne Gacy, Jr., both of whom confined their murderous activities to a single metropolitan area — Atlanta and Chicago, respectively. The mobility associated with serial murderers can result in a higher frequency of cruising, but not necessarily in greater geographic reach.

Hickey (1997) found three geographic categories of offender in his study of serial murder: (1) travelling killers (34%), who commit murder while moving through or relocating to other areas; (2) local killers (52%), who remain within a certain urban area, or a single state; and (3) place-specific killers (14%), who murder within their own home, workplace, or other specific site. Local serial murderers are responsible for fewer victims per offender than travelling or place-specific killers, both of whom are harder to apprehend. Linkage blindness is a significant problem with mobile offenders, and authorities are often not aware that a place-specific murderer is active. Hickey (1990) observes a shift in mobility patterns post-1975, with an increase in local serial killers and a reduction in out-of-state travelling and place-specific offenders. He suggests these shifts may be due to increased urbanization, advances in techniques of forensic analysis, and changes in methods of murder.

Newton (1992) studied 301 U.S. and 56 non-U.S. serial murderers from a 20-year period, and classifies them by hunting style into: (1) territorial killers (63% of U.S., 70% of non-U.S. cases), who stake out a defined area; (2) nomadic killers (29% of U.S., 15% of non-U.S. cases), who travel widely in their search of victims; and (3) stationary killers (8% of U.S., 15% of non-U.S. cases), who commit their crimes at home or work. Newton notes that serial murderers usually follow the same hunting style, which he feels expresses their view of life and who they are.

These results contradict the generally held assumption that serial killers are highly peripatetic (Egger, 1984; Keppel, 1989). Levin and Fox (1985) found "traveling serial killers ... are a minority to those ... who 'stay at home' and at their jobs, killing on a part-time basis" (p. 183). Serial murderers tend to be geographically stable, killing in areas they know. Turf is a valued commodity and Barrett (1990) suggests offenders avoid hunting in areas besieged by other killers, though this might be best explained by the scarcity of the phenomenon. Newton (1992) comments that the majority "rarely deviate from the selected game preserve" (p. 48). Perhaps executed serial murderer Donald "Pee Wee" Gaskins said it best: "I felt safer doing my killing and burying in my home state. I guess I'm just a Carolina Southern-boy at heart" (Gaskins & Earle, 1993, p. 161).

Serial murder victims are more often attacked outside their home than other homicide victims because of the crime's stranger nature, and potential victims are more vulnerable in areas where such killers have ready access. Hickey (1997) found female serial child killers are more likely than their male counterparts to be place-specific (33% vs. 13%), and male serial child killers more likely to be travellers (46% vs. 21%). This result reflects the institutional nature of the locations involved (e.g., hospitals, boarding houses, etc.) involved. Most employed female serial murderers use their occupational position to access victims (Scott, 1992; Segrave, 1992).

In their study of serial rape in England, Canter and Larkin (1993) applied the circle hypothesis as a means of dividing offenders into "marauders" or "commuters." An offence circle is the region enclosed by the circumference of the circle, the diameter of which is the line joining the two most distant crimes. Marauders are individuals whose residences act as the focus of their crimes. Commuters, on the other hand, travel from home into another area to commit their offences. The circle hypothesis suggests that marauders reside within their offence circle, and commuters reside without. Only 13% of the British serial rapists (n=45) had a home base outside of their offence circle. Finding little support for the commuter hypothesis, the research concluded that rapists, like most people, are typically "domocentric."

Kocsis and Irwin (1997) caution, however, that the generality of this conclusion is doubtful. In a study of Australian serial offenders, they noted that 71% of rapists, 82% of arsonists, and 48% of burglars resided within their offence circle. The FBI found 51% of U.S. serial rapists (n = 76) lived outside of their offence circle, and 76% outside of the convex hull polygon (see above) created by their crime site pattern (Warren et al., 1995). Alston (1994) had similar results to those of the FBI in his study of 30 British Columbia stranger sexual assault series; in 43.4% of the cases the offence circle did not contain an offender activity node. National differences in urban structure, neighbourhood density, and travel behaviour might contribute to the inconsistencies in these findings (Warren et al., 1995).

One of the problems with the circle hypothesis is its determination of hunting behaviour solely from the crime site point pattern (see Alston, 1994, for a discussion of other issues of concern). In cases involving large numbers of offences, a rapist may commute to several different areas in various directions, creating an offence circle that contains his residence. And in cases involving small numbers of crimes a marauder might find by chance all of his victims in the same direction, resulting in an offence circle that excludes their home base. Offence circles could therefore lead to both commuter and marauder designations, depending upon what point in a serial rapist's career they were generated.[49] This happened in both the Yorkshire Ripper and the Boston Strangler cases (Burn, 1984; Davies & Dale, 1995a; Frank, 1966). In other instances a nonuniform target backcloth may force a commuter pattern regardless of the offender's hunting style.

As part of a suggested taxonomy of rape series, Alston (1994) proposes marauders be defined as those offenders who consistently travel under 5 kilometres from a primary activity site (e.g., home or work) to the initial victim contact scene, and commuters as those who travel more than 5 kilometres. He observes the latter tend to stay close to the major thoroughfares used for their crime journeys. Davies and Dale (1995b) caution "that the commuter and marauder models may just be extremes of a continuum of patterns determined by topography and target availability" (p. 16).

9.2   Geography of Serial Murder

Descriptive accounts of serial murder and rape spatial patterns are useful, but a greater understanding of offender behaviour is gained by applying theories and techniques from environmental criminology and quantitative geography (Brantingham & Brantingham, 1984; R. V. Clarke, 1992, 1997; Garson & Biggs, 1992; Taylor, 1977). To this end, a seven-year research project on geographic profiling and target patterns of serial murderers was conducted at Simon Fraser University's (SFU) School of Criminology (Rossmo, 1995a). The study involved the collection and analysis of two forms of data: (1) macrolevel information on serial killers; and (2) microlevel information on offenders, victims, and locations for selected serial murders.

Within a geography of crime perspective, locations of crime sites are seen to be influenced by hunting style, target backcloth, and changes in offender activity space. Some of the related questions this study sought to answer include: (1) which crime location types, individually or jointly, are the best predictors of offender residence; (2) what do the characteristics of the crime site and surrounding area tell us about the offender; and (3) is it possible earlier crimes, committed before the killer gained experience and expanded his or her spatial repertoire, are better indicators of an offender's home area? The SFU serial murder data set provided the information necessary for an analysis concerned with these and other issues. Area and neighbourhood characteristics, victim types and activities, date and time periods, and offender mobility were examined. Data were also available to compute crime trip distances, size of hunting area, degree of pattern aggregation, and weekday of offence.

---

[49] The probability that n crimes of a marauder will appear to be those of a commuter is approximately: $(2^n - 1)/(2^{2n-2})$. The likelihood such a pattern could happen by chance is not insignificant for low values of n. For example, in a series of 4 crimes the probability is equal to 0.23.

9.2.1   Methodology

9.2.1.1   Serial Killer Data

The first database (henceforth referred to as the FBI serial killer data set) contains macrolevel information on serial killers. The main source for this data was an FBI NCAVC *Lexus/Nexus* newspaper computerized topical search file on serial murderers in the U.S. The crimes are therefore primarily, though not exclusively, North American. An attempt was made to clean and verify the information in the original list, and to eliminate those cases that are closer to a spree or mass murder classification. To this end, the FBI definition of serial murder was used (see Ressler et al., 1988). While there was no attempt to be comprehensive, an effort was made to update the data and include well-known foreign serial killers. The final list consists of 225 cases, including most well-known serial killers. Information in the FBI serial killer data set includes: (1) offender name; (2) moniker or media name; (3) sex; (4) associates; (5) number of confirmed victims; (6) number of suspected victims; (7) start date of murders; (8) end date of murders; and (9) cities, states or provinces, and countries of operation.

The data set on serial killers served two analytic purposes. First, it was the means by which frequencies, averages, and rates were computed for the macrolevel variables. Regional variation in serial murder was also examined through state comparisons of counts and rates (adjusted for both population and overall murder). Second, this list was the source for the microlevel serial murder data set. One of the critical elements of the selection criteria involved choosing those cases where the serial murderer's activity space and hunting style produced target patterns that are amenable to geographic profiling. This ultimately led to the development of the predator hunting typology, a necessary step in the articulation of the applicability and limits of geographic profiling. The larger data set made this process feasible.

9.2.1.2   Newspaper Sources

While the use of newspaper data in serial murder research is common, a few cautions are worth noting. Egger (1990) states that "it would appear that the mass media are currently the only source from which to quantify serial murders in this country [U.S.]" (p. 11). He searched *The New York Times Index* from January 1978 to June 1983 for cases of serial killers (1984, 1990). Simonetti (1984) perused the same index and associated microfilm files for stories of serial murder cases from January 1970 to November 1983. Jenkins (1988a, 1989) researched newspaper archives, including *The New York Times Index*, to compile a list of major cases of serial murder in the U.S. from 1900 to the present, finding just as much journalistic interest in this topic in the early part of the century as in the later.

Levin and Fox (1985) searched indices of six major American newspapers for serial and mass murder cases involving a minimum of four victims from 1974 to 1979. Hickey (1997) identified serial murder cases from 1800 to 1995 through a variety of sources including newspapers, journals, biographies, interviews, bibliographies, and computer abstract searches. Anytime the media are used as a source of information, it becomes important to ascertain the existence of possible reporting biases. Kiger (1990) warns that "newspaper stories are problematic sources of data because they are obviously dependent upon editorial decisions and because they may sensationalize (not to mention glorify) this phenomenon in order to increase circulation" (p. 37). The media may be inclined to focus on particularly heinous cases or those involving a large number of victims, and ignore African-American (Jenkins, 1993a) and foreign offenders. In his analysis of the Henry Lee Lucas serial murder case, Egger (1990) found newspaper accounts were often inaccurate in their descriptions of details and had to be treated as suspect.

Kiger (1990) further cautions that a string of murders must first be identified as part of the same series before the existence of a serial killer will even be suspected (see the earlier discussion on linkage blindness). Newspaper reporting inaccuracies and definitional problems further complicate media source research. For example, upon perusing case details in microfilmed newspaper articles, Simonetti (1984) found some so-called incidents of serial murder were actually mass murders. Jenkins (1989) discusses the problems of historical changes in media practice and coverage, and the tendency towards greater coverage of events that occur in large urban areas. He notes major metropolitan papers expanded their coverage of regional issues in the 1950s, and since 1960 the proportion of national newspaper chains has tripled (1992b). In subsequent research, however, he concludes that such concerns do not present major research difficulties or significant data biases (1989).

These problems suggest a potential research bias. Crimes of repetitive killers who hunt over wide geographic regions may, because of linkage blindness, be unidentified as serial murders. Those attacks lacking a consistent M.O. and spread out over long periods of time are even less likely to be connected. Some serial murders may be officially known only as a number of unrelated missing persons reports. Such crimes fall into the "dark figure" of serial murder and are not open to traditional methods of information gathering, possibly skewing data collection towards more geographically confined serial murderers. But this begs the question; if a murder series is not identified in the first instance, then there is no need to assist in its investigation. It is also possible that purported but unidentified serial murderers, such as Jack the Ripper or the Green River Killer, never actually existed. While that conclusion is unlikely in these particular cases, it is certainly feasible the press or police might incorrectly link a number of unconnected homicides (see Jenkins, 1989). This is apparently what happened with a 1984 to 1985 series of murders of women in Fort Worth, Texas (Jenkins, 1993b).

9.2.1.3 Offender, Victim, and Location Data

The second database (henceforth referred to as the SFU serial murder data set) contains microlevel information on offenders, victims, and locations for selected serial murder cases. It is based on a sample drawn from the FBI serial killer list, which served as a reasonable approximation of the overall population. While an accurate accounting of all serial murderers does not exist and most likely never will, the best efforts to date suggest the size of the modified FBI list is on the right order of magnitude (see Cavanagh, 1993; Hickey, 1997).

Specific criteria were employed to structure the sampling procedure. Only serial killers responsible for five or more victims, after 1960, who were residentially stable, operated by themselves or with a single partner, and who hunted in certain ways, were included (see Rossmo, 1995a, for complete details of the sampling methodology). The selection process helped to define the appropriate limits of the analysis and prevent misapplication. To have value in the investigation of an unsolved serial murder case, such a classification must be determinable from information likely to be known to police prior to the killer's apprehension. Research parameters were developed with this consideration in mind.

A sample of 10 cases was randomly drawn from those that met the selection criteria and used to examine the microlevel geography of serial murder. An additional three cases that violated various selection criteria were also studied in order to assess the impact of these violations. The resulting 13 cases served as the initial test group for the criminal geographic targeting algorithm used in geographic profiling.

Information in the SFU serial murder data set includes: (1) date of murder; (2) day of murder; (3) time of murder; (4) sequential case number; (5) weapon; (6) vehicle use; (7) degree of offender organization; (8) serial killer classification; (9) hunting typology; (10) victim traits (specific or nonspecific); (11) victim selection (random/nonpatterned or nonrandom/patterned); (12) victim activity; (13) offender residence (address, and spatial coordinates); (14) offender workplace (address, and spatial coordinates); and, for all known crime locations connected to each murder, (15) area description; (16) neighbourhood type; and (17) spatial coordinates. Appendix B contains the serial murderer, victim, and crime location data coding forms. Data coding procedures and guidelines can be found in Rossmo (1995a).

Through the use of a relational database management system, crime locations were hierarchically connected through the common murder, and murders linked through the common killer. Further data items were calcu-lated from these relationships, such as the distance from residence to crime site. A total of 13 serial murder cases, comprising 15 serial killers, 178 victims, and 347 crime locations constitute the SFU data set.

9.2.2   Serial Killer Characteristics

A breakdown of the characteristics for the 225 serial killers in the FBI data set is given in Table 9.2. The complete list is presented in Appendix A, Table A.1.

Table 9.2   Serial Killer Characteristics

Characteristic	Results
Offender Identity	
Known	93.8% (211)
Unknown	6.2% (14)
Sex	
Male	90.7% (204)
Female	9.3% (21)
Co-Killer	
Operated Alone	75.6% (170)
Operated With Partner	24.4% (55)
Mean Duration of Murder Activity	4.4 Years
Mean Number of Confirmed Victims	9.7
Mean Number of Suspected Victims	13.3
Mean Number of Different Cities	2.8
Mean Number of Different States	1.7

As there were 14 cases that remained unsolved with the identity of the offender unknown, the proportion of unsolved cases is 7.3% (there are 193 unique cases in the data set). The percentage of female offenders is compa-rable to that found in previous research (cf. Hickey, 1997; Newton; 1992), as is the estimate for mean duration of murder activity (cf. Hickey, 1991; Jen-kins, 1988b). One-quarter of the serial murderers operated with a partner, and the proportion of cases with more than one offender is 11.9%. This estimate is at the low end of the range found in previous studies (cf. Hickey, 1997; Jenkins, 1990; Simonetti, 1984; Newton, 1992). Team killers averaged 1.7 partners.[50]

Figure 9.1 presents the distributions for number of confirmed and sus-pected victims by case. The mean for the suspected number of victims was calculated after eliminating those cases that claimed 100 or more victims, as

---

[50] Interestingly, the hunting efficiency of solitary lions ranges from 8 to 19%, but increases to 30% in cooperative hunts (Barnard, 1984a; Schaller, 1972).

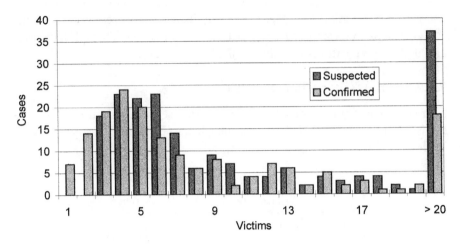

Figure 9.1 Confirmed and suspected victim numbers by case.

these figures were not considered reliable (the mean is 18.7 otherwise). The estimate for the mean number of different cities should be regarded with caution as the data appear to contain listings for both metropolitan areas (e.g., New York) and individual cities (e.g., Brooklyn, Queens).

9.2.2.1   State Comparisons

Many researchers have noted regional variations in multiple murder, but there is little consensus as to where the high rate areas are. The Pacific Northwest is often held out to be the location with the most incidents of serial murder (Egger, 1990; Mathers, 1989). Cavanagh (1993) found that 39.6% of serial murder victims were from the Pacific subregion, a proportion more than twice as great as the next highest subregion. Levin and Fox (1985) observe that multiple murderers usually strike in urban areas, most likely in New York, Texas, or on the West Coast, particularly Southern California. They are least likely to attack in the Deep South, with the exception of Texas. But 64% of the female serial killers in Keeney and Heide's (1994c) study were from the South, most commonly Florida (29%).

Hickey (1997) found a lack of regionality in serial murder, though California reported over half again the number of serial murder cases as New York, the next highest state. In Cavanagh's (1993) analysis, California had over four times the number of victims of New York, the next highest state. Hickey observes that population density, particularly in metropolitan areas, appears to be a more important correlate than region. Jenkins (1990) suggests that the geographical concentration of serial murder in the western U.S. may be partially attributable to "a culture of casual predatory sexuality," and differential access to vice facilities in Californian cities. Levin and Fox (1985) refer to Southern California, with its wealth of displaced individuals and potential victims, as a "playground for murder."

Table 9.3 displays a state-by-state (including the District of Columbia) comparison of population, murder and nonnegligent manslaughter offences and rates known to police, 1988 (Flanagan & Maguire, 1990), and serial murder counts and rates. The serial murder counts are an average of three studies: (1) cases of serial murder in which one or more victims were killed, 1800 to 1995 (Hickey 1997); (2) serial murder victims by state, mid-1800s to 1989 (Cavanagh, 1993); and (3) location of serial killer operation, 1880 to 1993 (Rossmo, 1995a). The serial murder rates are adjusted for both population (per 10,000,000 people) and overall murder (per 1000 offences).

States with the highest counts of serial murder (more than twice the mean) are, in order, California, New York, Florida, Illinois, Texas, Ohio, and Georgia. States with the highest per capita rates of serial murder (more than twice the overall rate for the U.S.) are, in order, Alaska, Nevada, California, District of Columbia, and Oregon. States with the highest rates of serial murder per all murders (more than twice the overall rate for the U.S.) are, in order, Alaska, Vermont, Utah, Wyoming, Idaho, Montana, Oregon, North Dakota, Nevada, Washington, Delaware, and Wisconsin. Figure 9.2 shows a map of per capita serial murder rates by state.

The degree of confidence in these findings should be tempered by the fact that each study used different methods of counting[51] and covered dissimilar time periods. Furthermore, many states had only small numbers of recorded serial murder cases and therefore little reliability should be placed in their ranking. Once population or overall murder levels (a proxy for both population and propensity for lethal violence) are accounted for, many of the geographic differences noted by previous researchers disappear. There is still some evidence, however, for higher serial murder rates in the west.

9.2.3 Case Descriptions

The serial murder cases selected for more detailed analysis include: (1) Richard Chase; (2) Albert DeSalvo; (3) Clifford Olson; (4) Angelo Buono and Kenneth Bianchi; (5) Peter Sutcliffe; (6) Richard Ramirez; (7) David Berkowitz; (8) Jeffrey Dahmer; (9) Joel Rifkin; and (10) John Collins. In order to explore the impact of violating certain selection criteria, an additional 3 cases were included: (1) Aileen Wuornos; (2) Ian Brady and Myra Hindley; and (3) Jerry Brudos. These 13 cases, representing 15 serial murderers, 178 victims, and 347 crime locations, comprise the microlevel SFU serial murder data set.

---

[51] Also, Hickey presents his frequency counts as ranges (e.g., Washington, 6 to 10 cases), requiring use of the midpoint (e.g., Washington, 8 cases).

Table 9.3   Serial Murder Counts and Rates by State

State	Population	Murders	Murder Rate	Count	Rate	Per Murder
Alabama	4,127,000	408	9.89	6.3	15.3	15.5
Alaska	513,000	29	5.65	7.7	149.4	264.4
Arizona	3,466,000	294	8.48	6	17.3	20.4
Arkansas	2,422,000	211	8.71	1.7	6.9	7.9
California	28,168,000	2936	10.42	193	68.5	65.7
Colorado	3,290,000	187	5.68	6	18.2	32.1
Connecticut	3,241,000	174	5.37	8	24.7	46
Delaware	660,000	34	5.15	3	45.5	88.2
District of Columbia	620,000	369	59.52	4	64.5	10.8
Florida	12,377,000	1416	11.44	47.5	38.4	33.5
Georgia	6,401,000	748	11.69	32.3	50.5	43.2
Hawaii	1,093,000	44	4.03	2.7	24.4	60.6
Idaho	999,000	36	3.6	5	50.1	138.9
Illinois	11,544,000	991	8.58	38.8	33.6	39.2
Indiana	5,575,000	358	6.42	13.3	23.9	37.2
Iowa	2,834,000	47	1.66	1.7	5.9	35.5
Kansas	2,487,000	85	3.42	3	12.1	35.3
Kentucky	3,721,000	229	6.15	3.7	9.9	16
Louisiana	4,420,000	512	11.58	12.3	27.9	24.1
Maine	1,206,000	37	3.07	1.7	13.8	45
Maryland	4,644,000	449	9.67	8	17.2	17.8
Massachusetts	5,871,000	208	3.54	5	8.5	24
Michigan	9,300,000	1009	10.85	23.3	25.1	23.1
Minnesota	4,306,000	124	2.88	2	4.6	16.1
Mississippi	2,627,000	225	8.56	4.3	16.5	19.3
Missouri	5,139,000	413	8.04	7.7	14.9	18.6
Montana	804,000	21	2.61	2.7	33.2	127
Nebraska	1,601,000	58	3.62	2.7	16.7	46
Nevada	1,060,000	111	10.47	10.3	97.5	93.1
New Hampshire	1,097,000	25	2.28	1.3	12.2	53.3
New Jersey	7,720,000	411	5.32	9.3	12.1	22.7
New Mexico	1,510,000	173	11.46	3	19.9	17.3
New York	17,898,000	2244	12.54	51.7	28.9	23
North Carolina	6,526,000	510	7.81	7.7	11.7	15
North Dakota	663,000	12	1.81	1.3	20.1	111.1
Ohio	10,872,000	585	5.38	32.7	30	55.8
Oklahoma	3,263,000	243	7.45	11.7	35.8	48
Oregon	2,741,000	139	5.07	16.7	60.8	119.9
Pennsylvania	12,027,000	660	5.49	12.7	10.5	19.2
Rhode Island	995,000	41	4.12	2	20.1	48.8
South Carolina	3,493,000	325	9.3	4.7	13.4	14.4
South Dakota	715,000	22	3.08	1.3	18.6	60.6
Tennessee	4,919,000	461	9.37	5	10.2	10.8
Texas	16,780,000	2022	12.05	36.8	22	18.2
Utah	1,691,000	47	2.78	9.7	57.2	205.7
Vermont	556,000	11	1.98	2.3	42	212.1
Virginia	5,996,000	468	7.81	5.3	8.9	11.4

Table 9.3   Serial Murder Counts and Rates by State (continued)

State	Population	Murders	Murder Rate	Count	Rate	Per Murder
Washington	4,619,000	264	5.72	23.3	50.5	88.4
West Virginia	1,884,000	93	4.94	2	10.6	21.5
Wisconsin	4,858,000	144	2.96	12	24.7	83.3
Wyoming	471,000	12	2.55	2	42.5	166.7
United States	245,810,000	20,675	8.41	718.2	29.2	34.7
Mean	4,820,000	405.4		14.1		

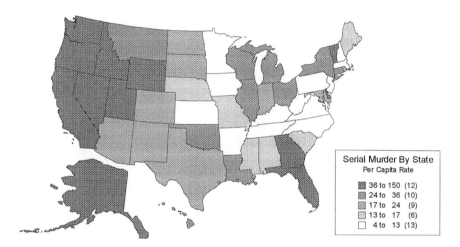

Figure 9.2   Serial murder rates by state.

Summary histories for each of the selected murder series follow. For the purposes of the study, a victim and associated crime sites were connected to a serial killer case if the offence was one of murder, attempted murder, or a violent crime (rape, sexual assault, kidnapping, abduction, or any attempt thereof), the circumstances of which were such that the person had a substantial likelihood of being killed.

While workplace is an important component of activity space, reliable information on occupation was not available for this sample, and offender work site was therefore not analyzed. Certain locations that appear to have been key offender anchor points were noted. All residences are included in cases involving two offenders or where the killer moved in the midst of the murder series.

9.2.3.1   Richard Chase

Richard Trenton Chase, the Vampire Killer, was a chronic paranoid schizophrenic who believed that his blood supply was being dried up by aliens
(Biondi & Hecox, 1992; Ressler & Shachtman, 1992). He therefore reasoned
the only way he could stay alive was through drinking the blood of others.
Released from a mental institution in 1976, Chase began a rampage of murder
in Sacramento County, California, in late December of 1977, killing six
people — male and female, adult and child — while engaging in postmortem
evisceration, anthropophagy, and vampirism.

Often used as an exemplar for the disorganized murderer type, Chase
lived in the area of his crimes, at one point leaving a vehicle stolen from one
of his victims just around the corner from his home. Consistent with a
disorganized murder series, Chase's hunting area was localized and limited
in size. With one exception, the body dump and encounter sites are equivalent. His last crime scene involved four victims. Apprehended in January 1978
through police neighbourhood canvassing efforts that were informed by a
psychological profile, Chase was eventually convicted of six counts of first-
degree murder. In 1980, he committed suicide by poison while in prison.

9.2.3.2   Albert DeSalvo

Albert DeSalvo, the Boston Strangler, murdered 13 women during the 1960s
in and around Boston, Massachusetts (Frank, 1966; James, 1991; Newton,
1990a; Time-Life, 1992b). Married with a family, he had a particularly abusive
childhood history and was eventually diagnosed as schizophrenic. DeSalvo
is believed to have committed over 300 sexual assaults and hundreds of
burglaries in four states before and after his murders. He began to strangle
his victims in June 1962, often leaving their bodies displayed with an elaborate bow tied in the ligatures around their necks.

DeSalvo commuted into Boston from his home in Malden and drove
aimlessly through rundown and "Bohemian" neighbourhoods in the Back
Bay area. He picked target locations from building types likely to house
students, transients, or the elderly. DeSalvo was often familiar with these
places from his travels throughout the city as his maintenance position for
a construction company required him to work at different sites. He conned
his way into a victim's apartment by pretending to be the building plumber.
DeSalvo was really a poacher who did not search for victims close to home.
The body dump and encounter sites in his crimes are equivalent.

A Medical-Psychiatric Committee mistakenly profiled his crimes as the
product of two separate individuals, in part because DeSalvo altered his
choice of victims, first killing elderly women and then younger females. His
final victim, killed on January 4, 1964, was left with a card reading "Happy
New Year" by her feet. DeSalvo then returned to sexual assaults and was

eventually arrested and jailed for rape. While confined to the state psychiatric hospital he confessed to, but was never tried for, the Boston stranglings. He died in 1973 after being stabbed during a prison fight.

9.2.3.3   Clifford Olson

From November 1980 to July 1981, 11 children disappeared from the Greater Vancouver area of British Columbia (Alston, 1994; Bayless, 1982; Ferry & Inwood, 1982; Mulgrew, 1990; Olson, 1989, 1992a, 1992b; Worthington, 1993). The remains of most victims were not discovered until Clifford Robert Olson confessed to their murders after his arrest by an RCMP surveillance team. Olson, 41, was a petty but chronic offender who spent only four years of his adult life out of prison. When he began his murder orgy he was free on bail for sex and firearms charges, and was wanted for child abuse charges in Nova Scotia, though the warrant was not enforceable outside that province (see Rossmo, 1987). He learned his future M.O. while in the B.C. Penitentiary from the letters and maps of fellow convict Gary Francis Marcoux, a brutal rapist and child killer.

Olson, a veteran con man, picked up victims from suburban shopping malls, arcades, and bus stops, luring them into his car with flashy business cards and promises of employment. Some he let go, others he murdered. His victims were of both sexes and ranged in age from 9 to 18 years; Olson's primary selection criterion appeared to be victim vulnerability. He drove extensively in his hunt for prey and once put 5569 kilometres on a rental car in just two weeks of July 1981.

Olson moved early in the murder series and his second residence was his main anchor point. Not only did he reside there for most of the murders, but he had lived in that particular neighbourhood several times in the past. It appears that Olson had two mental maps, one used in the search for victims, the other in his choice of dump sites. The first of these was local and centred on his residence and surrounding neighbourhood, while the second was regional and focused on Agassiz Mountain Prison. The body dump site area is much larger than the victim encounter site area. Olson was willing to travel greater distances to dispose of victims than to search for them; the former was an infrequent and risky event, the latter common and relatively safe.

One of the most controversial aspects of the case was the agreement by the Attorney General of British Columbia to pay Olson $100,000 in exchange for information about the locations of his victims' burial sites. Though this "cash-for-bodies" deal generated considerable reaction at the time, the resulting evidence was necessary in order to convict Olson of the multiple homicides. Sentenced to life imprisonment on 11 counts of first-degree murder, Olson still ranks as Canada's most prolific serial killer. He unsuccessfully

applied for a judicial review in 1996 under s. 745 of the *Criminal Code* of
Canada.

9.2.3.4   Angelo Buono and Kenneth Bianchi

The Hillside Stranglers, Angelo Buono and Kenneth Bianchi, were cousins
who ran a part-time prostitution ring (Gates & Shah, 1992; Levin & Fox,
1985; Newton, 1990a; Newton & Swoope, 1987; O'Brien, 1985; Schwarz,
1981; Time-Life, 1993; Wolf & Mader, 1986). When that enterprise failed
they impersonated police officers and picked up women from the streets of
Los Angeles to bring back to Buono's automobile upholstery shop-cum-
residence. There the victims were sexually assaulted and tortured before being
murdered. Their bodies were later dumped on the hillsides of the San Gabriel
Range.

These dump sites were chosen by Angelo Buono, the more dominant of
the two killers. He had grown up in the suburb of Glendale and knew the
Los Angeles area well, unlike Bianchi who was raised in Rochester, New York.
The crime locations produced a connected geographic pattern that was subsequently linked to Buono's home, and this fact was presented as corrobo-
rating evidence by the prosecution during trial. "The Stranglers were taking
advantage of the freeways, covering far more territory than would have been
possible in, say, New York or Boston, sketching the arterial form of the city
in the geographical pattern of their abductions and dumpings" (O'Brien,
1985, p. 179).

Buono and Bianchi murdered a total of 10 women from 1977 to 1978,
before they separated and Bianchi moved to the state of Washington. There
he killed two more women in January 1979, and was arrested by Bellingham
Police who subsequently made the connection between their case and the
Hillside Stranglings. Bianchi at first pretended to suffer from multiple personality disorder, and his alter ego "Steve" claimed responsibility for the
murders. When this ruse was unsuccessful, he testified against his cousin,
and after the longest trial in California history, both killers were sentenced
to life imprisonment.

9.2.3.5   Peter Sutcliffe

In the 5 years from 1975 to 1980, the Yorkshire Ripper attacked 20 women
in Northern England, murdering 13 of them (Burn, 1984; Doney, 1990;
James, 1992; Jones, 1989; "The killing ground," 1981; Kind, 1987a, 1987b;
Newton, 1990a; Nicholson, 1979; Time-Life, 1993). Like Jack the Ripper, his
namesake of a century past, Peter Sutcliffe sought out victims from the
prostitutes who worked the streets and bars of red-light districts. He attacked
these women in a frenzied fury with a claw hammer or sharpened screwdriver.

The Ripper Inquiry was the largest manhunt in British history, consuming enormous police resources and costing millions of dollars. Ironically, Sutcliffe was interviewed by detectives at least nine different times, a connection lost in the 24 tons of paper records generated by the investigation. When police presence became too great in the red-light districts of West Yorkshire, Sutcliffe responded by hunting in other cities and targeting women who did not work the streets. Because of his choice of victim, the target backcloth for these crimes was not uniform. Body dump and encounter sites are close to equivalent. Sutcliffe moved residence halfway through the murder series.

He was eventually arrested while parked with a prostitute in Sheffield by two patrol officers who found his murder weapons. Sutcliffe confessed and claimed to be acting on orders from God whose voice he heard originating from a gravestone. This led to considerable debate amongst psychiatrists over whether Sutcliffe was a paranoid schizophrenic or a sexual sadist. One doctor assessed him as an extremely dangerous person, and conjectured that the best forensic hospitalization could hope to accomplish was to turn him into just a dangerous one. Sutcliffe's own explanation to his brother for his murderous actions was that he was only cleaning up the streets. The case of *Regina v. Sutcliffe* in the Old Bailey resulted in 13 majority verdicts of guilty, and a life sentence without hope of parole for 30 years.

9.2.3.6 *Richard Ramirez*

Greater Los Angeles was terrorized for over a year by the Night Stalker, 25-year-old Richard Leyva Ramirez (Allen, 1993; Linedecker, 1991; Lyman, 1993; Newton, 1990a; Time-Life, 1992b). From 1984 to 1985 he murdered at least 15 people, tried to kill 8 others, and sexually assaulted another 10. His preferred M.O. involved shooting his victims in the head, but he also slashed their throats and brutally beat them.

An unemployed skid road habitué, he hunted at night in the middle-class, suburban neighbourhoods of the San Gabriel and San Fernando Valleys, breaking into the homes of his sleeping victims. For some unknown reason Ramirez seemed to target single-storey houses painted in light, pastel colours (usually white, yellow, or beige), typically located near freeway off-ramps.[52] Body dump and encounter sites are equivalent in this case. Several of the crime sites involved two victims, one of which occurred in San Francisco.

The Night Stalker was identified through old-fashioned witness observation and good patrol work, combined with state-of-the-art fingerprint technology involving cyanoacrylate resin fuming, laser enhancement, and a

---

[52] The Night Stalker's selection of targets close to freeway exits could be the result of opportunism (the first suitable houses encountered), or tactical considerations (proximity to escape routes). It might also be argued that little of the Los Angeles metropolitan area is any significant distance from a freeway.

computerized digital image search system. Ramirez was finally apprehended after a lengthy chase through the East Los Angeles barrio by citizens who recognized his mug shot from the newspaper.

Claiming to be a follower of Satan, he raved to the courtroom after his guilty verdict: "You don't understand me. You are not expected to. You are not capable of it" (Linedecker, 1991, p. 287). Some experts described Ramirez's crimes as simply pure evil. He himself stated he had "no morals, no scruples, no conscience." Ramirez was sentenced to the gas chamber, and now has a fan club of devoted Night Stalker "groupies" who regularly visit him on San Quentin's death row.

9.2.3.7 David Berkowitz

From the summer of 1976 to the summer of 1977, David Berkowitz shot 10 victims with a .44-calibre revolver, killing 6 of them (Carpozi, 1977; Lane & Gregg, 1992; "Murder and attempted murders," 1977; Newton, 1990a; Terry, 1987; Time-Life Books, 1992b). Known as the Son of Sam from a phrase in one of the taunting letters he sent to police and New York tabloids, Berkowitz later claimed to be obeying the murderous orders of a demon, manifested in the form of a dog belonging to his neighbour, Sam Carr.

Berkowitz hunted almost nightly through the New York boroughs of Queens, Brooklyn, and the Bronx, often returning to scenes of his former crimes. He sought out couples in parked cars, apparently attracted to women with long, dark, wavy hair. In a message left for police at one of the shooting sites, he wrote, "I love to hunt. Prowling the streets looking for fair game — tasty meat. The wemon of Queens are z prettyist of all. I must be the water they drink. I live for the hunt — my life. Blood for Papa...." (Terry, 1987, p. 55, uncorrected quote).

Body dump and encounter sites are equivalent in this case. Several of the crime sites involved two victims. After his first two attacks, Berkowitz moved from the Bronx to Yonkers, an address situated outside of his hunting area. At that point he became a poacher, commuting into the boroughs of New York City to commit his shootings. Berkowitz grew up in the Bronx, however, and it appears that his victim searches were based on the mental map he developed during that time.

Acting on information from a witness who saw the killer remove a summons from his illegally parked Ford Galaxie sedan shortly following the last shooting, police arrested Berkowitz at his Yonkers home. He pled guilty after being found sane. In 1979, while serving his murder sentence in Attica Prison, Berkowitz admitted he concocted the Son of Sam story, though some psychiatrists remain dubious about this recantation. Controversy remains over whether or not Berkowitz was a paranoid schizophrenic who suffered from delusions, but no one can deny his self-diagnosis. During his pretrial evaluation, Berkowitz drew a sketch of a jailed man surrounded by numerous walls. At the bottom he wrote, in classic understatement, "I am not well. Not at all" (Time-Life, 1992b, p. 183).

9.2.3.8   Jeffrey Dahmer

The infamous Jeffrey Dahmer admitted to police after his arrest that he murdered 17 men from 1978 to 1991 (Dahmer, 1994; Dvorchak & Holewa, 1991; Masters, 1993; Norris, 1992b). All but the first of his victims were killed in the four-year period from 1987 to 1991 while Dahmer worked night shift as a mixer for the Ambrosia Chocolate Company. Unlike many serial murderers, Dahmer did not own a vehicle and usually travelled by bus or taxi.

Dahmer typically preyed upon homosexual men he picked up in the gay bars along South 2nd Street in Milwaukee, Wisconsin. They were taken back to his place, drugged, and strangled. Dahmer then engaged in necrophilia, mutilation, and cannibalism. The corpses were dismembered and decapitated, and the body parts stored in the kitchen refrigerator or a 57-gallon barrel. Because earlier attempts to create zombies from his victims by drilling holes in their heads and pouring acid inside failed, Dahmer began to boil the flesh from their skulls in a plan to create an elaborate shrine of death.

Dahmer's first murder took place at his childhood home in Ohio. The next three murders occurred while he was living with his grandmother in West Allis, a suburb of Milwaukee. He then moved out on his own to first one, and then a second apartment building in Milwaukee. With the exception of the fifth murder, the rest of the killings happened in his second apartment. As Dahmer picked up most of his victims from gay bars, the target backcloth was nonuniform. Two of his victims were encountered in Chicago. Dahmer was an ambusher and the bodies of his victims were kept in his apartment.

When one of his prospective victims escaped, police discovered the hideous remains inside Dahmer's apartment and arrested him. He subsequently confessed. Determined by the court to be sane (in the legal sense), and found guilty of 16 counts of murder, Dahmer received the mandatory sentence of life imprisonment. The judge consecutively structured Dahmer's parole eligibility so as to forever prevent his release, but ultimately it did not matter. In November 1994, Dahmer was beaten to death by a fellow inmate in the maximum-security Columbia Correctional Institution.

9.2.3.9   Joel Rifkin

Joel Rifkin murdered New York street prostitutes, soliciting them in Lower Manhattan, strangling them, and then disposing of their remains in isolated locations (Eftimiades, 1993; Pulitzer & Swirsky, 1994a, 1994b). From 1989 to 1993, he killed at least 17 times. Rifkin had very specific victim selection criteria, preferring women who reminded him of the high school girls he knew during the 1970s. His murdered victims were dumped, often in 55-gallon oil drums, over a vast area that included Long Island, the rivers of New York City, New Jersey, and upstate New York. For the most part police did not connect the deaths and disappearances of Rifkin's victims, partly because of the high-risk nature of their occupations, and partly because of his method of body disposal.

Rifkin commuted from Long Island into New York City where he picked up his prostitute victims. The target backcloth for his encounter sites was nonuniform as was, to a lesser extent, that for his body dump sites. The former was constrained by the location of the red-light strolls, and the latter by the geography of the coastline and the degree of urban development.

Rifkin was arrested after a police chase that began when state troopers tried to stop him when they noticed his vehicle did not have a licence plate. They then discovered the decomposing body of his last victim under a tarpaulin in the rear of his pickup truck. During subsequent police interviews, he confessed to a total of 17 murders. Rifkin was found guilty after an unsuccessful insanity defence and sentenced to 25 years-to-life imprisonment. While in jail he wrote, "The Catch 22 of life, if you know you're crazy, then you're not" (Pulitzer & Swirsky, 1994b, p. 300).

9.2.3.10 John Collins

John Norman Collins preyed on coeds near the Eastern Michigan University (EMU) in Ypsilanti and was responsible for the Michigan Murders from 1967 to 1969 (James, 1991; Keyes, 1976; Lane & Gregg, 1992; Newton, 1990a). A senior EMU student himself, Collins worked one summer in the administration building and lived at the Theta Chi fraternity house close to campus. This lifestyle made him familiar with both his hunting grounds and potential victims.

Collins was fascinated by the novel *Crime and Punishment*, and once wrote in an English essay, "It's not society's judgment that's important, but the individual's own choice of will and intellect" (Keyes, 1976, p. 249). This was a paraphrase of Dostoevsky's student murderer Raskolnikov who believed that some men have an absolute right to commit wicked and criminal acts.

Collins picked up hitchhiking female students, then sexually assaulted and strangled, shot, stabbed, or beat them. Their decomposed bodies were found dumped on the outskirts of Ypsilanti and neighbouring Ann Arbor. He is believed responsible for a total of eight murders. Eastern Michigan University was Collins' primary anchor point. The target backcloth for his body dump sites was nonuniform as Collins chose isolated areas in which to dispose of his victims (the area north of EMU was largely undeveloped land). He committed one murder while on vacation in California.

Suspicions about Collins were confirmed through crime scene forensics after he strangled his last victim in the home of his uncle, a Michigan state trooper. On August 19, 1970, the jury returned with a verdict of guilty and

Collins was sentenced to confinement and hard labour for life in the Southern Michigan State Prison. Obviously, he was not one of those men who stood outside the law.

9.2.3.11 Aileen Wuornos

Aileen Wuornos murdered seven men across central Florida in under 12 months (Epstein, 1992; Kennedy, 1994; Lane & Gregg, 1992; Reynolds, 1992; Scott, 1992). While she has been incorrectly called the first female serial killer, Wuornos was one of the few such women who hunted her murder victims in a predatory fashion (Fox & Levin, 1994; Kelleher & Kelleher, 1998; Scott). A roadside prostitute of no fixed address, she hitchhiked from the Florida interstate entrances and truck stops in an effort to find customers. From November 1989 to November 1990, some of these men became her victims. They were shot and robbed, then their bodies and vehicles dumped in various locations over a vast area that stretched from the Atlantic Ocean to the Gulf of Mexico.

The exact locations of her victim encounter and murder sites are not known. Wuornos was nomadic and lived in different motels in various cities, but she appeared to have an anchor point located in Wildwood, Florida. It was from the I-75 truck stop here that she hitchhiked and picked up many of her clients.

After her arrest Wuornos argued self-defence, claiming that each of her seven victims had tried to rape her. She asserted her innocence, emphasizing that she was not a serial killer, only someone who had killed a series of men. Considered a compulsive liar, Wuornos was diagnosed with both borderline and antisocial personality disorders. Following a rather histrionic trial, the jury found Aileen Wuornos guilty of murder and sentenced her to death in the electric chair.

9.2.3.12 Ian Brady and Myra Hindley

The Moors Murderers, Ian Brady and Myra Hindley, hunted their victims in the Manchester area of England from 1963 to 1965 (Harrison, 1987; Williams, 1967). Brady converted Hindley to his neo-Nazi world view and involved her in a life of sexual sadism, pornography, and petty crime. The two lovers eventually turned to murder, killing five people, all children or teenagers. Brady and Hindley buried the bodies of their victims on Saddleworth Moor about an hour's drive east of the city, thereby earning the pair their infamous nickname. They moved to an outlying estate during the murder series, and for their last two crimes commuted into Manchester to search for victims.

Police found the corpse of the last victim in a back bedroom of the house where Brady and Hindley lived after receiving a tip from the latter's brother-in-law who witnessed the attack the night before. Extensive digging on the moors uncovered three of the victims' remains, though the body of the remaining victim has never been found. Brady was found guilty of three murders and Hindley of two. The killers escaped death twice: first when police discovered a plan by one of the victim's uncles to shoot them during the trial, and again when *The Murder (Abolition of Death Penalty) Act 1965* was passed a month after their arrest.

9.2.3.13 Jerry Brudos

Jerry Brudos, the Lust Killer, murdered at least four women in western Oregon from 1968 to 1969 (Lane & Gregg, 1992; Newton, 1990a; Rule, 1983a, Time-Life, 1992b). After strangling them, he mutilated their bodies in the garage beside his house before dumping their corpses, weighed down with automotive parts, in local rivers. His family was forbidden from entering the locked garage. After the first murder, Brudos moved from Portland to Salem. He used one of his dump sites twice.

Brudos had a shoe fetish and was attracted to some of his victims because of their footwear. He possessed a collection of 40 pairs of high-heeled shoes and often broke into homes to steal shoes or lingerie. Brudos liked to dress up and photograph the corpses of his victims. He amputated the foot of his first victim and stored it, shod, in the freezer.

Arrested after a tip from a suspicious college student whom he had dated, Brudos eventually confessed to police investigators. A search of his home revealed, amongst other bizarre souvenirs of the crimes, disturbing photographs of his captive victims. Brudos pled guilty and was sentenced to three consecutive life sentences. Incarcerated in the Oregon State Penitentiary, he became eligible for parole in 1999.

9.4 Serial Murder Characteristics

9.4.1 Offenders

A breakdown of the characteristics for the 15 offenders in the SFU serial murder data set is provided in Table 9.4. Percentages and frequencies, or means, are used as appropriate. This is a summary of the information collected in the *Data Coding Form #1: Serial Killers* (see Appendix B for the data coding form). Co-killer information is also presented indicating whether a serial murderer operated alone or with a partner.

Of the various serial murderer classifications discussed in the literature, only the FBI organized/disorganized dichotomy and the Holmes and De Burger typology are examined in the present research. The former was included because degree of organization influences offender activity space, and the latter because it is a commonly used typology.

Table 9.4   Serial Murder Offender Data

Characteristic	Results
Sex	
Male	87% (13)
Female	13% (2)
Co-Killer	
Operated Alone	73% (11)
Operated With Partner	27% (4)
Mean Total Number of Victims	12
Mean Total Number of Locations	23
Mean Duration of Murder Activity	2.7 years
Degree of Organization	
Organized	47% (7)
Somewhat Organized	20% (3)
Mixed	20% (3)
Somewhat Disorganized	7% (1)
Disorganized	7% (1)
Typology	
Visionary	20% (3)
Mission-Oriented	0% (0)
Lust	13% (2)
Thrill	13% (2)
Comfort	7% (1)
Power/Control-Oriented	47 % (7)
Residence Type	
Detached House	53% (8)
Semi-Detached House	0% (0)
Apartment	33% (5)
Hotel or Motel	7% (1)
Rooming or Lodging House	0% (0)
Trailer	0% (0)
Institution	0% (0)
Transient	7% (1)
Homeless	0% (0)

The mean values for total number of victims, total number of locations, and duration of murder activity are case, not offender, based. There was an average of 1.9 crime locations per victim in the sample. A lone offender was involved 85% of the time. Table 9.4 reveals no significant differences on these variables from the larger serial killer data set (see Table 9.2). Most of the offenders fit the power/control-oriented serial murder type. Mean level of organization was 2.1 (somewhat organized), assuming an interval coding scale. Detached house and apartment building were the most common offender residence types.

9.4.2 Victims

A breakdown of the characteristics for the 178 victims in the SFU serial murder data set is provided in Table 9.5. Percentages and frequencies, or means, are used as appropriate (percentages may add to more than 100 because of multiple responses). This is a summary of the information collected in the *Data Coding Form #2: Serial Murder Victims* (see Appendix B for the data coding form). Information is also presented on crime type (murder, attempted murder, rape, or other sexual assault, coded as the most serious offence), and secondary victim status (yes/same incident, yes/same day, or no). The latter field is used to distinguish cases of multiple victims, either murdered in the same incident, or else on the same day. Crime location set data is presented and discussed below.

Table 9.5   Serial Murder Victim Data

Characteristic	Results
Crime Type	
Murder	75.3% (134)
Attempted Murder	16.9% (30)
Rape	5.1% (9)
Other Sexual Assault	2.8% (5)
Secondary Victim	
Yes — Same Incident	12.9% (23)
Yes — Same Day	4.5% (8)
No	82.6% (147)
Sex of Victim	
Male	27.5% (49)
Female	72.5% (129)
Victim/Killer Relationship	
Stranger	93.8% (167)
Casual Acquaintance	6.2% (11)
Known	0% (0)
Killer Selection	
Nonrandom/Patterned	74.7% (133)
Random/Nonpatterned	25.3% (45)
Victim Traits	
Specific	47.8% (85)
Nonspecific	52.2% (93)

Table 9.5 Serial Murder Victim Data (continued)

Characteristic	Results
Victim Activity	
At Home	30.9% (55)
At Work	1.1% (2)
Commuting	6.2% (11)
Walking or Jogging	21.9% (39)
Hitchhiking	5.1% (9)
Other Travel	12.4% (22)
Visiting Friend	2.2% (4)
Outdoor Recreation	0% (0)
At Bar or Nightclub	10.7% (19)
At Other Social Event	5.1% (9)
Prostitution	22.5% (40)
Other	8.4% (15)
Killer Hunting Style — Search Method	
Hunter	31.6% (49)
Poacher	54.8% (85)
Troller	11.6% (18)
Trapper	1.9% (3)
Killer Hunting Style — Attack Method	
Raptor	78.7% (122)
Stalker	0% (0)
Ambusher	21.3% (33)
Control Method	
Firearm	6.7% (12)
Knife	3.4% (6)
Blunt Instrument	2.8% (5)
Strangulation	0.6% (1)
Physical Force	18.5% (33)
Intoxicant	16.9% (30)
Threat	6.2% (11)
Blitz Attack (Victim Immediately Killed)	51.1% (91)
Unknown	6.7% (12)
Murder Method	
Firearm	25.8% (46)
Knife	16.9% (30)
Blunt Instrument	21.3% (38)
Strangulation	37.6% (67)
Physical Force	2.2% (4)
Poison	0.6% (1)
Other	0.6% (1)
Unknown	3.9% (7)
No Murder Attempt	9% (16)

Table 9.5   Serial Murder Victim Data (continued)

Characteristic	Results
Attempt to Hide Body	
Displayed	7.3% (13)
Dumped	10.7% (19)
Other Not Hidden	34.3% (61)
Casually Hidden	10.1% (18)
Well Hidden	25.3% (45)
Other	12.4% (22)
Linked	
Linked	72.3% (112)
Unlinked	27.8% (43)

Percentages for hunting style/search method, hunting style/attack method, offender approach, and victim linkage are based on the 155 crimes not involving same-incident secondary victims. Cases classified as "other" for attempt to hide body typically involved escape of the victim. Almost three quarters of the victims in this sample were linked to the murder series at the time by police. Cases not connected usually involved the failure to recognize the existence of a serial killer rather than the inability to match a specific victim with a known series. If unrecognized offenders are not included, the percentage of linked crimes increases to 96%.

Cleary and Rettig (1994) suggest that stranger victims of serial killers are not randomly selected, but instead fit into a particular agenda known to the murderer. Similarly, Warren et al. (1995) observe that "serial rapists do not manifest random patterns when geographically choreographing their offenses" (p. 247). Three-quarters of the victim selections in this study were classified as nonrandom or patterned, and almost half of the victims possessed specific traits of interest to the offender. It would appear the "randomness" ascribed to serial murder refers more to its stranger nature (94% in this sample) than to any mathematical description of sampling process (i.e., method of victim selection).

Most of the victims were sought out by the offender either through poaching or hunting search methods. The former characteristic was originally thought to make a case unsuitable for geographic profiling. It appears, however, if criminals commute, they often do so in various directions. There is a substantial likelihood after a sufficient number of crimes that the offender's residence will be located within the hunting area. The findings of this study support the suggestion of Davies and Dale (1995b) that marauding (hunting) and commuting (poaching) are only ends of a continuum.

The raptor approach was the most common attack method. Ambushes were primarily associated with either hunting or poaching search behaviour. There were no instances of victims being stalked (as defined in the hunting typology) prior to attack,[53] despite commentary that serial and lust killers often engage in elaborate stalking as part of their careful, pre-crime planning (Holmes, 1991; Norris, 1988). Keeney and Heide (1994c) found little evidence of stalking behaviour on the part of female serial murderers, though over one third of the women in their study aggressively procured or lured victims.

Multiple responses were allowed for victim activity, and 225 actions were recorded. Disturbingly, almost one-third of the victims in this sample were attacked within their homes.[54] Other common activities included walking or jogging, and prostitution. Not quite three quarters of the victims were females. Multiple responses were allowed for control and murder methods, and 201 and 210 responses, respectively, were recorded. Over half of the victims were controlled through an immediate and deadly blitz attack. Strangulation was the preferred method of murder. Only one-quarter of the victims' bodies were well hidden by the killer.

9.4.3 Locations

A breakdown of characteristics for the 347 crime locations in the data set is given in Table 9.6. Percentages and frequencies, or means, are used as appropriate.[55] This is a summary of the information collected in the *Data Coding Form #3: Serial Murder Locations* (see Appendix B for the data coding form). Information regarding offence weekday and distance from offender residence to crime site (measured on a Manhattan metric) is also presented.

The crime location type counts are based on all 347 offence locations. The rest of Table 9.6 is based on 320 crime locations (those sites connected to same-incident secondary victims were excluded). Day of week is determined only from the encounter site dates. The other characteristics are presented for victim encounter sites, body dump sites, and all sites. For this purpose, the following crime locations types are classified as victim encounter sites (a total of 155 locations): (1) encounter; (2) encounter/attack; (3) encounter/attack/murder; and (4) encounter/attack/murder/body dump. The following crime locations types are classified as body dump sites (a total

---

[53] Stalking behaviour has been observed in cases of serial rape. The determination of victim routine activity overlaps to identify common ground or "fishing holes" used by the offender is a viable line of police inquiry.

[54] Schlesinger and Revitch (1999) found 53.7% of the sexual homicide victims (n=106) they examined were murdered within their residence. In the FBI rape study, 64% of the encounter sites were at the victim's home or workplace, and 70% were indoors (Warren et al., 1995); only 15% of the crimes involved transportation. Offenders who primarily raped indoors tended to be more selective in choice of victim.

[55] Percentages may add to more than 100 because of multiple responses.

Table 9.6   Serial Murder Location Data

Characteristic	Results		
Crime Location Type			
Encounter Site	27.7% (96)		
Encounter/Attack Site	2.3% (8)		
Encounter/Attack/Murder Site	1.4% (5)		
Encounter/Attack/Murder/Body Dump Site	19.9% (69)		
Attack Site	1.7% (6)		
Attack/Murder Site	11.0% (38)		
Attack/Murder/Body Dump Site	15.0% (52)		
Murder Site	2.6% (9)		
Murder/Body Dump Site	1.4% (5)		
Body Dump Site	13.5% (47)		
Body Dump/Vehicle Drop Site	0.9% (3)		
Vehicle Drop Site	2.3% (8)		
Found Evidence Site	0.3% (1)		
Day of Week	**Encounter Sites**		
Monday	12.9% (20)		
Tuesday	10.3% (16)		
Wednesday	8.4% (13)		
Thursday	16.8% (26)		
Friday	7.7% (12)		
Saturday	16.1% (25)		
Sunday	23.2% (36)		
Unknown	4.5% (7)		
Distance to Crime Site	**Encounter**	**Body Dump**	**All Sites**
Number of Crimes Sites	155	104	320
Mean Distance	21.8 km	33.7 km	25.8 km
0 Kilometres	1.3% (2)	16.3% (17)	11.9% (38)
0.1 — 1.0 kilometres	7.1% (11)	1.0% (1)	4.4% (14)
1.1 — 5.0 kilometres	14.8% (23)	2.9% (3)	8.8% (28)
5.1 — 10.0 kilometres	11.6% (18)	13.5% (14)	10.3% (33)
10.1 — 15.0 kilometres	15.5% (24)	5.8% (6)	9.4% (30)
15.1 — 20.0 kilometres	4.5% (7)	4.8% (5)	4.4% (14)
20.1 — 50.0 kilometres	34.2% (53)	29.8% (31)	29.1% (93)
Over 50 kilometres	5.2% (8)	20.2% (21)	10.6% (34)
Unknown	5.8% (9)	5.8% (6)	11.3% (36)
Crime Location Known to Police	**Encounter**	**Body Dump**	**All Sites**
Yes	70.3% (109)	67.3% (70)	60.9% (195)
No	29.7% (46)	32.7% (34)	39.1% (125)

Table 9.6   Serial Murder Location Data (continued)

Area Land Use	Encounter	Body Dump	All Sites
Residential	45.8% (71)	45.2% (47)	45% (144)
Commercial	43.2% (67)	3.8% (4)	24.4% (78)
Industrial	0% (0)	5.8% (6)	3.4% (11)
Institutional	3.2% (5)	1.0% (1)	1.9% (6)
Park	1.3% (2)	5.8% (6)	2.5% (8)
Rural or Agricultural	0.6% (1)	12.5% (13)	5.3% (17)
Wilderness or Uninhabited	1.3% (2)	21.2% (22)	9.1% (29)
Unknown	4.5% (7)	4.8% (5)	8.4% (27)

Site Description	Encounter	Body Dump	All Sites
Residence	29% (45)	17.3% (18)	27.2% (87)
Hotel or Motel	0.6% (1)	0% (0)	1.3% (4)
Public Building	1.3% (2)	0% (0)	0.6% (2)
School or Educational	0.6% (1)	0% (0)	0.3% (1)
Business or Shopping Site	11% (17)	1.0% (1)	7.8% (25)
Entertainment Site	5.8% (9)	0% (0)	2.8% (9)
Red-Light Zone	23.2% (36)	0% (0)	11.3% (36)
Vehicle	6.5% (10)	5.8% (6)	11.6% (37)
Public Transportation	10.3% (16)	1.0% (1)	5.3% (17)
Private Yard	1.3% (2)	5.8% (6)	2.5% (8)
Parking Lot	3.9% (6)	2.9% (3)	3.4% (11)
Street or Sidewalk	51% (79)	16.3% (17)	34.7% (111)
Alley, Lane, Pathway, or Trail	0.6% (1)	11.5% (12)	5.3% (17)
Highway or Ditch	5.8% (9)	3.8% (4)	5.6% (18)
Park	1.9% (3)	6.7% (7)	3.1% (10)
Farm, Field, or Open Area	0% (0)	11.5% (12)	4.1% (13)
River, Lake, or Marsh	0% (0)	20.2% (21)	7.2% (23)
Forest or Woods	0.6% (1)	21.2% (22)	8.4% (27)
Hills or Mountains	0% (0)	4.8% (5)	1.6% (5)
Desert or Wasteland	0% (0)	3.8% (4)	1.3% (4)
Other	0% (0)	4.8% (5)	2.5% (8)
Unknown	0% (0)	0% (0)	0.9% (3)

Site Classification	Encounter	Body Dump	All Sites
Inside Private	27.7% (43)	15.4% (16)	27.2% (87)
Inside Semi-Public	7.1% (11)	0% (0)	3.4% (11)
Inside Public	2.6% (4)	0% (0)	1.3% (4)
Outside Private	1.3% (2)	3.8% (4)	2.2% (7)
Outside Semi-Public	0% (0)	6.7% (7)	2.5% (8)
Outside Public	61.3% (95)	73.1% (76)	62.5% (200)
Unknown	0% (0)	1.0% (1)	0.9% (3)

Table 9.6   Serial Murder Location Data (continued)

Killer Travel Method	Encounter	Body Dump	All Sites
Vehicle	81.9% (127)	78.8% (82)	83.4% (267)
Public Transportation	8.4% (13)	6.7% (7)	7.2% (23)
On Foot	7.7% (12)	13.5% (14)	8.1% (26)
Other	1.3% (2)	0% (0)	0.6% (2)
Unknown	0.6% (1)	1.0% (1)	0.6% (2)
Victim or Killer Residence	Encounter	Body Dump	All Sites
Killer Residence	1.3% (2)	16.3% (17)	11.9% (38)
Victim Residence	25.2% (39)	1.9% (2)	12.8% (41)
Both	0% (0)	0% (0)	0% (0)
Neither	73.5% (114)	81.7% (85)	74.1% (237)
Unknown	0% (0)	0% (0)	1.3% (4)

of 104 locations): (1) attack/murder/body dump; (2) murder/body dump; (3) body dump; and (4) body dump/vehicle drop.

Figure 9.3 shows serial murder incidents by day of week (based on encounter site date). Almost 40% of the cases occurred on the weekend as evidenced by the Saturday/Sunday bulge in the radar chart. Consistent with the routine activity approach, this finding is explained both by the greater opportunity an offender has to hunt during the weekend, and by the increased availability of victims.[56]

The valid percentages of cases falling into various distance-to-crime site ranges are shown in Figure 9.4.[57] Excluding those cases where the offender kept the victim's remains at home, body dump sites tend to be located further than victim encounter sites from the killer's residence. This is probably the result of two factors. First, it appears that victim search activity occurs frequently while body disposal happens infrequently (see the case synopsis for Clifford Olson, for example). Second, optimal body disposal sites are often situated in uninhabited regions located some distance from urban areas.

The mean distance ratio between body dump and encounter sites is 11.6 (standard deviation = 25.9).[58] Ratios less than one usually involve incidents in which an attempt was made to hide the body. There is some relationship between this ratio and the distance from offender residence to encounter site. If the latter is less than 1.0 kilometres, then the mean distance ratio is 26.0;

[56] Warren et al. (1995) found no difference in serial rape occurrence by day of week, but did observe larger hunting areas associated to weekend offenders. Such a result is consistent with the greater victim search opportunities available to employed offenders on Saturdays and Sundays.
[57] Outliers were excluded.
[58] A crime was excluded if either the victim encounter or body dump occured at the offender's residence.

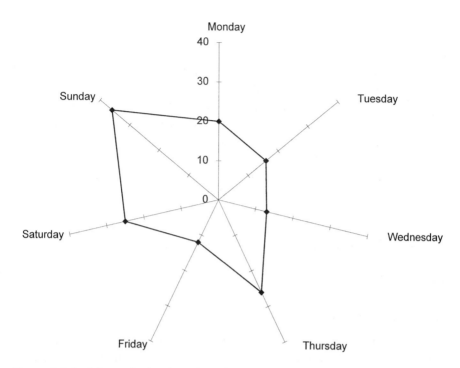

Figure 9.3 Serial murder by day of week.

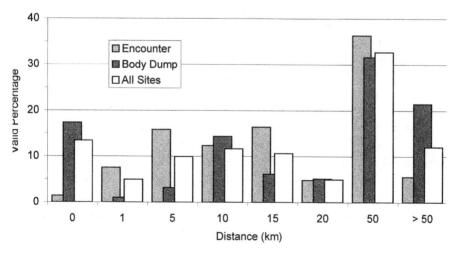

Figure 9.4   Distance to crime site.

otherwise it drops to 1.6. This appears to suggest a desire on the part of offenders to distance the remains of victims encountered relatively close to home.

While only 61% of all sites were known to police, this figure increased to 67% for body dump sites and 70% for encounter sites. These two location types are the most important in geographic profiling, and it is usually suffi- cient to know one or the other for the purposes of a criminal geographic targeting analysis (see Table 10.7). Approximately 12% of the crime sites were within the killer's residence. Such locations are likely unknown to police.

Multiple responses were allowed for site description, and 238 encounter site types, 144 body dump site types, and 476 total site types were recorded. Streets and residences are the most common crime locations. The "other" classification typically refers to deserted lots or waste ground. Residential and commercial land use predominated. The majority of incidents occurred in outside public places, followed by inside private places. Serial murderers prefer to travel by vehicle.

9.4.4   Crime Parsing

A crime is often treated as having a single location, but depending upon crime type there may be various sites connected to a single offence. These have different meanings to the offender and, consequently, distinctive choice prop- erties. For serial murder these location types include victim encounter, attack, murder, and body dump sites. For serial rape they include victim encounter, attack, rape, and victim release sites. Serial arson normally involves only one location, the fire setting site. While these particular actions can all occur in a single place, the majority of cases involve two or more locations.

Eight possible combinations, called crime location sets, result from the four different murder site types. Breaking an offence down into its crime location set is referred to as crime parsing. While the specific location set for a given crime is a function of victim selection and encounter site character- istics, it also implies something about the offender's mobility, search strategy, and level of organization. Generally, the greater the organization and mobility of an offender, the greater the potential complexity (i.e., the more separate locations) of the crime location set.

Table 9.7 presents the percentage breakdown for the eight crime location sets. Movement between victim encounter (E), attack (A), murder (M), and body dump (D) sites are represented by an arrow ($\rightarrow$). For example, $EAM{\rightarrow}D$ indicates that the encounter, attack, and murder sites were in the same place, but the body dump site was in a different location.

There was a high level of geographic consistency in the M.O. of this sample as most offenders repeatedly employed the same crime location set. Approximately 85% of the total number of serial murder victims (n = 178)

Table 9.7   Crime Location Sets

Crime Location Set	Percentage	Number of Sites	Percentage
E → A → M → D	1.7%	4	1.7%
E → A → MD	1.7%	3	26.4%
E → AM → D	21.3%		
EA → M → D	3.4%		
EA → MD	1.1%	2	33.1%
E → AMD	29.2%		
EAM → D	2.8%		
EAMD	38.8%	1	38.8%
Total	100%		100%

fell into the most common crime location set used by their killer, and 96% into either the first or second most common crime location set. This implies that crime location set might be used as an assessment characteristic for the linking of serial offences.[59]

An understanding of consistency, change, and progression in offender behaviour is an important principle of linkage analysis. Warren et al. (1995) found about half of the 119 quantified behaviours they examined from serial rape crime scenes remained consistent over time. Other offender behaviours either showed progression (e.g., degree of planning, protection of identity, and use of bindings), or exhibited inconsistent change. They suggest the pathological aspects are more constant. "The idea of consistency and change represents an important area of serial crime: in theory, it helps to define relevant dimensions of classificatory paradigms, which can inform investigative efforts to link crimes perpetrated by the same offender" (p. 255). Measures of consistency and change in offender geographic behaviour assist in this effort (see, for example, Dettlinger & Prugh, 1983).

9.4.5   Clusters

Short-term spatial selectivity has been observed in the hunting behaviour of animals and certain predators repeatedly visit the same forage sites (Smith, 1974a, 1974b; Smith & Sweatman, 1974). Geotropism is also found in serial killers, many of whom return to favoured sites to hunt victims, or dispose of bodies in cluster dumps or forest "graveyards" (Newton, 1992). Beyond convenience, these private "totem places" may also be significant to the offender's fantasies.

The Yorkshire Ripper and the Son of Sam were both known to revisit the areas of their previous crimes in pursuit of new victims (Ressler & Shachtman, 1992).

> When we went to New York to talk to the 'Son of Sam,' David Berkowitz," says [FBI Special Agent] Robert K. Ressler ... "he told us that on the nights when he couldn't find a victim to kill he would go back to the scene of an old crime to relive the crime and to fantasize about it. Now that's a heck of a piece of information to store somewhere to see whether other offenders do the same thing. (Porter, 1983, pp. 49–50)

LeBeau (1985) notes "the proclivity of chronic serial offenders to use repeatedly the same geographic and ecological space ... The geographical and ecological patterning of the serial offender may be tangible information which is discerned by police investigators and utilized in apprehension" (p. 397). He determined through nearest neighbour analysis that the mean distance between crime scenes for chronic serial rapists in San Diego varied from 0.12 to 0.85 miles, averaging 0.35 miles (1986). Büchler and Leineweber (1991) observe bank robbers in Germany follow similar patterns of escape, information which may help police connect crimes. Davies and Dale (1995b) found several cases of geographic "backtracking" in their study of British rapists. They propose national access to intelligence information on former crime sites, and people and places of significance to an offender is an important investigative resource. Serial killer Monte Rissell was apprehended only after he returned to his former rape sites in Alexandria, Virginia (Ressler & Shachtman, 1992).

An analysis of the pattern of crime sites in the SFU serial murder study showed a tendency towards aggregation (59% of R scale values were smaller than 1). One of the main influences on divergence from randomness is target backcloth; not surprisingly, a lack of uniformity leads to clustering. Another factor appears to be opportunity. If an offender was successful in a particular neighbourhood once, then why not again. Other potential targets may have been noticed and remembered during the commission of the first crime. In many ways, these influences are similar to those documented in repeat victimization studies of property crime (Farrell & Pease, 1993; Pease & Laycock, 1996). Fantasy also plays a role in drawing an offender back to a particular location. A crime site situated close to a previous offence is referred to as a contagion location, and is generally regarded for the purposes of geographic profiling as a nonindependent event.

9.4.6 Trip Distance Increase

While it has been suggested individual offender crime trips increase in distance over time, there has been little empirical testing of this hypothesis. In
an attempt to see what influence, if any, time had on the journey to crime,
distances travelled by serial murderers, both individual and collective analyses
were conducted. This approach is limited, however, as any particular journey
to crime may not have originated from the offender's residence. Also, a killer
could have been responsible for unknown murders, in addition to preceding
crimes such as burglary, robbery, or sexual assault. And some offenders
moved residence in the midst of their murder series, complicating journey-
to-crime comparisons.

The Manhattan distance from offender residence to location of victim
encounter was measured for every known crime in each killer's series. Where
two or more victims were attacked during the same day, only the first crime
was counted. The offences were chronologically ordered, outliers excluded,
and significant gaps ignored. Distance from offender residence to encounter
site was plotted against crime number (see Rossmo, 1995a).

Table 9.8 summarizes these results. Half of the serial murder cases showed
a significant increase (defined as a slope with an $R^2 > 0.300$), while the other
half exhibited no significant change; none showed a significant decrease in
crime trip distance. Average journeys varied considerably by offender (ranging from 1 to 40 km), therefore slopes were compared to each killer's mean
crime trip distance. This figure represents the incremental increase in crime
trip distance expressed as a proportion of the mean crime trip distance. The
overall mean percentage increase is 16% (standard deviation = 17).

Table 9.8   Crime Trip Distance Increase

Serial Murderer	Slope	Crime Trip Distance (km)			Proportion
		Minimum	Mean	Maximum	
Mean	2.66	4.47	24.44	57.95	0.16
Standard Deviation	3.97	7.39	13.20	50.31	0.17

Figure 9.5 shows crime trip distance changes in the aggregate. Wide
variations in hunting range distort the pooled data, therefore the
unweighted mean natural logarithm of crime trip distance was plotted
against offence number. Only those cases with a minimum of five crime
trips were included in the analysis. When a linear trend line is fitted to the
data, a significant increase over time is observed ($R^2 = 0.519$). A better fit
is found, however, with a third-order polynomial expression ($R^2 = 0.880$),
as shown in Figure 9.5.

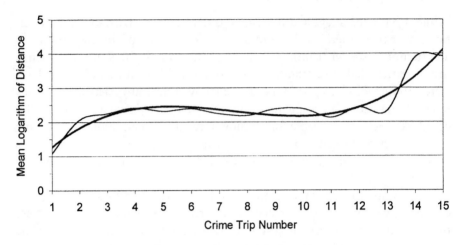

Figure 9.5   Mean logarithm of crime trip distance over time.

This raises an important issue. The above analysis assumes that increases over time in crime trip distance are linear, an assumption that may not be warranted. If journey-to-crime distance grows proportionately (e.g., if a given crime trip is, on average, 10% longer than the previous trip), then the relationship is best expressed through a power curve. Distances might also increase in steps or after significant thresholds (as suggested by Figure 9.5). Such a growth process could result from an offender first exploring directional alternatives before increasing crime trip distance. The exact nature of the relationship requires further research, preferably with larger data sets of offenders responsible for lengthier series of crimes.

The FBI maxim that the first crime in a series is the one closest to the offender's residence was tested. Of the serial murder cases in the SFU research, 50% involved at least one crime trip distance of a mile or less (Chase, Olson, Dahmer, Brady, Brudos, and Collins). First offence was closest in 41% of the cases, and distance to first crime averaged 40% of mean distance (standard deviation = 42). The FBI belief in offender residence proximity to first offence appears to be a reasonable though not universal rule, consistent with the increase of crime trip distance over time. It was found to apply in just under half of the cases.

The argument that journey-to-crime distances increase over time is based on the supposition that offenders learn from experience and increase their spatial knowledge accordingly. Warren et al. (1995) observed that serial rapists who travel greater distances appear to have longer criminal careers; they also found distance indicators to be significantly related to time between successive offences.

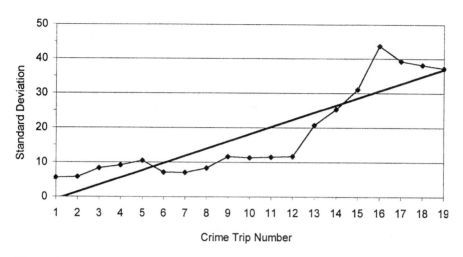

Figure 9.6   Crime trip distance mean standard deviation over time.

Expansion in hunting region, however, does not necessarily result in victims being selected exclusively from the perimeter of the search area. It does indicate that increasingly large target areas are available for the offender to hunt within. While this implies crime trip distances lengthen over time (albeit at a rate slower than the growth of the hunting area), it also suggests an increase in the variation of crime journeys. To examine this possibility, the standard deviation for crime trip distance was calculated in each serial murder case for every crime trip after the first. When the mean standard deviations for all cases are plotted against offence number (Figure 9.6), a significant increase is observed over time ($R^2 = 0.790$). This suggests that as a serial murderer's career progresses, his or her crime trips may increase in both distance and variation.

Fully half of the cases in the study, however, showed no significant increase in journey-to-crime distance over time. Indeed, the nearness and least-effort principles, and the tendency for crime locations to cluster, mitigate against expansion. Assuming learning underlies crime trip growth, why does an offender need to expand his or her spatial knowledge? The most obvious reasons include greater victim search opportunities and lowered risk of police detection. Previous crime sites become tarnished and unattractive because of the risk of increased community vigilance, as shown by the concern of child killer Westley Allan Dodd over losing his hunting ground.[60] Displacement, occasioned by police intervention or community response, was responsible on several occasions for the shift or expansion of a serial murderer's hunting area (e.g., Bianchi, Sutcliffe, Dahmer, Ramirez, and Berkowitz).

Increase in size of hunting area is most likely to occur in cases where an offender has the capability and need to learn, and will benefit from doing so. In this context, those with the capability to learn include organized mobile offenders who possess well-developed mental maps. Offenders with a need to learn include those whose hunting style, body disposal methods, or offence timing result in their crimes being linked, generating community fear and a significant police response. Offenders who benefit from learning include those who hunt close to home or prefer victim types that are available in several different areas (i.e., there is a uniform target backcloth).

The case of Joel Rifkin is a good example of an offender with little need to alter his crime trip distances, which were a consistent 37 kilometres from residence to victim encounter site. Rifkin was sane, drove an automobile, and was familiar with large areas of New York and Long Island. His victims were street prostitutes and their strangled bodies were dumped, often in steel drums, at remote sites that spanned thousands of square miles. Consequently, the murders were not linked and the police failed to realize that a serial killer was operating in their jurisdiction. Rifkin also lived a significant distance from the red-light district in Lower Manhattan where he picked up most of his victims.

---

[60] In times of short food supply, the nomadic Naskapi Indians employed scapulimancy – a technique in which a heat-cracked caribou shoulder is used as a map – to help them find game on the Labrador plateau. Anthropologists have theorized that this divination process produced effective results because of its randomizing effect, preventing grassland and tundra areas from being overhunted (Moore, 1957).

Geographic Profiling  10

10.1 Mapping and Crime Analysis

Crime mapping has become a common analytic practice in many police agencies. The capability to spatially manipulate and display offence-related data is the result of the power and availability of geographic information system (GIS) software. "GISs are automated systems for the capture, storage, retrieval, analysis, and display of spatial data" (Clarke, 1990, p. 11; see also Anderson, 1992; Garson & Biggs, 1992; Goodchild, Kemp, & Poiker, 1990a, 1990b; Miller, 1993; Tomlin, 1990; Waters, 1995a; Wendelken, 1995a). The ability to store and integrate geographic attributes and other data produces a powerful crime analysis tool.

Approximately 30% of police agencies with more than 100 officers now use computer-mapping software, and the International Association of Crime Analysts (IACA) estimates the need for GIS experts in law enforcement has grown ten-fold over the last 15 years (Waters, 1998). In a survey of 2004 U.S. police departments, 85% of respondents stated that mapping was a valuable tool and reported both increasing interest and implementation (Mamalian & La Vigne, 1999). This growth has been prompted largely by greater access to digital arrest, incident, and calls for service data. The survey found crime clustering and hot spot analyses were the most common mapping applications, and reported that mapped crimes allow comparisons with such external information as census, city planning, parks, property assessment, utility, and community data.

In 1996 the National Institute of Justice established the Crime Mapping Research Center (CMRC) to strategically support and guide this trend. According to Dr. Nancy La Vigne, Director of the CMRC, "[maps] make sense on an intuitive level. It's human nature to respond to this kind of

graphical representation. What you get is a far more sophisticated understanding of what's happening on the streets" (Waters, 1998, p. 47). This allows
patrol officers, detectives, and police managers to quickly comprehend local
crime patterns and trends. Not only is it possible to integrate a variety of
different data sources in a GIS crime map, but dimensions of both space and
time can be explored through this technique.

The Spatial and Temporal Analysis of Crime (STAC) software, developed
by the Illinois Criminal Justice Information Authority (ICJIA), was one of
the first systems designed for studying the existence, location, and size of
crime hot spots (Block, 1993a; Block & Block, 1995). It has been used to
analyze homicides, drug incidents, liquor-related crimes, rapid transit
impacts, gang turfs, and community problems. The New York Police Department (NYPD) has successfully pioneered the use of crime mapping and
organizational accountability in their CompStat (computer statistics) process. Geo-MIND (Geographically-linked Multi-Agency Information Network and Deconfliction) is an interdepartmental criminal information
network developed in Westchester and Rockland Counties, New York State,
to assist in tactical and strategic police decision making. It uses vehicle tracking, GIS mapping, and incident monitoring to manipulate and link information.

The potential application of geographic information systems to the investigation of serial murder was recognized several years ago. Because a GIS can
store geographic attributes and integrate spatial and other data for analytic
purposes, it is a useful tool in the reduction of linkage blindness and the
identification of crime series. "'Geographically coded information from
police records can be used to detect crime trends and patterns, confirm the
presence of persons within geographic areas, and identify areas for patrol
unit concentration'" (Rogers, Craig, & Anderson, 1991, p. 17, quoting from
a 1975 International Association of Chiefs of Police (IACP) report). Rogers
et al. suggest it might be possible to identify serial murder solvability factors
with a GIS through retrospective analyses of known cases. Such knowledge
may then be used to assist police investigators in their efforts to clear unsolved
murders. Much work has been done along these lines over the past decade.

Crime mapping and analysis may also help detect serial criminals. Techniques employed by epidemiologists to assess the likelihood of epidemic
disease outbreaks can be useful for determining if a predator is active in a
given area. The underlying concept is the same — the significance of a pattern
of incidents (crime or disease reports) is tested through spatial-temporal
clustering statistics to ascertain if the problem is real or merely a random
fluctuation. This method was applied in 1999 to help measure the probability
of a serial murderer targeting prostitutes in Vancouver's Downtown Eastside

after over 20 itinerant sex trade workers disappeared during a 30-month period.

Tactical crime analysis comprises those techniques used to assist investigators and patrol officers in the apprehension of active criminals (Gottlieb et al., 1998; see also Reuland, 1997). By comparison, strategic analysis is concerned with long-term trends and management issues such as the impact of changing demographics on crime rates. A common problem for tactical analysis is the prediction of where and when the next crime in a series of robberies or burglaries will take place. Time, weekday, weather, offence intervals, and other factors are examined to calculate an interval within which the next crime is most likely to happen. Estimating an offender's mean "cash burn" rate (the amount of money stolen divided by the number of days between successive crimes) can be helpful in determining when a burglar or robber will likely reoffend. And some success in using chaos theory to predict a time window for the next attack in a serial murder series has been reported (Egger, Lange, & Egger, 1996).

The spatial mean and standard distance of the crime sites in a connected series are commonly used to establish the most probable region for next offence occurrence. The precision of these pattern recognition methods is therefore related to the number of previous incidents, leading Gottlieb et al. (1998) to caution that future crime prediction can be a difficult task. These methods can be improved somewhat by more sophisticated analyses incorporating the influence of such factors as land use, demography, street networks, proximity to freeway exits, and other relevant landscape characteristics. Olligschlaeger (1997), for example, has demonstrated promise in the application of artificial neural networks to predict locations of "flare ups" of drug hot spots, using such input data as calls-for-service information, proportions of commercial and residential properties, and a seasonality index. The Arson Risk Prediction Index (ARPI) was developed as a computer-based model to predict arson proneness within Brooklyn neighbourhoods (Cook, 1985). Early warning signs of significance include number of apartment units, vacancy percentage, serious building code violations, past fires of unknown origin, and level of tax arrears. The top 50 buildings ranked with this system captured 30 to 40% of all potential arsons.

The U.S. Forest Service, in collaboration with the Drug Enforcement Agency (DEA), developed an expert system to locate illicit *Cannabis sativa L.* growth sites within the 856,000 acres of the Chattahoochee National Forest of Georgia (Fung & Potter, 1992). Relevant variables include topography and plant sun exposure, soil conditions and water balance, and remoteness, security, and privacy. The expert rules were grouped into the categories of topography (latitude, altitude, slope, vegetation), soil (nutrient content, soil texture, pH value), and proximity (distance from settlements, public facilities, transportation routes). The system had a reported prediction success rate of 80%.

Crime maps can be descriptive, analytic, or interactive (McEwen & Taxman, 1995). While the future of crime mapping is exciting (Sorensen, 1997), technology, praxis, and theory must move together. There is a need to transcend data and information, and move to knowledge and action (Berry, 1995). Wisdom is yet another issue. Progressing from information to knowledge is where criminology research can help. Eck (1997) correctly observes that theory significantly assists in the interpretation of mapped crime patterns.

10.2 Geography and Crime Investigation

> From a detective's point of view, no crime scene is better than a body in a house ... a body in the street offers less ... Not only are the opportunities for recovering physical evidence fewer, but the spatial relationship between the killer, the victim and the scene is obscured ... [But] even a body in an alley leaves a detective with questions: What was the dead man doing in that alley? Where did he come from? Who was he with?
>
> – Simon, 1991, pp. 76–78

One of the focuses of any police investigation is the crime scene and its evidentiary contents. What is often overlooked, however, is a geographic perspective on the actions preceding the offence, the spatial behaviour that led up to the crime scene. For any violent crime to occur there must have been an intersection of victim and offender in both time and place (Felson, 1998). How did this happen? What were the antecedents? What do the spatial elements of the crime tell us about the offender's actions and hunting patterns?

While police officers intuitively know the influence of place on crime, they are often unaware of the different ways in which geography can assist their work, of how looking beyond the crime scene tape provides additional clues (see Dettlinger & Prugh, 1983; Herbert, 1994). In spite of this general lack of utilization, there are some examples of the application of geographic principles in the effort to investigate crime and apprehend offenders.

Senior Superintendent Arvind Verma describes how the Indian Police Service in the Bihar province use geographical analysis in the investigation of certain kinds of offences (Rossmo, 1995c). Dacoities are a form of violent robbery dating back to 500 BC, involving gangs of five or more offenders. As these crimes customarily occur in the countryside, the lack of rural anonymity requires the dacoity gang to attack villages other than their own, and then only during those nights when the moon is new. There is usually little or no artificial lighting in rural India, and the lunar dark phase is a period of almost complete blackness that provides cover for criminal activities.

Upon being notified of a dacoity, police first determine the length of time between the occurrence of the crime and first light. Knowing the average speed that a person can travel cross-country on foot allows them to calculate a distance radius, centred on the crime site, that determines a circle within which the home village of the dacoity members most probably lies. There are few vehicles and if the criminals are not home by daylight, they run the risk of being observed by farmers who begin to work the fields at dawn.

Those villages of the same caste as the victim village within this circle are eliminated, as "brother" is not likely to harm "brother." If a sufficiently detailed description of the criminals has been obtained, dress, M.O., and other details can help determine the caste of the gang, allowing police to further concentrate on the most likely villages. Patrols then speed to intercept the dacoity members or investigate known offenders residing within the area.

Police dog handlers have noted patterns in the escape routes and movements of offenders fleeing from crime scenes (Eden, 1985, 1994). This predictability in the behaviour of those under stress has been observed in both actual trackings of suspects and in experimental reenactments using police dog quarries. Fleeing offenders tend to turn to the left if they are right handed, move to the right upon encountering obstacles, discard evidentiary items to their right, and stay near the outside walls when hiding in large buildings (Eden, 1985). Different patterns are found when conducting passive tracks for missing persons. Lost subjects tend to bear to the right in their wanderings, and men seem to favour downhill paths while women and children choose uphill routes (Eden, 1985).

A study of bank robbery escape patterns in the Federal Republic of Germany, conducted by the national police science research institute of the *Bundeskriminalamt* (BKA), produced several findings with implications for police response strategies (Büchler & Leineweber, 1991; see also Leineweber & Büchler, 1991). The research determined that most offenders (84.8%) plan their escapes, routes, and vehicle use. Professional criminals also assess bank location, distance from nearest police station, escape possibilities, and close-by hiding places. Bank robbers keep to this plan whenever possible, even if problems develop (which they often do).

Approximately 71% of the offenders are successful in their escape, most employing a two-stage flight process by switching vehicles or transportation modes between phases. The first stage generally lasts under 5 minutes, terminating within 2 kilometres of the bank in urban areas, and within 5 kilometres in rural areas. During this stage robbers typically flee on foot

(41.3%) or by car (44.4%). Escape during the second phase is most often by vehicle or, less commonly, on foot or by public transportation. Offenders with accomplices tend to use stolen cars, stay together, and eschew foot escapes. Robbers stay nearby if they commit a crime in an urban area, and try to get as far away as possible in a rural area. Overall, 20% of criminals remain in the vicinity of the bank. The most common destination is a residence, usually the home of the offender.

The typical police response in Germany to bank robbery is the formation of a *Ringalarmfahndung*, a circular blockade. This is an immediate and precise deployment of police personnel in an effort to apprehend the offenders by circumscribing the target area. The operation involves both dynamic (patrol) and static (control point) tactics. The study determined that it took an average of 26.7 minutes to form a blockade, a length of time that undoubtedly contributed to its low success rate (15 to 20%).

The BKA research recommended several improvements in the operational response to bank robbery. It was suggested that circular blockades be established no greater than 5 kilometres from urban crime scenes. Police search maps must be simple, accessible, and easy to use. Response time would be improved through tactical management at the local level, and police personnel, particularly in supervisory positions, should receive regular training in blockade formation. Finally, the importance of search information updates and enhanced interregional communication needs to be recognized.

Police investigations have also been helped through mapping and its ability to display geographic patterns. During a 1996 murder in Lowell, Massachusetts, police used a map to show how a trail of the victim's property, beer cans, and other physical evidence followed the offender's likely escape route, graphically linking the stabbing scene with the murderer's apartment residence (Cook, 1998). And after the St. Petersburg Police Department arrested the suspects in a gruesome 1997 mutilation drug killing, detectives conducted a unique geographic analysis for the Florida murder trial (Moland, 1998). They tracked the offenders' mobile telephone usage and associated cellular antennae sites in the Tampa Bay area, and correlated these locations with those where victim body parts and other items of physical evidence were recovered. The resulting map provided compelling evidence for the jury and both suspects were found guilty.

When the McLean County Sheriff's Office in Illinois asked the Mid-States Organized Crime Information Center (MOCIC) for assistance in the 1995 investigation of a series of almost 60 farm building burglaries, a geographic analysis revealed two interesting map patterns (Wood, 1998). First, most of the offences were situated close to a highway, leading to the theory the offenders were part of a travelling criminal group. Second, the crimes clustered around small rural cemeteries, suggesting the burglars might be using them as look-out positions to case targets. These ideas were confirmed and police were able to prevent any further crimes.

Former police officer Chet Dettlinger observed a geographic pattern in the Atlanta Child Murders (Dettlinger & Prugh, 1983; see also "Investigators believe many killers," 1981). For each victim Dettlinger mapped home address, place last seen, and body dump site. He noted these locations clustered along 12 major streets in Atlanta that were connected in a boot-shaped configuration. Questioning the value of such a map, police denied the existence of any geographic pattern. But in the midst of one of these clusters lay Penelope Road — the home of Wayne Williams, later arrested for the murders.

During 1977, in an effort to focus the Hillside Stranglers investigation, the Los Angeles Police Department (LAPD) tried to determine the most likely location of the scene of the homicides. It was correctly suspected that the victims had been murdered in the residence of one of the offenders. The police knew where the women were abducted, where their bodies were dumped, and the distances between (Gates & Shah, 1992). The LAPD computer analysts viewed the problem in terms of a Venn diagram, with the centre of each circle representing victim availability, the circumference representing offender movement capacity, and the radius representing offender mobility (C. Holt, personal communication, February 22, 1993).

Vectors drawn from the point where the victims were abducted to the location where their bodies were found were resolved to a common radius, which defined a circle encompassing an area of just over 3 square miles. The LAPD saturated this "sphere of concern" with 200 police officers in an attempt to find the murderers. While they were not successful, it is possible that the heavy police presence inhibited the killers, and prompted serial murderer Kenneth Bianchi's move from Los Angeles to Bellingham, Washington. The LAPD later realized the centre of this zone was close to co-killer Angelo Buono's automobile upholstery shop (Gates & Shah, 1992).

Geographic techniques were also used in the Yorkshire Ripper investigation. With the murders still unsolved after five and a half years, Her Majesty's Inspector of Constabulary Lawrence Byford implemented a case review process (Kind, 1987a). An Advisory Group, comprised of senior police officers and a Home Office forensic scientist, met in December 1980 to examine the investigation (Doney, 1990; Kind). Detectives had become divided over the issue of where the killer lived. One school of thought, led by the chief investigating officer, held the Ripper was from the Sunderland area, while other investigators believed he was local to West Yorkshire where most of the crimes had occurred (Nicholson, 1979). After an intensive investigative review the Byford advisory team came to the latter conclusion.

They applied two "navigational metrical tests" to the spatial and temporal data associated with the crimes to confirm their deduction (Kind, 1987a). The first test involved the calculation of the centre of gravity (spatial mean) for the 17 crimes believed to be linked to the Yorkshire Ripper.[61] The second test consisted of plotting time of offence against length of day (approximated by the month). The Advisory Team theorized the killer would be unwilling to attack late at night if his return home was too far. The tests determined the centre of gravity for the Ripper crimes lay near Bradford, and found the later attacks were those located in the West Yorkshire cities of Leeds and Bradford; these results supported the team's original hypothesis that the killer was local. The Advisory Group's interim report recommended "a special team of high-grade detectives be dedicated to enquiries in the Bradford area" (Kind, 1987a, p. 390).

In January 1981, Peter William Sutcliffe was arrested by two patrol officers in Sheffield's red-light district. Sutcliffe, a truck driver who later confessed to being the Yorkshire Ripper, resided in Heaton, a suburb of Bradford. While the resolution of the case occurred independent of the recommendations of the Advisory Group's report, their suggestion to focus on the Bradford area was valid, and if made sooner, might have led to an earlier case closure and helped save lives (Kind, 1987a).

Russian police used geography to set a trap for the USSR's worst serial murderer (Conradi, 1992). Dozens of women and children had been found slashed and mutilated in the lesopolosa (forest strips) of the Rostov-on-Don region over a period of 12 years (Cullen, 1993). Investigators believed the offender travelled for employment and used local commuter trains to find potential victims whom he lured into nearby woodland. Studies of aerial surveillance maps were unsuccessful in determining the killer's point of origin, and a computer biorhythm analysis of offence time, weekday, season, weather, and location was inconclusive (Lourie, 1993). So in an effort to better the odds of snaring the murderer along miles of rail line, Operation Forest Strip deployed 360 officers to maneuver him into key target areas. Uniformed officers guarded, in an obvious manner, all train stations except three near the forested areas where it was felt the killer would likely strike. These stations, and the surrounding lesopolosa, were surveilled by plain-clothes officers. The strategy led to the identification and arrest in November 1990 of former schoolteacher Andrei Chikatilo. He was later convicted of 53 murders and executed by gunshot.

Newton and Newton (1985) applied "geoforensic analysis" to a series of unsolved female homicides that occurred from 1983 to 1985 in Fort Worth,

---

[61] The analysis was based on 13 murders and 4 assaults, but the actual toll at the time was 13 murders and 7 attempted murders; the Byford Advisory Team missed one victim, and included an unrelated murder.

Texas. They found localized serial murder or rape forms place-time patterns different from those in "normal" criminal violence. The unsolved Fort Worth murders were analyzed with both quantitative (areal associations, crime site connections, centrographic analysis) and qualitative (landscape analysis) techniques.

Newton and Swoope (1987) utilized similar techniques in a retrospective analysis of the Hillside Stranglers case. Geographic centres (spatial means) were calculated for points of fatal encounter, body or car dump sites, and victim residences. They found the centre of the body dump sites lay close to the residence of murderer Angelo Buono, and that a search radius based at this point decreased with the addition of each new crime location. A conspicuous void in the crime pattern became evident when the crime locations were plotted on a map of Los Angeles; there was an area surrounding the home of Buono within which no crimes occurred. Newton and Swoope point out such a "coal-sack effect," resulting from an offender avoiding criminal activity close to home, has investigative significance.

Barrett (1990) documented several experience-based observations by police regarding the connection between crime locations and area of offender residence. If the murder and body dump sites are different, then the killer generally lives in the area where the victim was attacked. Conversely, if the victim was left at the murder scene then the killer is probably not local.[62] A crime scene close to a major road is an indication the murderer may not be from the area, while a crime scene a mile or more from a major road suggests the killer is local. A hidden body may mean the offender is more or less geographically stable and wishes to reuse the dump site, while an unconcealed body suggests the murderer is transient and unconcerned if police discover the victim.

Detective Constable Rupert Heritage of the Surrey Police and Professor David Canter, a psychologist at The University of Liverpool, have produced offender profiles for several British criminal investigations. They note that "one of the most successful components of the reports we have given to police forces has been an indication of where the assailant might live" (Canter, 1994, p. 283). Their first major inquiry was Operation Hart, set up to apprehend the Railway Killer who raped and murdered several females in the Greater London area from 1982 to 1986 (Lane & Gregg, 1992).

Blood typing reduced the register of over 5000 suspect names to 1999. Number 1505 on this list was John Francis Duffy, a carpenter for British Rail. The chronological pattern in the crime locations suggested a process of learning and planning on the part of the offender. The profile reasoned the

---

[62] This observation is inconsistent with the earlier finding that disorganized killers, who tend to live close to their crime sites, usually leave the victim's body at the murder scene. It may be that Barrett is referring to only organized offenders.

earlier attacks were closer to the Railway Killer's home and therefore he probably lived in the region circumscribed by the first three offences — the Kilburn/Cricklewood area of northwest London. This focus helped lead police to Duffy who was subsequently sentenced to seven life terms (Copson, 1993). An element of luck played into the analysis as Canter (1994) later admitted further research did not substantiate the "triangle hypothesis."

In another case, Heritage and Canter located the home area of the Tower Block Rapist in Birmingham (Canter, 1994). Responsible for a number of sexual assaults on elderly women from 1986 to 1988, Adrian Babb hunted in blocks of high-rise apartments situated in the Edgbaston and Druids Heath districts, on the edge of the city centre. The attacks revealed a strong sense of area familiarity, but at the same time, confidence in anonymity. This suggested the offender resided close by, but not in the immediate neighbour-hood. Furthermore, the rapist's comfort in prowling through the victims' high-rise apartment buildings, labelled "streets in the sky," indicated he lived in such a structure himself. The target area was a patchwork of distinct territories divided by Birmingham's busy arterial routes, and this pattern, informed by victimology and demographic information, was used as the basis for inferring the offender's mental map. The analysis correctly predicted the location of Babb's home base in nearby Highgate.

It should not be forgotten that criminals also use maps. Both David Berkowitz, the Son of Sam, and Sylvestre Matuschka, the Hungarian train wrecker, plotted their future crimes on maps. The Zodiac Killer mailed a code with a map marking where his next bomb was planted to *The San Francisco Chronicle*. While he shot and stabbed at least 8 victims in the Bay area, murdering 6, Zodiac claimed 37 kills (Graysmith, 1976). His confirmed attacks occurred from 1966 to 1969, but his correspondence with newspapers, police, and others stretched over 12 years. A letter to the *Chronicle* newspaper postmarked June 26, 1970, included a cipher and a map providing clues to the location of a bomb intended for a school bus: "The Map coupled with this code will tell you where the bomb is set. You have untill next Fall to dig it up" (King, 1996, p. 302). A further hint was provided on July 26, 1970: "P.S. The Mt. Diablo Code concerns Radians & # inches along the radians" (King, p. 305).

Zodiac's Phillips 66 service station roadmap focused on Mt. Diablo ("Devil's Mountain") in Contra Costa County, across the Bay from San Francisco. Mt. Diablo was used to help plot latitude and longitude after the Civil War. A compass symbol was hand drawn in the middle of the map, the centre of which contained the Naval Radio Station (Graysmith, 1976). The bomb was never found, the mystery of the map never solved, and the Zodiac Killer never apprehended.

10.3 Offender Residence Prediction

As early as 1986, LeBeau recognized the investigative potential of geostatistical techniques and crime pattern research for reducing the offender search area in rape cases. Until the development of geographic profiling in 1990, however, there was no tested systematic method beyond centrography for approaching this problem. Taylor (1977) states that geographic patterns should be viewed through the processes that produce them. Accordingly, crime pattern theory was utilized as a heuristic for the construction of an algorithmic model for locating offender residence (see Benfer et al., 1991). The research of Brantingham and Brantingham interprets offenders' activity spaces in order to describe where crimes are most likely to occur. Geographic profiling is, in effect, an attempt to invert this model, by using crime locations as the basis for predicting most probable area of offender residence or workplace. So while the two models have different purposes and inputs, their underlying concepts and ideas are similar.

10.3.1 Criminal Geographic Targeting

In the simplest case, offenders' residences lie at the centre of their crime patterns and can be found through the spatial mean. The intricacy of most criminal activity spaces, however, indicates that more complex patterns are the norm. George Rengert (1996) proposes four hypothetical spatial patterns for the geography of crime sites: (1) uniform pattern, with no distance-decay influence; (2) bull's-eye pattern, exhibiting distance decay and spatial clustering around the offender's anchor point; (3) bimodal pattern, with crimes clustered around two anchor points; and (4) teardrop pattern, centred around the offender's primary anchor point, with a directional bias towards a secondary anchor point. Crime patterns are also distorted by a variety of other real world factors — movement follows street layouts, traffic flows affect mobility, variations exist in zoning and land use, and crimes cluster dependent upon the nature of the target backcloth. The spatial mean is therefore limited in its ability to determine criminal residence.

Many researchers have noted the importance of direction as well as distance in the analysis of spatial patterns of criminal behaviour. Rengert and Wasilchick (1985) found a directional bias towards burglars' workplace and recreation sites. Canter and Hodge (1997) noticed that while crimes of U.S. and British serial killers generally grouped around their homes, they were also biased towards other activity sites. In their Sheffield study, Baldwin and Bottoms (1976) observed that crime disproportionately occurs in the city centre, indicating offender preference for such a bearing. Nonparametric assessments of spatial autocorrelation in the orientation of criminal travel

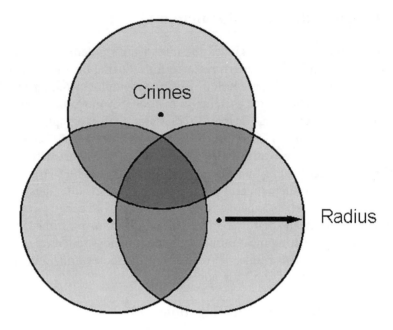

Figure 10.1   Journey-to-crime Venn diagram.

suggests that directional information can assist in certain police investigations (Costanzo, Halperin, & Gale, 1986).

Environmental criminology establishes a framework within which journey-to-crime research, centrography, and other geographic principles may be combined to create a method for determining offender residence from crime locations. Set theory provides a useful first approach for addressing this problem (Taylor, 1977). The ATF/FBI research on serial arsonists found that 70% set fires within 2 miles of their home. Figure 10.1 shows a Venn diagram for three hypothetical serial arsons.[63] The medial circles surrounding each crime location are defined by a radius equal to journey-to-crime distance d, within the range of which percentage p of the offender's arsons occur ($d = 2$ miles; $p \geq 0.70$). The probability of the offender's residence lying within the area circumscribed by a single circle is therefore also p. Because the crimes are connected, the lune overlap areas between any two circles is more likely to contain the offender's residence. The highest probability is in the middle region where all three of the circles intersect.

The residence of the offender is most likely within (in decreasing order of probability): (1) the middle intersection; (2) the lunes; (3) the circles; and (4) the background area. The areal probabilities for the four different spaces

---

[63] This procedure is akin to constructing an intersection of investigative frames through the use of geographic information (Kind, 1987b).

delineated by the Venn diagram in Figure 10.1 are given in Equations 10.1 to 10.4:

$$p(C_i) = p_d(1 - p_d)^2 \qquad\qquad (10.1)$$

$$p(C_i \cap C_j) = p_d^2 (1 - p_d) \qquad\qquad (10.2)$$

$$p(C_i \cap C_j \cap C_k) = p_d^3 \qquad\qquad (10.3)$$

$$p((C_i \cap C_j \cap C_k)') = (1 - p_d)^3 \qquad\qquad (10.4)$$

where:

$p(A)$ is the probability the offender's residence lies within area A;

C_x is the area around crime site x circumscribed by radius d; and

p_d is the probability the offender's crime journey is less than or equal to d.

Relative probabilities for the points within the various areas are obtained by dividing the areal probabilities by area size (or number of "points"). This process is a simple dichotomous function dependent only upon whether a point lies within one of the circles or not. Points in the overlaps of two, or all three of the circles, are given double or triple the value, respectively.

This process is conceptually similar to the function of the criminal geo-graphic targeting algorithm, the primary tool used in geographic profiling, but dichotomizing distance oversimplifies journey-to-crime patterns. The Brantingham and Brantingham model suggests the criminal search process is more correctly modeled by a distance-decay curve, incorporating a buffer zone centred around the residence of the offender. A more sophisticated method of predicting offender residence location results therefore by replac-ing the circles in Figure 10.1 with a Pareto function $f(d)$, in a fuzzy logic approach that better describes journey-to-crime behaviour (Kosko & Isaka, 1993; Yager & Zadeh, 1994): the value assigned to point (x, y), located at distance d from crime site i, equals $f(d_i)$. The final value for point (x, y) is determined by adding together the n values derived for that point for the n different crime sites.

Research conducted at Simon Fraser University and the Vancouver Police Department following this approach led to the development of the criminal geographic targeting (CGT) model which has been developed into a com-puterized geographic profiling system. Crime site coordinates are analyzed with a patented criminal hunting algorithm that produces a probability sur-face showing likelihood of offender residence within the hunting area. A three-dimensional depiction of this probability is referred to as a jeopardy surface. A two-dimensional perspective integrated with a street map is termed a geoprofile. These are discussed further, and examples shown, below.

The hunting area is defined as the rectangular zone oriented along the street grid containing all crime locations. These locations may be victim encounter points, murder scenes, body dump sites, or some combination thereof. The term hunting area is therefore used broadly in the sense of the geographic region within which the offender chose — after some form of search or hunting process — a series of places for criminal action. Locations unknown to authorities, including those where the offender searched for victims or dump sites but was unsuccessful or chose not to act, are obviously not included.

While the primary purpose of determining offender hunting area is calculation of search area size, there may be other value in such measures. The FBI used convex hull polygons to analyze the point patterns formed by serial rapists (Warren et al., 1995). For local serial rapists (travel under 20 miles), the mean CHP area was 7.14 square miles. The average CHP size was larger for commuters than for marauders (11.38 vs. 7.62 mi^2), for rapists who burgled (15.24 vs. 2.49 mi^2), and for offenders who lived outside of the CHP area enclosing their crimes (23.53 vs. 3.22 mi^2). If replicated, this last finding could be useful in helping narrow offender residence area in cases of serial rape.

Any geometric method of determining hunting area has strengths and weaknesses, and the optimal approach depends ultimately upon the under-lying purpose. Many predators exhibit a high hunting to offending ratio. *A priori*, we do not know where this hunting area is — we only know the locations of the reported, and connected, crimes. Technically, a geoprofile stretches to infinity; the hunting area is only a standardized method of displaying results so that important information is shown, and unimportant information is not. Special methods are used to deal with unusual patterns, including elimination of outliers, division of crimes into separate analyses, and geometric transformations of point patterns (e.g., rotations, "straight-ening," trimming, reflections, etc.). The decision on how to proceed is ulti-mately based on the crime locations and their underlying landscape, guided by theory and methodology. Criminal geographic targeting considers offender hunting methods and mental maps within a framework informed by routine activity, rational choice, and pattern theories.

The CGT analysis uses a Manhattan metric. This may appear to be a less than optimal approach for crimes in cities characterized by concentric, as opposed to grid, street layouts. Model testing and experiences with European cases have demonstrated otherwise. The Manhattan metric slightly overesti-mates travel in a concentric street layout, but crow-flight distance in turn results in a small underestimate. Neither are far off; on average, the Manhattan distance is approximately 1.273 times the length of the crow-flight distance (Larson & Odoni, 1981). Wheel distance, or path routing, is the most accurate estimate of shortest available travel distance — which may or may not be the actual route taken. It is less the physical distance than its psychological perception that is important. Factors such as traffic congestion, travel time, cost, and familiarity will influence "distance," regardless of the metric used.

The CGT model follows a four-step process:

1. Map boundaries delineating the offender's hunting area are first calculated from the crime locations. In the case of a Manhattan grid oriented along northerly and easterly axes, borders are determined by adding edges equal to 1/2 the mean x and y interpoint distances to the most eastern and western, and northern and southern points, respectively (for a discussion of alternative techniques for dealing with edge effects, see Boots & Getis, 1988):

$$y_{high} = y_{max} + (y_{max} - y_{min})/2\,(C-1) \tag{10.5}$$

$$y_{low} = y_{min} - (y_{max} - y_{min})/2\,(C-1) \tag{10.6}$$

$$x_{high} = x_{max} + (x_{max} - x_{min})/2\,(C-1) \tag{10.7}$$

$$x_{low} = x_{min} - (x_{max} - x_{min})/2\,(C-1) \tag{10.8}$$

where:
y_{high} is the y value of the northernmost boundary;
y_{low} is the y value of the southernmost boundary;
y_{max} is the maximum y value for any crime site;
y_{min} is the minimum y value for any crime site;
x_{high} is the x value of the easternmost boundary;
x_{low} is the x value of the westernmost boundary;
x_{max} is the maximum x value for any crime site;
x_{min} is the minimum x value for any crime site; and
C is the number of crime sites.

2. For every point on the map, Manhattan distances to each crime location are determined. While there are an infinite number of mathematical points in an area, the model uses a finite number of pixels (40,000) based on the measurement resolution of the x and y scales.
3. The distance is used as an independent variable in a distance decay function; if the distance is less than the radius of the buffer zone,

however, the function is reversed. Values are computed for each crime location (e.g., 12 crime locations equates to 12 values for every map point).

4. These values are summed[64] to produce a final score for each map point. The higher the resultant score, the greater the probability that point contains the offender's anchor point. The score function is presented in Equation 10.9:

$$P_{ij} = k \sum_{n=1}^{C} \left[\phi / \left(\left| x_i - x_n \right| + \left| y_j - y_n \right| \right)^f + \right.$$

$$\left. (1 - \phi) \left(B^{g-f} \right) / \left(2B - \left| x_i - x_n \right| - \left| y_j - y_n \right| \right)^g \right]$$

(10.9)

where:

$$| x_i - x_n | + | y_j - y_n | > B \supset \phi = 1 \tag{10.10}$$

$$| x_i - x_n | + | y_j - y_n | \le B \supset \phi = 0 \tag{10.11}$$

and:

P_{ij} is the resultant probability for point ij;
ϕ is a weighting factor;
k is an empirically determined constant;
B is the radius of the buffer zone;
C is the number of crime sites;
f is an empirically determined exponent;
g is an empirically determined exponent;
x_i, y_j are the coordinates of point ij; and
x_n, y_n are the coordinates of the nth crime site.

A three-dimensional surface is produced when the probability for every point on the map is calculated, which can be represented by an isopleth or "fishnet" map with different scores on the z-axis representing probability density (Garson & Biggs, 1992). These maps, a form of virtual reality (in the term's original sense), are generated through computer-aided mathematical visualization techniques. They are referred to as jeopardy surfaces.

The probability surface may be viewed from a top-down perspective and shown two-dimensionally, similar to how a topographic map displays altitude (Harries, 1990). When overlaid on a city map of the targeted region, specific.

---

[64] Alternatively, the logarithms of the values can be summed (a process equivalent to generating the product).

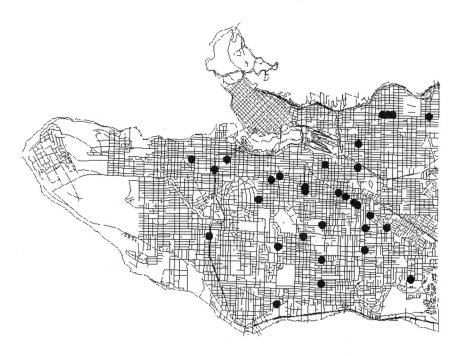

Figure 10.2   Vancouver robberies — crime sites.

streets or blocks can be prioritized according to the CGT probability values. The resulting map is termed a geoprofile. Figures 10.2, and Chapter 10 Colour Figures 1 and 2 (following page 230) show, respectively, the crime sites, jeopardy surface, and geoprofile for a series of armed robberies of insurance agencies in Vancouver, British Columbia. A geoprofile can also be expressed as a series of confidence intervals; Figure 10.3 displays a hypothetical example for the District of Columbia.

A geoprofile dictates less where an offender lives than it describes an optimal search process. A search that starts in the highest (i.e., most probable) area and works down is more likely to find the offender's residence sooner than a random process would. Search efficiency is therefore an indicator of the performance of the CGT model, and can be measured by determining the proportion of the total hunting area covered before the offender's residence is encountered. This ratio is referred to as the hit score percentage, and the actual size of the region it represents is called the search area. These terms are discussed further later in the chapter. Parameter specification optimizes predictive ability, but sophistication must be balanced with robustness; complicated models may perform better under specific conditions, but at the cost of losing their general applicability.

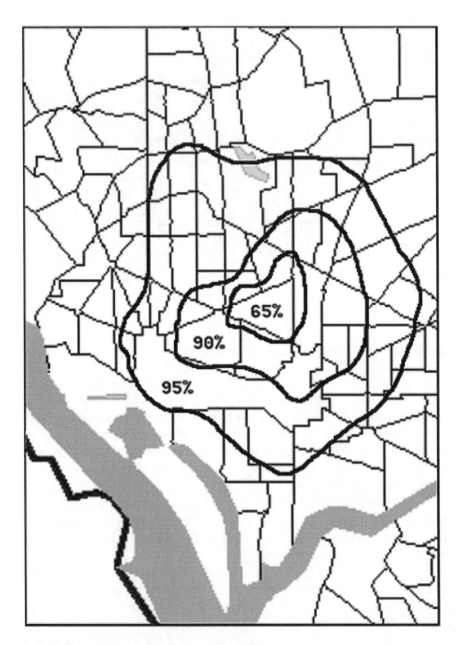

Figure 10.3 Geoprofile confidence intervals.

10.3.2 Performance

Table 10.1 presents information on crime patterns and CGT test results from the SFU serial murder data set, including number of crime sites, size of hunting and search areas, and hit score percentages (the implications of

Table 10.1   Crime Site Patterns and CGT Results

Serial Murderer	Crime Sites	Hunting Area	Area/Crime Site	CGT Hit Score %	Search Area
		Victim Encounter/Body Dump Sites			
Chase	5	8.0 km^2	1.6 km^2	**1.7%**	0.1 km^2
DeSalvo	14	1256 km^2	89.7 km^2	**17.8%**	223 km^2
Ramirez	21	6393 km^2	304 km^2	**9.8%**	625 km^2
Berkowitz	10	816 km^2	81.7 km^2	**4.7%**	38.2 km^2
		Victim Encounter Sites			
Olson	15	299 km^2	20.0 km^2	**3.0%**	9.1 km^2
Buono	9	487 km^2	54.1 km^2	**9.4%**	45.6 km^2
Bianchi				**3.2%**	15.6 km^2
Collins	7	62.6 km^2	8.9 km^2	**1.1%**	0.7 km^2
Dahmer	10	6.8 km^2	0.7 km^2	**8.7%**	0.6 km^2
Brudos	6	5726 km^2	954 km^2	**2.2%**	128 km^2
		Body Dump Sites			
Olson[65]	11	14,262 km^2	1,297 km^2	12.5%	1779 km^2
Buono and Bianchi	9	305 km^2	33.94 km^2	9.2%	28.0 km^2
Sutcliffe Res 1	20	9547 km^2	477 km^2	4.9%	465 km^2
Res 2				2.4%	232 km^2
Rifkin	16	25,278 km^2	1580 km^2	7.2%	1829 km^2
Collins[66]	7	368 km^2	52.54 km^2	23.8%	87.6 km^2
Wuornos Body	6	16,980 km^2	2830 km^2	**3.8%**	643 km^2
Vehicle	7	14,970 km^2	2139 km^2	5.4%	813 km^2

[65]The hit score percentage and search area for Agassiz Mounain Prison was 2.5% (352 km^2); aspects of the case suggest this location was a significant offender anchor point.
[66]The hit score percentage and search area for Eastern Michigan University was 15% (55.3 km^2); aspects of the case suggest this location was a significant offender anchor point.

which are discussed below). Case data are divided into victim encounter/body dump (i.e., there was no victim transport), victim encounter, and body dump sites. A minimum of five different locations of the same crime site type connected to a single residence was necessary for a site type to be individually analyzed (see Rossmo, 1995a, for full study details). Table 10.2 shows the comparative CGT hit score percentages for those cases where more than one type of crime site was available for examination. Generally, encounter sites result in lower hit scores than body dump sites, though in some cases best performance is achieved from the use of all site types (optimal crime site selection in geographic profiling is discussed below).

Table 10.2   CGT Comparative Site Type Results[67]

Serial Murderer	CGT Hit Score % (Encounter Sites)	CGT Hit Score % (Body Dump Sites)	CGT Hit Score % (All Sites)
Chase		1.7%	1.1%
Olson	3.0%	12.5%	1.3%
Buono and Bianchi	9.4%	9.2%	6.3%
Collins	1.1%	23.8%	1.2%
Wuornos	5.4%	3.8%	10.8%
Brudos	2.2%		2.9%
Mean	4.2%	10.2%	3.9%

[67]Combined locations for Chase include body dump and vehicle drop sites; for Collins, encounter, murder, and body dump sites; and for Wuornos, body dump and vehicle drop sites.

10.3.3 Validity, Reliability, and Utility

10.3.3.1 Validity

For geographic profiling to distinguish itself from geomancy, it should meet certain standards. Scientific methodologies must fulfil three important criteria — validity, reliability, and utility (see Oldfield, 1995). Specification of a methodology's limitations is also important (Poythress et al., 1993). The CGT model works on the assumption that a relationship, modeled on some form of distance-decay function, exists between crime location and offender residence. The process can be thought of as a mathematical method for assigning a series of scores to the various points on the map representing a criminal's hunting area. For the CGT model to be valid, the score it assigns to the point containing the offender's residence (referred to as the "hit score") should be relatively high; that is, there should be few points within the hunting area with equal or higher scores. This relationship can be shown as a distribution curve indicating the number of points with various scores (see Figure 10.4, derived from the CGT analysis of the Olson case). A uniform distribution assigns the same score to every point, producing a horizontal line. (If N is the total number of points on a map, then the probability associated with each point is $1/N$.)

The success of the CGT model is measured by the hit score percentage — the ratio of the total number of points with scores equal or higher to the hit score, to the total number of points within the hunting area. This is equivalent to the percentage of the total area that must be searched before the offender's residence is found, assuming an optimal search process (i.e., one that started in the locations with the highest scores and then worked down). The extent of the search area — the territory police have to search in order to find the offender — is equal to the size of the hunting area multiplied by the hit score percentage. The mean hit score percentage is 50% with a uniform distribution. This means

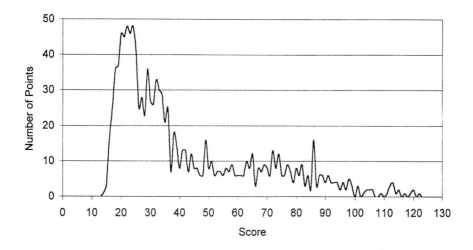

Figure 10.4 CGT score distribution.

that, on average, any police system based on this distribution can expect to locate an offender in half of the hunting area. Investigating suspects alphabetically, tips chronologically, or canvassing from the northwest to the southeast are all examples of such systems.

The validity of the CGT model can be determined by plotting groupings of hit score percentages against those from a uniform distribution (i.e., what is expected by chance) in a Lorenz curve, and then applying an index of dissimilarity or concentration. One such measure is the Gini coefficient (Goodall, 1987; Taylor, 1977). In this case it is equal to:

$$G = \sum_{n=1}^{N} |x_n - y_n|/2 \qquad (10.12)$$

where:

- G is the Gini coefficient;
- N is the total number of observations;
- x_n is the nth member of the uniform percentage frequency; and
- y_n is the nth member of the hit score percentage frequency.

The Gini coefficient ranges from 0 to 100, with 0 indicating exact correspondence between the two sets of percentage frequencies, and 100 indicating a complete lack of correspondence. The more successful or valid the CGT model, the closer the Gini coefficient is to 100. The distribution of CGT hit score percentages found in the SFU serial murder study was compared to that expected by chance (testing and learning data sets were different). Specific CGT hit score percentages used in calculating the index of dissimilarity are marked in bold in Table 10.1. Degree of offender choice was the basis for determining which score to use when different scenarios were available. This meant that encounter sites were preferred over body dump sites, unless the former were unknown or the target backcloth was patchy (e.g., a red-light district). Also, the dominant residence was used in cases involving more than one offender. Based on 5% intervals, the Gini coefficient for the study sample equals 85, indicating a high level of validity.

An alternative measure of performance can be obtained by doubling the mean hit score percentage; the lower this value the greater the predictive power of the model. This measure ranges from 0, indicating optimal performance, to 1, the value expected by chance. The mean hit score percentage for the above cases is 6.0%, therefore this measure is equal to approximately 0.12. All else being equal, this suggests an area search conducted through a geoprofile would find, on average, the offender's residence in 12% of the time that a random search would take. The relative performance of the CGT model is therefore approximately 830% (100/12).

Results of the SFU serial murder study show a mean CGT hit score percentage of 6.0% and a median of 4.2% (standard deviation = 4.8); the average number of crime locations was 11.6 (see Table 10.1). Performance ranged from a low of 1.1% to a high of 17.8%. A review of solved operational cases by the Vancouver Police Department Geographic Profiling Section found similar results, with a mean CGT hit score percentage of 5.5% and a median of 4.8% (standard deviation = 4.6); the average number of crime locations was 19.1. Performance ranged from a low of 0.2% to a high of 17.2%. Figure 10.5 shows the distribution of CGT hit score percentages for the SFU serial murder data and a sample of VPD operational cases.

The theoretical maximum efficiency of the CGT model was estimated through Monte Carlo testing, using a computer program to generate random crime site coordinates based on a fixed-buffered distance-decay function.[65] The testing produced the "learning curve" in Figure 10.6, which displays the relationship between number of crime sites and median hit score percentage (standard deviation is also shown). Because the distribution is not normal (see Figure 10.5) the median is a better indicator of typical performance than the mean. Functions based on these curves are used in geographic profiling

---

[65] This function produces a pattern similar to Rengert's (1996) bull's-eye distribution. The CGT model showed a small drop in performance when tested on other forms of crime site geography (teardrop, bimodal, or uniform spatial patterns).

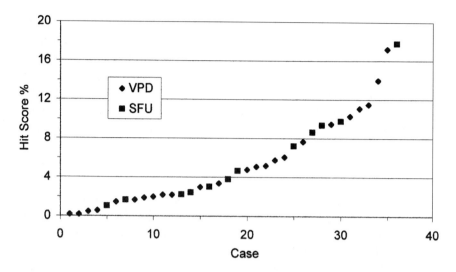

Figure 10.5 CGT operational performance.

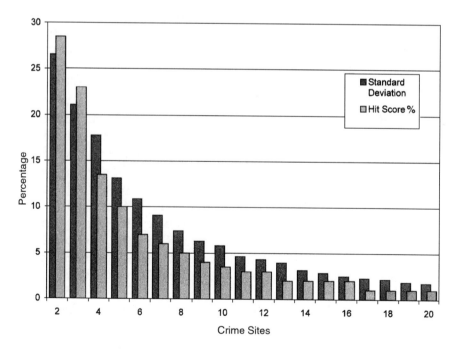

Figure 10.6 CGT model learning curve.

to help determine performance, but these estimates should be considered optimal, rather than expected, performance levels of the model.

This process establishes that a minimum of 5 crime locations are necessary to produce a median hit score percentages of 10%, and 6 crime locations for a mean hit score percentage of 10%. The mean CGT hit score percentage (6.0%) in the SFU serial murder study was higher than that predicted from Monte Carlo testing (mean = 3.8%, median = 3.0%) for an average of 11.6 crime sites. This degradation reflects the impact of real world complexity, and is most likely attributable to departures from uniformity in target backcloth (see note 68).

10.3.3.2 Reliability

The CGT model is reliable as the process is a computerized mathematical procedure; however, but there is an element of subjectivity in determining which crime sites in a given case are useful predictors of offender residence. Theory, methodology, and experience help structure this interpretation process (Benfer et al., 1991). The following guidelines should be considered when choosing the input locations for a geographic profile:

- Generally, there should be a minimum of five distinct locations, of the same type, available for analysis. It is usually assumed that the offender has not moved or been displaced during the time period of these crimes, but if this has occurred, then more locations are required. A geographic assessment may be appropriate in cases involving fewer locations (see Section 10.4.2.1 below).

- Only crime locations that are accurately known should be used. For example, encounter sites may be imprecise if they have to be inferred from last known victim sighting. In some investigations, the locations of certain sites may be completely unknown.

- Analyses of the crime site type with the most locations results in lower expected CGT hit score percentages. Multiple offences in the same immediate area should not be double counted. The degree of spatial-temporal clustering must be assessed as crime sites too close in time and space are probably non-independent events (see previous discussion on clusters). Contagion locations should be excluded from a CGT analysis.

- Combining different site types to increase the total number of locations available for analysis can be advantageous when the number of crimes is minimal. But two potential problems exist with this approach. The first is that locations may be significantly correlated; this is particularly likely when the offender travels directly to the dump site from the encounter site. For example, the Yorkshire Ripper picked up prostitutes, parked a short distance away, and then killed and dumped their bodies. While not identical, the encounter and body dump sites in this series are close to being equivalent. The Hillside Stranglers, by contrast, originated their victim disposal trips from Buono's home where the murders took place. The second problem occurs when combined crime locations produce a hunting area larger than that found with a single site type, resulting in the possibility of a greater search area, even though the hit score percentage is smaller. This problem is most likely to occur if the two crime site areas are incongruent. Clifford Olson appeared to use different mental maps for his victim searches and body dumps. Aileen Wuornos dumped victim's bodies and abandoned their vehicles at different sites, the former suggestive of where she was coming from, and the latter of where she was going to.

- Preference should be given to the crime site type that affords the greatest degree of choice to the offender. Site types with constrained target backcloths tell us little about the criminal. If victim specificity leads to spatial bias then encounter locations may not be the best profiling option. Similarly, body dump sites in isolated areas may reveal only general detail about an urban killer.

The limitations of the CGT model are set by the hunting typology. Because the process assumes the offender's anchor point lies within the hunting area, it cannot determine the residence of poaching offenders who commute. Experience has shown, however, that often some form of secondary anchor point draws a poacher into the crime area — a workplace, former residence, or the home of a friend or relative. The results of the geoprofile then point to the secondary site, and to the degree the offender can be associated with this location, investigators will find the geographic profile of value.

10.3.3.3 Utility

No matter how valid or reliable a particular technique, it will have little value if it cannot be used within the practical context of a police investigation (Baeza, 1999). Even a highly accurate CGT prediction (i.e., a small hit score percentage) will not lead police investigators to an offender's door. Certain psychics have allegedly been successful in finding criminal offenders,[66] missing people, and buried bodies (Lyons & Truzzi, 1991; but see Kocsis et al., 1999). Geographic profiling cannot do this. The process is an information management system, and to that end it must be compatible with the overall police investigation.

Table 10.3   Urban Population Density

Urban Residential Area	Total Population	Private Households
Metropolitan District	580/km²	220/km²
Core City	4190/km²	1770/km²
High Density Neighbourhood	19,800/km²	13,530/km²
Medium Density Neighbourhood	6290/km²	3430/km²
Low Density Neighbourhood	2380/km²	790/km²

The scope of the search area for a given CGT hit score percentage depends upon the size of the hunting area. With a small hunting area the geoprofile can outline the streets or blocks where the offender most probably resides; with a large hunting area it will indicate the cities or towns. The resolution of an analysis is bounded by its information input. Investigative strategies based on a geographic profile must consider both expected hit score percentage and search area size. Some tactics possible at the local level are not feasible on a larger scale.

Table 10.3 lists average population and household estimates for five urban area types in Vancouver, British Columbia (1991 Canada Census data; *Vancouver local areas 1981–1991*, 1994). Figures are provided for metropolitan district, core city, and high, medium, and low density residential neighbourhoods (these estimates are somewhat high in that many areas contain uninhabited regions such as industrial sectors, parks, water, farmland, or wilderness). While numbers vary by city and region, it can be seen that even a search area as small as one square kilometre contains hundreds of people. This suggests there may be limited investigative value in a map that only delineates the most probable area of offender residence. In other words, geographic profiling does not result in an "x" that marks the spot; instead, it provides an optimal search strategy. It is therefore important that the profile be properly integrated with the overall investigation.

The Paperbag Rapist was responsible for at least 79 attacks in Greater Vancouver from 1977 to 1985 (Alston, 1994; Eastham, 1989). These covered an area of 1873 square kilometres (723 mi²). After John Horace Oughton was identified as a suspect, an undercover policewoman gained access to his apartment and observed a pin map on the wall showing the locations of his crimes. He was being careful not to follow a pattern. Despite efforts to avoid this, Oughton still left behind a "fingerprint" of his mental map; in a retro-

---

[66] Moscow police have allegedly used a pair of psychics with the ability to sense "death's geography" to help them locate bodies. But a Russian clairvoyant contacted during the Chikatilo murder investigation incorrectly told police there were two offenders, who lived high up a mountain (Lourie, 1993). A British medium claims to have accurately predicted the Yorkshire Ripper's name and street address 18 months prior to the arrest of Peter Sutcliffe (Lyons & Truzzi, 1991; see also Nicholson, 1979); her assertion cannot be substantiated.

spective analysis the geoprofile located his home in only 0.08% of the total hunting area. However, this still translated into a region of 1.4 square kilometres (0.6 mi^2), or approximately 1130 households and 3400 people. Suspects can be prioritized in such a situation, but resource limitations make door-to-door canvassing, for example, unfeasible. In other words, tactics and analysis must be harmonious.

The utility of the CGT model is demonstrated by the various geographically-based investigative strategies that this process makes possible. Some examples of such applications include suspect prioritization by address, directed patrol saturation tactics, and the retrieval of computerized database information on the basis of location, licence plate registration, telephone number, and postal or zip code. These and other examples are discussed in the following chapter.

10.4 Geographic Profiling

Clues derived from crime site location and place can be of significant assistance to law enforcement agencies in the investigation of repetitive offences. "Locating where an offender might be is the cornerstone of any detective work ... and provides the foundations from which discovery of the criminal's identity may proceed" (Canter, 1994, p. 282). The probable spatial behaviour of the offender may be determined from information contained in crime site locations, their geographic connections, and the characteristics and demography of the surrounding neighbourhoods.

Criminal apprehension efforts are assisted when some idea of offender residence area exists. This information allows police departments to focus their investigative activities, prioritize suspects, and concentrate saturation patrol efforts in those zones where the criminal predator is most likely to reside. Such investigative approaches are part of geographic profiling (Rossmo, 1992, 1993a, 1995a).

Geographic profiling is a strategic information management system designed to support serial violent crime investigations. It is part of the police behavioural science response, and has relationships to both linkage analysis and psychological profiling. It meets the definition of offender profiling: "an approach to police investigations whereby an attempt is made to deduce a description of an unknown offender based on evaluating minute details of the crime scene, the victim, and other available evidence" (Copson, 1995, p. 1; see also Dale, 1996). Not all types of offenders or crimes can be geographically profiled, but in appropriate cases the process produces practical results.

Geographic profiling is a police-provided service for law enforcement agencies or prosecuting offices, available upon official request (MacKay,

1994). The first such profile was prepared in 1990. To date, requests have come from a variety of federal, provincial, state, and local law enforcement agencies, including the RCMP, the FBI, and Scotland Yard. The cases involve crimes of serial murder, serial rape and sexual assault, serial arson, serial robbery, serial exposers, sexual homicide, and kidnapping.

The implementation of geographic profiling within the policing community is a direct result of the SFU study on target patterns of serial murderers. This is an example of criminological research, done in an academic university setting, having practical policy and procedural implications for the criminal justice system. While the original research focused on serial killers, the hunting patterns of serial rapists, arsonists, and other repetitive violent offenders are similar and can also be geographically profiled. This resemblance is not surprising considering what the relevant theory tells us. Murder and violent sex crimes comprise the two single largest categories in geographic profiling casework, followed by arson and robbery.

10.4.1 Profiling Considerations

A geographic profile is only one part of what is usually a large and complex police investigation. Understanding its role in the overall picture and its relationship to other behavioural science methods is helpful. The following sequence outlines how geographic profiling typically fits into a criminal investigation:

1. Occurrence of a crime series;
2. Traditional investigative techniques;
3. Linkage analysis;
4. Criminal profile;
5. Geographic profile; and
6. New investigative strategies.

The ability to identify the existence of a serial offender is the starting point of the process. The extent and accuracy of the linkage analysis is important as the more crimes, the more accurate the geographic profile. But providing there is no spatial bias, and not too many locations are missed, unlinked crimes are not a critical problem. The CGT algorithm is also quite robust and its results are not significantly affected by the mistaken inclusion of an unconnected crime; generally, at least 90% of the information should be accurate.

If traditional investigative methods are successful, then there is unlikely to be a need for profiling. The development of new investigative strategies based on the profile is the topic of the following chapter. That leaves the relationship between geographic and psychological profiling.

While primarily empirical, geographic profiling has both quantitative (objective) and qualitative (subjective) components. The objective component uses a series of geostatistical techniques and quantitative measures, such as the CGT program, to analyze and interpret the point pattern formed by target sites. Because the validity of these measures depends upon number of locations, they are inappropriate for smaller crime series. The subjective component of geographic profiling is based upon the reconstruction and interpretation of the offender's mental map (Homant & Kennedy, 1998). A criminal profile is not a necessary precursor for a geographic profile, but the insights it provides to offender personality, behaviour, and lifestyle are useful, particularly in cases involving only a few locations. A geographic profile, in turn, helps refine a psychological profile, focus its application, and increase its utility. The two types of profiles optimize each other, and act in tandem to help investigators develop a "picture" of the person responsible for the crimes in question.

For example, in 1996 the RCMP investigated a series of 14 arsons of house carports in Burnaby, British Columbia, and requested psychological and geographic profiles. When a suspect who closely matched both profiles came to the attention of the investigator, he carefully focused on him, initiating surveillance and then interviewing strategies. The offender confessed. He closely matched the criminal profile, and literally lived across the street from the highest part of the geoprofile, in 0.6% of the hunting area (0.02 mi²).

Many different crime factors and environmental elements are considered in the construction and interpretation of a geographic profile. The most relevant ones include:

1. Crime locations — Offence locations and times are the most important data in a geographic profile. Also significant are the number and types of crime sites, their parsing, and the crime location set.
2. Offender type — The type and number of offender(s) affect crime geography. If multiple criminals living apart are involved, the geoprofile will focus on the dominant one's residence. Large, amorphous gangs may not be suitable for geographic profiling because of changing group composition. Psychological profiling assists in interpreting offender behaviour by providing information on personality, background, and level of organization.
3. Hunting style — Criminal hunting methods influence both encounter and body dump site target patterns. Hunting style must be considered when preparing a geographic profile.

4. Target backcloth — Constrained or patchy target backcloths limit the degree of offender choice, affecting the importance of certain crime site types for the profile.

5. Arterial roads and highways — People, including criminals, do not travel as the crow flies. Not only must they follow street layouts, but they are most likely to travel along major arterial routes, freeways, or highways.

6. Bus stops and rapid transit stations — Offenders without vehicles may use public transit or travel along bicycle and jogging paths. The locations and routes of these should be taken into consideration.

7. Physical and psychological boundaries — People are constrained by physical boundaries such as rivers, ocean, lakes, ravines, and highways. Psychological boundaries also influence movement. For example, a criminal of low socioeconomic status may avoid an upper class area, or a black offender might not wish to go into a white neighbourhood.

8. Zoning and land use — Zoning (e.g., residential, commercial, industrial) and land use (e.g., stores, bars, businesses, transportation centres, major facilities, government buildings, military institutions) provide keys as to why someone may be in a particular area. Police in Britain conduct site surveys and location inventories in the area surrounding a crime to help identify what may have brought an offender to a particular location. Similarly, information about the peak area in a geoprofile provides insight to a criminal's anchor point, and zoning classification helps determine if this is a residence or workplace. For example, the geographic profile for a series of bank robberies occurring during the early afternoon pointed towards a commercially zoned area. Time and location factors correctly suggested an offender who was committing the crimes during his lunch break from work.

9. Neighborhood demographics — Some sex offenders prefer victims of a certain racial or ethnic group. These groups may be more common in certain neighbourhoods than in others, affecting spatial crime patterns.

10. Victim routine activities — The pattern of routine victim movements provides insight to how the offender is searching for targets.

11. Singularities — Single offences that do not appear to fit the overall pattern of the crime series may provide important clues and should be carefully reviewed.

12. Displacement — Media coverage or uniformed police presence can cause spatial displacement, affecting the locations of subsequent crime sites.

Crime locations are the basis of a geographic profile, and a given murder can involve separate encounter, attack, murder, and body dump sites. But other locations that are not crime sites per se may also be connected to an offence. Examples of such locations include credit or bank card use, mailings, telephone calls, vehicle rentals or drops, witness sightings, and found property or evidence sites. In these cases, it may be possible to geographically profile a single crime, depending upon the number and types of locations.

In October 1995 two teenage girls in the municipality of Abbotsford, British Columbia, were attacked on the street at night by a man with a baseball bat. One victim was murdered and dumped in the Vedder Canal, some 20 miles away; the other was left for dead, but she somehow managed to revive and make her way to a nearby hospital. A few days later, the Abbotsford Killer began a series of bizarre actions starting with several taunting 911 telephone calls. He then stole and defaced the murder victim's gravestone and dumped it in the parking lot of a local radio station. Finally, he threw a note wrapped around a wrench through a house window; in the note, he admitted to other sexual assaults. These actions provided 13 different sites for the geographic profile. He was eventually caught through a local-based strategy initiated by the Abbotsford Police Department. His residence was in the top 7.7% of the geoprofile (0.6 mi^2).

A geoprofile may result in two peak areas, an indication the offender has more than one anchor point. Manley Eng, responsible for a series of arsons in Saanich and Victoria, British Columbia, left a crime pattern that resulted in dual peaks — one which contained his residence, and the other, his probation office. Information regarding land use, zoning, and area characteristics help interpret such outcomes. Examples of multiple anchor points include:

- Residence and work sites;
- Residence and social or family sites;
- Present and previous residences; and
- Two or more offenders living apart.

Between 1994 and 1998 the Mardi Gra Bomber was responsible for a total of 36 explosive devices, most in the Greater London area. These were mailed or delivered to locations near bank machines, supermarkets, payphones, businesses, and residences. Even though the targets and delivery methods varied, the underlying spatial pattern of the crimes remained consistent. Scotland Yard requested a geographic profile which produced two high probability regions; a primary area around Chiswick in west London, and a secondary peak in southeast London. When police detectives arrested two elderly brothers, it turned out they lived in Chiswick, and their family resided in southeast London. The geoprofile identified the convicted offender's home in the top 3.4% (9.1 mi²) of the hunting area.

Investigators may benefit from a geographic perspective on their crimes, independent of a formal profile. It is not just what offenders do, but also what they do not do, that is of interest. Some specific questions worth considering include:

1. Locations — What are the locations connected to this crime or crime series? Where are they? What are the distances and travel times between them?
2. Time — When did the crimes occur (i.e., time, weekday, date)? What was the weather on those dates? What are the time lags between crimes?
3. Site selection — How were the crime locations accessed? What else is in their general area? How might the offender have known of these locations? What criminal purpose or function did they serve?
4. Target backcloth — What is the geographic arrangement and availability of the target group? What degree of control did the offender have over the choice of crime locations? Has displacement (spatial or temporal) occurred?
5. Hunting — What hunting method did the offender use? Why were these sites chosen, and not other possible locations? What was the offender's probable mode of transportation?

10.4.2 Operational Procedures

10.4.2.1 Information Requirements

Certain operational procedures are followed in the request for and preparation of a geographic profile. Assessing the appropriateness of the crimes, collection of necessary information, and coordination between the profiler and the investigator are necessary. The following is the content of a standard letter sent by the Vancouver Police Department to investigators requesting a geographic profile. It outlines basic information requirements and procedural details:

> Geographic profiling is an investigative support technique for serial violent crime investigations. The process analyzes the locations connected to a series of crimes to determine the most probable area of offender residence. It should be regarded as an information management system designed to help focus an investigation, prioritize tips and suspects, and suggest new strategies to complement traditional methods.

> A preliminary assessment is necessary to determine if a case is appropriate for geographic profiling. This is best done by directly contacting the Van-

couver Police Department Geographic Profiling Section (GPS). If it is determined that a profile is appropriate, then an official letter of request must be sent to the Chief Constable. This letter should indicate the serious nature of the crimes, the fact that an initial discussion with the GPS has already occurred, and that all costs involved in the preparation of the profile will be covered. The Vancouver Police Department provides this service at no charge to requesting law enforcement and prosecution agencies, but any expenses incurred must be borne by the requesting agency.

A case information package should be prepared and forwarded to the GPS. The accuracy of the profile is determined by the quality of the information on which it is based. This package should include the following:

A list of all locations connected to those crimes believed to be part of the series (e.g., victim encounter sites, crime scenes, body dump/victim release sites, offender directions of travel, etc. This list should be in chronological order, and include complete address information, and date, weekday, and time of offence;
A street map with all crime locations precisely marked;
Case summaries;
A criminal profile (if available);
The investigating officer's business card; and
Any other relevant information.

Further information may be required (e.g., crime scene photographs, demographic data, bus routes, etc.). If necessary, the GPS will advise the investigating officer of what additional information is required. All GPS casework is kept strictly confidential.

The requesting agency must decide if they wish to have the geographic profile prepared on-site. An on-site profile is more thorough, accurate, and complete, and is recommended in more serious cases. All travel and accommodation expenses (e.g., airfare, taxis, airport tax, hotel, meals, etc.) are the responsibility of the requesting agency, and must be reimbursed to the GPS within 30 days of expenditure.

In most cases the GPS will prepare a written report, complete with colour maps, indicating the area of most probable offender residence. This will be mailed, by normal post (unless otherwise specified), to the investigating officer. While this report explains the theory, process, and output of geographic profiling, and suggests certain investigative strategies, it is recommended that the officer consult with the GPS if there are any questions or if further explanation is required. If additional crimes occur or new information comes to light, an update on the profile may be necessary. When the offender is apprehended, the GPS would appreciate being notified so that the accuracy and utility of the geographic profile can be assessed. It is important to realize that a profile is only one tool of many, and the requesting agency is responsible for intelligently combining it with the other techniques available to an investigation. If there are any questions regarding geographic profiling, the GPS can be contacted directly.

Not every case may be geographically profiled. While a preliminary review is necessary to determine suitability, generally a profile may be developed when the following conditions have been met:

1. A series of crimes has occurred that have been linked together with a reasonable degree of certainty (i.e., they are likely the responsibility of the same offender);
2. There are at least five crime sites in the series (although in some circumstances it may be possible to provide an assessment with fewer locations); and
3. The investigation is of a serious enough nature to justify the time and effort required to produce the profile.

A geographic assessment may be appropriate in those instances where a full profile cannot be prepared, for example, in cases involving only a few crime sites. Time-distance-speed calculations, journey-to-crime estimates, mental map interpretations, Thiessen polygons, and other methods of analysis have been successfully used in both geographic profiles and assessments. Thiessen polygons (also known as a Voronoi or Dirichlet polygons) define catchment areas around central positions, and any point within a given polygon is closer to its centre than to any other "competing" centre. The technique can be applied in cases involving certain offender hunting styles. For example, plotting the locations of playgrounds as Thiessen polygon centres may determine the probable residence area for a pedophile. This method was employed to determine the catchment regions around high schools in St. Catharines, Ontario, for the Green Ribbon Task Force investigation of the abductions and murders of two teenage girls. The killers, Paul Bernardo and Karla Homolka, identified through DNA, resided near the school attended by the second victim. The geographic profile correctly predicted an offender residence area of 10 square kilometres (0.5% of the total hunting area).

10.4.2.2 Requesting a Geographic Profile

A geographic profile takes approximately two weeks to complete, though response time depends upon current case load. Requests are prioritized according to level of community risk — murder over rape, current cases over historical ones, active offenders over intermittent criminals. The process of profile preparation follows a set outline, the main steps of which include:

1. Thorough perusal of the case file, including investigation reports, witness statements, autopsy reports, and criminal profile (if available);
2. Detailed examination of crime scene and area photographs;
3. Interviews with lead investigators and crime analysts;
4. Visits to each of the crime sites, when possible;
5. Review of neighbourhood and demographic information;
6. Study of street, land use, and transit maps;
7. Analysis; and
8. Report preparation.

The Vancouver Police Department established the world's first geographic profiling capability in 1990, with a mandate to provide services to the international police community. It has assisted in over 100 investigations, involving 1500 crimes, for agencies such as Scotland Yard, the FBI, the New York Police Department, and the RCMP. Requests have come from across Canada and the U.S., as well as from Britain, Germany, Belgium, Greece, South Africa, Mexico, Australia, New Zealand, and the Middle East. The service is now also available from the RCMP, the Ontario Provincial Police, and the British National Crime Faculty. Their profilers successfully completed an intensive understudy training program in Vancouver, the details of which are described below. Several other agencies have expressed interest in setting up similar units. Currently, the possibility of the Police Fellowship of Profilers (ICIAF) also becoming the international professional body for geographic profilers is being examined.

Contact details for qualified geographic profilers[67] are listed below:

Detective Inspector D. Kim Rossmo
Geographic Profiling Section
Vancouver Police Department
312 Main Street
Vancouver, British Columbia
V6A 2T2 Canada
Telephone: (604) 717-3247

Corporal Scot M. Filer
Geographic Profiling Unit
Pacific Region ViCLAS Centre
Royal Canadian Mounted Police
"E" Division Headquarters
4949B Heather Street

---

[67] The RCMP will be adding an additional geographic profiling position to its Behavioural Sciences and Special Services Branch at Ottawa Headquarters in late 1999.

Vancouver, British Columbia
V5Z 1K6 Canada
Telephone: (604) 264-2955

Detective Sergeant Brad J. Moore
Geographic Profiling Unit
Behavioural Sciences Section
Ontario Provincial Police
General Headquarters
Lincoln M. Alexander Building
777 Memorial Avenue
Orillia, Ontario
L3V 7V3 Canada
Telephone: (705) 329-6487

Detective Sergeant Neil Trainor
Serious Crime Analysis Section
National Crime Faculty
Foxley Hall, Bramshill
Nr. Hook, Hampshire
RG27 0JW
England, United Kingdom
Telephone: (01256) 602660

10.4.3 Understudy Training Program

The Geographic Profiling Understudy Program is designed to provide comprehensive training to members of those agencies wishing to establish their own geographic profiling capability. Modeled after the FBI Police Fellowship training, the program commenced in September 1997 at the Vancouver Police Department Geographic Profiling Section, and the first successful graduates completed their studies in the fall of 1998.

The following criteria were established as a general guide to assist police agencies in the selection of suitable understudy candidates. Applicants should:

- Have extensive service involving patrol duties and at least 3 years recent experience in the investigation of crimes of interpersonal violence, including homicide or sexual assault, and have a documented and superior level of investigative skill in this area;
- Have demonstrated an ability to work effectively with outside police and other law enforcement agencies;

- Have demonstrated above average oral and written communication skills;
- Have a documented high level of interpersonal skills;
- Agree to remain in geographic profiling duties, on a full-time basis, for at least 5 years following a 2-year understudy program;
- Be willing to travel on short notice (as both an understudy candidate and a geographic profiler);
- Have the ability to dedicate long hours to academic pursuits as required (both as an understudy candidate and as a geographic profiler);
- Be mathematically competent with an ability to master basics of probability and statistics;
- Be computer literate and have the ability to accurately read maps;
- Have a documented high level of self-motivation and the ability to work without supervision;
- Have the ability to learn psychological and geographical concepts and techniques;
- Have a demonstrated ability to grasp abstract concepts and complex scenarios;
- Have a documented aptitude for thoroughness in conducting complex investigations;
- Have demonstrated a balance of tenacity and open-mindedness in his or her duties;
- Have demonstrated a proficiency in public speaking and presenting lectures to both small and large groups; and
- Have a high level of credibility in the police community, particularly with investigative units both within and outside their own agency.

Suitable candidates embark upon a year of study under the tutelage of a mentor who must be a fully qualified geographic profiler. The training program is divided into four blocks:

1. Probability, statistics, and computer systems;
2. Violent and sexual crime, and offence linkage;
3. Violent sexual offenders and criminal profiling; and
4. Quantitative spatial techniques and geographic profiling.

The first three blocks are done through distance education, under the supervision of the understudy's mentor. The fourth block (four months) is a residency at the mentor's agency, involving both reviews of previous files and casework in active investigations. The sequence of the training blocks is

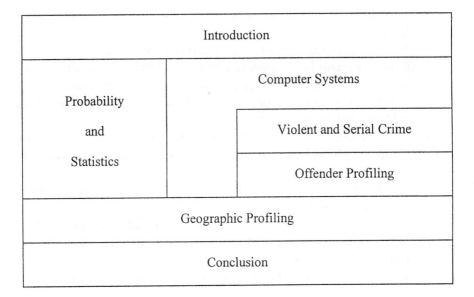

Figure 10.7 Understudy training program.

shown in Figure 10.7. To successfully conclude the program, the understudy must pass a qualifying examination at the end of the training period.

The graduate then returns to his or her home agency with the status of associate geographic profiler. At this stage, he or she is operational and works active cases, preparing geographic profiles and assessments as appropriate. The associate is on probation for one year and remains linked to the mentor for support and guidance. He or she is not allowed to train new candidates or testify as an expert in court. The associate is also required to conduct a research project that adds to the body of knowledge in the area of geography of crime. Upon the successful completion of this component of the program, the associate becomes a fully qualified geographic profiler. The candidate's agency is responsible for all expenses and the mentor's agency has right of refusal for unsuitable individuals; a memorandum of understanding is signed between the two agencies outlining details of the training arrangement. The qualification process and the candidate's continuing education are important for the development of professional skills and expertise (see U.S. Department of Justice, 1995).

10.4.4 The Rigel Computer System

Rigel[68] is a computerized geographic profiling workstation based on the patented CGT algorithm. It incorporates an analytic engine, GIS capability,

---

[68] *Rigel* is pronounced "RI-jul."

database management, and powerful visualization tools. Crime locations, which are broken down by type (e.g., victim encounter, murder, and body dump sites for a homicide), provide the input and are entered by the optional means of street address, latitude/longitude, or digitization. This reflects the realities of policing in which crimes can happen anywhere — houses, parking lots, back alleys, highways, parks, rivers, mountain ravines, and so on. Latitude and longitude coordinates can be determined from a handheld global positioning system (GPS) that reads the user's position from a satellite fix.

Scenarios, wherein crime locations are weighted based upon certain theoretical and methodological principles, are next created and examined.[69] Output is a map of the most likely area of offender residence. Suspect addresses can be evaluated according to their hit score percentage on a z-score histogram, allowing the prioritization of known criminals, registered sex offenders, task force tips, and other information. Examples of *Rigel* output for a GIS map are shown in Figure 10.2 and Chapter 10 Colour Figures 1 and 2, and examples for an image map are shown in Figure 11.1, and Chapter 11 Colour Figures 1 and 2.

Rigel was developed by Environmental Criminology Research Inc. (ECRI) of Vancouver, British Columbia, and the system currently runs on a high-end Sun UltraSPARC workstation (a Java-based version was scheduled for completion in late 1999). This provides the computing power for the 1,000,000 or so calculations of the CGT algorithm a typical analysis requires. Geoprofiles and jeopardy surfaces can be rotated and visually manipulated in a variety of ways, facilitating their interpretation. Orthodigital photographs may be overlaid on the peak geoprofile area, assisting the user in viewing land use within the region of interest. Large databases can be searched and their entries prioritized by address. These include sex offender registries, major case management programs, and crime linkage systems, such as ViCLAS. *Rigel* is designed to enable law enforcement agencies to make the best use of their limited resources. It is the main tool used in geographic profiling.

Its namesake Rigel (β Orionis) is a supergiant forming part of the winter constellation Orion (Menzel & Pasachoff, 1983). It is a hot blue star, 50,000 times as bright as our Sun, and 1400 light years away. Rigel, meaning "foot" in Arabic, constitutes the heel of Orion. In Greek mythology, Orion was a mighty giant hunter who was loved by Artemis, the goddess of the moon and hunt; but she was tricked by her twin brother, Apollo, into shooting him with an arrow. In her sorrow Artemis placed Orion in the night sky with his hunting dogs, facing Taurus, the bull. Legend holds that her grief is why the Moon looks so sad and cold (Levy, 1994). The symbolism in the name *Rigel*[70]

---

[69] Expert system support to structure this process and guide the profiler is planned for the near future.

[70] *Orion* was the name of the software prototype.

for the CGT-based geographic profiling software originates from the idea that the system is designed to support the hunter — the police detective — in his or her efforts to apprehend criminal offenders, just as Rigel the star supports Orion, the constellation hunter.

Investigative Applications  11

11.1 Strategies and Tactics

A variety of police strategies and tactics can be used more effectively and efficiently with a geographic profile. While specific applications are best determined by the investigators responsible for the case in question, suggestions for effective approaches are presented below. Their development has been an interactive process involving detectives, profilers, and academics. Case examples are used to illustrate these strategies, but it should be made clear that the crimes were not solved by geographic profiling; they were resolved by the assigned investigators. Profiling plays a support role, the importance of which can vary, and it is only one of many techniques in the investigator's tool box.

While the most common anchor point is the offender's residence, some cases involve other bases of criminal activity. Clifford Olson used body dump locations near Agassiz Mountain Prison where he had once been incarcerated. John Collins hunted in the area around Eastern Michigan University where he was a student and summer employee. Aileen Wuornos based her "hitch-hooking" from truck stops and freeway entrances in the town of Wildwood. Inmate records, enrollment and employee registries, and field checks were all potentially useful sources of investigative information in these cases. As important as residence is in structuring activity space, the value of business and institutional records should not be overlooked.

11.1.1 Suspect Prioritization

The geographic profile, in conjunction with a psychological profile, can help focus follow-up investigative work. The problem in many serial violent crime investigations is one of too many suspects rather than one of too few. Profiling can help reassess and prioritize hundreds or even thousands of suspects, leads, and tips.

The South Side Rapist in Lafayette, Louisiana, committed a series of 14 burglary rapes from 1984 to 1995. Detective McCullan Gallien refused to close the file, and requested a geographic profile which resulted in the identification of a neighborhood previously not considered. This was used as the basis for suspect and tip prioritization. One tip involved a sergeant with the Lafayette Parish Sheriff's Department who both fit the FBI's psychological profile and lived in the peak area of the geoprofile at the time of the crimes. DNA obtained from surveillance of the suspect matched samples from the crime scenes. The offender confessed, pled guilty, and was sentenced to life in prison. The geoprofile located the rapist's address in the top 2.2% (0.5 mi^2) of the hunting area. Figure 11.1 and Chapter 11 Colour Figures 1 and 2 show, respectively, the crime sites, jeopardy surface (top 20%), and geoprofile (top 15%) for this case. Residences of the offender are marked with blue dots in Colour Figure 2; his home during the main period of the attacks was the centre dot.

11.1.2   Police Information Systems

Additional investigative leads may be obtained from information contained in various computerized police dispatch and record systems. Such systems include computer aided dispatch (CAD) systems, records management systems (RMS), the RCMP Police Information Retrieval System (PIRS), and the like (Fowler, 1990; Rebscher & Rohrer, 1991). Offender profile details and case specifics can help further focus the search.

For example, police may be investigating a series of sexual assaults that have been psychologically profiled as the crimes of an anger retaliatory rapist. Such an offender is "getting even with women for real or imagined wrongs ... the attack is an emotional outburst that is predicated on anger" (Hazelwood, 1995, p. 163). His rapes are often initiated by conflicts with a significant woman in his life and he will frequently select victims who symbolize the source of that conflict. A search of CAD data for domestic disturbance calls on the dates of the rapes to see which ones originated from the area where the geographic profile suggests that the offender most likely resides could produce viable suspects. This process is particularly powerful with police record systems integrated with geographic information systems.

Police agencies with computerized records containing description, address, and M.O. of local offenders can also use profiling information, including probable area of residence, as the basis for developing search criteria. Many departments have such files for specific types of criminals, such as parolees or sex offenders (Brahan, Valcour, & Shevel, 1994; Pilant, 1994; Skogan & Antunes, 1979). The latter commonly have nuisance crimes (e.g.,

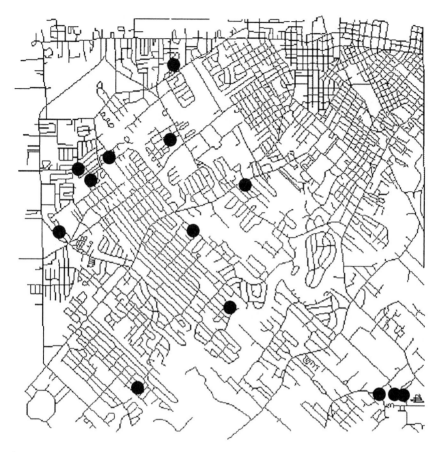

Figure 11.1   Lafayette South Side Rapist — crime sites.

loitering, trespassing, peeping, etc.) in their backgrounds, and the locations
of their past offences may overlap with the present ones.

11.1.3   Task Force Management

Task force operations formed to investigate a specific series of crimes often
collect and collate their information in some form of computerized major
case management system, such as the British HOLMES or FBI Rapid Start
programs (Federal Bureau of Investigation, 1996; U.S. Department of Justice,
1991b). Cases suffering from information overload will benefit from the
prioritization of data and the application of correlation analysis (Keppel &
Birnes, 1995). Geographic profiling can assist in these tasks through the
ranking of street addresses, postal or zip codes, and telephone number
(NNXs) areas.

This process can also be linked to information available in CD-ROM telephone directory databases listing residential and business names, telephone numbers, addresses, postal or zip codes, business headings, and standard industrial classification (SIC) codes. The details of the specific task force computer database software, including information fields, search time, number of records, and correlational abilities, determine the most appropriate form the geographic profile should take to maximize its usefulness to the police investigation.

11.1.4 Sex Offender Registries

Violent sex offender registries are a useful information source for geographic profiling in cases of serial sex crimes (Popkin, 1994). By providing a list of addresses of known sex criminals, these registries can be used with a geographic profile to help prioritize suspects. The U.S. *Violent Crime Control and Law Enforcement Act of 1994* "requires states to enact statutes or regulations which require those determined to be sexually violent predators or who are convicted of sexually violent offenses to register with appropriate state law enforcement agencies for ten years after release from prison," or risk the reduction of Federal grant money (U.S. Department of Justice, 1994a).

Sex offender registries are powerful tools for monitoring and controlling criminal predators who, unfortunately, are more prevalent than is commonly believed. Washington State established the first such registry, and according to the Seattle Police Department Special Assault Unit, in May of 1995 the City of Seattle had a total of 859 registered sex offenders, an average of 10 per square mile. This figure does not include the 20% of released sex offenders who fail to register.

11.1.5 Government and Business Databases

Data banks are often geographically based and information from parole and probation offices, mental health outpatient clinics, social services offices, schools, and other agencies located in prioritized areas can also prove to be of value (it has been estimated that approximately 85% of our records contain an address). LeBeau (1992) discusses the case of a serial rapist who emerged as a suspect after police checked parolee records for sex offenders. Private businesses may also contain information of interest. In one case involving a series of sexual assaults, the criminal profile suggested the offender was likely a frequent user of pornography. An SIC code search for video stores on a CD-ROM telephone directory produced a list, which was then prioritized by address according to the geoprofile. Investigators could then use this information to focus on prioritized stores, showing composite suspect sketches, and checking frequent renters of adult video titles, knowing most people frequent video stores close to home. Similarly, prioritization of automobile service stations is useful if a suspect vehicle description has been obtained.

11.1.6 Motor Vehicle Registrations

A geographic profile can be integrated with suspect vehicle and offender descriptions to search registered motor vehicle and driver's licence files, contained in provincial or state computer record systems. This is often done by first using the geoprofile to prioritize postal or zip codes most likely associated with the offender's residence. The description and geographic parameters act as a linear program to produce a small set of records containing the appropriate data. This strategy results in areas of manageable size for major police investigations.

A case example involving a violent child sex offender illustrates this point. The postal codes for the neighbourhood within which he was attacking children were prioritized from the geoprofile. Planning and zoning maps were then used to eliminate industrial, commercial, and other nonresidential areas. Socioeconomic and demographic census data were also consulted to reevaluate the priority of those neighbourhoods that were inconsistent with the socioeconomic level of the offender as suggested by the criminal profile.

The final list of postal codes, ranked by priority of probability, could then be used to conduct a computer search of the provincial motor vehicle department records which contain postal codes as part of the address associated with the vehicle registered owner and driver's licence files. Suspect vehicle and offender descriptions had been developed by detectives, and this information was combined with the geographic data to effectively focus the search.

For example, a new red station wagon driven by a tall white middle-aged male, with dark hair, may seem to be somewhat vague information. But the description actually contains several parameters: (1) vehicle style — station wagon; (2) vehicle colour — red; and (3) vehicle year range — last 5 years. Additional focus results from the various driver descriptors (e.g., sex, race, age range, height, hair colour, etc.), though the assumption that the driver is the vehicle's registered owner may be incorrect. These parameters can narrow down hundreds of thousands of records to a few dozen vehicles or drivers when combined with a prioritized list of postal or zip codes. This is sufficient discrimination to allow detailed police follow-up (see Ressler & Shachtman, 1992, for an example of a murder investigation involving a computerized vehicle search without such geographic discrimination).

11.1.7 Patrol Saturation and Stakeouts

The geoprofile can be used as the basis for directing saturation patrol and police stakeouts. This strategy is particularly effective if the crimes occur during specific time periods. Many criminals spend a significant amount of time searching for targets, while others wait in particular areas for suitable victims and the right circumstances. Police have a much greater chance of observing an offender prowling or loitering than in an assault simply because considerable more time is spent hunting than attacking. It has been estimated that some criminals exhibit hunt to attack ratios in excess of 10:1.

Kentucky police, correctly anticipating the movements of a serial killer from the pattern of his crimes, set up road blocks in a park to question late night motorists (Barrett, 1990). This tactic gathered over 2000 names for the purpose of cross-comparison with other investigative information. Through a geographic analysis of the crime sites in the Atlanta Child Murders, Dettlinger came to the conclusion the killer was commuting along certain city routes (Dettlinger & Prugh, 1983). But his suggestion that stakeouts be established at the crucial points in this spatial pattern went unheeded by police, and five more bodies would be dumped near these locations before Task Force officers staking out a Chattahoochee River bridge pulled over Wayne Williams.

11.1.8   Response Plans

Additional police responses in the event of a new crime may be developed with a geographic profile. Many criminals return home after committing a crime, and patrol units can be directed to the area of probable offender residence, in addition to responding to the crime scene. Particular attention should be paid to the most logical routes from the crime site to the high profile area, and to relevant major arterial streets, freeways, and off-ramps. Roadblocks may also be an option. This strategy is only appropriate for those cases in which there is no significant time delay in reporting of the crime. Depending on the size of the hunting area, the offender's probable escape routine might also suggest possibilities for locating witnesses. Gasoline stations, cafés, pubs, and other services along the likely routes between the crime sites and the peak geoprofile area can be identified and canvassed. Closed circuit television (CCTV) and commercial video cameras can similarly be checked.

In serial murder cases, police response plans can be developed in the event of the discovery of a new body dump site. Some killers reuse previous body dump sites; other offenders have been known to repeatedly visit their crime sites between killings for the purposes of fulfilling sexual fantasies. If the discovery of a new body dump site can be kept secret from the media, police surveillance may catch the offender revisiting the location.

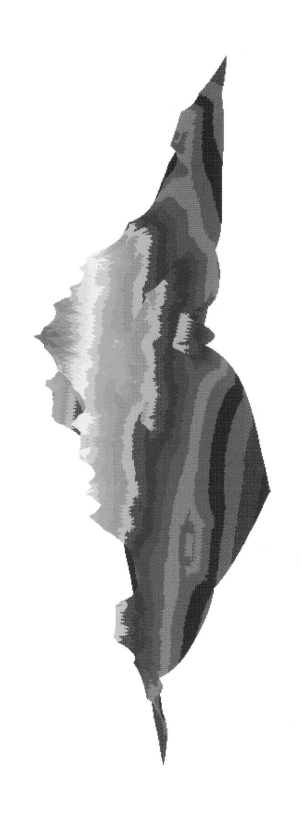

Chapter 10, Colour Figure 1 Vancouver robberies —Jeopardy surface.

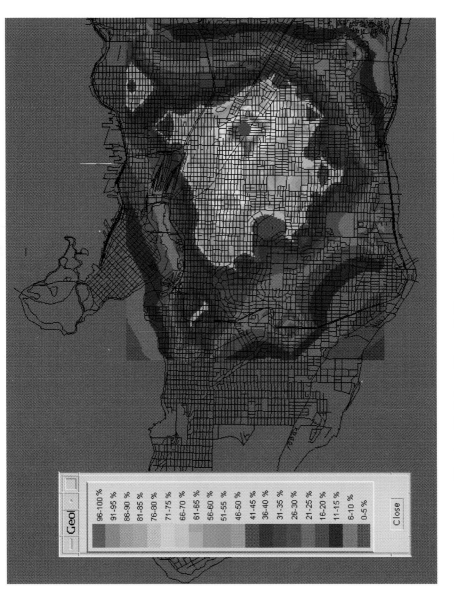

96-100 %	
91-95 %	
86-90 %	
81-85 %	
76-80 %	
71-75 %	
66-70 %	
61-65 %	
56-60 %	
51-55 %	
46-50 %	
41-45 %	
36-40 %	
31-35 %	
26-30 %	
21-25 %	
16-20 %	
11-15 %	
6-10 %	
0-5 %	

Geol

Close

Chapter 10, Colour Figure 2 Vancouver robberies — GeoProfile.

Chapter 11, Colour Figure 1 Lafayette South Side Rapist — Jeopardy surface.

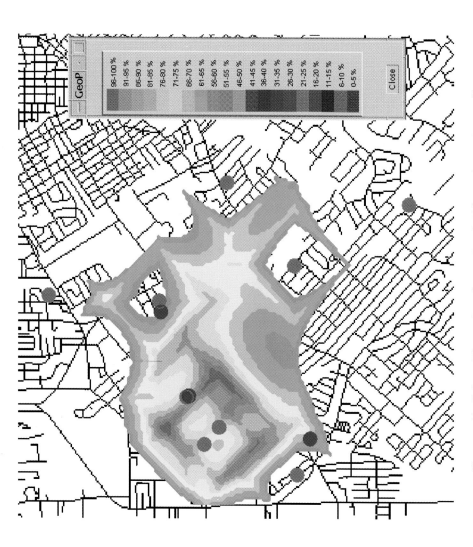

Chapter 11, Colour Figure 2 Lafayette South Side Rapist — GeoProfile.

11.1.9 Mail Outs

Information regarding the offender can be mailed or delivered to those households and businesses located within the peak area of the geoprofile. This is accomplished through the geographic prioritization of postal or zip codes; postal workers in the appropriate letter carrier walks can then delivery the information packages at commercial rates, allowing thousands of premises to be covered for only a few hundred dollars. The purpose of this approach is two-fold. First, people are more likely to respond to an individualized request stating the offender resides in their neighbourhood than they are to generalized television broadcasts or newspaper stories. Second, this method generates high quality information as it comes from those individuals in a better position to know the offender from either home or work. Less focused methods often produce low quality responses and information overload problems. The mail-out tactic is viable only if the offender description information is sufficient and reliable; preferably, a suspect composite sketch is available. Personality details generated from a psychological profile can also be included.

11.1.10 Neighbourhood Canvasses

A thorough police canvass in the area where a victim was abducted, attacked, or dumped is a useful and proven investigative approach. Such efforts may also be directed within the neighbourhood of probable offender residence. Prioritized areas can focus door-to-door canvassing, interviews, grid searches, information sign posting, and community cooperation and media campaigns. Police departments have used this approach to target areas for leaflet distribution, employing prioritized letter carrier walks for strategic household mail delivery. LeBeau (1992) notes the case of a serial rapist in San Diego who was arrested through canvassing efforts in an area targeted by analysis of the crime locations. The Vampire Killer, serial murderer Richard Trenton Chase, was caught in the same manner after a psychological profile predicted he would be living near a recovered vehicle stolen from one of the victims (Biondi & Hecox, 1992).

Neighbourhood canvasses and grid searches sometimes cover vast areas. John Joubert left the body of his first victim, a young newsboy, in high grass beside a gravel road outside of Omaha (Ressler & Shachtman, 1992). This was 4 miles from where police located the victim's bicycle, resulting in an extensive building-to-building search. A circle with a radius of 4 miles has an area of 50 square miles (130 km^2). Methods to geographically prioritize searches of this size have obvious value.

11.1.11 News Media

Investigative media strategies may use a geographic profile in attempts to generate new tips. Summary results or full profiles can be released, depending on the details of the specific case and the status of the investigation. Because of the risk of displacement, both spatially and temporally, this approach needs to be carefully considered. Factors such as the number of crimes, the rate of offending, the reliability of suspect descriptions, and the availability of other investigative initiatives must be assessed. Television shows, including *CrimeStoppers*, news broadcasts, and special crime programs are the most effective medium because of their visual nature and large coverage. Newspapers and magazines can also be used. Mainstream media might be supplemented with neighbourhood newspapers and community postings in key locations. Media strategies involving geographic profiling and surveillance activities should not be conducted at the same time as the former will hinder the latter. An optimal approach would first involve surveillance, followed by a media campaign.

During 1995, a series of 32 armed robberies targeting primarily insurance agencies plagued Vancouver, British Columbia. Three investigative strategies were predicated upon the geographic profile. First, a search was conducted of the Vancouver Police Department's Records Management System for known robbery offenders, matching the criminals' descriptions, who resided within the top 5% of the geoprofile. This failed to produce viable matches; it later turned out that neither offender had a previous conviction for robbery.

Second, a simplified geoprofile, displaying only the top 2% (0.7 mi^2), was generated for patrol officers. Previous research found robbers usually return home after the commission of their crime; it was therefore suggested that in addition to responding to a crime scene after the report of a new robbery, patrol members should also search the most likely area of offender residence, with particular attention paid to logical routes of travel. This tactic also was unsuccessful; the offenders were using stolen cars and no reliable vehicle descriptions were ever obtained (the geoprofile was used by police units to search for stolen automobiles that might be "laid down" prior to a new robbery). The third tactic involved releasing the results of the geoprofile on television through *CrimeStoppers*. This approach was helpful in that the robberies immediately stopped. Detectives identified the offenders by reassessing their tips. The primary robber's address was located within the top 1.5% of the peak geoprofile area. Figures 10.2, and Chapter 10 Colour Figures 1 and 2 show, respectively, the crime sites, jeopardy surface, and full geoprofile for this case. The residence of the offender is marked with a blue dot in Chapter 10 Colour Figure 2.

11.1.12 Bloodings

During a sexual murder or rape investigation, British police may conduct large-scale DNA testing of all men from the area of the crime ("How the DNA 'Database,'" 1995). The first such case was the Narborough Murder Enquiry, when "all unalibied male residents in the villages between the ages of seventeen and thirty-four years would be asked to submit blood and saliva samples voluntarily in order to 'eliminate them' as suspects in the footpath murders" (Wambaugh, 1989, pp. 220-221). Close to 4,000 men from the villages of Narborough, Littlethorpe, and Enderby were tested during the investigation.

Because considerable police resources and laboratory costs are involved in such "bloodings," British police conduct intelligence-led DNA screens in which individuals are prioritized based on proximity to scene, criminal record, age, and other relevant criteria (National Crime Faculty, 1996). In cases of serial crime, geographic profiling can further refine the selection process through targeting by address, or postal or zip code, resulting in more efficient and systematic testing procedures. Canadian police are also beginning to use this strategy. A series of 11 sexual assaults including a rape occurred within the space of just over a month in Mississauga, Ontario. The investigation by the Peel Regional Police resulted in 312 suspects. Combining the geographic and psychological profiles with description and interview information, detectives prioritized the suspects into groups and obtained DNA samples from the most probable individuals. The offender was identified in the first lot. He resided within the top 2.2% (0.03 mi^2) of the area under consideration.

11.1.13 Peak-of-Tension Polygraphy

In presumed homicides with known suspects but no bodies, polygraphists have had success in narrowing down the search area for the victim's remains through peak-of-tension (POT) tests (Hagmaier, 1990; see also Cunliffe & Piazza, 1980; Lyman, 1993; Raskin, 1989). Peak-of-tension polygraphy involves monitoring a subject's reaction to photographs, objects, or maps, as opposed to answering verbal questions. A deceptive response to queries concerning the type of location where the victim's body was hidden (e.g., cave, lake, marsh, field, forest, etc.) can help focus a search. Because POT tests often involve maps or pictures, their usefulness is enhanced when results are combined with a geographic profile.

11.1.14 Fugitive Location

In cases where the identity but not the whereabouts of a criminal fugitive is known, geographic profiling may be able to assist in determining probable hiding places. Sightings, purchases, credit or bank card transactions, telephone calls, cellular telephone switch sites, crimes, and other locational information can be used as input for the profile. This process is also applicable to extortion and kidnapping investigations.

11.1.15 Missing Bodies

In certain missing person cases that are suspected homicides, geographic profiling can help determine probable body dump site areas. In November 1993, a teenage boy was found shot dead in his parked car, and his girlfriend kidnapped, outside St. Antoine, New Brunswick. The murderer was identified through rifle ballistics but he disappeared before arrest. After unsuccessfully pursuing various leads and tips, the RCMP began to theorize that the missing female victim had been killed and the offender had committed suicide. Two searches by police and military teams of the rural Bouctouche region failed to find evidence of either body. A geographic profile was then prepared and it identified two prioritized search areas using techniques of path analysis, journey-to-crime estimates, and time-distance-speed calculations. A third search effort located effects of the offender in a river under a railway trestle, and the body of the female victim in a field; the former was found in the highest prioritized area of the geoprofile, and the latter in the second highest.

11.1.16 Trial Court Expert Evidence

While geographic profiling is primarily an investigative tool, it also has a role in the courtroom. In addition to analyzing the geographic patterns of unsolved crimes for investigative insights, the spatial relationship between the locations of a crime series and an accused offender's activity sites can be assessed in terms of the probability of their congruence (Rossmo, 1994a). When combined with other forensic identification findings (e.g., a DNA profile), such information increases evidential strength and likelihood of guilt. The question of how to most appropriately quantify the weight of forensic identification evidence and rare trait possession is called the generalized island problem (see Balding & Donnelly, 1994). Geographic profiles can also be used as supporting grounds for search warrant affidavits.

On the cold winter morning of January 31, 1969, nursing assistant Gail Miller left home and walked to the bus stop to go to work (Karp & Rosner, 1991). She never made it. She was pulled into an alley, raped, and stabbed. David Milgaard, a 16-year-old youth from Regina, was later arrested, tried, and convicted of her murder. He was sentenced to life imprisonment but maintained his innocence throughout 23 years of incarceration.

In 1990, an alternative suspect surfaced. Larry Fisher was a serial rapist who lived in Riversdale, a block away from Miller's bus stop, at the time of the murder. After lobbying efforts by Milgaard's family, the Minister of Justice ordered a review of the case by the Supreme Court of Canada. As part of the review, a geographic assessment of the crimes, Milgaard, and Fisher was undertaken (Boyd & Rossmo, 1992).

"True to his controlling, orderly nature, Fisher committed his rapes in a comfort zone, which in the winter of 1969 was alleys in the working-class Saskatoon neighbourhood where he lived and Gail Miller died" (Milgaard & Edwards, 1999, p. 211). There were strong parallels in M.O. and crime site microenvironment between Fisher's rapes and the Miller murder — same immediate area, identical location type (alleys protected from observation by garages, fences, and vegetation), similar hunting style, same attack method, clothing manipulation, use of a knife, and brutality of sexual assault (Boyd & Rossmo, 1992). The similarity is even more striking given the rarity of stranger sexual assault in Saskatoon in 1969.

Conversely, the circumstances of Milgaard on the morning of the murder did not support an opportunity to commit the crime. The geographic profile suggested that Fisher was the more probable suspect, but profiling is insufficient for the establishment of either guilt or innocence. More compelling, a time-distance-speed analysis cast doubt on the accuracy of statements made by certain witnesses for the prosecution. In 1997, advanced DNA testing methods in Britain resulted in Milgaard's exoneration and the arrest and charge of Fisher for Miller's murder (see Connors, Lundregan, Miller, & McEwen, 1996).

11.2 Jack the Ripper

No one knows who Jack the Ripper was. And no one knows for certain what motivated him (Abrahamsen, 1992). But he was, in a macabre way, a man for his times. The turmoil of the Industrial Revolution in Britain upset the standard social order, generating new ambitions, conflicts, and frustrations. Urbanization, crowding, and change led to anomie and the creation of the alienated loner. Harsh and inhumane conditions, an indifference towards children, and a savage lifestyle all conspired to create an environment conducive to violence and sexual deviance. It is not surprising the psychological and social infrastructures of the 19th century produced the first modern serial killer (Leyton, 1986).

Many of the rookeries in Victorian London were demolished during a series of social reforms, but the slums of Whitechapel and Spitalfields survived and predictably endured an influx of criminals displaced by the city's urban renewal (see Brantingham & Brantingham, 1984). The late 1800s saw almost a million people dwelling in the slums east of Aldgate Pump; 4000 houses in Whitechapel alone one year were condemned as uninhabitable, though little was done about it for years (Rumbelow, 1988). Liquid sewage filled the cellars of houses and people kept their windows — those not yet broken — shut because of the stench from without. The majority of families, often up to nine people, lived in one room. Incest was common in these crowded conditions, even amongst children as young as 10.

Many East End youth died before they were five. It would not be unusual for a mother to send her young children into the streets until after midnight, while she engaged in the business of prostitution to make sufficient money to feed them. Often children fell off their seats at school from exhaustion or cried from the pain of chronic starvation. Yet these unfortunates at least had a home. Many others slept on the streets or in dustbins, under stairways or bridges. Those who managed to scrape together enough money could rent a room in a lodging house, and such buildings held 8500 nightly in Whitechapel. Within these doss houses, flea-infested wallpaper hung in strips and stairway handrails were missing, long ago burnt for firewood. If you could not afford a straw mattress, two pence bought you the privilege of a place along a rope to lean against and sleep (Rumbelow, 1977).

Women's work included scrubbing, sweatshop tailoring, hop picking, and sack or matchbox making, all with a complete lack of safety standards. Seventeen hours of backbreaking labour paid 10 pence, less the cost of materials. Prostitution was a viable alternative, paying anywhere from a loaf of stale bread to three pence. It was estimated that one woman in 16 engaged in this trade, for a total of 1200 prostitutes in Whitechapel and 80,000 in London (Rumbelow, 1988). The environment in the slums of London was such that Irish playwright George Bernard Shaw commented, after the second of the Ripper killings, that perhaps "the murderer was a social reformer who wanted to draw attention to social conditions in the East End" (C. Wilson, 1960, p. 60).

Little is known about Jack the Ripper beyond his handiwork. The first canonical murder took place on Bank Holiday, Friday, August 31, 1888, in Buck's Row. The victim was Polly Nichols, a 42-year-old alcoholic with grey hair and five missing front teeth. She had five children from a broken marriage. The Ripper cut her throat from ear to ear, back to the vertebrae, and sliced open her abdomen from pelvis to stomach. The autopsy found she sustained stab wounds to the vagina (Howells & Skinner, 1987).

The next killing took place in a yard at No. 29 Hanbury Street, on Saturday, September 8, 1888. Annie Chapman was 45 years of age, stout, pugnacious, and missing two of her front teeth. An alcoholic, she was separated from her husband and two children, one of them a cripple. She was found with her neck cut so deeply it appeared as if an attempt had been made to take off her head. Her abdomen was laid open and her intestines placed on her shoulder. Parts of her vagina and bladder had been removed.

On Sunday, September 30, 1988, a double murder occurred. The Ripper first attacked Elizabeth Stride in a courtyard next to the International Working Men's Educational Club on Berner Street. Stride was a 45-year-old alcoholic missing her front teeth and the roof of her mouth. She bore nine children, but claimed her husband and two offspring had perished in a steamboat disaster. The Ripper had cut her throat, severing the windpipe. The mutilation was minimal as he was interrupted by a carriage entering the courtyard.

Within the hour a second body was discovered in Mitre Square, in the City of London. Catherine Eddowes, 43 years, was, like her fellow victims, an alcoholic with a broken marriage. She carried all her worldly possessions in her pockets. Her throat was deeply cut, and her abdomen laid open from breast downwards, the entrails "flung in a heap about her neck." Her ear was almost cut off and a kidney taken, the latter apparently later mailed to the authorities.

The final and most horrific murder occurred in 13 Miller's Court, on Friday, November 9, 1888. Mary Kelly, only 20 years of age and 3 months pregnant, was already a widow with alcohol problems. A bizarre sight greeted those who discovered her body. Her head and left arm were almost severed, her breasts and nose cut off, thighs and forehead skinned, entrails wrenched away, and her body parts piled on the bedside table. Jack the Ripper had all the time he needed to satiate his bizarre desires in Miller's Court, and while debate continues on whether he was responsible for other prostitute murders that occurred around this time, most investigators believe he stopped, for whatever reason, after the mutilation of Mary Kelly (Wilson & Odell, 1987).

In 1988 the FBI prepared a criminal personality profile for the Jack the Ripper murders (Begg, Fido, & Skinner, 1991; Douglas & Olshaker, 1995; The secret identity of Jack the Ripper, 1988). After an analysis of the crime scenes, police and autopsy reports, photographs, victimology, and area demographics, the following key crime scene elements were identified:

- Blitz attacks and lust murders;
- High degree of psychopathology exhibited at the crime scenes;
- No evidence of sexual assault;
- Possible manual strangulation;
- Postmortem mutilation and organ removal, but no torture;
- Elaboration of ritual;
- Victims selected on the basis of accessibility;
- All the crimes took place on a Friday, Saturday, or Sunday, in the early morning hours; and

- Unreported attacks might have occurred.

With the caution that profiling deals in probabilities and generalities, not certainties, the FBI report suggests that Jack the Ripper:

- Was a white male, 28–36 years of age;
- Was of average intelligence, lucky not clever;
- Was single, never married, and had difficulty in interacting with people in general and women in particular;
- Was nocturnal and not accountable to anyone;
- Blended in with his surroundings;
- Had poor personal hygiene, and appeared disheveled;
- Was personally inadequate with a low self-image and diminished emotional responses;
- Was a quiet loner, withdrawn and asocial;
- Was of lower social class;
- Lived or worked in Whitechapel, and committed the crimes close to home;
- Had a menial job with little or no interaction with the public;
- Was employed Monday to Friday, possibly as a butcher, mortician's helper, medical examiner's assistant, or hospital attendant (the proximity of London Hospital was noted in the profile);
- Was the product of a broken home, and lacked consistent care and stable adult role models as a child;
- Was raised by a dominant female figure who drank heavily, consorted with different men, and physically, possibly sexually, abused him;
- Set fires and abused animals as a child;
- Hated, feared, and was intimidated by women;
- Internalized his anger;
- Was mentally disturbed and sexually inadequate, with much generalized rage directed against women;
- Desired power, control, and dominance;
- Behaved erratically;
- Engaged in sexually motivated attacks to neuter his victims;
- Drank in local pubs prior to the murders;
- Hunted nightly, and was observed walking all over Whitechapel during the early morning hours;
- Did not have medical knowledge or surgical expertise;
- Was probably interviewed by police at some point;
- Did not write any of the "Jack the Ripper" letters, and would not have publicly challenged the police; and
- Did not commit suicide after the murders stopped.

The geographic concentration of the Ripper crimes has long made their "topography" of interest to researchers (Fido, 1987). The murders were all within a mile of each other, and the total hunting area was just over half a square mile in size. In 1998 a geographic profile was produced for the Jack the Ripper case based on body dump sites. The peak area of the geoprofile focused on the locale around Flower and Dean Street and Thrawl Street.

Flower and Dean Street and Thrawl Street no longer exist as they used to, but in 1888 they lay between Commercial Street to the west and Brick Lane to the east, north of Whitechapel Road; during the time of the Whitechapel murders they contained several doss houses. Dorset Street lay less than two blocks to the north along Commercial Street. This was the vice-ridden neighbourhood that East End social reformers referred to as the "wicked quarter-mile" (Begg, Fido, & Skinner, 1991). It appears that the notorious rookery played a key role in the Jack the Ripper mystery, and there is some supporting evidence for the geographic profile results.

All the victims resided within a couple of hundred yards of each other in the Thrawl, Flower and Dean, Dorset, and Church Street doss houses off Commercial Street (Fido, 1987; Underwood, 1987):

- Polly Nichols used to reside at 18 Thrawl Street; just before her death she was evicted and moved into the White House at 56 Flower and Dean Street, a doss house that slept both men and women.
- Annie Chapman's primary residence was Crossingham's Common Lodging House at 35 Dorset Street.
- Elizabeth Stride occasionally lived in a common lodging house at No. 32 Flower and Dean Street, and reportedly was there the night of her murder.
- Catherine Eddowes usually stayed in Cooney's Lodging House at No. 55 Flower and Dean Street, and had slept there two nights before her murder.
- Mary Kelly lived and died in McCarthy's Rents at 13 Miller's Court, off Dorset Street (it was actually the back room of 26 Dorset Street, situated across the road from Crossingham's Common Lodging House). She had previously resided in George Street, between "Flow-ery Dean" and Thrall Street. Kelly was seen picking up a man on Commercial Street between Thrall and Flower and Dean Streets the night of her murder.

These residences were suspiciously close to each other, covering less than 1.5% of the total hunting area. It is difficult to assess the significance of this finding as the locale had a concentration of slum lodging houses where most

Spitalfields Parish prostitutes lived at one time or another. These women were also highly transient.

Two blocks north of Flower and Dean Street was the Ten Bells Pub (now known as the Jack the Ripper Public House) on Church Street and Commercial Street, across from Spitalfields Market; all the Ripper victims were known to have drank here. Possibly Whitechapel Road and Commercial Street/Road were arterial routes used by the killer.

Part of Eddowes' blood-stained apron was cut away by her killer, and the missing segment was later found in the passageway to a staircase for the Wentworth Model Dwellings, No. 108-119 Goulston Street. Located just south of Wentworth Street, the new flats were one third of a mile away and a 10-minute walk from Mitre Square where Eddowes was murdered. It appeared the bloodied apron piece was used to wipe a knife clean. The following graffito was written in chalk above on the black brick wall (Rumbelow, 1988):

> The Juwes are not
> The men that
>   Will be
> Blamed for nothing

This location, between Mitre Square and Flower and Dean Street, is on the likely route home if Jack the Ripper indeed lived in the infamous "wicked quarter-mile." Some police theorized at the time the Ripper's route led to the vicinity of Flower and Dean Street, and others believed this should be the epicentre for their manhunt (Fido, 1987).

While the geographic profile for the Whitechapel murders is interesting and has some supporting evidence, we cannot assess its accuracy. The killer's address, like his identity, remains unknown. In 1992, it was claimed the diary of Jack the Ripper had been found (Harrison, 1993). Such a discovery would finally solve the world's most famous mystery, but perhaps leave the world a less colourful place. Fortunately — depending upon your viewpoint — forensic tests discredited the diary, leaving the puzzle still intact (Butts, 1994).

Conclusion

12

We were just hunting humans. I guess because we thought they were the hardest things to hunt, but humans are the easiest things to hunt ... Sad to say, but it's true."

—Convicted Canadian murderer; Boyd, 1988, p. 258

The ease with which predators hunt humans has its roots in the nature of our society — most people do not expect to encounter random violence during the course of their normal lives. But while serial murder, rape, and arson are uncommon, their impact can be significant, stretching beyond the immediate and secondary victims to the community at large. And for reasons that no one yet fully understands, the incidence of serial murder in North America appears to be growing.

Attempts to expand our knowledge in this area are a challenge to both criminology and law enforcement. Even the offenders themselves may not understand why they do what they do. Albert DeSalvo, the Boston Strangler, could not explain his hunting processes to interviewers: "I was just driving — anywhere — not knowing where I was going. I was coming through back ways, in and out and around. *That's the idea of the whole thing. I just go here and there. I don't know why*" (Frank, 1966, pp. 289–290). But while the motivations of criminal predators may be difficult to fathom, such an under-standing is not necessary for the task of interpreting their crime patterns. As Felson and Clarke (1998) observe, "highly unusual crime can follow very routine patterns" (pp. 16–17).

Environmental criminology provides a general framework for addressing questions related to offender spatial behaviour, and crime pattern theory suggests a specific method for determining probable area of criminal resi-dence. Geographic profiling is an example of the practical application of criminological theory to the real world of police investigation. "Some of our [offender profiling] hypotheses ... seem now to have passed into the general realm of established detective knowledge ... It is this gradual building of elements of certainty by scientific rigour that is the object of the researchers" (Copson, 1993, pp. 20–21).

This book has sought to help explain one small part of the phenomenon of serial violent crime — the geography of offender hunting patterns. Geographic profiling owes a debt to the work and efforts of many researchers, and hopefully has helped inform the field in turn. But while we have answers to some questions, many new ones have been raised.

- What more can temporal patterns tell us?
- What are the similarities and differences between offender types?
- How can psychological and geographic profiles be better integrated?
- How do we improve our offender typologies?
- Can the locations of future crimes be reliably predicted?
- How do past anchor points influence and structure an offender's mental map?
- Can the criminal investigative process be improved by adopting principles from the field of information theory?

Further study is required to properly examine these and other issues.

Geographic profiling is a decision support tool for criminal inquiries. It does not solve cases; rather, it focuses an investigation by providing both an optimal search strategy and a means of managing large volumes of information. Crime locations and their patterns provide clues that, when properly interpreted, can be used to help find the offender. Like all police tactics, it reaches its potential when employed as part of a package of techniques. Because address information is so common, a number of different strategies have been developed that can be integrated with other investigative approaches. This results in the more effective and efficient use of limited police resources.

On average, geographic profiling determines the location of offender residence within 5% of the total hunting area, performance that is significantly better than what could be expected by chance. The underlying theory also provides guidelines for consistent and reliable decision making regarding the appropriate use of crime sites for this type of analysis. Furthermore, a variety of investigative strategies have been developed to maximize the utility of the process. As much of our information is address based, it is likely that additional applications will be developed in the future.

Any increase in our ability to apprehend criminal predators is desirable from both community and law enforcement perspectives (see Newark &

Sullivan, 1995). But for an investigative methodology to be of value, more is required than tests of validity and reliability. Police detectives must: (1) be aware of and give credibility to the technique; (2) request the service and have it delivered in a timely fashion; and (3) understand the method's capabilities and limitations, and utilize its results appropriately. Also, finding the offender is only half of the police investigative equation; gathering sufficient evidence for a charge and conviction is the other, equally critical, half (Eastham, 1989, p. 33).

Taylor (1997) suggests that: "The technique [of geographic profiling] holds the strongest promise for assisting police in investigations of serial murderers, serial rapists, and serial arsonists" (p. 5). Its full potential, however, results from its integration with other behavioural science techniques, forensic analysis, eyewitness reports, and investigative information. A classic example of such a strategic approach can be found in Operation Lynx, the largest police manhunt in Britain since the Yorkshire Ripper Inquiry. The investigative team's focus was five linked rapes that had occurred in three different cities – Leeds, Leicester, and Nottingham – from 1982 to 1995. Detectives had collected DNA evidence, suspect descriptions, and a partial fingerprint too small to search via AFIS. They also connected the use of a stolen credit card to one of the cases, producing 20 locations upon which to base a geographic profile. Parameters of sex, age, criminal record, and residence area were used to conduct a manual search of fingerprint files. A print match was found in the second police station on the geographically prioritized list, and DNA confirmed the result. At the time of the rapes the offender, Clive Barwell, was living in the top 3.0% (21 mi2) of the geoprofile. In October 1999 he pled guilty to four counts and was sentenced to eight life terms in prison.

Waters (1998) states that geographic profiling is "at the cutting edge of a revolution in crime-mapping strategy and technology. By organizing vast amounts of information and translating that information into maps, a growing coterie of geographer-criminologists is helping to change the way we cope with crime" (p. 47). The use of geography for criminal investigation and offender profiling strikes a chord within practitioners. This resonance is perhaps best explained by the old police truism: "When all else fails, return to the scene" (Barrett, 1990, p. 90).

Appendix A
Serial Murderer Data Set

Table A.1 FBI Serial Killer Data Set[72]

Surname	Given Name	Media Name	Co-Killer	Murders	Start	End	State
Anderson	Allen			7	1976	1976	CA
Angelo	Richard			4	1987	1987	NY
Ball	Joe			14	1936	1938	TX
Banks	George			13		1982	PA
Bankston	Clinton			5	1987	1987	GA
Barboza	Daniel			59	1963	1986	EC
Barfield	Velma			6	1969	1978	NC
Barnes	James			7	1988	1988	MI
Beck	Martha	Lonely Hearts Killers	1	20	1947	1949	NY
Bell	Larry			6	1975	1985	SC
Berdella	Robert			6	1984	1988	MO
Berkowitz	David	Son of Sam		6	1976	1977	NY
Best	Alton			6	1986	1987	MD
Bianchi	Kenneth	Hillside Stranglers	1	12	1977	1979	CA
Biegenwald	Richard			6	1958	1982	NY
Bishop	Arthur			5	1979	1983	UT
Bittaker	Lawrence	Murder Mac	1	5	1979	1979	CA
Bonin	William	Freeway Killer	1	21	1972	1980	CA
Brady	Ian	Moors Murderers	1	10	1963	1965	UK
Briggen	Joseph			12		1902	CA
Brooks	David		2	31	1970	1973	TX
Brooks	John			9	1986	1986	LA
Brown	Debra		1	8	1984	1984	OH
Brudos	Jerry	Lust Killer		5	1968	1969	OR
Bunday	Thomas			5	1979	1981	AK
Bundy	Carol	Sunset Strip Slayer	1	6	1980	1980	CA

Table A.1 FBI Serial Killer Data Set[72] (continued)

Surname	Given Name	Media Name	Co-Killer	Murders	Start	End	State
Bundy	Theodore			36	1973	1978	WA
Buono	Angelo	Hillside Stranglers	1	10	1977	1978	CA
Butts	Vernon	Freeway Killer	1	9	1979	1980	CA
Carignan	Harvey	Want-Ad Killer		5	1949	1975	MN
Carpenter	David	Trailside Killer		7	1979	1981	CA
Carr	Robert			5			CT
Carson	Michael		1	3	1981	1983	CA
Carson	Suzan		1	3	1981	1983	CA
Carter	Dean			6	1983	1984	CA
Chase	Richard	Vampire Killer		6	1977	1978	CA
Chikatilo	Andrei	Rostov Ripper		53	1978	1990	SR
Christensen	William			16	1982	1982	PA
Christopher	Joseph	.22 Caliber Killer		6	1980	1981	NY
Clark	Douglas	Sunset Strip Slayer	1	6	1980	1980	CA
Code	Nathaniel			10	1985	1987	LA
Cole	Carroll			35	1946	1979	NV
Coleman	Alton		1	8	1984	1984	OH
Collins	John	Michigan Murderer		8	1967	1969	MI
Cooks	Jesse	Zebra Murders	4	15	1973	1974	CA
Copeland	Faye		1	13	1985	1989	MO
Copeland	Ray		1	13	1985	1989	MO
Corll	Dean	Candy Man	2	31	1970	1973	TX
Corona	Juan			25	1971	1971	CA
Cottingham	Richard	Mid-Town Torso Killer		6	1977	1980	NY
Craine	Louis			4	1985	1987	CA
Creech	Thomas			42	1965	1981	OH
Dahmer	Jeffrey	Milwaukee Cannibal		17	1978	1991	WI
Danielson	Robert			5			WI
Daugherty	Jeffrey			5	1976	1976	FL
Davis	Bruce			30	1969	1971	NY
DeSalvo	Albert	Boston Strangler		13	1962	1964	MA
Diaz	Robert			60	1981	1981	CA
Dodd	Westley			6	1989	1989	WA
Duffy	John	Railway Killer		3	1985	1986	UK
Eaton	Dennis			4		1989	VA
Eveans	Tammy			3	1987	1989	IL
Eyler	Larry			23	1982	1984	IL
Fernandez	Raymond	Lonely Hearts Killers	1	20	1947	1949	NY
Fischer	Joseph			100	1955	1979	NY
Fish	Albert			15	1910	1934	NY
Franklin	Joseph			4	1977	1980	UT

Table A.1 FBI Serial Killer Data Set[72] (continued)

Surname	Given Name	Media Name	Co-Killer	Murders	Start	End	State
Gacy	John			33	1972	1978	IL
Gallego	Charlene		1	8	1978	1980	CA
Gallego	Gerald		1	10	1978	1980	CA
Gary	Carlton	Stocking Strangler		9	1970	1978	GA
Gaskins	Donald			100	1953	1982	SC
Gecht	Robin	Chicago Rippers	3	18	1981	1982	IL
Gein	Ed			7	1954	1957	WI
Glatman	Harvey	Lonely-Hearts Killer		3	1957	1958	CA
Glaze	Billy			3	1986	1987	MN
Gohl	Billy			39	1909	1912	WA
Goode	Arthur			4	1976	1976	FL
Gore	David		1	6	1981	1983	FL
Graham	Gwendolyn		1	6	1987	1987	MI
Graham	Harrison			7	1986	1987	PA
Granviel	Kenneth			7	1974	1975	TX
Green	Larry	Zebra Murders	4	15	1973	1974	CA
Green	Ricky			4	1985	1986	TX
Greenwood	Vaughn	Skid Row Slasher		11	1964	1975	CA
Gretzler	Douglas		1	17	1973	1973	AZ
Grissom	Richard			5	1977	1989	KS
Groves	Vincent			15			CO
Gruber	Maria		3	39	1982	1989	AU
Gunness	Belle			19	1900	1908	IL
Hance	William	Forces of Evil		4	1977	1978	GA
Hansen	Robert			24	1975	1983	AK
Harris	Anthony	Zebra Murders	4	15	1973	1974	CA
Harvey	Donald			55	1970	1987	OH
Hatcher	Charles			16	1969	1982	MO
Heirens	William			4	1945	1946	IL
Henderson	Robert			16			NC
Henley	Elmer		2	31	1970	1973	TX
Hindley	Myra	Moors Murderers	1	10	1963	1965	UK
Hoch	Johann			25	1890	1905	IL
Holladay	Glenn			4		1986	AL
Holland	James			6	1967	1987	UT
Humphrey	Edward			5		1990	FL
Hunter	Richard			4	1986	1986	GA
Jennings	Wilbur			4	1983	1984	CA
Johnson	Martha			4	1977	1982	GA
Jones	Genene			11	1981	1982	TX
Joubert	John			3	1982	1983	NE
Judy	Steven			7	1973	1979	IN
Justus	Buddy			3	1978	1978	FL
Kearney	Patrick	Trash-Bag Killer		28	1968	1977	CA

Table A.1 FBI Serial Killer Data Set[72] (continued)

Surname	Given Name	Media Name	Co-Killer	Murders	Start	End	State
Kelbach	Walter		1	6	1966	1966	UT
Kemper	Edmund	Coed Killer		10	1964	1973	CA
Kibbe	Roger	I-5 Strangler		7	1986	1987	CA
Kirker	James			300		1852	
Koedatich	James			3			FL
Kokoraleis	Andrew	Chicago Rippers	3	18	1981	1982	IL
Kokoraleis	Thomas	Chicago Rippers	3	18	1981	1982	IL
Kraft	Randy	Score-Card Killer		67	1972	1983	CA
Kurten	Peter	Monster of Dusseldorf		12	1892	1930	GE
Lake	Leonard		1	25	1983	1985	CA
Lance	Myron		1	6	1966	1966	UT
Lassor	Raymond			3	1984	1984	RI
Leidolf	Irene		3	39	1982	1989	AU
Long	Bobby Joe			10	1984	1984	FL
Long	Royal			3	1981	1984	SD
Lopez	Roberto			3		1983	CA
Lucas	Henry Lee		1	100	1960	1982	MI
Macek	Richard			8	1974	1974	IL
Mansfield	Billy			5	1975	1980	CA
Marcus	Jerry			7	1971	1987	MS
Marquette	Richard			6	1961	1975	OR
Mathurin	Jean-Thierry	Monster of Montmartre	1	38	1984	1987	FR
Maxwell	Bobby Joe	Skid Row Stabber		10	1978	1979	CA
Mayer	Stefanie		3	39	1982	1989	AU
McCrary	Danny		2	22	1971	1972	CO
McCrary	Sherman		2	22	1971	1972	CO
McKnight	Anthony			7	1985	1986	CA
Michasevich	Gennaday			36	1973	1988	SR
Miley	Gregory			5			CA
Miller	Don			4	1980	1981	CA
Miyazaki	Tsutomu			3	1988	1989	JP
Moore	Manuel	Zebra Murders	4	15	1973	1974	CA
Morin	Stephan			30	1981	1981	TX
Mudgett	Hermann	H. H. Holmes		200	1891	1896	IL
Mullin	Herbert			13	1972	1973	CA
Murrell	John			500		1835	TN
Nash	Steven			6		1958	CA
Nelson	Earle	Gorilla Murderer		25	1926	1927	CA
Ng	Charles		1	25	1981	1985	CA
Nilsen	Dennis			15	1978	1983	UK
Norris	Roy	Murder Mac	1	50	1979	1979	CA
O'Neall	Darren			6	1985	1987	WA
Olson	Clifford			11	1980	1981	BC
Owen	Duane			5	1984	1984	CO
Panzram	Carl			22	1923	1929	KS

Table A.1 FBI Serial Killer Data Set[72] (continued)

Surname	Given Name	Media Name	Co-Killer	Murders	Start	End	State
Paulin	Thierry	Monster of Montmartre	1	38	1984	1987	FR
Pennell	Steven			5	1987	1988	DE
Player	Michael	Skid Row Slayer		11	1986	1986	CA
Ponte	Kenneth			9	1988	1989	MA
Price	Craig			4	1987	1989	RI
Puente	Dorothea			8	1985	1988	CA
Rahman	Yusef			4	1989	1989	NY
Ralston	Larry			4			OH
Ramirez	Richard	Night Stalker		18	1984	1985	CA
Rhoades	Paul			3	1987	1987	ID
Rifkin	Joel			17	1989	1993	NY
Rios	Joe			4	1987	1987	TX
Rissell	Monte			5	1975	1976	VA
Rogers	Dayton	Molalla Forest Killer		7	1972	1987	OR
Ross	Michael			6	1982	1984	CT
Ross	Rickey	Strawberry Killer		3	1988	1988	CA
Sapp	John			10	1975	1985	CA
Shawcross	Arthur			13	1972	1990	NY
Siebert	Daniel			13	1979	1986	AL
Silka	Michael			9			AK
Silva	Mauricio			4	1978	1984	CA
Simon	J. C.	Zebra Murders	4	15	1973	1974	CA
Smith	Lemuel			6	1958	1981	NY
Smith	Nathaniel			4		1982	KS
Smith	William			8	1981	1984	OR
Snyder	David			4	1982	1984	MD
Solomon	Morris			7	1986	1987	CA
Spencer	Timothy	Southside Strangler		5	1984	1987	VA
Spisak	Frank			3	1982	1982	OH
Spreitzer	Edward	Chicago Rippers	3	18	1981	1982	IL
Stafford	Roger		1	9	1978	1978	OK
Stafford	Vern		1	9	1978	1978	OK
Stano	Gerald			41	1969	1980	FL
Steelman	Willie		1	17	1973	1973	AZ
Sutcliffe	Peter	Yorkshire Ripper		13	1975	1980	UK
Taylor	Raymond		2	22	1971	1972	CO
Tenneson	Michael			5	1987	1987	CO
Threinen	David			6	1975	1975	SK
Tinning	Marybeth			9	1972	1985	NY
Toole	Ottis		1	25	1961	1983	FL
Toppan	Jane			31	1880	1901	MA
Travaglia	Michael			4		1980	PA
Trimboli	Ronald			3	1985	1985	TX
Tuchlin	Pawel			9	1979	1983	PO

Table A.1 FBI Serial Killer Data Set[72]   (continued)

Surname	Given Name	Media Name	Co-Killer	Murders	Start	End	State
Unsub		Aurora Killings		4	1984	1984	CO
Unsub		Baltimore Murders		5	1987		MD
Unsub		BTK Killer		7	1974	1979	KS
Unsub		Fort Worth Killings		9	1984	1985	TX
Unsub		Green River Killer		49	1982	1984	WA
Unsub		Jack the Ripper		5	1888	1888	UK
Unsub		Redhead Murders		6	1984	1985	TN
Unsub		Salt Lake City Murders		3	1986		UT
Unsub		San Mateo Killings		5	1980	1985	CA
Unsub		Skid Row Killer		9	1974	1975	CA
Unsub		Skid Row Slasher		10		1987	CA
Unsub		Southside Slayer		17	1983	1987	CA
Unsub		Torso Murderer		18	1934	1938	OH
Unsub		Zodiac Killer		37	1968	1969	CA
Wagner	Waltraud		3	39	1982	1989	AU
Walker	Gary			5	1984	1984	OK
Washington	David			3		1976	FL
Waterfield	Frederick		1	6	1981	1983	FL
Watts	Coral	Sunday Morning Slasher		19	1979	1982	TX
Whisenhant	Thomas			4	1963	1976	
Wilder	Christopher			12	1984	1984	FL
Williams	Wayne	Atlanta Child Murderer		29	1979	1981	GA
Wood	Catherine		1	6	1987	1987	MI
Woodfield	Randall	I-5 Killer		18	1979	1981	WA
Wuornos	Aileen			7	1989	1990	FL

[72]*UNSUB* means unknown subject (i.e., the offender has not been identified). *Media Name* refers to the nickname used by the press to describe the serial killer or murders. *Co-Killer* lists the number of accomplices. *Murders* lists the number of suspected victims. *Start* refers to the year of first known murder. *End* refers to the year of last known murder. *State* lists one of the U.S. states, Canadian provinces, or countries that the serial killer is known to have murdered in (some offenders operated in more than one area). *Official* two-letter U.S. Postal Service or Canada Post abbreviations are used. For cases outside of the U.S. or Canada, the following codes were substituted: *AU* (Austria); *EC* (Ecuador); *FR* (France); *GE* (Germany); *JP* (Japan); *PO* (Poland); and *SR* (USSR).

Appendix B
Data Coding Forms

DATA CODING FORM #1: SERIAL MURDER OFFENDERS

1. Sequential Number   __ __
2. Surname   _____
3. Given Names _____
4. Moniker   _____
5. Sex 1 Male   2 Female
6. Total Number of Victims   __ __
7. Total Number of Locations   __ __ __
8. Start Date   __ __.__ __.__ __
9. End Date   __ __.__ __.__ __
10. Degree of Organization
    1 Organized   2 Somewhat Organized   3 Mixed
    4 Somewhat Disorganized   5 Disorganized
11. Typology
    1 Visionary   2 Mission-Oriented   3 Lust
    4 Thrill   5 Comfort   6 Power/Control-Oriented
12. Residence Type
    1 Detached House   2 Semi-Detached House   3 Apartment
    4 Hotel/Motel
    5 Rooming/Lodging House   6 Trailer   7 Institution
    8 Transient 9 Homeless
13. Residence Address   _____
14. Residence City   _____
15. Residence State   __ __
16. Residence X Coordinate   __ __
17. Residence Y Coordinate   __ __
18. Workplace Type   _____
19. Workplace Address   _____
20. Workplace City   _____

21. Workplace State   __ __
22. Workplace X Coordinate   __ __
23. Workplace Y Coordinate   __ __
24. Scale (km/unit)   __ __ __ __
25. Data File   mur __ __ __ .dat
26. Comments   _____
27. References   _____

DATA CODING FORM #2: SERIAL MURDER VICTIMS

1. Sequential Number   __ __ __ __
2. Surname   _____
3. Sex   1 Male   2 Female
4. Victim/Killer Relationship   1 Stranger   2 Casual Acquaintance
   3 Known
5. Killer Selection   1 Nonrandom/Patterned   2 Random/Nonpatterned
6. Victim Traits   1 Specific   2 Nonspecific
7. Victim Activity
   01 At Home   02 At Work   03 Commuting
   04 Walking/Jogging   05 Hitchhiking
   06 Other Travel   07 Visiting Friend   08 Outdoor Recreation
   09 At Bar/Nightclub
   10 At Other Social Event   11 Prostitution
8. Killer Hunting Style
   1 Hunter   2 Poacher   3 Stalker   4 Troller   5 Trapper
9. Killer Approach
   1 Confidence Approach   2 Surprise Attack   3 Blitz Assault
10. Control Method
    1 Firearm   2 Knife   3 Blunt Instrument   4 Strangulation
    5 Physical Force
    6 Intoxicant   7 Threat   8 Blitz Attack (Victim Immediately Killed)
11. Murder Method
    1 Firearm   2 Knife   3 Blunt Instrument
    4 Strangulation   5 Physical Force   6 Poison
12. Crime Location Set
    1 E→A→M→D   2 E→A→MD   3 E→AM→D   4 EA→M→D
    5 EA→MD   6 E→AMD   7 EAM→D   8 EAMD
13. Attempt To Hide Body
    1 Displayed   2 Dumped   3 Other Not Hidden   4 Casually
    Hidden   5 Well Hidden
14. Linked   1 Linked   2 Unlinked
15. Comments   _____

DATA CODING FORM #3: SERIAL MURDER LOCATIONS

1. Sequential Number   __ __ __ __ __
2. Crime Location Type
   1 Location Victim Last Seen   **2** Encounter Site   **3** Attack Site
   4 Murder Scene
   5 Body Dump Site   **6** Vehicle Recovery Site   **7** Found Evidence
   Site   **8** Witness Site
3. Crime Location Address   _____
4. Crime Location City   _____
5. Crime Location State   __ __
6. Crime Location X Coordinate   __ __
7. Crime Location Y Coordinate   __ __
8. Crime Location Known During Police Investigation   **1** Yes   **2** No
9. Area Land Use
   1 Residential   **2** Commercial   **3** Industrial   **4** Institutional
   5 Park   **6** Rural/Agricultural   **7** Wilderness/Uninhabited
10. Site Description
    01 Residence   **02** Hotel/Motel   **03** Public Building
    04 School/Educational
    05 Business/Shopping Site   **06** Entertainment Site
    07 Red-Light Zone
    08 Vehicle   **09** Public Transportation   **10** Private Yard
    11 Parking Lot
    12 Street/Sidewalk   **13** Alley/Lane/Pathway/Trail   **14** Highway/Ditch
    15 Park
    16 Farm/Field/Open Area   **17** River/Lake/Marsh   **18** Forest/Woods
    19 Hills/Mountains   **20** Desert/Wasteland
11. Site Classification
    1 Inside Private   **2** Inside Semi-Public   **3** Inside Public
    4 Outside Private   **5** Outside Semi-Public   **6** Outside Public
12. Date   __ __.__ __.__ __
13. Time Arrived ____:____   To Time Left ____:____ = Total Time
    At Scene ____:____
14. Killer Travel Method   **1** Vehicle   **2** Public Transportation   **3** On Foot
15. Victim or Killer Residence
    1 Killer Residence   **2** Victim Residence   **3** Both   **4** Neither
16. Comments   _____

Glossary

action space See *activity space.*

activity displacement See *functional displacement.*

activity node An individual's past and present homes, current and previous work sites, and residences of partners, friends, and family members.

activity site Any location routinely visited by an individual (e.g., workplace, friend's residence, neighbourhood bar, etc.)

activity space Those places regularly visited by a person in which the majority of their activities are carried out. It comprises an individual's activity sites and the routes used to travel between them, and is contained within the awareness space.

ambusher An offender who attacks a victim once he or she has been enticed to a location, such as a residence or workplace, controlled by the offender.

anchor point The base from which an individual resides or regularly operates; usually the single most important location in a person's life.

anisotropic surface A surface exhibiting different physical properties, such as ease of movement, in various directions.

arson site The location where an offender commits an arson.

ASPD Antisocial personality disorder.

attack site The location where an offender first attacks the victim.

awareness space Locations and areas that a person is aware of and possesses at least a minimum level of knowledge about. It contains, but is larger than, the activity space.

behavioural science The scientific study and analysis of human behaviour. This term is often used to describe the investigative study of criminal behaviour.

body dump site   The location where an offender disposes of the murder victim's body.

Brantingham and Brantingham crime site selection model   A model of crime geometry within the environmental criminology perspective developed at Simon Fraser University. It suggests that crimes are most likely to occur in those areas where an offender's awareness space intersects with perceived suitable targets.

buffer zone   An area centred around the criminal's residence within which targets are viewed as less desirable because of the perceived risk associated with operating too close to home.

CCA   *Comparative case analysis.*

centre of minimum travel   See *median centre.*

centrography   A form of spatial analysis that focuses on the central tendency of a point pattern.

centroid   See *spatial mean.*

CGT   *Criminal geographic targeting.*

choropleth map   A thematic map that uses colours or shading to depict variations in areally-based data.

CIA   *Criminal investigative analysis.*

circle hypothesis   The hypothesis that marauders reside within their offence circle, while commuters reside without. See *marauder, commuter.*

clustering   The degree of site proximity or grouping in a point pattern. See *dispersion.*

cluster dump   Bodies of several murder victims buried or dumped in the same location or general area.

collateral material   Articles not directly associated with a sex offender's crimes but that provide evidence or information regarding sexual preferences, interests, or activities. These can be erotic, educational, introspective, or intelligence material.

commuter An offender who travels from home into another area to commit his or her crimes. A commuter usually resides outside of the offence circle. See *circle hypothesis.*

comparative case analysis (CCA)   See *linkage analysis.*

contagion location A crime site situated close to a previous offence. Such a location is generally regarded for the purposes of geographic profiling as a nonindependent event.

CPA *Crime pattern analysis.*

crime attractor A place that attracts offenders through its reputation for crime opportunities.

crime generator A high-traffic location that experiences crime as a by-product of the large number of people who regularly visit there.

crime interval The period of time (usually expressed in days) between successive crimes. Crime intervals are used to calculate the mean crime interval and standard deviation.

crime location A geographic location associated with a given crime. There may be several different locations connected to a single crime; for example, in a homicide there may be victim encounter, attack, murder, and body dump sites.

crime location set The number and grouping of the different locations associated with a crime.

crime parsing The breaking down of a crime into its crime location set.

crime pattern analysis (CPA) See *linkage analysis.*

crime pattern theory See *pattern theory.*

crime scene profiling See *criminal profiling.*

crime trip An offender's journey to any location associated with a crime.

crime trip distance See *journey-to-crime distance.*

criminal geographic targeting (CGT) A computerized spatial profiling model that determines the most probable area of offender residence through the production of a jeopardy surface or geoprofile from a criminal hunting algorithm. It is the primary methodology used in geographic profiling.

criminal investigative analysis (CIA) Techniques of psychological profiling and related methods developed and used by the FBI and the ICIAF.

criminal profiling The inference of offender characteristics from offence characteristics. See *psychological profiling.*

crow-flight distance The shortest distance between two points, measured "as the crow flies." Compare with *Manhattan distance* and *wheel distance.*

curvilinear distance See *wheel distance.* Also known as curvimetre distance.

curvimetre distance   See *wheel distance*. Also known as curvilinear distance.

Dirichlet polygon   See *Thiessen polygon.*

disorganized (asocial) offender   See *disorganized offender.*

disorganized offender   A criminal personality type used in psychological profiling based on an offender's lifestyle and the condition of their crime scenes. Disorganized offenders usually act spontaneously and do not plan their crimes. They may suffer from some form of psychosis such as paranoid schizophrenia.

dispersion   The degree of site spread in a point pattern. See *clustering.*

displacement   A change in an offender's pattern of behaviour as the result of crime prevention efforts, community wariness, or police investigative strategies. There are five types of displacement: spatial (territorial), temporal, target, tactical, and functional (activity).

distance decay   The reduction in probability of spatial interaction with the increase in distance. Most crime trips follow a distance-decay pattern as measured from the offender's residence.

EAMD   Acronym for encounter, attack, murder, and body dump sites.

ecological fallacy   The assumption that results from a higher level of geographic analysis apply to a lower level (in particular, the individual level).

ECRI   Environmental Criminology Research Inc.

EDA   *Equivocal death analysis.*

encounter site   The location where an offender first comes into contact with the victim.

environmental criminology   An area of criminology focusing on the criminal event rather than just the offender. The primary concern of environmental criminology is the crime setting or place, the where and when, of the criminal act.

equivocal death analysis (EDA)   A retrospective psychological analysis of the most probable manner of death (accidental, suicidal, or homicidal) in suspicious cases. Also known as psychological autopsy.

fishing hole   A location with a high probability for a criminal predator of finding a potential victim, who may then be followed to a different location before being attacked. See *crime attractor* and *hunting ground.*

forensic behavioural science   Behavioural science as applied to the investigative and court processes. See *behavioural science.*

functional displacement   A type of displacement resulting from an offender engaging in a different type of criminal behaviour, often resulting from changes in opportunities. Also known as activity displacement. See *displacement*.

geographic displacement   See *spatial displacement*.

geographic information system (GIS)   A computer software system designed to store geographic attributes and integrate spatial and other data for analytic purposes.

geographic profiling   An information management strategy for serial violent crime investigation that analyzes crime site information to determine the most probable area of offender residence.

geography of crime   The study of the geography associated with crime, targets, and criminals.

geoprofile   A two-dimensional jeopardy (probability) surface overlaid on a map of the hunting area.

GIS   *Geographic information system*.

global positioning system   A handheld device that provides latitude and longitude coordinates based on a satellite fix.

GPS   *Global positioning system*.

hit percentage   See *hit score percentage*.

hit score   The CGT likelihood value (z-score) associated with the location of an offender's residence or anchor point. See *z-score*.

hit score percentage   An indicator of search efficiency used in geographic profiling, measured by determining the proportion of the total hunting area covered before the offender's residence is encountered. The smaller this number, the better the focus of the geoprofile.

HITS   Homicide Investigation Tracking System, the Washington State-based computerized linkage analysis system for murders and sexual offences.

HOLMES   Home Office Large Major Enquiry System, the major case management system used by British police forces.

hot spot   A small geographic area containing a disproportionate number of criminal offences.

hunter   An offender who sets out specifically to hunt for a victim, basing the search from his or her residence.

hunting area   A rectangular zone bounded by the crime locations. It is the area within which the geoprofile is generated.

hunting behaviour   The victim search and attack processes engaged in by an offender.

hunting ground   The territory within which an offender searches for victims. See *fishing hole* and *trap line*.

ICIAF   *International Criminal Investigative Analysis Fellowship.*

indirect personality assessment (IPA)   A behavioural evaluation of a criminal suspect to assist in the determination of the most effective interview, cross-examination, and other investigative techniques.

International Criminal Investigative Analysis Fellowship (ICIAF)   An association of police criminal profilers, originally initiated by the FBI but now an independent professional body. Also known as the Police Fellowship.

IPA   *Indirect personality assessment.*

isoline map   See *isopleth map*.

isopleth map   A map depicting isopleths (also known as isolines), or lines of equal data value.

isotropic surface   A surface exhibiting equal physical properties, such as ease of movement, in all directions.

jeopardy surface   A three-dimensional probability surface, produced by the CGT algorithm, depicting the most probable area of offender residence.

journey-to-crime distance   The distance between a crime site and the offender's residence.

linkage analysis   The comparison of crimes to determine whether they were committed by the same offender(s). Linkages can be established through physical evidence, eyewitnesses, or behavioural similarities such as modus operandi (M.O.) and signature. Also known as crime pattern analysis.

linkage analysis system   A computerized database that searches for behavioural similarities between crimes in an effort to connect them.

linkage blindness   The inability to link connected crimes together, usually resulting from a lack of coordination and information sharing between law enforcement agencies.

macrolevel spatial analysis   The study of geographic phenomena on a national or international level.

major case management system   A computer system designed to store, collate, compare, and analyze investigative information in serious crimes.

Manhattan distance   Distance measured along an orthogonal (e.g., northing and easting) grid layout of street blocks. See *wheel distance.*

Manhattan metric   Measurement using Manhattan distances.

marauder   An offender whose residence acts as the focus for his or her crimes. A marauder usually resides within the offence circle. See *circle hypothesis.*

mass arson   An arson incident in which several fires are set simultaneously, or within a relatively short time period in the same general area.

mass murder   A murder incident in which several victims are killed simultaneously, or within a relatively short time period in the same general area.

mean centre   See *spatial mean.*

median centre   The position from which travel to all the points in a spatial distribution (i.e., the sum of the distances) is minimized.

median distance   The radius of a circle encompassing one half of the points in a spatial distribution.

mental map   Cognitive images or representations of familiar geographic areas such as neighbourhoods or cities.

mesolevel spatial analysis   The study of geographic phenomena on a regional or intercity level.

microenvironment   The immediate environment surrounding a site, on the scale of a block or intersection.

microlevel spatial analysis   The study of geographic phenomena on an individual, neighbourhood, or urban level.

multiple murder   Mass, spree, or serial murder.

murder site   The location where an offender murders the victim.

nearest neighbour analysis   Various statistical analyses of nearest neighbour distances.

nearest neighbour distances   Various measure of distances between points and their closest (or k-nearest) neighbours as a means of quantifying location spacing. See *point pattern statistics.*

offence circle   The circle formed from a diameter produced by the line connecting the two crime sites in a connected offence series most distant from each other.

offence interval   See *crime interval.*

offender profiling   A general approach to criminal profiling including psychological, geographic, and statistical profiling methods. See *criminal profiling.*

organized nonsocial offender   See *organized offender.*

organized offender   A criminal personality type used in psychological profiling based on an offender's lifestyle and the condition of their crime scenes. Organized offenders usually plan their crimes. They are typically intelligent, and sane but psychopathic.

Orion   See *Rigel.*

parsing   See *crime parsing.*

path routing   A path that follows the shortest possible street route. While this can be measured simply in terms of distance, more sophisticated techniques incorporate estimates of path travel time. See *wheel distance.*

pattern theory   A multidisciplinary approach that combines rational choice and routine activity theory to explain the distribution of crime and criminal behaviour. Offender target choice is affected by their interactions with the physical and social environments. Also known as crime pattern theory.

poacher   An offender who sets out specifically to search for a victim, basing the search from an activity site other than his or her residence, or who travels to another city during the victim search process. See *commuter.*

point pattern   The two-dimensional pattern produced by a series of spatial locations.

point pattern statistics   Statistical measures derived from various distance calculations within a point pattern. See *nearest neighbour distances.*

Police Fellowship   See *International Criminal Investigative Analysis Fellowship.*

premeditated opportunism   The practice of exploiting criminal opportunities after an initial degree of preparation and planning.

principle of least action   The minimization of quantities within dynamic systems (e.g., energy, distance, time, change, effort, cost, etc.).

profiling   See *criminal profiling.*

psychological autopsy   See *equivocal death analysis.*

psychological profiling   The identification of the major personality and behavioural characteristics of an individual based upon an analysis of the crimes he or she has committed. Also known as criminal personality assessment or criminal behaviour profiling.

rape site   The location where an offender rapes the victim.

raptor An offender who attacks a victim directly upon encounter.

rational choice theory   A theoretical perspective in which crime and criminal behavior are viewed as the outcomes of choices influenced by the offender's rational consideration of the risk, effort, and reward associated with different decisions.

release site   See *victim release site.*

remission   A period of inactivity, ranging from weeks to years, between the crimes of a serial offender. It can result from either episodic behaviour or temporal displacement.

Rigel   The geographic profiling computer software based on the CGT algorithm. The prototype version was named *Orion.*

routine activities   The activities and behaviours engaged in by people on a regular (e.g., daily, weekly, seasonal) basis.

routine activity theory   The opportunity structure for crime based upon the convergence in space and time of motivated offenders, suitable targets, and the absence of capable guardians.

routine pathway   The regularly used streets or routes connecting a related set of activity nodes.

scenario   The selection of crime locations and their associated weighting used in a given geoprofile.

search area   The hit score percentage translated into area size.

serial arson   Three or more separate arson events with an emotional cooling-off period between fires.

serial murder   Three or more separate murder events with an emotional cooling-off period between homicides.

serial rape   Three or more separate rape events with an emotional cooling-off period between attacks.

singularity   A single offence that does not appear to fit the overall pattern in a crime series.

spatial displacement   A type of displacement resulting from an offender relocating his or her criminal activity in response to a perceived increase in the risk of apprehension or reduction in opportunity. Also known as geographic or territorial displacement. See *displacement*.

spatial mean   A univariate measure of the central tendency of a point pattern, the geographic "centre of gravity." Also known as the centroid or mean centre.

spree arson   Three or more arsons at different locations with no emotional cooling-off period in between. The fires are all the result of a single event. Spree arson is an intermediate classification between mass and serial arson.

spree murder   Three or more murders at different locations with no emotional cooling-off period in between. The killings are all the result of a single event. Spree murder is an intermediate classification between mass and serial murder.

stalker   An offender who upon encountering a victim, follows them to attack at a later place and time.

standard distance   A measure of spatial dispersion analogous to the standard deviation.

structural backcloth   See *target backcloth*.

tactical displacement   A type of displacement resulting from an offender using alternative strategies or changing his or her modus operandi to achieve the same criminal goals. Tactical displacement is usually the result of learning. See *displacement*.

target backcloth   A spatial opportunity structure configured by both geographic and temporal distributions of suitable crime targets or victims across the physical landscape. Nonuniform or patchy target backcloths are characterized by varying levels of target availability in different areas. Also known as structural backcloth. See *anisotropic surface*.

target displacement   A type of displacement resulting from an offender modifying the selection of premises, objects, or subjects as targets for his or her criminal activities. See *displacement*.

target location   The various geographic sites connected to a crime series including victim encounter, attack, murder, and body dump sites.

target-rich environment   An area containing a high density of potential victims or targets. See *fishing hole*.

temporal displacement   A type of displacement resulting from an offender shifting his or her criminal activity to a different time period in response to perceived changes in risk or opportunity environments. Activity shifts to a period (e.g., time of day, day of week, etc.) with acceptable levels of risk and target availability; this may involve an extended period of offender inactivity. See *displacement, remission.*

territorial displacement   See *spatial displacement.*

Thiessen polygon   A catchment area around a central position; the area within that polygon is closer to its centre than to any other "competing" centre. Also known as a Voronoi or Dirichlet polygon.

trap line   A linear fishing hole, typically stretched along a street or commercial strip. See *hunting ground.*

trapper   Trappers have occupations or positions where potential victims come to them (e.g., nursing), or by means of some subterfuge, victims are enticed into their homes or other locations they control (e.g., by placing want ads).

troller   An offender who, while involved in other, nonpredatory activities, opportunistically encounters a victim.

VICAP   Violent Criminal Apprehension Program, the U.S. national computerized linkage analysis system for murders.

ViCLAS   Violent Crime Linkage Analysis System, the Canadian national computerized linkage analysis system for murders and sexual offences.

victim release site   The location where an offender releases the victim, often used in the context of a rape or sexual assault case.

victim trail   The path taken by a victim (e.g., going home from work), at some unknown point along which they were encountered by the offender.

victimology   In the context of profiling, the type (e.g., physical appearance, occupation, actions, etc.) of victim selected by an offender and that person's behaviour during the crime.

Voronoi polygon   See *Thiessen polygon.*

watering hole   See *fishing hole.*

wheel distance   The distance along a street network. Also known as curvimetre distance or path route.

z-score   The CGT likelihood value associated with a given location.

Bibliography

Abel, G.G., Mittelman, M.S., & Becker, J.V. (1985). Sexual offenders: Results of assessment and recommendations for treatment. In M.H. Ben-Aron, S.J. Hucker, & C.D. Webster (Eds.), *Clinical criminology: The assessment and treatment of criminal behaviour* (pp. 191-205). Toronto: M&M Graphics.

Abrahamsen, D. (1973). *The murdering mind.* New York: Harper & Row.

Abrahamsen, D. (1992). *Murder & madness: The secret life of Jack the Ripper.* New York: Donald I. Fine.

Adams, D. E. (1989, November). *DNA analysis in the FBI Laboratory.* Paper presented at the meeting of the American Society of Criminology, Reno, NV.

Adhami, E., & Browne, D. P. (1996). *Major crime enquiries: Improving expert support for detectives* (Special Interest Series: Paper XX). London: Police Research Group, Home Office Police Department.

Aitken, C. G. G., Connolly, T., Gammerman, A., & Zhang, G. (1994). *Statistical analysis of the CATCHEM data.* Unpublished manuscript, Police Research Group, Home Office Police Department, London.

Aitken, C. G. G., Connolly, T., Gammerman, A., Zhang, G., Bailey, D., Gordon, R., & Oldfield, R. (1995). Statistical modelling in specific case analysis. *Jurimetrics.*

Aitken, C. G. G., Connolly, T., Gammerman, A., Zhang, G., & Oldfield, R. (1995). *Predicting an offender's characteristics: An evaluation of statistical modelling* (Special Interest Series: Paper 4). London: Police Research Group, Home Office Police Department.

Akiyama, Y. (1981). Murder victimization: A statistical analysis. *FBI Law Enforcement Bulletin, 50*(3), 1-4.

Akiyama, Y., & Pfeiffer, P. C. (1984). Arson: A statistical profile. *FBI Law Enforcement Bulletin, 53*(10), 8-14.

Aldeman, R. H. (1970). *The bloody Benders.* London: Michael Joseph.

Allen, H. E. (1990). Serial killer captured. *The Trooper, 28*(1), 2-6.

Allen, J. (1993, August). The lady-killer. *Mirabella*, pp. 76-81.

Allen-Hagen, B. (1989). *Stranger abduction homicides of children* (OJJDP Publication No. NCJ-115213). Washington, DC: U.S. Government Printing Office.

Allen-Hagen, B., & Sickmund, M. (1993, July). *Juveniles and violence: Juvenile offending and victimization* (OJJDP Publication Fact Sheet #3). Washington, DC: U.S. Government Printing Office.

Allmand, W. (1976). *Statement of the Solicitor General of Canada, the Honourable Warren Allmand, on the abolition of capital punishment.* Ottawa: Department of Justice.

Alston, J. D. (1994). *The serial rapist's spatial pattern of target selection.* Unpublished master's thesis, Simon Fraser University, Burnaby, BC.

Alston, J. D. (1998, November). *Using GIS in geographic profiles of serial offenders.* Paper presented at the meeting of the American Society of Criminology, Washington, DC.

American Psychiatric Association. (1987). *Diagnostic and statistical manual of mental disorders* (3rd ed. rev.). Washington, DC: Author.

American Psychiatric Association. (1994). *Diagnostic and statistical manual of mental disorders* (4th ed.). Washington, DC: Author.

Amir, A. (1971). *Patterns in forcible rape.* Chicago: University of Chicago Press.

Anderson, D. (1992, July). Tracking crime with GIS – Geographic information systems. *Law Enforcement Technology,* pp. 58-59.

Andranovich, G. D., & Riposa, G. (1993). *Doing urban research.* Newbury Park, CA: Sage.

Andrews, D. A., & Bonta, J. (1994). *The psychology of criminal conduct.* Cincinnati: Anderson.

Anselin, L. (1998). Exploratory spatial data analysis in a geocomputational environment. In P. A. Longley, S. M. Brooks, R. McDonnell, & B. MacMillan (Eds.), *Geocomputation: A primer* (pp. 77-94). Chichester: John Wiley & Sons.

Appleby, T., & Roberts, D. (1992, May 2). The other man. *The Toronto Globe and Mail,* pp. D1-D4.

Are serial killers on the rise? (1985, September 9). *U.S. News and World Report,* p. 14.

Ault, Jr., R. L. (1986). NCAVC's research and development program. *FBI Law Enforcement Bulletin, 55*(12), 6-8.

Ault, Jr., R. L., & Hazelwood, R. R. (1995). Indirect personality assessment. In R. R. Hazelwood & A. W. Burgess (Eds.), *Practical aspects of rape investigation: A multidisciplinary approach* (2nd ed.) (pp. 205-218). Boca Raton, FL: CRC Press.

Ault, Jr., R. L., & Reese, J. T. (1980). A psychological assessment of crime profiling. *FBI Law Enforcement Bulletin, 49*(3), 22-25.

Austin, V. (1996, July). *An investigation into offender profiling: Assessing the performance of automated profiling on criminal identification, using fuzzy logic.* Paper presented at the Third International Conference on Forensic Statistics, Edinburgh, UK.

Austrian writer held in murders. (1992, March 1). *The Vancouver Province,* p. A13.

Babbie, E. R. (1989). *The practice of social research* (5th ed.). Belmont, CA: Wadsworth.

Bachman, R. (1994). *Violence against women* (BJS Publication No. NCJ-145325). Washington, DC: U.S. Government Printing Office.

Bachman, R., & Saltzman, L. E. (1995). *Violence against women: Estimates from the redesigned survey* (BJS Publication No. NCJ-154348). Washington, DC: U.S. Government Printing Office

Baeza, J. J. (1999). Task-Force management. In B. E. Turvey, *Criminal profiling: An introduction to behavioral evidence analysis* (pp. 415-428). San Diego: Academic Press.

Bailey, K. D. (1982). *Methods of social research* (2nd ed.). New York: Macmillan.

Bailey, W. G. (Ed.). (1989). *The encyclopedia of police science.* New York: Garland.

Balding, D. J., & Donnelly, P. (1994). Inference in forensic identification. *Journal of the Royal Statistical Society, 157*(3), 1-20.

Baldwin, J., & Bottoms, A. E. (1976). *The urban criminal: A study in Sheffield.* London: Tavistock Publications.

Ball, M. S., & Smith, G. W. H. (1992). *Analyzing visual data.* Sage university paper series on qualitative research methods, 24. Newbury Park, CA: Sage.

Ball, R. A., & Curry, G. D. (1995). The logic of definition in criminology: Purposes and methods for defining "gangs." *Criminology, 33,* 225-245.

Bandura, A. (1976). Social learning analysis of aggression. In E. Ribes-Inesta & A. Bandura (Eds.), *Analysis of delinquency and aggression* (pp. 203-232). New York: J. Wiley.

Barak, G. (1996). *Representing O.J.: Murder, criminal justice and mass culture.* Guilderland, NY: Harrow and Heston.

Baring-Gould, W. S. (Ed.). (1967). The annotated Sherlock Holmes. New York: Clarkson N. Potter.

Barker, M. (1989). *Criminal activity and home range: A study of the spatial offence patterns of burglars.* Unpublished master's thesis, University of Surrey, England.

Barnard, C. J. (1984a). The evolution of food-scrounging strategies within and between species. In C. J. Barnard (Ed.), *Producers and scroungers: Strategies of exploitation and parasitism* (pp. 95-126). London: Croom Helm.

Barnard, C. J. (Ed.). (1984b). *Producers and scroungers: Strategies of exploitation and parasitism.* London: Croom Helm.

Barnes, G. C. (1995). Defining and optimizing displacement. In J. E. Eck & D. A. Weisburd (Eds.), *Crime and place: Crime prevention studies, Vol. 4* (pp. 95-113). Monsey, NY: Criminal Justice Press.

Barrett, G. M. (1990). *Serial murder: A study in psychological analysis, prediction, and profiling.* Unpublished master's thesis, University of Louisville, Louisville, KY.

Bartol, C. R. (1996). Police psychology: Then, now, and beyond. *Criminal Justice and Behavior, 23,* 70-89.

Bartol, C. R., & Bartol, A. M. (1986). *Criminal behavior: A psychosocial approach* (2nd ed.). Englewood Cliffs, NJ: Prentice-Hall.

Bates, S. (1987). *Spatial and temporal analysis of crime* (Research Bulletin). Chicago: Illinois Criminal Justice Information Authority.

Bawa, M. S. (1994). *Final report. Geographic profiling of serial crime investigation: A report on secondary research and a market survey.* Unpublished manuscript, Simon Fraser University, University/Industry Liaison Office, Burnaby. BC.

Bayless, A. (1982, Summer/Fall). Paying a murderer for evidence. *Criminal Justice Ethics*, pp. 47-55.

Beavon, D. J. K., Brantingham, P. L., & Brantingham, P. J. (1994). The influence of street networks on the patterning of property offenses. In R. V. Clarke (Ed.), *Crime prevention studies, Vol. 2* (pp. 115-148). Monsey, NY: Criminal Justice Press.

Begg, P., Fido, M., & Skinner, K. (1991). *The Jack the Ripper A to Z.* London: Headline.

Beirne, P. (1999). For a nonspeciesist criminology: Animal abuse as an object of study. *Criminology, 37*, 117-147.

Bekerian, D. A., & Jackson, J. L. (1997). Critical issues in offender profiling. In J. L. Jackson & D. A. Bekerian (Eds.), *Offender profiling: Theory, research and practice* (pp. 209-220). Chichester: John Wiley & Sons.

Belanger, M. (1996, November). *The journey to crime on the New York City subway.* Paper presented at the meeting of the American Society of Criminology, Chicago, IL.

Bellamy, L. C. (1995). *Is displacement an inevitable consequence of situational crime prevention measures?* Unpublished manuscript, Rutgers University, School of Criminal Justice, Newark, NJ.

Ben-Aron, M. H., Hucker, S. J., & Webster, C. D. (Eds.). (1985). *Clinical criminology: The assessment and treatment of criminal behaviour.* Toronto: M & M Graphics.

Benfer, R. A., Brent, Jr., E. E., & Furbee, L. (1991). *Expert systems.* Sage university paper series on quantitative applications in the social sciences, 77. Newbury Park, CA: Sage.

Bennett, T., & Wright, R. T. (1984). *Burglars on burglary: Prevention and the offender.* Aldershot, Hants: Gower.

Bennett, W. W., & Hess, K. M. (1998). *Criminal investigation* (5th ed.). Belmont, CA: Wadsworth.

Bensimon, P. (1997). Characteristics of handguns and personality traits in murderers. *International Criminal Police Review, (462-463)*, 59-70.

Benson, K. (1992). Map to the future. *Police, 16*(8), 98-100, 163-165.

Berkman, E. J. (1989). Mental illness as an aggravating circumstance in capital sentencing. *Columbia Law Review, 89*, 291-309.

Berry, J. K. (1995). *Spatial reasoning for effective GIS.* Fort Collins, CO: GIS World Books.

Beyer, J. C., & Enos, W. F. (1981). Death scene checklist. *FBI Law Enforcement Bulletin, 50*(8), 1-5.

Bigbee, D., Tanton, R. L., & Ferrara, P. B. (1989, October). Implementation of DNA analysis in American crime laboratories. *The Police Chief*, pp. 86-89.

Bils, J. (1994, March 23). How lawyer kept secret of dead client: 21 killings. *The San Francisco Examiner*, p. A2.

Biondi, R., & Hecox, W. (1988). *All his father's sins*. New York: Simon & Schuster.

Biondi, R., & Hecox, W. (1992). *The Dracula Killer*. New York: Simon & Schuster.

Bishop, M. G. (1946, April). Speak to me of murder. *Headquarters Detective*, pp. 20-23, 70-73.

Blackburn, R., & Maybury, C. (1985). Identifying the psychopath: The relation of Cleckley's criteria to the interpersonal domain. *Personal Individual Differences, 6*, 375-386.

Blair, D. (1993). The science of serial murder [Review of *Whoever fights monsters*]. *American Journal of Criminal Law, 20*, 293-297.

Blalock, Jr., H. M. (1972). *Social statistics* (2nd ed.). New York: McGraw-Hill.

Blanche, T., & Schreiber, B. (1998). *Death in paradise: An illustrated history of the Los Angeles County Department of Coroner*. Los Angeles: General Publishing Group.

Block, C. R. (1990, December). *Hot spots and isocrimes in law enforcement decision making*. Paper presented at the conference on Police and Community Responses to Drugs: Frontline Strategies in the Drug War.

Block, C. R. (1993a). Automated spatial analysis as a tool in violence reduction. *CJ the Americas, 6*(1), 7-8, 10.

Block, C. R. (1993b). Lethal violence in the Chicago Latino community. In A. V. Wilson (Ed.), *Homicide: The victim/offender connection* (chap. 15). Cincinnati: Anderson.

Block, C. R., & Block, R. L. (Eds.). (1992). *Questions and answers in lethal and non-lethal violence: Proceedings of the First Annual Workshop of the Homicide Research Working Group* (NIJ Publication No. NCJ-142058). Washington, DC: U.S. Government Printing Office.

Block, C. R., & Block, R. L. (Eds.). (1993). *Questions and answers in lethal and non-lethal violence: Proceedings of the Second Annual Workshop of the Homicide Research Working Group* (NIJ Publication No. NCJ-147480). Washington, DC: U.S. Government Printing Office.

Block, C. R., & Block, R. L. (Eds.). (1995). *Trends, risks, and interventions in lethal violence: Proceedings of the Third Annual Spring Symposium of the Homicide Research Working Group* (NIJ Publication No. NCJ-154254). Washington, DC: U.S. Government Printing Office.

Block, C. R., & Dabdoub, M. (Eds.). (1993). *Workshop on crime analysis through computer mapping; Proceedings: 1993*. Chicago: Illinois Criminal Justice Information Authority.

Block, C. R., & Green, L. A. (1994). *The geoarchive handbook: A guide for developing a geographic database as an information foundation for community policing.* Chicago: Illinois Criminal Justice Information Authority.

Block, C. R., Dabdoub, M., & Fregly, S. (Eds.). (1995). *Crime analysis through computer mapping.* Washington, DC: Police Executive Research Forum.

Block, R. L. (1998, November). *Gang activities and gang territories: Identifying gang turfs though police records.* Paper presented at the meeting of the American Society of Criminology, Washington, DC.

Block, R. L., & Block, C. R. (1995). Space, place and crime: Hot spot areas and hot places of liquor-related crime. In J. E. Eck & D. A. Weisburd (Eds.), *Crime and place: Crime prevention studies, Vol. 4* (pp. 145-183). Monsey, NY: Criminal Justice Press.

Block, R. L., & Davis, S. (1995, July). *The criminology of dangerous places and areas: The environs of rapid transit stations.* Paper presented at the Seminar on Environmental Criminology and Crime Analysis, Cambridge, UK.

Block, R. L., Felson, M., & Block, C. R. (1985). Crime victimization rates for incumbents of 246 occupations. *Sociology and Social Research, 69,* 442-451.

Boar, R., & Blundell, N. (1983). *The world's most infamous murders.* New York: Berkley Books.

Boggs, S. (1965). Urban crime patterns. *American Sociological Review, 30,* 899-908.

Boots, B. N., & Getis, A. (1988). *Point pattern analysis.* Sage university paper series on scientific geography, 8. Beverly Hills: Sage.

Bottoms, A. E., & Wiles, P. (1992). Explanations of crime and place. In D. J. Evans, N. R. Fyfe, & D. T. Herbert (Eds.), *Crime, policing and place: Essays in environmental criminology* (pp. 11-35). London: Routledge.

Bourget, D., & Bradford, J. M. W. (1989). Female arsonists: A clinical study. *The Bulletin of American Academic Psychiatry Law, 17,* 293-300.

Boyanowsky, E. O. (1990, June). *Grains of truth in the wasteland of fear.* Paper presented at the World Conference of the International Society for Research on Aggression, Banff, AB.

Boyd, N. (1988). The last dance: Murder in Canada. Scarborough, ON: Prentice-Hall.

Boyd, N., & Rossmo, D. K. (1992). *Milgaard v. The Queen: Finding justice — Problems and process.* Burnaby, BC: Criminology Research Centre, Simon Fraser University.

Brahan, J. W., Valcour, L., & Shevel, R. (1994). The investigator's notebook. In *Applications and innovations in expert systems.* Cambridge: Cambridge University Press.

Brantingham, P. J. (1987). Violent crime in Canada, the U.S., and Europe. In J. M. MacLatchie (Ed.), *Violence in contemporary Canadian society* (pp. 43-49). Ottawa: John Howard Society of Canada.

Brantingham, P. J., & Brantingham, P. J. (1991, February). *Niches and predators: Theoretical departures in the ecology of crime.* Paper presented at the conference of the Western Society of Criminology, Berkeley, CA.

Brantingham, P. J., Brantingham, P. J., & Brantingham, P. L. (1998, February). *Utilizing biometric behavior models to understand and control criminal behavior.* Paper presented at the conference of the Western Society of Criminology, Newport Beach, CA.

Brantingham, P. J., & Brantingham, P. L. (1975). The spatial patterning of burglary. *Howard Journal of Penology and Crime Prevention, 14,* 11-24.

Brantingham, P. J., & Brantingham, P. L. (1978). A theoretical model of crime site selection. In M. D. Krohn & R. L. Akers (Eds.), *Crime, law, and sanctions: Theoretical perspectives* (pp. 105-118). Beverly Hills: Sage.

Brantingham, P. J., & Brantingham, P. L. (Eds.). (1981a). *Environmental criminology.* Beverly Hills: Sage.

Brantingham, P. J., & Brantingham, P. L. (Eds.). (1981b). *Environmental criminology* (1991 reissue). Prospect Heights, IL: Waveland Press.

Brantingham, P. J., & Brantingham, P. L. (1981c). Introduction: The dimensions of crime. In P. J. Brantingham & P. L. Brantingham (Eds.), *Environmental criminology* (pp. 7-26). Beverly Hills: Sage.

Brantingham, P. J., & Brantingham, P. L. (1984). *Patterns in crime.* New York: Macmillan.

Brantingham, P. J., & Brantingham, P. L. (1998). Environmental criminology: From theory to urban planning practice. *Studies on Crime and Crime Prevention, 7,* 1-30.

Brantingham, P. J., Brantingham, P. L., & Wong, P. S. (1991). How public transit feeds private crime: Notes on the Vancouver "Skytrain" experience. *Security Journal, 2,* 91-95.

Brantingham, P. J., & Jeffery, C. R. (1981). Afterword: Crime space, and criminological theory. In P. J. Brantingham & P. L. Brantingham (Eds.), *Environmental criminology* (pp. 227-237). Beverly Hills: Sage.

Brantingham, P. J., Mu, S., & Verma, A. (1993, October). *An ecology of crime in Vancouver.* Paper presented at the meeting of the American Society of Criminology, Phoenix, AZ.

Brantingham, P. L., & Brantingham, P. J. (1975). Residential burglary and urban form. *Urban Studies, 12,* 273-284.

Brantingham, P. L., & Brantingham, P. J. (1978). A topological technique for regionalization. *Environment and Behavior, 10,* 335-353.

Brantingham, P. L., & Brantingham, P. J. (1981). Notes on the geometry on crime. In P. J. Brantingham & P. L. Brantingham (Eds.), *Environmental criminology* (pp. 27-54). Beverly Hills: Sage.

Brantingham, P. L., & Brantingham, P. J. (1993a). Nodes, paths and edges: Considerations on the complexity of crime and the physical environment. *Journal of Environmental Psychology, 13*, 3-28.

Brantingham, P. L., & Brantingham, P. J. (1993b). Environment, routine and situation: Toward a pattern theory of crime. In R. V. Clarke & M. Felson (Eds.), *Routine activity and rational choice* (pp. 259-294). New Brunswick, NJ: Transaction.

Brantingham, P. L., & Brantingham, P. J. (1995). Criminality of place: Crime generators and crime attractors. *European Journal on Criminal Policy and Research: Crime Environments and Situational Prevention, 3*(3), 5-26.

Brantingham, P. L., & Brantingham, P. J. (1997, June). *Theoretical models of crime hot spot generation.* Paper presented at the Seminar on Environmental Criminology and Crime Analysis, Oslo, Norway.

Brantingham, P. L., Brantingham, P. J., & Verma, A. (1992, November). *Crime pattern analysis using point-set and algebraic topology.* Paper presented at the meeting of the American Society of Criminology, New Orleans, LA.

Brantingham, P. L., Brantingham, P. J., & Wong, P. S. (1990). Malls and crime: A first look. *Security Journal, 1*, 175-181.

Breo, D. L., & Martin, W. J. (1993). *The crime of the century: Richard Speck and the murder of eight student nurses.* New York: Bantam Books.

Brewer, C. A., MacEachren, A. M., Pickle, L. W., Herrmann, D. (1997). Mapping mortality: Evaluating color schemes for choropleth maps. *Annals of the Association of American Geographers, 87*, 411-438.

Brewer, V. E., & Edison, Jr., W. G. (1996, November). *Analysis of differentials between cleared and uncleared homicides in Houston, Texas, 1984-1994: A preliminary report.* Paper presented at the meeting of the American Society of Criminology, Chicago, IL.

Brittain, R. P. (1970). The sadistic murderer. *Medical Science and the Law, 10*, 198-207.

Britton, P. (1997). *The Jigsaw Man.* London: Bantam Press.

Brooks, P. R. (1982). *The investigative consultant team: A new approach for law enforcement cooperation.* Washington, DC: Police Executive Research Forum.

Brooks, P. R. (1984, November). *VICAP.* Lecture presented at Washington Criminal Justice Training Center seminar, Seattle, WA.

Brooks, P. R., Devine, M. J., Green, T. J., Hart, B. L., & Moore, M. D. (1987, June). Serial murder: A criminal justice response. *The Police Chief,* pp. 40-44.

Brooks, P. R., Devine, M. J., Green, T. J., Hart, B. L., & Moore, M. D. (1988). *Multi-Agency investigative team manual.* Washington, DC: National Institute of Justice.

Brown, J. R. (1994, March). DNA analysis: A significant tool for law enforcement. *The Police Chief,* pp. 51-52.

Brown, Jr., J. S. (1991a). The historical similarity of 20th century serial sexual homicide to pre-20th century occurrences of vampirism. *American Journal of Forensic Psychiatry, 12*(2), 11-24.

Brown, Jr., J. S. (1991b). The psychopathology of serial sexual homicide: A review of the possibilities. *American Journal of Forensic Psychiatry, 12*(1), 13-21.

Brown, P. J. B., Hirschfield, A., & Batey, P. W. J. (1991). Applications of geodemographic methods in the analysis of health condition incidence data. *Papers in Regional Science, 70,* 329-344.

Brown, S. (1997, November). *Public attitudes toward the treatment of sex offenders.* Paper presented at the meeting of the American Society of Criminology, San Diego, CA.

Brown, W. (1952). *The Lonely Hearts Killers.* New York: Collier Books.

Brunet, R. (1995, February 13). The menace of sex offenders. *British Columbia Report,* pp. 36-40.

Brussel, J. A. (1968). Casebook of a crime psychiatrist. New York: Bernard Geis Associates.

Büchler, H., & Leineweber, H. (1991). The escape behavior of bank robbers and circular blockade operations by the police. In E. Kube & H. U. Störzer (Eds.), *Police research in the Federal Republic of Germany: 15 years research within the "Bundeskriminalamt"* (pp. 199-208). Berlin: Springer-Velag.

Buckley, J. B. (1996). *Public transit and crime: A routine activities/ecological approach.* Unpublished master's thesis, Simon Fraser University, Burnaby, BC.

Bugliosi, V., & Gentry, C. (1974). *Helter skelter.* New York: Bantam Books.

Bullock, C. A., & Waldo, G. P. (1992, November). *Homicides in Florida: Female murderers.* Paper presented at the meeting of the American Society of Criminology, New Orleans, LA.

Bullock, H. A. (1955). Urban homicide in theory and fact. *Journal of Criminal Law, Criminology and Police Science, 45,* 565-575.

Bundeskriminalamt Kriminalistisches Institut. (1998). *Methods of case analysis: An international symposium.* (BKA Research Series vol. 38.2). Wiesbaden, Germany: Author.

Bunge, E. (1991). The role of pattern recognition in forensic science: An introduction to methods. In E. Kube & H. U. Störzer (Eds.), *Police research in the Federal Republic of Germany: 15 years research within the "Bundeskriminalamt"* (pp. 253-265). Berlin: Springer-Velag.

Burfeind, J. W., Doyle, D. P., & Cooper, J. M. (1992, November). *The University of Montana Sexual Victimization Survey: Preliminary findings.* Paper presented at the meeting of the American Society of Criminology, New Orleans, LA.

Burger, D. (Ed.). (1991). *Death row 1992.* Carlsbad, CA: Glenn Hare Publications.

Burgess, A. G., Burgess, A. W., & Hazelwood, R. R. (1995). Classifying rape and sexual assault. In R. R. Hazelwood & A. W. Burgess (Eds.), *Practical aspects of rape investigation: A multidisciplinary approach* (2nd ed.) (pp. 193-203). Boca Raton, FL: CRC Press.

Burgess, A. W., Hartman, C. R., Ressler, R. K., Douglas, J. E., & McCormack, A. (1986). Sexual homicide: A motivational model. *Journal of Interpersonal Violence, 1*, 251-272.

Burgess, A. W., Hazelwood, R. R., Rokous, F. E., Hartman, C. R., & Burgess, A. G. (1988). Serial rapists and their victims: Reenactment and repetition. In R. A. Prentky & V. L. Quinsey (Eds.), *Human sexual aggression: Current perspectives* (pp. 277-295). New York: Annals of the New York Academy of Sciences.

Burgess, E. W. (1925). The growth of the city. In R. E. Park, E. W. Burgess, & R. D. McKenzie (Eds.), *The city* (pp. 47-62). Chicago: University of Chicago Press.

Burgess, R. L. (1980). Family violence: Implications from evolutionary biology. In T. Hirschi & M. Gottfredson (Eds.), *Understanding crime: Current theory and research* (pp. 91-101). Beverly Hills: Sage.

Burke, T. W. (1994, March). *Multiple personality and the law.* Paper presented at the meeting of the Academy of Criminal Justice Sciences, Chicago, IL.

Burke, T. W., & Rowe, W. F. (1989, October). DNA analysis: The challenge for police. *The Police Chief,* pp. 92-95.

Burn, G. (1984). *Somebody's husband, somebody's son.* New York: Penguin.

Burnside, S., & Cairns, A. (1995). *Deadly innocence.* New York: Warner Books.

Burrough, P. A. (1986). *Principles of geographic information systems for land resources assessment* (Monographs on Soil and Resources Survey No. 12). Oxford: Clarendon Press.

Burton, C. (1998). *The CATCHEM Database: Child murder in the United Kingdom.* Paper presented at the International Homicide Investigators Association Symposium, Zutphen, The Netherlands.

Buser, L. W. (1994). The bone experts. *Police, 18*(3), 37-40, 74.

Butts, W. (1994). The diary of Jack the Ripper [Review of *The diary of Jack the Ripper: The discovery, the investigation, the debate*]. *Manuscripts, 66*, 131-133.

Byford, L. (1984, September). Lessons to be learned. *Police Review,* pp. 1870-1871.

Cahill, T. (1986). *Buried dreams.* New York: Bantam Books.

Came, B. (1989, December 18). Montreal Massacre. *Maclean's,* pp. 14-17.

Cameron, D., & Frazer, E. (1987). *The lust to kill.* New York: New York University Press.

Canada's Postal Code Directory 1995. (1995). Ottawa: Canada Post Corporation.

Canadian Centre for Justice Statistics. (1982). *Homicides: Canada and selected countries* (Juristat Service Bulletin vol. 2, no. 1). Ottawa: Statistics Canada.

Canadian Centre for Justice Statistics. (1984). *Homicide in Canada: Statistical highlights —1983* (Juristat Service Bulletin vol. 4, no. 6). Ottawa: Statistics Canada.

Canela-Cacho, J. A., Blumstein, A., & Cohen, J. (1997). Relationship between the offending frequency (λ) of imprisoned and free offenders. *Criminology, 35*, 133-175.

Canter, D. V. (1977). *The psychology of place.* London: Architectural Press.

Canter, D. V. (1989). Offender profiles. *The Psychologist*, 2(1), 12-16.

Canter, D. V. (1994). *Criminal shadows*. London: HarperCollins.

Canter, D. V., & Alison, L. J. (Eds.). (1997). *Criminal detection and the psychology of crime*. Aldershot, Hants: Ashgate Publishing.

Canter, D. V., & Gregory, A. (1994). Identifying the residential location of rapists. *Journal of the Forensic Science Society*, 34, 169-175.

Canter, D. V., & Heritage, R. (1990). A multivariate model of sexual offence behaviour: Developments in 'offender profiling.' I. *Journal of Forensic Psychiatry*, 1, 185-212.

Canter, D. V., & Hodge, S. (1997). *Predatory patterns of serial murder*. Unpublished manuscript, The University of Liverpool, Institute of Investigative Psychology and Forensic Behavioural Science, Liverpool.

Canter, D. V., & Larkin, P. (1993). The environmental range of serial rapists. *Journal of Environmental Psychology*, 13, 63-69.

Canter, D. V., & Tagg, S. (1975). Distance estimation in cities. *Environment and Behaviour*, 7, 59-80.

Canter, P. (1993). State of the statistical art: Point pattern analysis. In C. R. Block & M. Dabdoub (Eds.), *Workshop on crime analysis through computer mapping; Proceedings: 1993* (pp. 199-210). Chicago: Illinois Criminal Justice Information Authority.

Canter, P. (1995). State of the statistical art: Point-Pattern analysis. In C. R. Block, M. Dabdoub, & S. Fregly (Eds.), *Crime analysis through computer mapping* (pp. 151-160). Washington, DC: Police Executive Research Forum.

Capone, D. L., & Nichols, Jr., W. W. (1975). Crime and distance: An analysis of offender behaviour in space. *Proceedings, Association of American Geographers*, 45-49.

Capone, D. L., & Nichols, Jr., W. W. (1976). Urban structure and criminal mobility. *American Behavioral Scientist*, 20, 199-213.

Caputi, J. (1990). The new founding fathers: The lore and lure of the serial killer in contemporary culture. *Journal of American Culture*, 13(3), 1-11.

Cardarelli, A. P., & Cavanagh, D. (1992, November). *Uncleared homicides in the United States: An exploratory study of trends and patterns*. Paper presented at the meeting of the American Society of Criminology, New Orleans, LA.

Carlisle, A. L. (1993). The divided self: Toward an understanding of the dark side of the serial killer. *American Journal of Criminal Justice*, 17(2), 23-36.

Carpozi, Jr., G. (1977). *Son of Sam: The .44-Caliber Killer*. New York: Manor Books.

Cartel, M. (1985). *Disguise of sanity: Serial mass murderers*. Toluca Lake, CA: Pepperbox Books.

Casti, J. (1998, May 9). Easy does it. *New Scientist*, pp. 44-47.

Cater, J. G. (1997). The social construction of the serial killer. *RCMP Gazette*, 59(2), 2-21.

Cavanagh, D. P. (1993, October). *An experimental procedure for estimating the incidence of serial murder in the United States.* Paper presented at the meeting of the American Society of Criminology, Phoenix, AZ.

Cavanagh, K., & MacKay, R. E. (1991). Violent Crime Analysis Section. *RCMP Gazette, 53*(1), 5-7.

Cawthorne, N. (1994). *Sex killers.* London: Boxtree.

Caywood, T. (1998). Routine activities and urban homicides. *Homicide Studies, 2,* 64-82.

Caywood, T., & Jentzen, J. (1994, March). *A partial replication of the application routine activities approach to urban homicides.* Paper presented at the meeting of the Academy of Criminal Justice Sciences, Chicago, IL.

Chaiken, J., Greenwood, P., & Petersilia, J. (1991). The Rand study of detectives. In C. B. Klockars (Ed.), *Thinking about police: Contemporary readings* (2nd ed.) (pp. 170-187). New York: McGraw-Hill.

Chappell, D. (1965). *The development and administration of the English law relating to breaking and entering.* Unpublished doctoral dissertation, University of Cambridge, Cambridge.

Chappell, D. (1984). Crime and law enforcement. In D. Daume & J. E. Davis (Eds.), *1984 Britannica book of the year* (pp. 256-261). Chicago: Encyclopedia Britannica.

Chappell, D. (1990). *Preventing violence: An international perspective* (A/Conf. 144/G/Australia/2). Canberra: Australian Institute of Criminology.

Cheatwood, D. (1992, November). *The effects of weather on homicide: A consideration of social and physiological factors.* Paper presented at the meeting of the American Society of Criminology, New Orleans, LA.

Cheatwood, D. (1993). Notes on the theoretical, empirical and policy significance of multiple-offender homicides. In A. V. Wilson (Ed.), *Homicide: The victim/offender connection* (chap. 21). Cincinnati: Anderson.

Cheney, M. (1976). *The Coed Killer.* New York: Walker.

Chester, G. (1993). *Berserk!: Motiveless random massacres.* New York: St. Martin's Press.

Chin, P., & Tamarkin, C. (1991, August 12). The door of evil. *People,* pp. 32-37.

Chisholm, P. (1993, January 4). The fear index. *Maclean's,* p. 24.

Clark, A. N. (1990). *The New Penguin dictionary of geography.* London: Penguin Books.

Clark, D. (1995, May). In pursuit of human predators. *The Financial Post Magazine,* pp. 18-20.

Clark, G. (1995, November 8). Serial crimes on-line. *The Vancouver Province,* p. A10.

Clark, W. A. V. (1986). *Human migration.* Sage university paper series on scientific geography, 7. Beverly Hills: Sage.

Clarke, G. (1989, November). *Legal issues pertaining to DNA typing.* Paper presented at the meeting of the American Society of Criminology, Reno, NV.

Clarke, J. W. (1988). *Last rampage.* New York: Berkley Books.

Clarke, K. B. (1992). Michael Bruce Ross. *Police, 16*(1), 46-48, 76.

Clarke, K. C. (1990). *Analytical and computer cartography.* Englewood Cliffs, NJ: Prentice Hall.

Clarke, R. V. (Ed.). (1992). *Situational crime prevention: Successful case studies.* New York: Harrow and Heston.

Clarke, R. V. (Ed.). (1993). *Crime prevention studies, Vol. 1.* Monsey, NY: Criminal Justice Press.

Clarke, R. V. (Ed.). (1994a). *Crime prevention studies, Vol. 2.* Monsey, NY: Criminal Justice Press.

Clarke, R. V. (Ed.). (1994b). *Crime prevention studies, Vol. 3.* Monsey, NY: Criminal Justice Press.

Clarke, R. V. (Ed.). (1997). *Situational crime prevention: Successful case studies* (2nd ed.). Guilderland, NY: Harrow and Heston.

Clarke, R. V., & Felson, M. (1993a). Introduction: Criminology, routine activity, and rational choice. In R. V. Clarke & M. Felson (Eds.), *Routine activity and rational choice* (pp. 1-14). New Brunswick, NJ: Transaction.

Clarke, R. V., & Felson, M. (Eds.). (1993b). *Routine activity and rational choice.* New Brunswick, NJ: Transaction.

Classifying sexual homicide crime scenes. (1985). *FBI Law Enforcement Bulletin, 54*(8), 12-17.

Cleary, S., Klein, L., & Luxenburg, J. (1994, March). *Toward an analysis of serial murder victims.* Paper presented at the meeting of the Academy of Criminal Justice Sciences, Chicago, IL.

Cleary, S., & Luxenburg, J. (1993, October). *Serial murderers: Common background characteristics and their contribution to causation.* Paper presented at the meeting of the American Society of Criminology, Phoenix, AZ.

Cleary, S., & Luxenburg, J. (1994, November). *Classifying the serial killer according to personality type and victim selection pattern.* Paper presented at the meeting of the American Society of Criminology, Miami, FL.

Cleary, S., & Rettig, R. P. (1994, November). *A profiling matrix for serial killers.* Paper presented at the meeting of the American Society of Criminology, Miami, FL.

Cleckley, H. (1982). *The mask of sanity.* New York: Mosby.

Cleveland, W. A. (Ed.). (1985). 1985 Britannica world data. In D. Daume & J. E. Davis (Eds.), *1985 Britannica book of the year* (pp. 609-960). Chicago: Encyclopædia Britannica.

Cluff, J., Hunter, A., & Hinch, R. (1997). Feminist perspectives on serial murder. *Homicide Studies, 1,* 291-308.

Coburn, G. M. B. (1988). *Patterns of homicide in Vancouver: 1980-1986.* Unpublished master's thesis, Simon Fraser University, Burnaby, BC.

Codrescu, A. (1992, October 15). The original Iron Maiden. *American Way*, pp. 68-72, 92-110.

Cohen, B. (1980). *Deviant street networks: Prostitution in New York City.* Lexington, MA: Lexington Books.

Cohen, L., & Felson, M. (1979). Social change and crime rate trends: A routine activity approach. *American Sociological Review, 44*, 588-608.

Coleman, J. C. (1976). *Abnormal psychology and modern life* (5th ed.). Glenview, IL: Scott, Foresman.

Collins, P. I., Johnson, G. F., Choy, A., Davidson, K. T., & MacKay, R. E. (1998). Advances in violent crime analysis and law enforcement: The Canadian Violent Crime Linkage Analysis System. *Journal of Government Information, 25*, 277-284.

Collins, R., & Johnson, A. (1990, January 10). Teen hooker murdered. *Calgary Herald*, pp. A1-A2.

Connors, E., Lundregan, T., Miller, N., & McEwen, J. T. (1996). *Convicted by juries, exonerated by science: Case studies in the use of DNA evidence to establish innocence after trial* (National Institute of Justice Research Report No. NCJ-161258). Washington, DC: U.S. Government Printing Office.

Conradi, P. (1992). *The Red Ripper.* London: Virgin.

Conviction of Williams ends 23 slaying inquiries. (1982, March 2). *The New York Times*, p. A10.

Cook, P. (1998). Mapping a murderer's path. In N. G. La Vigne & J. Wartell (Eds.), *Crime mapping case studies: Successes in the field* (pp. 123-128). Washington, DC: Police Executive Research Forum.

Cook, R. (1985, October). Predicting arson. *Byte*, pp. 239-245.

Coon, C. S. (1976). Populations, human. In *The new encyclopædia Britannica* (Vol. 14, pp. 839-848). Chicago: Encyclopædia Britannica.

Copson, G. (1993, May). *Offender profiling.* Presentation to the Association of Chief Police Officers Crime Sub-Committee on Offender Profiling, London, England.

Copson, G. (1995). *Coals to Newcastle? Part 1: A study of offender profiling* (Special Interest Series: Paper 7). London: Police Research Group, Home Office Police Department.

Copson, G., & Holloway, K. (1996). *Review of the scientific status of the 'abuser/exploiter' model of sexual offending.* Unpublished manuscript.

Cornish, D. B. (1993). Theories of action in criminology: Learning theory and rational choice approaches. In R. V. Clarke & M. Felson (Eds.), *Routine activity and rational choice* (pp. 351-382). New Brunswick, NJ: Transaction.

Cornish, D. B., & Clarke, R. V. (1986a). Introduction. In D. B. Cornish & R. V. Clarke (Eds.), *The reasoning criminal: Rational choice perspectives on offending* (pp. 1-16). New York: Springer-Verlag.

Cornish, D. B., & Clarke, R. V. (Eds.). (1986b). *The reasoning criminal: Rational choice perspectives on offending.* New York: Springer-Verlag.

Costanzo, C. M., Halperin, W. C., & Gale, N. (1986). Criminal mobility and the directional component in journeys to crime. In R. M. Figlio, S. Hakim, & G. F. Rengert (Eds.), *Metropolitan crime patterns* (pp. 73-95). Monsey, NY: Criminal Justice Press.

Coston, J. (1992). *To kill and kill again.* New York: Penguin Books.

Coucelis, H., Golledge, R., Gale, N., & Tobler, W. (1987). Exploring the anchor point hypothesis of spatial cognition. *Journal of Environmental Psychology, 7,* 99-122.

Cox, D. R., & Hinkley, D. V. (1974). *Theoretical statistics.* London: Chapman and Hall.

Cox, K. R., & Golledge, R. G. (Eds.). (1969). *Behavioral problems in geography.* Evanston, IL: Northwestern University Press.

Cox, M. (1991). *The confessions of Henry Lee Lucas.* New York: Simon & Schuster.

Craven, D. (1996). *Female victims of violent crime* (NIJ Publication No. NCJ-162602). Washington, DC: U.S. Government Printing Office.

Crime scene and profile characteristics of organized and disorganized murderers. (1985). *FBI Law Enforcement Bulletin, 54*(8), 18-25.

Criminal Code, R.S.C. 1985, Chap. C-46.

Criminal Intelligence Service Canada. (1990). *Organized Crime Committee report 1990.* Ottawa: Canadian Association of Chiefs of Police.

Criminal personality profiling now available in Canada. (1992). *Blue Line Magazine,* 4(6), 16.

Crockett, A. (Ed.). (1990). *Serial murderers.* New York: Windsor.

Cromwell, P. F. (Ed.) (1996). *In their own words: Criminals on crime.* Los Angeles: Roxbury Publishing.

Cromwell, P.F. (Ed.) (1999). *In their own words: Criminals on crime* (2nd ed.). Los Angeles: Roxbury Publishing

Cromwell, P. F., Olson, J. N., & Avary, D. W. (1990). *Residential burglary: An ethnographic analysis.* Washington, DC: National Institute of Justice.

Cromwell, P.F., Olson, J.N., & Avary, D.W. (1991). *Breaking and entering: An ethnographic analysis of burglary.* Newbury Park, CA: Sage.

Cryan, M. P. (1988). Halt program joins VICAP in hunting serial criminals. *Trooper Magazine,* (May/June), 8-9.

Cullen, R. (1993). *The Killer Department.* New York: Ballantine Books.

Cunliffe, F., & Piazza, P. B. (1980). *Criminalistics and scientific investigation.* Englewood Cliffs, NJ: Prentice-Hall.

Curtis, L. A. (1974). *Criminal violence.* Lexington, MA: Lexington Books.

Cusson, M. (1993). A strategic analysis of crime: Criminal tactics as responses to precriminal situations. In R. V. Clarke & M. Felson (Eds.), *Routine activity and rational choice* (pp. 295-304). New Brunswick, NJ: Transaction.

Dahmer, L. (1994). *A father's story.* London: Little, Brown.

Dale, A. (1996). Modelling criminal offences. *The Police Journal.*

Dale, A., & Davies, A. (1994a). *Developments in the analysis of rapists speech.* Unpublished manuscript, Police Research Group, Home Office Police Department, London.

Dale, A., & Davies, A. (1994b). *The geography of rape.* Unpublished manuscript, Police Research Group, Home Office Police Department, London.

Daly, M., & Wilson, M. (1988). *Homicide.* New York: Aldine de Gruyter.

Daly, M., & Wilson, M. (1994). Evolutionary psychology of male violence. In J. Archer (Ed.), *Male violence* (pp. 253-288). London: Routledge.

Daly, M., & Wilson, M. (1995, November). *Foraging theory for criminologists.* Paper presented at the meeting of the American Society of Criminology, Boston, MA.

Damore, L. (1981). *In his garden.* New York: Dell.

Danson, T. S. B. (1995). *Sexual predator law (Protecting our children).* Unpublished manuscript, Canadian Police Association, Ottawa.

Daubert v. Merrell Dow Pharmaceuticals, Inc., 509 U.S. 579 (1993).

Davey, F. (1994). *Karla's web: A cultural investigation of the Mahaffy-French murders.* Toronto: Viking.

Davies, A. (1996a). *Modus operandi and the stranger rapist.* Unpublished manuscript, Police Research Group, Home Office Police Department, London.

Davies, A. (1996b). *A preliminary analysis of the relationship between rapists' criminal careers and their victims' perceptions of offence behaviour.* Unpublished manuscript, Police Research Group, Home Office Police Department, London.

Davies, A., & Dale, A. (1995a). *Locating the rapist.* Unpublished manuscript, Police Research Group, Home Office Police Department, London.

Davies, A., & Dale, A. (1995b). *Locating the stranger rapist* (Special Interest Series: Paper 3). London: Police Research Group, Home Office Police Department.

Davies, A., & Dale, A. (1996). Locating the stranger rapist. *Medical Science and the Law, 36,* 146-156.

Davies, A., Wittebrood, K., & Jackson, J. L. (1997). Predicting the criminal antecedents of a stranger rapist from his offence behaviour. *Science & Justice, 37,* 161-170.

Davies, A., Wittebrood, K., & Jackson, J. L. (1998). *Predicting the criminal record of a stranger rapist.* (Special Interest Series: Paper 12). London: Police and Reducing Crime Unit, Home Office.

Davis, J. A. (1998). A psychological profile and autopsy of a serial killer: Jeffrey Dahmer. *Canadian Journal of Clinical Medicine, 5,* 188-199.

Davis, J. E. (1958). *An introduction to tool marks, firearms and the striagraph.* Springfield, IL: Charles C. Thomas.

Dawson, J. M. (1993). *Murder in large urban counties, 1988* (BJS Publication No. NCJ-140614). Washington, DC: U.S. Government Printing Office.

Dawson, J. M., & Langan, P. A. (1994). *Murder in families* (BJS Publication No. NCJ-143498). Washington, DC: U.S. Government Printing Office.

de Cocq, M. (1997). *Interpol crime analysis booklet*. Lyon, France: International Criminal Police Organization.

De Forest, P. R., Gaensslen, R. E., & Lee, H. C. (1983). *Forensic science: An introduction to criminalistics*. New York: McGraw-Hill.

de Kleuver, E. E. (1997, June). *Geographical aspects in rape cases*. Paper presented at the Seminar on Environmental Criminology and Crime Analysis, Oslo, Norway.

de Kleuver, E. E., & van den Eshof, P. (1995, November). *Geographical aspects in sexual assault and rape cases*. Paper presented at the meeting of the American Society of Criminology, Boston, MA.

De Smedt, M., Pattyn, M., Rongvaux, D., & Vervaecke, S. (1998, June). *Is crime analysis a matter of scientific techniques or of strategic police management*. Paper presented at the Seminar on Environmental Criminology and Crime Analysis, Barcelona, Spain.

Decker, S., Wright, R. T., & Logie, R. (1993). Perceptual deterrence among active residential burglars: A research note. *Criminology, 31*, 135-147.

Dees, T. M. (1994, March). Automation of forensic ballistics. *Law Enforcement Technology*, pp. 44, 47.

DeFrances, C. J., & Smith, S. K. (1994). *Crime and neighborhoods* (BJS Publication No. NCJ-147005). Washington, DC: U.S. Government Printing Office.

DeFrances, C. J., & Titus, R. M. (1993, May). *The environment and residential burglary outcomes*. Paper presented at the Seminar on Environmental Criminology and Crime Analysis, Miami, FL.

DeMont, J. (1994, October 31). Murder, he wrote. *Maclean's*, pp. 56-57.

Dennis, G. (1993). "The Night Stalker": Richard Ramirez. *Police, 17*(3), 51-54, 86-88.

Depue, R. L. (1986). An American response to an era of violence. *FBI Law Enforcement Bulletin, 55*(12), 2-5.

Dettlinger, C., & Prugh, J. (1983). *The List*. Atlanta: Philmay Enterprises.

Devine, M. (1989, November 4). Chilling profile of a 'charming psychopath.' *The Sydney Daily Telegraph*, p. 3.

Devine, M., & Kennedy, L. (1989, November 4). Second murder in 24 hours. *The Sydney Daily Telegraph*, pp. 1-2.

Di Maio, V. J. M. (1985). *Gunshot wounds: Practical aspects of firearms, ballistics, and forensic techniques*. Boca Raton, FL: CRC Press.

Dickson, G. (1958). *Murder by numbers*. London: Robert Hale.

Dietz, M. L. (1995, June). Killer coverage. *Fremens*, p. 1.

Dietz, P. E. (1985). Sex offender profiling by the FBI: A preliminary conceptual model. In M. H. Ben-Aron, S. J. Hucker, & C. D. Webster (Eds.), *Clinical criminology: The assessment and treatment of criminal behaviour* (pp. 207-219). Toronto: M & M Graphics.

Dietz, P. E., Hazelwood, R. R., & Warren, J. I. (1990). The sexually sadistic criminal and his offences. *The Bulletin of American Academic Psychiatry Law, 18*, 163-178.

Dillon, M. (1989). *The Shankill Butchers: A case study of mass murder.* London: Hutchinson.

DiRosa, A. (1992). The FBI's Violent Crimes and Major Offenders Program. *FBI Law Enforcement Bulletin, 61*(7), 12-13.

DNA profiling. (1995, January). *DNA Database,* p. 2.

Dobson, J. C. (1989, February 28). *"Focus on the Family" Newsletter.* Pomona, CA.

Dodge, R. W. (1985). *Locating city, suburban, and rural crime* (BJS Publication No. NCJ-99535). Washington, DC: U.S. Government Printing Office.

Dodge, R. W. (1987). *Series crimes: Report of a field test* (BJS Publication No. NCJ-104615). Washington, DC: U.S. Government Printing Office.

Doney, R. H. (1990). The aftermath of the Yorkshire Ripper: The response of the United Kingdom police service. In S. A. Egger (Ed.), *Serial murder: An elusive phenomenon* (pp. 95-112). New York: Praeger.

Dostoyevsky, F. (1982). *Crime and punishment* (D. Magarshack, Trans.). New York: Greenwich House. (Original work published 1866).

Douglas, J. E., & Burgess, A. E. (1986). Criminal profiling: A viable investigative tool against violent crime. *FBI Law Enforcement Bulletin, 55*(12), 9-13.

Douglas, J. E., Burgess, A. W., Burgess, A. G., & Ressler, R. K. (1992a). *Crime classification manual.* New York: Lexington Books.

Douglas, J. E., Burgess, A. W., Burgess, A. G., & Ressler, R. K. (1992b). *Pocket guide to the crime classification manual.* New York: Lexington Books.

Douglas, J. E., & Munn, C. (1992). Violent crime scene analysis: Modus operandi, signature, and staging. *FBI Law Enforcement Bulletin, 61*(2), 1-10.

Douglas, J. E., & Olshaker, M. (1995). *Mindhunter: Inside the FBI's elite serial crime unit.* New York: Simon & Schuster.

Douglas, J. E., Ressler, R. K., Burgess, A. W., & Hartman, C. R. (1986). Criminal profiling from crime scene analysis. *Behavioral Sciences & the Law, 4,* 401-421.

Douglas, K. (1999, September 4). Basic instinct. *New Scientist,* pp. 32-35.

Drukteinis, A. M. (1992). Serial murder — The heart of darkness. *Psychiatric Annals, 22,* 532-538.

Du Clos, B. (1993). *Fair game.* New York: St. Martin's Press.

Duchesne, D. (1997). *Street prostitution in Canada* (Juristat Service Bulletin vol. 17, no. 2). Ottawa: Statistics Canada.

Duncanson, J. (1991, October 13). Evidence surfaces to link slayings to drifter. *The Toronto Star,* pp. A1, A4.

Duplain, R. (1990a). DNA codes help nab killer. *Blue Line Magazine, 2*(2), 25.

Duplain, R. (1990b). Terror on the Miramichi. *Blue Line Magazine, 2*(2), 24-25.

Durand-Hansen, D. (1998, November). *Necrophilic partialism: A paraphilia.* Paper presented at the meeting of the American Society of Criminology, Washington, DC.

Dussich, J. P. J., & Shinohara, S. (1997, November). *Nonreporting of sexual assault in Japan.* Paper presented at the meeting of the American Society of Criminology, San Diego, CA.

Dvorchak, R. J., & Holewa, L. (1991). *Milwaukee massacre.* New York: Dell.

Eastham, M. W. (1989). Blindfold/Paperbag Rapist. *The RCMP Quarterly, 54*(2), 30-37.

Easton, S., & Berry, S. (1988, October 9). Scary silence. *The Vancouver Province,* pp. 14-15.

Ebert, B. W. (1987). Guide to conducting a psychological autopsy. *Professional Psychology: Research and Practice, 18,* 52-56.

Eck, J. E. (1993, Summer). The threat of crime displacement. *Problem-Solving Quarterly,* pp. 1-2.

Eck, J. E. (1997). What do those dots mean? Mapping theories with data. In D. A. Weisburd & J. T. McEwen (Eds.), *Crime mapping and crime prevention: Crime prevention studies, Vol. 8* (pp. 379-406). Monsey, NY: Criminal Justice Press.

Eck, J. E., & Weisburd, D. A. (Eds.). (1995a). *Crime and place: Crime prevention studies, Vol. 4.* Monsey, NY: Criminal Justice Press.

Eck, J. E., & Weisburd, D. A. (1995b). Crime places in crime theory. In J. E. Eck & D. A. Weisburd (Eds.), *Crime and place: Crime prevention studies, Vol. 4* (pp. 1-33). Monsey, NY: Criminal Justice Press.

Eckert, W. G., & James, S. H. (1989). *Interpretation of bloodstain evidence at crime scenes.* New York: Elsevier.

Eden, R. S. (1985). *Dog training for law enforcement.* Calgary: Detselig.

Eden, R. S. (1994). On automatic pilot. *Police, 18*(3), 20-21.

Eftimiades, M. (1993). *Garden of graves.* New York: St. Martin's Press.

Egger, S. A. (1984). A working definition of serial murder and the reduction of linkage blindness. *Journal of Police Science and Administration, 12,* 348-357.

Egger, S. A. (1985). *Serial murder and the law enforcement response.* Unpublished doctoral dissertation, Sam Houston State University, Huntsville, TX.

Egger, S. A. (1989). Serial murder. In W. G. Bailey (Ed.), *The encyclopedia of police science* (pp. 578-581). New York: Garland.

Egger, S. A. (1990). *Serial murder: An elusive phenomenon.* New York: Praeger.

Egger, S. A. (1998). *The killers among us: An examination of serial murder and its investigation.* Upper Saddle River, NJ: Prentice-Hall.

Egger, S. A., & O'Reilly-Fleming, T. (1993). *Newsletter of the International Research Association for the Study of Multiple Murder, 1*(1).

Egger, S. A., Lange, R., & Egger, K. A. (1996, November). *Chaos from chaos: Using chaos and facet theory to predict the date of the serial killer's next kill.* Paper presented at the meeting of the American Society of Criminology, Chicago, IL.

Eisner, R. (1989). Guidelines for DNA fingerprinting. *Diagnostics & Clinical Testing, 27,* 14-15.

Elkind, P. (1989). *The death shift*. New York: Penguin Books.

Elliott, P. (1996, February). What took so long? *Canadian Living*, pp. 41-47.

Ellis, B. E. (1991). *American psycho*. New York: Vintage Books.

Englade, K. (1988). *Cellar of horror*. New York: St. Martin's Press.

Engstad, P. A. (1975). Environmental opportunities and the ecology of crime. In R. A. Silverman & J. J. Teevan, Jr. (Eds.), *Crime in Canadian society* (pp. 193-211). Toronto: Butterworth.

Enns, G. (1989, May 15). Some saw true Christian; others, master manipulator. *Sarasota Herald-Tribune*, pp. 1A, 8A-9A.

Epstein, S. (1992, November). *The first female: The case of Aileen Wuornos*. Paper presented at the meeting of the American Society of Criminology, New Orleans, LA.

Erlanson, O. A. (1946). The scene of sex offences. *Journal of Criminal Law & Criminology*, 31, 339-342.

Evans, D. J., Fyfe, N. R., & Herbert, D. T. (Eds.). (1992). *Crime, policing and place: Essays in environmental criminology*. London: Routledge.

Experts say mass murders are rare but on the rise. (1988, January 3). *The New York Times*, p. 16.

Fair, K. (1994). Kenneth McDuff. *Police, 18*(7), 56-58.

Falk, G. (1990). *Murder: An analysis of its forms, conditions, and causes*. Jefferson, NC: McFarland.

Farr, L. (1992). *The Sunset Murders*. New York: Simon & Schuster.

Farrell, G., & Pease, K. (1993). *Once bitten, twice bitten: Repeat victimisation and its implications for crime prevention* (Crime Prevention Unit Series Paper No. 46). London: Police Research Group, Home Office Police Department.

Farrington, D. P., & Lambert, S. (1993, October). *Predicting violence and burglary offenders from victim, witness and offence data*. Paper presented at the meeting of the First NISCALE Workshop on Criminality and Law Enforcement, The Hague, The Netherlands.

Fattah, E. A. (Ed.). (1986). *From crime policy to victim policy: Reorienting the justice system*. Houndsmills, UK: Macmillan Press.

Fattah, E. A. (1987). Victims of violence. In J. M. MacLatchie (Ed.), *Violence in contemporary Canadian society* (pp. 306-311). Ottawa: John Howard Society of Canada.

Fattah, E. A. (1991). *Understanding criminal victimization: An introduction to theoretical victimology*. Scarborough, ON: Prentice-Hall Canada.

Federal Bureau of Investigation. (1990). [*Lexus/Nexus* newspaper computerized topical search file on serial murder]. Quantico, VA: Unpublished Behavioral Science Unit files.

Federal Bureau of Investigation. (1996). *Rapid Start Information Management System: Reference Guide*. Washington, DC: Author.

Fedorowycz, O. (1996). *Homicide in Canada – 1995* (Juristat Service Bulletin vol. 16, no. 11). Ottawa: Statistics Canada.

Fedorowycz, O. (1997). *Homicide in Canada –1996* (Juristat Service Bulletin vol. 17, no. 9). Ottawa: Statistics Canada.

Feeney, F. (1986). Robbers as decision-makers. In D. B. Cornish & R. V. Clarke (Eds.), *The reasoning criminal: Rational choice perspectives on offending* (pp. 53-71). New York: Springer-Verlag.

Feeney, F. (1996). Robbers as decision makers. In P. F. Cromwell (Ed.), *In their own words: Criminals on crime* (pp. 87-97). Los Angeles: Roxbury Publishing.

Fein, R. A., Vossekuil, B., & Holden, G. A. (1995). *Threat assessment: An approach to prevent targeted violence* (NIJ Publication No. NCJ-155000). Washington, DC: U.S. Government Printing Office.

Felson, M. (1986). Linking criminal choices, routine activities, informal control, and criminal outcomes. In D. B. Cornish & R. V. Clarke (Eds.), *The reasoning criminal: Rational choice perspectives on offending* (pp. 119-128). New York: Springer-Verlag.

Felson, M. (1987). Routine activities and crime prevention in the developing metropolis. *Criminology, 25,* 911-931.

Felson, M. (1994a, November). *Why the routine activity approach applies to violence.* Paper presented at the meeting of the American Society of Criminology, Miami, FL.

Felson, M. (1994b). *Crime and everyday life.* Thousand Oaks, CA: Pine Forge Press.

Felson, M. (1995, November). *I've got rhythms: Crime rhythms and routine activities.* Paper presented at the meeting of the American Society of Criminology, Boston, MA.

Felson, M. (1996, November). *Crime circuits and circuit breakers.* Paper presented at the meeting of the American Society of Criminology, Chicago, IL.

Felson, M. (1997, June). *The fractal spread of crime.* Paper presented at the Seminar on Environmental Criminology and Crime Analysis, Oslo, Norway.

Felson, M. (1998). *Crime and everyday life* (2nd ed.). Thousand Oaks, CA: Pine Forge Press.

Felson, M., & Clarke, R. V. (1998). *Opportunity makes the thief: Practical theory for crime prevention* (Police Research Series: Paper 98). London: Policing and Reducing Crime Unit, Home Office.

Felson, R. B. (1993). Predatory and dispute-related violence: A social interactionist approach. In R. V. Clarke & M. Felson (Eds.), *Routine activity and rational choice* (pp. 103-125). New Brunswick, NJ: Transaction.

Felson, R. B., & Steadman, H. J. (1983). Situational factors in disputes leading to criminal violence. *Criminology, 21,* 59-74.

Ferracuti, F. (1968). European migration and crime. *Collected Studies in Criminological Research, 3,* 9-76.

Ferry, J., & Inwood, D. (1982). *The Olson murders.* Langley, BC: Cameo Books.

Fido, M. (1987). *The crimes, detection and death of Jack the Ripper.* London: Weidenfeld and Nicolson.

Figlio, R. M., Hakim, S., & Rengert, G. F. (Eds.). (1986). *Metropolitan crime patterns.* Monsey, NY: Criminal Justice Press.

Fingleton, B. (1976). Alternative approaches to modelling varied spatial behaviour. *Geographic Analysis, 8,* 95-101.

Finkelhor, D., Hotaling, G., & Sedlak, A. (1990). *Missing, abducted, runaway, and thrownaway children in America – First report: Numbers and characteristics, national incidence studies, executive summary.* Washington, DC: U.S. Government Printing Office.

Fishbein, D. (1998). "Building bridges." *ACJS Today, 17*(2), 1, 3-5.

Fishbein, D. H., Lozovsky, D., & Jaffe, J. H. (1989). Impulsivity, aggression and neuroendocrine responses to serotonergic stimulation in substance abusers. *Biological Psychiatry, 25,* 1049-1066.

Fisher, B. A. J. (1993). *Techniques of crime scene investigation* (5th ed.). Boca Raton, FL: CRC Press.

Fisher, B. S., Sloan, J. J., & Wilkins, D. L. (1993, October). *The spatial and temporal patterns of fear of crime: An examination of their characteristics.* Paper presented at the meeting of the American Society of Criminology, Phoenix, AZ.

Fitzpatrick, E. (1993, November 5). A killer's graveyard. *The Sydney Morning Herald,* pp. 1, 4.

Flanagan, T. J., & Maguire, K. (Eds.). (1990). *Sourcebook of criminal justice statistics – 1989* (U.S. Department of Justice, BJS Publication No. NCJ-124224). Washington, DC: U.S. Government Printing Office.

Fletcher, J. S. (1995). *Deadly thrills.* New York: Penguin Books.

Flowers, A. (1993). *Blind fury.* New York: Windsor.

Foin, Jr., T. C. (1976). *Ecological systems and the environment.* Boston: Houghton Mifflin.

Ford, D. A. (1990). Investigating serial murder: The case of Indiana's "Gay Murders." In S. A. Egger (Ed.), *Serial murder: An elusive phenomenon* (pp. 113-133). New York: Praeger.

Forst, B. (1993, October). *The analytics of criminal investigation: Putting Sherlock Holmes in a box.* Paper presented at the meeting of the American Society of Criminology, Phoenix, AZ.

Forst, B. (1996a). Evidence, probabilities, and legal standards for the determination of guilt: Beyond the O.J. trial. In G. Barak (Ed.), *Representing O.J.: Murder, criminal justice and mass culture* (pp. 22-28). Guilderland, NY: Harrow and Heston.

Forst, B. (1996b, November). *The logic of inference and decision making in criminal investigation*. Paper presented at the meeting of the American Society of Criminology, Chicago, IL.

Forth, A. E., Hart, S. D., & Hare, R. D. (1990). Assessment of psychopathy in male young offenders. *Psychological Assessment: A Journal of Consulting and Clinical Psychology, 2*, 342-344.

Foucault, M. (Ed.). (1975). *I, Pierre Riviere, having slaughtered my mother, my sister, and my brother...* (F. Jellinek, Trans.). Lincoln, NE: University of Nebraska Press. (Original work published 1973).

Fowler, K. (1990). The serial killer. *RCMP Gazette, 52*(3), 1-11.

Fowler, R. D. (1986, May). Howard Hughes: A psychological autopsy. *Psychology Today*, pp. 22-25, 28-33.

Fowles, J. (1963). *The collector*. London: Pan Books.

Fox, J. A., & Levin, J. (1992, April). *Serial murder: A survey*. Paper presented at the First International Conference on Serial and Mass Murder: Theory, Research and Policy, Windsor, ON.

Fox, J. A., & Levin, J. (1994). *Overkill: Mass murder and serial killing exposed*. New York: Plenum Press.

Fox, J. A., & Levin, J. (1995a). Serial murder: A survey. In T. O'Reilly-Fleming (Ed.), *Serial and mass murder: Theory, research and policy*. Toronto: Canadian Scholars' Press.

Fox, J. A., & Levin, J. (1995b). Special concerns of surviving victims of multiple murder: In memory of the victims of the Montreal Massacre. In T. O'Reilly-Fleming (Ed.), *Serial and mass murder: Theory, research and policy* (pp. 181-184). Toronto: Canadian Scholars' Press.

Fox, J. A., & Levin, J. (1996a). A psycho-social analysis of mass murder. In T. O'Reilly-Fleming (Ed.), *Serial and mass murder: Theory, research and policy* (pp. 55-76). Toronto: Canadian Scholars' Press.

Fox, J. A., & Levin, J. (1996b). Special concerns of surviving victims of multiple murder: In memory of the victims of the Montreal Massacre. In T. O'Reilly-Fleming (Ed.), *Serial and mass murder: Theory, research and policy* (pp. 181-184). Toronto: Canadian Scholars' Press.

France, D. L., Griffin, T. J., Swanburg, J. G., Lindemann, J. W., Davenport, G. C., Trammell, V., Travis, C. T., Kondratieff, B., Nelson, A., Castellano, K., Hopkins, D., & Adair, T. (1997). NecroSearch revisited: Further multidisciplinary approaches to the detection of clandestine graves. In W. D. Haglund & M. H. Sorg (Eds.), *Forensic taphonomy: The postmortem fate of human remains* (pp. 497-509). Boca Raton, FL: CRC Press.

Frank, G. (1966). *The Boston Strangler*. New York: Penguin Books.

Frye v. United States, 293 F.2d 1013, 104.

Fung, D. S., & Potter, W. D. (1992). *An expert system to predict illicit cannabis growth sites in northeast Georgia*. In Proceeding Third Annual Symposium of the International Association of Knowledge Engineers (pp. 563-569). Gaithersburg, MD: IAKE.

Fyfe, J. J., Goldkamp, J. S., & White, M. D. (1997). *Strategies for reducing homicide: The Comprehensive Homicide Initiative in Richmond, California* (BJA Monograph No. NCJ-168100). Washington, DC: U.S. Government Printing Office.

Gabor, T. (1978). Crime displacement: The literature and strategies for its investigation. *Crime and Justice, 6,* 100-106.

Gabor, T., & Gottheil, E. (1984). Offender characteristics and spatial mobility: An empirical study and some policy implications. *Canadian Journal of Criminology, 26,* 267-281.

Gabrish and Balcerzak v. Board of Fire and Police Commissioners for the City of Milwaukee (Milwaukee County Cir. Court, Wisc., April 27, 1994).

Gainesville murders studied. (1992, May). *Law Enforcement Technology,* p. 9.

Ganey, T. (1989). *Innocent blood.* New York: St. Martin's Press.

Garland, N. M., & Stuckey, G. B. (2000). *Criminal evidence for the law enforcement officer* (4th ed.). New York: McGraw-Hill.

Garson, G. D., & Biggs, R. S. (1992). *Analytic mapping and geographic databases.* Sage university paper series on quantitative applications in the social sciences, 87. Newbury Park, CA: Sage.

Gaskins, D., & Earle, W. (1993). *Final truth.* New York: Windsor.

Gates, D. F., & Shah, D. K. (1992). *Chief.* New York: Bantam Books.

Gaudette, B. D. (1990). DNA typing: A new service to Canadian police. *RCMP Gazette, 52*(4), 1-7.

Geake, E. (1993, October 23). How PCs predict where crime will strike. *New Scientist,* p. 17.

Geberth, V. J. (1981, September). Psychological profiling. *Law and Order,* pp. 46-52.

Geberth, V. J. (1990a, May). The serial killer and the revelations of Ted Bundy. *Law and Order,* pp. 72-77.

Geberth, V. J. (1990b). *Practical homicide investigation: Tactics, procedures, and forensic techniques* (2nd ed.). New York: Elsevier.

Geberth, V. J. (1994, April). State-Wide and regional information systems. *Law and Order,* pp. 1-6.

Geberth, V. J. (1996). *Practical homicide investigation: Tactics, procedures, and forensic techniques* (3rd ed.). Boca Raton, FL: CRC Press.

Gentleman, J. F., & Reed, P. B. (1987). *Measuring the effects of legal change: Capital punishment in Canada, 1961-83.* Paper presented at the meeting of the American Statistical Association.

Georges-Abeyie, D. E., & Harries, K. D. (Eds.). (1980). *Crime: A spatial perspective.* New York: Columbia University Press.

Gibney, B. (1984). *The Beauty Queen Killer.* New York: Windsor.

Gibson, E. (1975). *Homicide in England and Wales 1967-1971* (Home Office Statistical Department Report No. 31). London: Her Majesty's Stationery Office.

Gilmour, W., & Hale, L. E. (1991). *Butcher, baker.* New York: Penguin Books.

Ginsburg, P. E. (1993). *The shadow of death: The hunt for a serial killer.* New York: Charles Scribner's Sons.

Gleick, E. (1994, December 12). The final victim. *People*, pp. 126-132.

Glover, J. D., Witham, D. C. (1989). The Atlanta serial murders. *Policing*, 5(1), 2-16.

Godfrey, E. (1984). *By reason of doubt.* Toronto: James Lorimer.

Godwin, G.M. (1998). Victim target networks as solvability factors in serial murder. *Social Behavior and Personality, 26,* 75-83.

Godwin, G. M. (2000). *Hunting serial predators: A multivariate classification approach to profiling violent behavior.* Boca Raton, FL: CRC Press.

Godwin, G.M., & Canter, D. V. (1997). Encounter and death: The spatial behavior of U.S. serial killers. *Policing: An International Journal of Police Strategy and Management, 20,* 24-38.

Godwin, J. (1978). *Murder U.S.A.: The ways we kill each other.* New York: Ballantine Books.

Goertzen, H. (1975, August 14). Four children strangled, according to A-G Dept. *The Saskatoon Star-Phoenix,* p. 1.

Goldstein, H. (1990). *Problem-Oriented policing.* New York: McGraw-Hill.

Gollmar, R. H. (1981). *Edward Gein.* New York: Windsor.

'Good boy' charged in deaths of 3 women. (1995, January 21). *The Saskatoon Star-Phoenix,* p. A11.

Goodall, B. (1987). *The Penguin dictionary of human geography.* Harmondsworth, Middlesex: Penguin.

Goodchild, M. F. (1987). *Spatial autocorrelation.* Norwich: Geo Abstracts.

Goodchild, M. F., Kemp, K. K., & Poiker, T. (1990a). *Introduction to GIS* (NCGIA Core Curriculum). National Center for Geographic Information and Analysis.

Goodchild, M. F., Kemp, K. K., & Poiker, T. (1990b). *Technical issues in GIS* (NCGIA Core Curriculum). National Center for Geographic Information and Analysis.

Goode, E. (1994, September 19). Battling deviant behavior. *U.S. News and World Report*, pp. 74, 76.

Goodman, J., & Waddell, B. (1987). *The Black Museum.* London: Harrap.

Gottlieb, S. L., Arenberg, S., & Singh, R. (1998). *Crime analysis: From first report to final arrest.* Montclair, CA: Alpha Publishing.

Gould, A. (1994). *Criminal acts I: The Canadian true crime annual.* Toronto: Macmillan Canada.

Gould, P. (1966). *On mental maps.* Michigan Inter-University Community of Mathematical Geographers Discussion Paper Series, 9. Ann Arbor, MI: University of Michigan.

Gould, P. (1975). Acquiring spatial information. *Economic Geography, 51,* 87-99.

Gould, P., & White, R. (1986). *Mental maps* (2nd ed.). London: Routledge.

Graham, H. D., & Gurr, T. R. (Eds.). (1979). *Violence in America: Historical & comparative perspectives* (rev. ed.). Beverly Hills: Sage.

Grau, J. J. (Ed.). (1993). *Criminal and civil investigation handbook* (2nd ed.). New York: McGraw-Hill.

Gray, H. (1974). *Gray's anatomy.* Philadelphia: Running Press.

Gray, L. S. (1981, May). Death in Atlanta. *Black Enterprise*, p. 15.

Gray, M. (1992, June 29). Russia's ripper. *Maclean's*, pp. 38-39.

Graysmith, R. (1976). *Zodiac.* New York: Berkley.

Graysmith, R. (1990). *The Sleeping Lady: The Trailside Murders above the Golden Gate.* New York: Penguin Books.

Great Britain road atlas. (1995). Sevenoaks, Kent: Geographers' A-Z Map Company.

Green, E. (1993). *The intent to kill: Making sense of murder.* Baltimore: Clevedon Books.

Green, L. A. (1994). Controlling drug hotspots through civil law enforcement: Displacement and diffusion effects. *Justice Quarterly, 11.*

Green, L. A. (1995). Cleaning up drug hot spots in Oakland, California: The displacement and diffusion effects. *Justice Quarterly, 12,* 737-754.

Green, T. J., & Whitmore, J. E. (1993, June). VICAP's role in multiagency serial murder investigations. *The Police Chief,* pp. 38-45.

Greenberg, D. F. (1979). *Mathematical criminology.* New Brunswick, NJ: Rutgers.

Greenfeld, L. A. (1996). *Child victimizers: Violent offenders and their victims* (BJS Publication No. NCJ-158625). Washington, DC: U.S. Government Printing Office.

Greenfeld, L. A. (1997). *Sex offenses and offenders* (BJS Publication No. NCJ-163931). Washington, DC: U.S. Government Printing Office.

Greenfeld, L. A., & Rand, M. R. (1998). *Violence by intimates: Analysis of data on crimes by current or former spouses, boyfriends, and girlfriends* (BJS Publication No. NCJ-167237). Washington, DC: U.S. Government Printing Office.

Greenfeld, L. A., & Stephan, J. J. (1993). *Capital punishment 1992* (BJS Publication No. NCJ-145031). Washington, DC: U.S. Government Printing Office.

Gregory, J., & Lees, S. (1996). Attrition in rape and sexual assault cases. *The British Journal of Criminology, 36,* 1-17.

Grescoe, T. (1996, May-June). A policeman and a scholar. *Vancouver Magazine,* pp. 38-42.

Griffiths, C. T., & Verdun-Jones, S. N. (1989). *Canadian criminal justice.* Toronto: Butterworths.

Groth, A. N., Burgess, A. W., & Holmstrom, L. L. (1977). Rape: Power, anger and sexuality. *American Journal of Psychiatry, 134,* 1239-1243.

Grubin, D. (1999, March). *Offender profiling: Art or science.* Lecture presented at New Scotland Yard, Directorate of Intelligence, London, UK.

Grubin, D., & Gunn, J. (1990, December). *The imprisoned rapist and rape.* Unpublished manuscript, Institute of Psychiatry, Department of Forensic Psychiatry, London.

Grubin, D., Kelly, P., & Ayis, A. (1996). *Linking serious sexual assaults.* Unpublished manuscript, Police Research Group, Home Office Police Department, London.

Grubin, D., Kelly, P., & Ayis, A. (1997). *Linking serious sexual assaults.* Draft briefing note, Police Research Group, Home Office Police Department, London.

Guillen, T., & Seven, R. (1989, July 14). Police also seek link to 17 other slayings. *The Seattle Times*, p. A8.

Gurr, T. R. (Ed.). (1989a). *Violence in America: Vol. 1. The history of crime.* Newbury Park, CA: Sage.

Gurr, T. R. (Ed.). (1989b). *Violence in America: Vol. 2. Protest, rebellion, reform.* Newbury Park, CA: Sage.

Haga, F. O. F., Vasu, M. L., & Pelfrey, W. V. (1993, October). *Domestic violence versus predatory assault.* Paper presented at the meeting of the American Society of Criminology, Phoenix, AZ.

Haglund, W. D. (1997a). Dogs and coyotes: Postmortem involvement with human remains. In W. D. Haglund & M. H. Sorg (Eds.), *Forensic taphonomy: The postmortem fate of human remains* (pp. 367-381). Boca Raton, FL: CRC Press.

Haglund, W. D. (1997b). Scattered skeletal human remains: Search strategy considerations for locating missing teeth. In W. D. Haglund & M. H. Sorg (Eds.), *Forensic taphonomy: The postmortem fate of human remains* (pp. 383-394). Boca Raton, FL: CRC Press.

Haglund, W. D., & Sorg, M. H. (Eds.). (1997). *Forensic taphonomy: The postmortem fate of human remains.* Boca Raton, FL: CRC Press.

Hagmaier, B. (1990, September). *Ted Bundy, a case study.* Lecture presented at the FBI National Academy retraining session, Bellingham, WA.

Haines, M. (1990). *True crime stories: Book IV.* Toronto: Toronto Sun.

Haines, M. (1994). *Multiple murderers.* Toronto: Toronto Sun.

Hakim, S., & Rengert, G. F. (Eds.). (1981). *Crime spillover.* Beverly Hills: Sage.

Hale, R. L. (1993). The application of learning theory to serial murder, *or "You too can learn to be a serial killer."* American Journal of Criminal Justice, 17(2), 37-45.

Hall, N., & Kines, L. (1995, September 16). The killers among us. *The Vancouver Sun*, pp. A4-A5.

Hall, N., & Pemberton, K. (1989a, February 4). Riddle of 14 hooker slayings. *The Vancouver Sun*, pp. A1, A10.

Halvorsen, D. (1990, January 4). State Supreme Court hears Billy Glaze appeal. *Minneapolis Star Tribune*, pp. 1B, 7B.

Hanfland, K. A. (1982). *Distance/Suspect age-group relationship – Crime scene to suspect residence.* Unpublished manuscript.

Hanfland, K. A., Keppel, R. D., & Weis, J. G. (1997). *Case management for missing children homicide investigation*. Seattle: Washington State Office of the Attorney General.

Hanson, R. K. (1998, November). *Predicting sexual offense recidivism: A comparison of rapists and child molesters*. Paper presented at the meeting of the American Society of Criminology, Washington, DC.

Harada, Y. (1996, September). *Koban-Based information system as an information foundation for community policing*. Paper presented at the meeting of the International Criminological Symposium on Internal Security in an Open Democratic Society, Wiesbaden, FRG.

Hare, R. D. (1986). Criminal psychopaths. In J. C. Yuille (Ed.), *Police selection and training: The role of psychology* (pp. 187-206). Dordrecht: Martinus Nijhoff.

Hare, R. D. (1993). *Without conscience: The disturbing world of the psychopaths among us*. New York: Simon & Schuster.

Hare, R. D., & McPherson, L. M. (1984). Violent and aggressive behavior by criminal psychopaths. *International Journal of Law and Psychiatry, 7*, 35-50.

Hare, R. D., Harpur, T. J., Hakstian, A. R., Forth, A. E., Hart, S. D., & Newman, J. P. (1990). The Revised Psychopathy Checklist: Reliability and factor structure. *Psychological Assessment: A Journal of Consulting and Clinical Psychology, 2*, 338-341.

Hare, R. D., Hart, S. D., & Harpur, T. J. (1991). Psychopathy and the DSM-IV criteria for antisocial personality disorder. *Journal of Abnormal Psychology, 100*, 391-398.

Hare, R. D., McPherson, L. M., & Forth, A. E. (1988). Male psychopaths and their criminal careers. *Journal of Consulting and Clinical Psychology, 56*, 710-714.

Harlow, C. W. (1991). *Female victims of violent crime* (BJS Publication No. NCJ-126826). Washington, DC: U.S. Government Printing Office.

Harmon, R. B., Rosner, R., & Wiederlight, M. (1985). Women and arson: A demographic study. *Journal of Forensic Sciences, 30*, 467-477.

Harpur, T. J., Hare, R. D., & Hakstian, A. R. (1989). Two-Factor conceptualization of psychopathy: Construct validity and assessment implications. *Psychological Assessment: A Journal of Consulting and Clinical Psychology, 1*, 6-17.

Harries, K. (1990). *Geographic factors in policing*. Washington, DC: Police Executive Research Forum.

Harries, K. (1995). The ecology of homicide and assault: Baltimore City and County, 1989-91. *Studies on Crime and Crime Prevention, 4*, 44-60.

Harrington, J., & Burger, R. (1993). *Eye of evil*. New York: St. Martin's Press.

Harris, T. (1988). *The silence of the lambs*. New York: St. Martin's Press.

Harrison, F. (1987). *Brady and Hindley: Genesis of the Moors Murders*. London: Grafton Books.

Harrison, S. (1993). *The diary of Jack the Ripper: The discovery, the investigation, the debate*. New York: Hyperion.

Hart, S. D., Forth, A. E., & Hare, R. D. (1990). Performance of criminal psychopaths on selected neuropsychological tests. *Journal of Abnormal Psychology, 99*, 374-379.

Hart, S. D., Hare, R. D., & Harpur, T. J. (1992). The Psychopathy Checklist-Revised (PCL-R): An overview for researchers and clinicians. In J. C. Rosen & P. McReynolds (Eds.), *Advances in psychological assessment: Vol. 8* (pp. 103-130). New York: Plenum Press.

Harvey, S. (1993, November 5). A bloody trail of multiple murders and serial killers. *The Sydney Morning Herald*, p. 4.

Haynes, K. E., & Fotheringham, A. S. (1984). *Gravity and spatial interaction models.* Sage university paper series on scientific geography, 2. Beverly Hills: Sage.

Hazelwood, R. R. (1986). The NCAVC training program: A commitment to law enforcement. *FBI Law Enforcement Bulletin, 55*(12), 23-26.

Hazelwood, R. R. (1987). Analyzing the rape and profiling the offender. In R. R. Hazelwood & A. W. Burgess (Eds.), *Practical aspects of rape investigation: A multidisciplinary approach* (pp. 169-199). New York: Elsevier.

Hazelwood, R. R. (1995). Analyzing the rape and profiling the offender. In R. R. Hazelwood & A. W. Burgess (Eds.), *Practical aspects of rape investigation: A multidisciplinary approach* (2nd ed.) (pp. 155-181). Boca Raton, FL: CRC Press.

Hazelwood, R. R., & Burgess, A. W. (1987a). An introduction to the serial rapist: Research by the FBI. *FBI Law Enforcement Bulletin, 56*(9), 16-24.

Hazelwood, R. R., & Burgess, A. W. (Eds.). (1987b). *Practical aspects of rape investigation: A multidisciplinary approach.* New York: Elsevier.

Hazelwood, R. R., & Burgess, A. W. (Eds.). (1995). *Practical aspects of rape investigation: A multidisciplinary approach* (2nd ed.). Boca Raton, FL: CRC Press.

Hazelwood, R. R., Dietz, P. E., & Warren, J. I. (1992). The criminal sexual sadist. *FBI Law Enforcement Bulletin, 61*(2), 12-20.

Hazelwood, R. R., & Douglas, J. E. (1980). The lust murderer. *FBI Law Enforcement Bulletin, 49*(4), 18-22.

Hazelwood, R. R., & Lanning, K. V. (1995). Collateral material and sexual crimes. In R. R. Hazelwood & A. W. Burgess (Eds.), *Practical aspects of rape investigation: A multidisciplinary approach* (2nd ed.) (pp. 183-192). Boca Raton, FL: CRC Press.

Hazelwood, R. R., Reboussin, R., & Warren, J. I. (1989). Serial rape: Correlates of increased aggression and the relationship of offender pleasure to victim resistance. *Journal of Interpersonal Violence, 4*, 65-78.

Hazelwood, R. R., Ressler, R. K., Depue, R. L., & Douglas, J. E. (1995). Criminal investigative analysis: An overview. In R. R. Hazelwood & A. W. Burgess (Eds.), *Practical aspects of rape investigation: A multidisciplinary approach* (2nd ed.) (pp. 115-126). Boca Raton, FL: CRC Press.

Hazelwood, R. R., & Warren, J. I. (1989a). The serial rapist: His characteristics and victims (Part 1). *FBI Law Enforcement Bulletin, 58*(1), 1-9.

Hazelwood, R. R., & Warren, J. I. (1989b). The serial rapist: His characteristics and victims (Part 2). *FBI Law Enforcement Bulletin, 58*(2), 10-16.

Hazelwood, R. R., & Warren, J. I. (1990). The criminal behavior of the serial rapist. *FBI Law Enforcement Bulletin, 59*(2), 11-16.

Hazelwood, R. R., & Warren, J. I. (1995a). The relevance of fantasy in serial sexual crime investigation. In R. R. Hazelwood & A. W. Burgess (Eds.), *Practical aspects of rape investigation: A multidisciplinary approach* (2nd ed.) (pp. 127-137). Boca Raton, FL: CRC Press.

Hazelwood, R. R., & Warren, J. I. (1995b). The serial rapist. In R. R. Hazelwood & A. W. Burgess (Eds.), *Practical aspects of rape investigation: A multidisciplinary approach* (2nd ed.) (pp. 337-359). Boca Raton, FL: CRC Press.

Hazelwood, R.R., & Warren, J.I. (forthcoming). Impulsive vs. ritualistic sexual offenders. *Aggression and Violent Behavior.*

Heilbroner, D. (1993, August). Serial murder and sexual repression. *Playboy,* pp. 78-79, 147-150.

Heimer, M. (1971). *The cannibal.* London: Xanadu.

Hellman, D. A. (1981). Criminal mobility and policy recommendations. In S. Hakim & G. F. Rengert (Eds.), *Crime spillover* (pp. 135-150). Beverly Hills: Sage.

Herbeck, D. (1990, July 12). The serial killers' confidant. *The Buffalo News,* pp. B7, B9.

Herbert, D. T., & Johnston, R. J. (Eds.). (1982). *Geography and the urban environment: Vol. 5.* Chichester: John Wiley and Sons.

Herbert, S. (1994, November). *The normative ordering of police territoriality.* Paper presented at the meeting of the American Society of Criminology, Miami, FL.

Heritage, R. (1994, March). *Act frequency to a profiling typology for sexual conduct.* Paper presented at the meeting of the Academy of Criminal Justice Sciences, Chicago, IL.

Hess, H. (1996, March 27). Computer sniffs out serial criminals. *The Toronto Globe and Mail,* p. A6.

Hesseling, R. (1993, October). *Displacement, a review of the empirical literature.* Paper presented at the meeting of the American Society of Criminology, Phoenix, AZ.

Hewings, G. J. D. (1985). *Regional input-output analysis.* Sage university paper series on scientific geography, 6. Beverly Hills: Sage.

Hickey, E. W. (1986). The female serial murderer 1800-1986. *Journal of Police and Criminal Psychology, 2*(2), 72-81.

Hickey, E. W. (1987). [Review of *Mass murder: America's growing menace*]. *Journal of Criminal Law & Criminology, 78,* 441-443.

Hickey, E. W. (1990). The etiology of victimization in serial murder: An historical and demographic analysis. In S. A. Egger (Ed.), *Serial murder: An elusive phenomenon* (pp. 53-71). New York: Praeger.

Hickey, E. W. (1991). *Serial murderers and their victims.* Pacific Grove, CA: Brooks/Cole.

Hickey, E. W. (1996). An interview with a serial murderer. In P. F. Cromwell (Ed.), *In their own words: Criminals on crime* (pp. 117-127). Los Angeles: Roxbury Publishing.

Hickey, E. W. (1997). *Serial murderers and their victims* (2nd ed.). Belmont, CA: Wadsworth.

Hickey, G. (1990, September 17). The hunt for a serial killer. *The Richmond News Leader.*

Higgins, S. E. (1990, August). Portrait of a serial arsonist. *Firehouse,* pp. 54-57.

Hinch, R., & Scott, H. (1995, November). *Explaining female serial murderers: Theoretical issues.* Paper presented at the meeting of the American Society of Criminology, Boston, MA.

Hirschfield, A. (1994, November). *Crime and the spatial concentration of disadvantage in Northern Britain: An analysis using geographical information systems.* Paper presented at the meeting of the American Society of Criminology, Miami, FL.

Hirschfield, A., & Bowers, K. (1997, June). *Crime, disadvantage and community safety on Merseyside: Bridging the gap between research and practice.* Paper presented at the Seminar on Environmental Criminology and Crime Analysis, Oslo, Norway.

Hirschi, T. (1969). *Causes of delinquency.* Berkeley, CA: University of California Press.

Hirschi, T., & Gottfredson, M. (Eds.). (1980). *Understanding crime: Current theory and research.* Beverly Hills: Sage.

Hirschi, T., & Gottfredson, M. (1990). *A general theory of crime.* Stanford, CA: Stanford University Press.

Hodder, I., & Orton, C. (1976). *Spatial analysis in archaeology.* Cambridge: Cambridge University Press.

Hole, J. (1990, October 9). Joan's tragedy: Murdered at home as police waited outside. *The Sydney Morning Herald,* pp. 1, 4.

Hollandsworth, S. (1993, May). See no evil. *Texas Monthly,* pp. 92-97, 128-140.

Holmes, R. M. (1989). *Profiling violent crimes: An investigative tool.* Beverly Hills: Sage.

Holmes, R. M. (1991). *Sex crimes.* Newbury Park, CA: Sage.

Holmes, R. M., & De Burger, J. E. (1985, September). Profiles in terror: The serial murderer. *Federal Probation, 49,* 29-34.

Holmes, R. M., & De Burger, J. E. (1988). *Serial murder.* Newbury Park, CA: Sage.

Holmes, R. M., & Holmes, S. T. (1994). *Murder in America.* Thousand Oaks, CA: Sage.

Holmes, R. M., & Holmes, S. T. (1996). *Profiling violent crimes: An investigative tool* (2nd ed.). Thousand Oaks, CA: Sage.

Holmes, R. M., & Holmes, S. T. (1998a). *Serial murder* (2nd ed.). Thousand Oaks, CA: Sage.

Holmes, R. M., & Holmes, S. T. (Eds.). (1998b). *Contemporary perspectives on serial murder.* Thousand Oaks, CA: Sage.

Holmes, R. M., & Rossmo, D. K. (1996). Geography, profiling, and predatory criminals. In R. M. Holmes & S. T. Holmes, *Profiling violent crimes: An investigative tool* (2nd ed.) (pp. 148-165). Thousand Oaks, CA: Sage

Homant, R. J. (1998). [Review of Offender profiling: Theory, research and practice]. *Criminal Justice and Behavior, 25*, 507-510.

Homant, R. J. (forthcoming). Crime scene profiling in premises security litigation. *Security Journal.*

Homant, R. J., & Kennedy, D. B. (1997). *Psychological aspects of crime scene profiling: Validity research.* Unpublished manuscript, University of Detroit Mercy, Department of Criminal Justice and Security Administration, Detroit, MI.

Homant, R. J., & Kennedy, D. B. (1998). Psychological aspects of crime scene profiling: Validity research. *Criminal Justice and Behavior, 25*, 319-343.

Honeycombe, G. (1982). *The murders of the Black Museum.* London: Mysterious Press.

House, J. C. (1993). *Facet theory and stranger sexual assault behaviour: Investigative classification in Canadian offenders.* Unpublished master's thesis, University of Surrey, England.

House, J. C. (1997). Towards a practical application of offender profiling: The RNC's Criminal Suspect Prioritization System. In J. L. Jackson & D. A. Bekerian (Eds.), *Offender profiling: Theory, research and practice* (pp. 177-190). Chichester: John Wiley & Sons.

How the DNA 'Database' & 'Caseworking' Units will function! (1995, February). *DNA Database,* p. 2.

Howard, C. (1979). *Zebra.* New York: Berkley Books.

Howells, M., & Skinner, K. (1987). *The Ripper legacy.* London: Sphere Books.

Howlett, J. B., Hanfland, K. A., & Ressler, R. K. (1986). The Violent Criminal Apprehension Program – VICAP: A progress report. *FBI Law Enforcement Bulletin, 55*(12), 14-22.

Huff, T. G. (1994, August). Fire-Setting fire fighters: Arsonists in the fire department – Identification and prevention. *On Scene.*

Huff, T. G. (n.d.). Filicide by fire – The worst crime? *Fire and Arson Investigator.*

Humes, E. (1991). *Buried secrets: A true story of serial murder.* New York: Penguin Books.

Humphrey, J. A., & Porter, S. (1993, October). *Unsolved homicide: A partial test of Black's theory of the behavior of law.* Paper presented at the meeting of the American Society of Criminology, Phoenix, AZ.

Icove, D. J. (1981). *Principles of incendiary crime analysis: The arson pattern recognition system (APRS) approach to arson information management.* Quantico, VA: National Center for the Analysis of Violent Crime.

Icove, D. J. (1986). Automated crime profiling. *FBI Law Enforcement Bulletin, 55*(12), 27-30.

Icove, D. J., & Crisman, H. J. (1975). Application of pattern recognition in arson investigation. *Fire Technology, 11*(1), 35-41.

Icove, D. J., & Estepp, M. H. (1987). Motive-Based offender profiles of arson and fire-related crimes. *FBI Law Enforcement Bulletin, 56*(4), 17-23.

Icove, D. J., & Horbert, P. R. (1990, December). Serial arsonists: An introduction. *The Police Chief,* pp. 46-48.

Icove, D. J., Wherry, V. B., & Schroeder, J. D. (1980). *Combating arson for profit: Advanced techniques for investigators.* Columbus, OH: Battelle Press.

Inciardi, J. A., & Pottieger, A. E. (Eds.). (1978). *Violent crime: Historical and contemporary issues.* Beverly Hills: Sage.

Indermaur, D. (1996). Offenders' perspectives on violent property crime. In P. F. Cromwell (Ed.), *In their own words: Criminals on crime* (pp. 98-106). Los Angeles: Roxbury Publishing.

Infamous murders. (1989). London: Macdonald.

Innes, C. A., & Greenfeld, L. A. (1990). *Violent state prisoners and their victims* (BJS Publication No. NCJ-124133). Washington, DC: U.S. Government Printing Office.

Institutional Research and Development Unit, FBI Academy. (1981). *Evaluation of the psychological profiling program.* Unpublished manuscript.

International Association of Chiefs of Police. (1975). *Geographic base files for law enforcement.* Gaithersburg, MD: Author.

Interviewing techniques for sexual homicide investigation. (1985). *FBI Law Enforcement Bulletin, 54*(8), 26-31.

Investigators believe many killers, acting separately, slew children in Atlanta. (1981, March 15). *The New York Times,* pp. A1, A32-A33.

Iversen, G. R. (1984). *Bayesian statistical inference.* Sage university paper series on quantitative applications in the social sciences, 43. Beverly Hills: Sage.

Jackman, T., & Cole, T. (1992). *Rites of burial.* New York: Windsor.

Jackson, J. L. (1994, March). *An expert/novice approach to offender profiling.* Paper presented at the meeting of the Academy of Criminal Justice Sciences, Chicago, IL.

Jackson, J. L., & Bekerian, D. A. (1997a). Does offender profiling have a role to play? In J. L. Jackson & D. A. Bekerian (Eds.), *Offender profiling: Theory, research and practice* (pp. 1-7). Chichester: John Wiley & Sons.

Jackson, J. L., & Bekerian, D. A. (Eds.). (1997b). *Offender profiling: Theory, research and practice.* Chichester: John Wiley & Sons.

Jackson, J. L., & Herbrink, J. C. M. (1996). *Profiling organised crime: An impossible task* (NISCALE Working Paper). Leiden, The Netherlands: The Netherlands Institute for the Study of Criminality and Law Enforcement.

Jackson, J. L., van den Eshof, P., & de Kleuver, E. E. (1994). *Offender profiling in The Netherlands* (Report NSCR WD94-03). Leiden, The Netherlands: The Netherlands Institute for the Study of Criminality and Law Enforcement.

Jackson, J. L., van Koppen, P. J., & Herbrink, J. C. M. (1993a). *Does the service meet the needs? An evaluation of consumer satisfaction with specific profile analysis and investigative advice as offered by the Scientific Research Advisory Unit of the National Criminal Intelligence Division (CRI), The Netherlands* (NISCALE Report NSCR 93-05). Leiden, The Netherlands: The Netherlands Institute for the Study of Criminality and Law Enforcement.

Jackson, J. L., van Koppen, P. J., & Herbrink, J. C. M. (1993b). *An expert/novice approach to offender profiling* (NISCALE Working Paper). Leiden, The Netherlands: The Netherlands Institute for the Study of Criminality and Law Enforcement.

Jacobs, J. (1961). *The death and life of great American cities.* New York: Random House.

Jacobs, J. (1992). *Systems of survival.* New York: Random House.

Jacoby, J. E. (Ed.). (1979). *Classics of criminology.* Prospect Heights, IL: Waveland Press.

Jaffe, F. A. (1983). *A guide to pathological evidence for lawyers and police officers* (2nd ed.). Toronto: Carswell.

Jaffe, P., Wolfe, D. A., Wilson, S. K., & Zak, L. (1986). Similarities in behavioral and social maladjustment among child victims and witnesses to family violence. *American Journal of Orthopsychiatry, 56,* 142-146.

Jahnke, A. (1989, November). The killing season. *Boston Magazine,* pp. 134-137, 195-199.

Jakle, J. A., Brunn, S., & Roseman, C. C. (1976). *Human spatial behavior: A social geography.* Prospect Heights, IL: Waveland Press.

James, C. A. M. (1992). *Peter William Sutcliffe: 'The Yorkshire Ripper'.* Unpublished manuscript, Simon Fraser University, School of Criminology, Burnaby, BC.

James, E. (1991). *Catching serial killers.* Lansing, MI: International Forensic Services.

James, P. D., & Critchley, T. A. (1971). *The maul and the pear tree: The Ratcliffe Highway murders 1811.* London: Penguin Books.

Jasanoff, S. (1989, Fall). Science on the witness stand. *Issues in Science and Technology,* pp. 80-87.

Jayewardene, C. H. S. (1975). The nature of homicide: Canada 1961-70. In R. A. Silverman & J. J. Teevan, Jr. (Eds.), *Crime in Canadian society* (pp. 279-310). Toronto: Butterworth.

Jeffers, H. P. (1991). *Who killed Precious?* New York: Pharos Books.

Jeffery, C. R. (1977). *Crime prevention through environmental design* (2nd ed.). Beverly Hills: Sage.

Jeffery, C. R., & Zahm, D. L. (1993). Crime prevention through environmental design, opportunity theory, and rational choice models. In R. V. Clarke & M. Felson (Eds.), *Routine activity and rational choice* (pp. 323-350). New Brunswick, NJ: Transaction.

Jenkins, P. (1988a). Myth and murder: The serial killer panic of 1983-5. *Sam Houston State University Criminal Justice Research Bulletin, 3*(11).

Jenkins, P. (1988b). Serial murder in England 1940-1985. *Journal of Criminal Justice, 16,* 1-15.

Jenkins, P. (1989). Serial murder in the United States 1900-1940: A historical perspective. *Journal of Criminal Justice, 17,* 377-392.

Jenkins, P. (1990). Sharing murder: Understanding group serial homicide. *Journal of Crime and Justice, 13,* 125-147.

Jenkins, P. (1992a). *Intimate enemies: Moral panics in contemporary Great Britain.* New York: Aldine de Gruyter.

Jenkins, P. (1992b). A murder "wave"? Trends in American serial homicide 1940-1990. *Criminal Justice Review, 17,* 1-19.

Jenkins, P. (1993a). African-Americans and serial homicide. *American Journal of Criminal Justice, 17*(2), 47-60.

Jenkins, P. (1993b). Chance or choice: The selection of serial murder victims. In A. V. Wilson (Ed.), *Homicide: The victim/offender connection* (chap. 22). Cincinnati: Anderson.

Jenkins, P. (1994). *Using murder: The social construction of serial homicide.* New York: Aldine de Gruyter.

Jerath, B. K., & Jerath, R. (1993). *Homicide: A bibliography* (2nd ed.). Boca Raton, FL: CRC Press.

Johnson, G. (1994). ViCLAS: Violent Crime Linkage Analysis System. *RCMP Gazette, 56*(10), 9-13.

Johnson, G., Killmier. B., & Sellinger, J. A. (1996, October). *Violent Crime Linkage Analysis System.* Paper presented at the conference of the International Association of Chiefs of Police, Phoenix, AZ.

Johnson, H. A. (1988). *History of criminal justice.* Cincinnati: Anderson.

Johnston, R. J. (1973). On frictions of distance and regression coefficients. *Area, 5,* 187-191.

Johnston, R. J. (1975). Map pattern and friction of distance parameters: A comment. *Regional Studies, 9,* 281-283.

Jones, M. (1989, November 6). The hunt for a vicious killer. *Sydney Daily Mirror,* pp. 20-21.

Jones, R. G. (Ed.). (1960). *Unsolved! Classic true murder cases.* New York: Peter Bedrick Books.

Jones, R. G. (Ed.). (1989). *The mammoth book of murder.* New York: Carroll & Graf.

Jones, V., & Collier, P. (1993). *True crime – Volume 2: Serial killers & mass murderers.* Forestville, CA: Eclipse Books.

Kaihla, P. (1989, December 18). A lethal choice for a murderer. *Maclean's,* p. 16.

Kalish, C. B. (1988). *International crime rates* (BJS Publication No. NCJ-110776). Washington, DC: U.S. Government Printing Office.

Kanji, G. K. (1993). *100 statistical tests.* London: Sage.

Kappeler, V. E., Sluder, R. D., & Alpert, G. P. (1994). *Forces of deviance: Understanding the dark side of policing.* Prospect Heights, IL: Waveland Press.

Karlsson, T. (1996, November). *The creation of the serial killer.* Paper presented at the meeting of the American Society of Criminology, Chicago, IL.

Karp, C., & Rosner, C. (1991). *When justice fails.* Toronto: McClelland & Stewart.

Kearney, J. J. (1989, November). *Future applications of DNA technology in forensic science.* Paper presented at the meeting of the American Society of Criminology, Reno, NV.

Keeney, B. T., & Heide, K. M. (1994a, November). *Serial murder: A more accurate and inclusive definition.* Paper presented at the meeting of the American Society of Criminology, Miami, FL.

Keeney, B. T., & Heide, K. M. (1994b, November). *Serial murder: Refining the definition to capture the involvement of men and women.* Paper presented at the meeting of the American Society of Criminology, Miami, FL.

Keeney, B. T., & Heide, K. M. (1994c). Gender differences in serial murderers: A preliminary analysis. *Journal of Interpersonal Violence, 9.*

Kelleher, M. D., & Kelleher, C. L. (1998). *Murder most rare: The female serial killer.* Praeger Publishers: Westport, CT.

Kelly, K. F., Rankin, J. J., & Wink, R. C. (1987). Method and applications of DNA fingerprinting: A guide for the non-scientist. *The Criminal Law Review,* 105-110.

Kennedy, D. (1991). *William Heirens: His day in court.* Chicago: Bonus Books.

Kennedy, D. (1994). *On a killing day.* New York: Shapolsky Publishers.

Kennedy, D. B. (1990). Facility site selection and analysis through environmental criminology. *Journal of Criminal Justice, 18,* 239-252.

Kennedy, D. B. (1993). Architectural concerns regarding security and premises liability. *Journal of Architectural and Planning Research, 10,* 105-129.

Kennedy, D. B., & Homant, R. J. (1997). Problems with the use of criminal profiling in premises security litigation. *Trial Diplomacy Journal, 20,* 223-229.

Kennedy, L. W., & Forde, D. R. (1990). Routine activities and crime: An analysis of victimization in Canada. *Criminology, 28,* 137-152.

Kenrick, D. T., & Sheets, V. (1993, October). *Homicidal fantasies.* Paper presented at the meeting of the American Society of Criminology, Phoenix, AZ.

Keppel, R. D. (1989). *Serial murder: Future implications for police investigations.* Cincinnati: Anderson.

Keppel, R. D. (1995). Signature murders: A report of several related cases. *Journal of Forensic Sciences, 40,* 670-674.

Keppel, R. D., & Birnes, W. J. (1995). *The Riverman: Ted Bundy and I hunt for the Green River Killer.* New York: Simon & Schuster.

Keppel, R. D., & Birnes, W. J. (1997). *Signature killers.* New York: Simon & Schuster.

Keppel, R. D., & Weis, J. G. (1993a). HITS: Catching criminals in the Northwest. *FBI Law Enforcement Bulletin, 62*(4), 14-19.

Keppel, R. D., & Weis, J. G. (1993b). *Improving the investigation of violent crime: The Homicide Investigation and Tracking System* (NIJ Publication No. NCJ 141761). Washington, DC: U.S. Government Printing Office.

Keppel, R. D., & Weis, J. G. (1994). Time and distance as solvability factors in murder cases. *Journal of Forensic Sciences, 39,* 386-401.

Kerr, P. (1992). *A philosophical investigation.* New York: Penguin Books.

Kesterton, M. (1997, April 25). Profiling a killer. *The Toronto Globe and Mail,* p. A20.

Keyes, E. (1976). *The Michigan Murders.* New York: Simon & Schuster.

Kiger, K. (1990). The darker figure of crime: The serial murder enigma. In S. A. Egger (Ed.), *Serial murder: An elusive phenomenon* (pp. 35-52). New York: Praeger.

The killing ground. (1981, May 24). *The Sunday Times,* p. 13.

Kind, S. S. (1987a). Navigational ideas and the Yorkshire Ripper investigation. *Journal of Navigation, 40,* 385-393.

Kind, S. S. (1987b). *The scientific investigation of crime.* Harrogate: Forensic Science Services.

Kind, S. S. (1988). Science and the hunt for the criminal. *Impact of Science on Society, 154,* 113-123.

Kind, S. S. (1989, March). The science of crime detection. *Police Review,* pp. 554-555.

Kind, S. S. (1990, July). Who goes in the frame? *Police Review,* pp. 1446-1447.

Kind, S. S. (1991). Concepts and practice in forensic science – The particularly unitary tag. *The Criminologist, 15,* 144-148.

Kind, S. S. (1993). Correlation and coincidence in crime investigation: An essay. *The Criminologist, 17,* 2-6.

Kines, L. (1995, October 17). New unit to target serial killers, rapists. *The Vancouver Sun,* p. B1.

Kines, L. (1996, March 11). Years of study put to use in search for Abbotsford killer. *The Vancouver Sun,* pp. A1-A2.

King, B. (Ed.) (1996). *Lustmord: The writings and artifacts of murderers.* Burbank, CA: Bloat.

King, G. C. (1992). *Blood lust.* New York: Penguin Books.

King, G. C. (1993). *Driven to kill.* New York: Windsor.

King, L. J. (1984). *Central place theory.* Sage university paper series on scientific geography, 1. Beverly Hills: Sage.

Kinsey, R., Lea, J., & Young, J. (1986). *Losing the fight against crime.* Oxford: Basil Blackwell.

Kish, L. (1965). *Survey sampling.* New York: John Wiley & Sons.

Klaus, P. A. (1994). *The costs of crime to victims* (BJS Publication No. NCJ-145865). Washington, DC: U.S. Government Printing Office.

Klaus, P. A., & DeBerry, M. (1985). *The crime of rape* (BJS Publication No. NCJ-96777). Washington, DC: U.S. Government Printing Office.

Kleemans, E. R. (1997, June). *Repeat burglary victimization: Results of empirical research in The Netherlands.* Paper presented at the Seminar on Environmental Criminology and Crime Analysis, Oslo, Norway.

Klockars, C. B. (Ed.). (1983). *Thinking about police: Contemporary readings.* New York: McGraw-Hill.

Klockars, C. B., & Mastrofski, S. D. (Eds.). (1991). *Thinking about police: Contemporary readings* (2nd ed.). New York: McGraw-Hill.

Knight, R. A., Warren, J. I., Reboussin, R., & Soley, B. J., (1998). Predicting rapist types from crime-scene variables. *Criminal Justice and Behavior, 25,* 46-80.

Knoke, D., & Kuklinski, J. H. (1982). *Network analysis.* Sage university paper series on quantitative applications in the social sciences, 28. Beverly Hills: Sage.

Knutsson, J. (1997, June). *There is a where but also a when.* Paper presented at the Seminar on Environmental Criminology and Crime Analysis, Oslo, Norway.

Kocsis, R. N. (1999). Criminal profiling of crime scene behaviours in Australian sexual murders. *Australian Police Journal, 53,* 113-116.

Kocsis, R. N., & Davies, K. (1997). An introduction to criminal profiling. *Police Issues & Practice Journal, 5*(4), 31-35.

Kocsis, R. N., & Irwin, H. J. (1997). An analysis of spatial patterns in serial rape, arson, and burglary: The utility of the circle theory of environmental range for psychological profiling. *Psychiatry, Psychology and Law, 4,* 195-206.

Kocsis, R. N., & Irwin, H. J. (1998). The psychological profile of serial offenders and a redefinition of the misnomer of serial crime. *Psychiatry, Psychology and Law, 5,* 197-213.

Kocsis, R. N., Irwin, H. J., & Hayes, A. F. (1998). Organised and disorganised criminal behaviour syndromes in arsonists: A validation study of a psychological profiling concept. *Psychiatry, Psychology and Law, 5,* 117-131.

Kocsis, R. N., Irwin, H. J., Hayes, A. F., & Nunn, R. (forthcoming). Expertise in psychological profiling: A comparative assessment. *Journal of Interpersonal Violence.*

Kolarik, G. (1990). *Freed to kill: The true story of serial murderer Larry Eyler.* New York: Avon Books.

Kosko, B., & Isaka, S. (1993). Fuzzy logic. *Scientific American, 269*(1), 76-81.

Kposowa, A. J. (1999). The effects of occupation and industry on the risk of homicide victimization in the United States. *Homicide Studies, 3,* 47-77.

Krippendorff, K. (1986). *Information theory: Structural models for qualitative data.* Sage university paper series on quantitative applications in the social sciences, 62. Beverly Hills: Sage.

Krohn, M. D., & Akers, R. L. (Eds.). (1978). *Crime, law, and sanctions: Theoretical perspectives.* Beverly Hills: Sage.

Kube, E., & Störzer, H. U. (Eds.). (1991). *Police research in the Federal Republic of Germany: 15 years research within the "Bundeskriminalamt."* Berlin: Springer-Velag.

Kubik, R. (1996, Winter). New tool for imaging. *Canadian Resources*, pp. 2-5.

Kumar, K. S. (1993, October). *Comparing "solved" and "unsolved" homicides.* Paper presented at the meeting of the American Society of Criminology, Phoenix, AZ.

La Vigne, N. G. (1997, June). *How hot is that spot?: The utility and application of place-based theories of crime.* Paper presented at the Seminar on Environmental Criminology and Crime Analysis, Oslo, Norway.

La Vigne, N. G. (1998, June). *Mapping an opportunity surface of crime.* Paper presented at the Seminar on Environmental Criminology and Crime Analysis, Barcelona, Spain.

La Vigne, N. G., & Wartell, J. (Eds.). (1998). *Crime mapping case studies: Successes in the field.* Washington, DC: Police Executive Research Forum.

Lambert, P., & Podesta, J. S. (1998, February 16). Nightmare alley. *People*, pp. 163-166.

Lane, B., & Gregg, W. (1992). *The encyclopedia of serial killers.* New York: Diamond Books.

Lane, R. (1997). *Murder in America: A history.* Columbus, OH: Ohio State University Press.

Langan, P. A., & Harlow, C. W. (1994). *Child rape victims, 1992* (BJS Publication No. NCJ-147001). Washington, DC: U.S. Government Printing Office.

Langan, P. A., & Innes, C. A. (1985). *The risk of violent crime* (BJS Publication No. NCJ-97119). Washington, DC: U.S. Government Printing Office.

Langbein, L. I., & Lichtman, A. J. (1978). *Ecological inference.* Sage university paper series on quantitative applications in the social sciences, 10. Beverly Hills: Sage.

Lange, J. E. T. (1985, March). The adventure of the nine thinking men. *Mensa Bulletin*, pp. 9-10.

Lange, J. E. T., & DeWitt, Jr., K. (1990a). *The Ripper Syndrome: A perspective on serial murder.* Unpublished manuscript.

Lange, J. E. T., & DeWitt, Jr., K. (1990b, February). *What the FBI doesn't know about serial killers and why.* Paper presented at the Metropolitan Washington Mensa Regional Gathering, Arlington, VA.

Langevin, R. (1983). *Sexual strands: Understanding and treating sexual anomalies in men.* Hillsdale, NJ: Lawrence Erlbaum Associates.

Langevin, R., & Handy, L. (1987). Stranger homicide in Canada: A national sample and a psychiatric sample. *Journal of Criminal Law & Criminology, 78,* 398-429.

Lanning, K. V. (1986). Child molesters: A behavioral analysis. *FBI Law Enforcement Bulletin, 44*(10), 1-15.

Lanning, K. V. (1989, October). Satanic, occult, ritualistic crime: A law enforcement perspective. *The Police Chief*, pp. 62-84.

Lanning, K. V. (1995). Child molestation – Law enforcement typology. In R. R. Hazelwood & A. W. Burgess (Eds.), *Practical aspects of rape investigation: A multidisciplinary approach* (2nd ed.) (pp. 323-335). Boca Raton, FL: CRC Press.

Larsen, R. W. (1980). *Bundy: The deliberate stranger*. New York: Bantam Books.

Larson, R. C., & Odoni, A. R. (1981). *Urban operations research*. Englewood Cliffs, NJ: Prentice-Hall.

Latvian kindergarten killer planned murder spree. (1999, February 24). *Reuters World Report*.

Lau, E. (1989). *Runaway*. Toronto: Harper & Collins.

Law Reform Commission of Canada. (1984). *Homicide* (Working Paper 33). Ottawa: Minister of Supply and Services Canada.

Layton, M. (Ed.). (1993). *Policing in the global community: The challenge of leadership*. Burnaby, BC: Simon Fraser University.

Lea, J., & Young, J. (1984). *What is to be done about law and order?* Harmondsworth, Middlesex: Penguin.

LeBeau, J. L. (1984). Rape and racial patterns. *Journal of Offender Counselling, Services, & Rehabilitation, 9*, 125-148.

LeBeau, J. L. (1985). Some problems with measuring and describing rape presented by the serial offender. *Justice Quarterly, 2*, 385-398.

LeBeau, J. L. (1986). *The geographical profiling of serial and non-serial rape offenders.* Unpublished manuscript, Southern Illinois University, Carbondale, IL.

LeBeau, J. L. (1987a). The journey to rape: Geographic distance and the rapist's method of approaching the victim. *Journal of Police Science and Administration, 15*, 129-136.

LeBeau, J. L. (1987b). The methods and measures of centrography and the spatial dynamics of rape. *Journal of Quantitative Criminology, 3*, 125-141.

LeBeau, J. L. (1987c). Patterns of stranger and serial rape offending: Factors distinguishing apprehended and at large offenders. *Journal of Criminal Law & Criminology, 78*, 309-326.

LeBeau, J. L. (1991). *The spatial behaviors of serial rapists.* Unpublished manuscript, Southern Illinois University, Carbondale, IL.

LeBeau, J. L. (1992). Four case studies illustrating the spatial-temporal analysis of serial rapists. *Police Studies, 15*, 124-145.

LeBeau, J. L. (1994, November). *The rhythms of violence.* Paper presented at the meeting of the American Society of Criminology, Miami, FL.

LeBeau, J. L., & Corcoran, W. T. (1990). Changes in calls for police service with changes in routine activities and the arrival and passage of weather fronts. *Journal of Quantitative Criminology, 6,* 269-291.

LeBeau, J. L., & Langworthy, R. H. (1992, November). *The journey to get stung.* Paper presented at the meeting of the American Society of Criminology, New Orleans, LA.

LeBourdais, I. (1966). *The trial of Steven Truscott.* Toronto: McClelland and Stewart.

Legall, P. (1992, July 15). Profiles in evil. *The Hamilton Spectator,* p. B4.

Leineweber, H., & Büchler, H. (1991). Preventing bank robbery: The offense from the robber's perspective. In E. Kube & H. U. Störzer (Eds.), *Police research in the Federal Republic of Germany: 15 years research within the "Bundeskriminalamt"* (pp. 209-222). Berlin: Springer-Velag.

Leith, R. (1983). *The Torso Killer.* New York: Windsor.

Lenarduzzi, R., & Jones, M. (1989, November 3). Society killer victim no. 4. *Sydney Daily Mirror,* pp. 1-2.

Levin, J., & Fox, J. A. (1985). *Mass murder.* New York: Plenum Press.

Levin, J., & Fox, J. A. (1994, November). *The role of sociopathy in typologies of serial murder.* Paper presented at the meeting of the American Society of Criminology, Miami, FL.

Levy, D. H. (1994). *Skywatching.* Alexandria, VA: Time-Life Books.

Lewis, D.O. (1998). *Guilty by reason of insanity.* New York: Random House.

Leyton, E. (1986). *Hunting humans.* Toronto: McClelland-Bantam.

Leyton, E. (1995). *Men of blood: Murder in everyday life.* Toronto: McClelland & Stewart.

Leyton, E., O'Grady, W., & Overton, J. (1992). *Violence and public anxiety: A Canadian case.* St. John's, NF: Institute of Social and Economic Research.

Lindsey, R. (1984, January 21). Officials cite a rise in killers who roam U.S. for victims. *The New York Times,* pp. 1, 7.

Linedecker, C. L. (1980). *The man who killed boys.* New York: St. Martin's Press.

Linedecker, C. L. (1987). *Thrill killers.* New York: Knightsbridge.

Linedecker, C. L. (1990). *Hell ranch.* New York: Tom Doherty.

Linedecker, C. L. (1991). *Night Stalker.* New York: St. Martin's Press.

Linedecker, C. L., & Burt, W. A. (1990). *Nurses who kill.* New York: Windsor.

Lines, K. (1999, September). Police Profilers. *The Police Chief,* p. 49.

Lipson, N. (1992, August). Granny killer's wife: Was she to be next? *New Idea,* pp. 38-40.

Loeber, R. (1990). Development and risk factors of juvenile antisocial behavior and delinquency. *Clinical Psychology Review, 10,* 1-41.

Longley, P. A., Brooks, S. M., McDonnell, R., & MacMillan, B. (Eds.). (1998). *Geocomputation: A primer.* Chichester: John Wiley & Sons.

Lourie, R. (1993). *Hunting the devil.* New York: HarperCollins.

Lowe, J. C., & Moryadas, S. (1975). *The geography of movement.* Boston: Houghton Mifflin.

Lowman, J. (1982). Crime, criminal justice policy and the urban environment. In D. T. Herbert & R. J. Johnston (Eds.), *Geography and the urban environment* (Vol. 5, pp. 81-94). Chichester: John Wiley and Sons.

Lowman, J. (1983). *Geography, crime and social control.* Unpublished doctoral dissertation, University of British Columbia, Vancouver.

Lowman, J. (1984). *Vancouver field study of prostitution.* Ottawa: Department of Justice.

Lowman, J. (1986). Conceptual issues in the geography of crime: Toward a geography of social control. *Annals of the Association of American Geographers, 76*(1), 81-94.

Lowman, J. (1989). *Street prostitution: Assessing the impact of the law, Vancouver.* Ottawa: Department of Justice.

Lowman, J., & Fraser, L. (1995). *Violence against persons who prostitute: The experience in British Columbia.* Ottawa: Department of Justice.

Lowrie, P., & Wells, S. (1991, November 16). Genetic fingerprinting. *New Scientist: Inside Science.*

Lucas, R. (1986). An expert system to detect burglars using a logic language and a relational database. 43-54.

Luce, R. D. (1959). *Individual choice behavior.* New York: John Wiley & Sons.

Lunde, D. T. (1976). *Murder and madness.* San Francisco: Stanford.

Lundsgaarde, H. P. (1977). *Murder in Space City: A cultural analysis of Houston homicide patterns.* New York: Oxford University Press.

Lyman, M. D. (1993). *Criminal investigation: The art and the science.* Englewood Cliffs, NJ: Regents/Prentice Hall.

Lynch, K. (1960). *The image of the city.* Cambridge, MA: MIT Press.

Lyons, A., & Truzzi, M. (1991). *The blue sense: Psychic detectives and crime.* New York: Mysterious Press.

Macdonald, J. E., & Gifford, R. (1989). Territorial cues and defensible space theory: The burglar's point of view. *Journal of Environmental Psychology, 9,* 193-205.

Macdonald, J. M. (1961). *The murderer and his victim.* Springfield, IL: Charles C. Thomas.

Macdonald, J. M. (1963). The threat to kill. *American Journal of Psychiatry, 120,* 125-130.

Macdonald, J. M., & Michaud, D. L. (1992). *Criminal interrogation.* Denver: Apache Press.

MacKay, R. E. (1994). Violent Crime Analysis. *RCMP Gazette, 56*(5), 11-14.

MacLatchie, J. M. (Ed.). (1987). *Violence in contemporary Canadian society.* Ottawa: John Howard Society of Canada.

MacLean, R., & Veniot, A. (1990). *Terror: Murder and panic in New Brunswick.* Toronto: McClelland & Stewart.

MacNamara, M. (1990, November). Playing for time. *Vanity Fair,* pp. 80-92.

Maeder, T. (1980). *The unspeakable crimes of Dr. Petiot.* London: Penguin Books.

Makin, K. (1989a, April 1). Terror, recriminations follow trail of Green River Killer: Public is beginning to identify with the plight of prostitutes. *The Toronto Globe and Mail,* pp. A1, A9.

Makin, K. (1989b, April 3). Deadly social chameleons: Serial killers hide behind cloak of respectability. *The Toronto Globe and Mail,* pp. A1, A14.

Makin, K. (1992). *Redrum the innocent.* Toronto: Viking.

Makower, J., & Bergheim, L. (1986). *The map catalog.* New York: Tilden Press.

Malette, L., & Chalouh, M. (Eds.). (1991). *The Montreal Massacre* (M. Wildeman, Trans.). Charlottetown, PE: Gynergy Books.

Maltz, M. D., Gordon, A. C., & Friedman, W. (1991). *Mapping crime in its community setting: Event geography analysis.* New York: Springer-Verlag.

Maltz, M. D., & Zawitz, M. W. (1998). *Displaying violent crime trends using estimates from the National Crime Victimization Survey* (BJS Publication No. NCJ-167881). Washington, DC: U.S. Government Printing Office.

Mamalian, C. A. & La Vigne, N. G. (1999). *The use of computerized crime mapping by law enforcement: Survey results* (NIJ Publication). Washington, DC: U.S. Government Printing Office.

Mandelsberg, R. G. (Ed.). (1993). *Hooker killers.* New York: Windsor.

Mann, R. W., & Ubelaker, D. H. (1990). The forensic anthropologist. *FBI Law Enforcement Bulletin, 59*(7), 20-23.

Manners, T. (1995). *Deadlier than the male.* London: Pan Books.

Mardia, K. V., Coombes, A., Kirkbride, J., Linney, A., & Bowie, J. L. (1996). On statistical problems with face identification from photographs. *Journal of Applied Statistics, 23,* 655-675.

Marques, J. K., Day, D. M., Nelson, C., & Miner, M. H. (1989). *The Sex Offender Treatment and Evaluation Project: Third report to the Legislature in response to PC 1365.* Sacramento: California State Department of Mental Health.

Marron, K. (1988). *Ritual abuse.* Toronto: McClelland-Bantam.

Marshall, I., & Zohar, D. (1997). *Who's afraid of Schrödinger's Cat?: An A-to-Z guide to all the new science ideas you need to keep up with the new thinking.* New York: William Morrow and Company.

Marshall, W. L., & Barrett, S. (1990). *Criminal neglect: Why sex offenders go free.* Toronto: McClelland-Bantam.

Martin, R. M. (1992). *There are two errors in the the title of this book: A sourcebook of philosophical puzzles, problems, and paradoxes.* Peterborough, ON: Broadview Press.

Marvell, T. B., & Moody, C. E. (1998). The impact of out-of-state prison population on state homicide rates: Displacement and free-rider effects. *Criminology, 36*, 513-535

Mason, B. (1997). New software targets serial criminals. *RCMP Gazette, 59*(2), 25.

Masters, B. (1985). *Killing for company: The case of Dennis Nilsen.* London: Hodder and Stoughton.

Masters, B. (1991, November). Dahmer's inferno. *Vanity Fair,* pp. 182-189, 264-269.

Masters, B. (1993). *The shrine of Jeffrey Dahmer.* London: Hodder & Stoughton.

Masters, B. (1994, September 25). Mind over murder. *Night & Day,* pp. 38-42.

Mathers, R. (1989, July). *Psychological profiling.* Lecture presented at the Justice Institute of British Columbia, Police Academy seminar, Central Saanich, BC.

Mathews, E. K. (1992). Daniel Eugene Remeta. *Police, 16*(8), 81-86, 154-157.

Mawson, A. R. (1980). Aggression, attachment behavior, and crimes of violence. In T. Hirschi & M. Gottfredson (Eds.), *Understanding crime: Current theory and research* (pp. 103-116). Beverly Hills: Sage.

McCready, B., & Heide, K. M. (1994, November). *Male serial murderers from minority groups: A preliminary analysis.* Paper presented at the meeting of the American Society of Criminology, Miami, FL.

McDougal, D. (1992). *Angel of darkness.* New York: Warner Books.

McEwen, J. T., & Taxman, F. S. (1995). Applications of computer mapping to police operations. In J. E. Eck & D. A. Weisburd (Eds.), *Crime and place: Crime prevention studies, Vol. 4* (pp. 259-284). Monsey, NY: Criminal Justice Press.

McFeely, T. (1991, November 25). Satanic sacrifices. *British Columbia Report,* pp. 42-43.

McIver, J. P. (1981). Criminal mobility: A review of empirical studies. In S. Hakim & G. F. Rengert (Eds.), *Crime spillover* (pp. 20-47). Beverly Hills: Sage.

McKay, S. (1985, July 8). Coming to grips with random killers. *Maclean's,* pp. 44-45.

McLintock, B. (1995, February 5). Computer cop ready to work. *The Vancouver Province,* p. A13.

The men who murdered. (1985). *FBI Law Enforcement Bulletin, 54*(8), 2-6.

Menzel, D. H., & Pasachoff, J. M. (1983). *A field guide to the stars and planets* (2nd ed.). Boston: Houghton Mifflin.

Menzies, R. (1985). *Doing violence: Psychiatric discretion and the prediction of dangerousness.* Unpublished doctoral dissertation, University of Toronto, Toronto.

Meredith, N. (1984, December). The murder epidemic. *Science, 84,* 43-48.

Methvin, E. H. (1993, December). Stalking the Seattle Specter. *Reader's Digest,* pp. 115-120.

Michaud, S. G. (1994). *Lethal shadow.* New York: Penguin Books.

Michaud, S. G., & Aynesworth, H. (1983). *The only living witness.* New York: Penguin Books.

Michaud, S. G., & Aynesworth, H. (1989). *Ted Bundy: Conversations with a killer.* New York: Penguin Books.

Michaud, S. G., & Hazelwood, R. R. (1998). *The evil that men do: FBI profiler Roy Hazelwood's journey into the minds of sexual predators.* New York: St. Martin's Press.

Miethe, T. D., & McCorkle, R. C. (1998). *Crime profiles: The anatomy of dangerous persons, places, and situations.* Los Angeles: Roxbury Publishing.

Milgaard, J., & Edwards, P. (1999). *A mother's story: The fight to free my son David.* Toronto: Doubleday Canada.

Miller, J. V. (1991). The FBI's forensic DNA analysis program. *FBI Law Enforcement Bulletin, 60*(7), 11-15.

Miller, T. (1993a). Ray & Faye Copeland. *Police, 17*(9), 62-66.

Miller, T. (1993b). *The Copeland killings.* New York: Windsor.

Miller, T. (1993, May). GIS catches criminals. *GIS World,* pp. 42-43.

Miller, T. (1994, January). Computers track the criminal's trail. *American demographics,* pp. 13-14.

Miller, T. R., Cohen, M. A., & Wiersema, B. (1996a). *The extent and costs of crime victimization: A new look* (NIJ Publication). Washington, DC: U.S. Government Printing Office.

Miller, T. R., Cohen, M. A., & Wiersema, B. (1996b). *Victim costs and consequences: A new look* (NIJ Publication No. NCJ-155282). Washington, DC: U.S. Government Printing Office.

Mind of a serial killer. (1992, October 18). *Nova* (show #1912, transcript). Denver: Journal Graphics.

Mischel, W. (1976). *Introduction to personality* (2nd ed.). New York: Holt, Rinehart and Winston.

Mitchell, E. W. (1997). *The aetiology of serial murder: Towards an integrated model.* Unpublished master's thesis, University of Cambridge, Cambridge, UK.

Moland, R. S. (1998). Graphical display of murder trial evidence. In N. G. La Vigne & J. Wartell (Eds.), *Crime mapping case studies: Successes in the field* (pp. 69-79). Washington, DC: Police Executive Research Forum.

Molnar, G., Keitner, L., & Harwood, B. T. (1984). A comparison of partner and solo arsonists. *Journal of Forensic Sciences, 29,* 574-583.

Monaco, R., & Burt, B. (1993). *The Dracula Syndrome.* New York: Avon Books.

Monahan, J. (1994). The causes of violence. *FBI Law Enforcement Bulletin, 63*(1), 11-15.

Monmonier. M. (1991). *How to lie with maps.* Chicago: University of Chicago Press.

Montgomery, J. E. (1993). Organizational survival: Continuity or crisis? In M. Layton (Ed.), *Policing in the global community: The challenge of leadership* (pp. 133-142). Burnaby, BC: Simon Fraser University.

Moore, G. (1993, July 14). Why men become monsters. *Seattle Weekly,* pp. 16-20, 22.

Moore, K., & Reed, D. (1988). *Deadly medicine*. New York: St. Martin's Press.

Moore, M. (1993, December 27). Plotting a strategy to curtail crime. *PC Week*, pp. 35, 38.

Moore, O. K. (1957). Divination – A new perspective. *American Anthropologist, 59*, 69-74.

Morrill, R., Gaile, G. L., & Thrall, G. L. (1988). *Spatial diffusion*. Sage university paper series on scientific geography, 10. Beverly Hills: Sage.

Morris, N., & Miller, M. (1987). *Predictions of dangerousness in the criminal law* (NIJ Publication No. NCJ-104599). Washington, DC: U.S. Government Printing Office.

Morrison, H. (Ed.). (1991). *Serial killers and murderers*. Lincolnwood, IL: Publications International.

Morrow, F. (1992). Ronald White. *Police, 16*(3), 51-54.

Mott, N. L. (1999). Serial murder: Patterns in unsolved cases. *Homicide Studies, 3*, 241-255.

Mulgrew, I. (1990). *Final payoff: The true price of convicting Clifford Robert Olson*. Toronto: Seal Books.

Mullins, S. (1992). Donald "Pee Wee" Gaskins. *Police, 16*(2), 44-46, 90-91.

Mumford, L. (1961). *The city in history: Its origins, its transformations, and its prospects*. New York: Harcourt, Brace & World.

Murad, T. A. (1997). The utilization of faunal evidence in the recovery of human remains. In W. D. Haglund & M. H. Sorg (Eds.), *Forensic taphonomy: The postmortem fate of human remains* (pp. 395-404). Boca Raton, FL: CRC Press.

Murder and attempted murders – New York City. (1977). *The New York Times Annual Index*, p. 874.

Nachmias, D., & Nachmias, C. (1976). *Research methods in the social sciences*. New York: St. Martin's Press.

Namboodiri, K. (1984). *Matrix algebra*. Sage university paper series on quantitative applications in the social sciences, 38. Beverly Hills: Sage.

Nash, J.R. (1992). *World encyclopedia of 20th century murder*. New York: Paragon House.

National Crime Faculty. (1996). *Intelligence led DNA screening: A guide for investigating officers*. Bramshill: Author.

Nelson, R. (1990, December). What really happened on the IOWA? *Popular Science*, pp. 84-87, 120-121.

Nettler, G. (1982). *Killing one another*. Cincinnati: Anderson.

New service available to police: Criminal investigative analysis/Criminal personality profiling. (1993). *Canadian Police Association Yearbook 1992, 4*(50), 81-85.

New system helps locate violent offenders. (1995). *Blue Line Magazine, 7*(11).

Newark, S., & Sullivan, S. (1995, Summer). High risk offenders: Unmasked. *Canadian Police Association Express*, pp. 14-20.

Newman, O. (1972). *Defensible space: Crime prevention through urban design.* New York: Macmillan.

Newman, O. (1996). *Creating defensible space.* Washington, DC: U.S. Department of Housing and Urban Development.

Newton, Jr., M. B., & Newton, D. C. (1985, October). *Geoforensic identification of localized serial crime: Unsolved female homicides, Fort Worth, Texas, 1983-85.* Paper presented at the meeting of the Southwest Division, Association of American Geographers, Denton, TX.

Newton, Jr., M. B., & Swoope, E. A. (1987). *Geoforensic analysis of localized serial murder: The Hillside Stranglers located.* Unpublished manuscript.

Newton, M. (1990a). *Hunting humans: The encyclopedia of serial killers, Volume 1.* New York: Avon Books.

Newton, M. (1990b). *Hunting humans: The encyclopedia of serial killers, Volume 2.* New York: Avon Books.

Newton, M. (1992). *Serial slaughter: What's behind America's murder epidemic?* Port Townsend, WA: Loompanics Unlimited.

Newton, M. (1994). *Silent rage.* New York: Dell.

Newton, M. (1998). *Rope: The twisted life and crimes of Harvey Glatman.* New York: Simon & Schuster.

Newton, M., & Newton, J. A. (1989). *The FBI most wanted: An encyclopedia.* New York: Garland.

Ng, Y. (1981). *Ideology, media, and moral panics: An analysis of the Jacques murder.* Unpublished master's dissertation, University of Toronto, Toronto.

Nichols, Jr., W. W. (1980). Mental maps, social characteristics, and criminal mobility. In D. E. Georges-Abeyie & K. D. Harries (Eds.), *Crime: A spatial perspective* (pp. 156-166). New York: Columbia University Press.

Nicholson, M. (1979). *The Yorkshire Ripper.* London: W. H. Allen.

Nickel, S. (1989). *Torso: The story of Eliot Ness and the search for a psychopathic killer.* Winston-Salem, NC: John F. Blair.

Nobile, P. (1989). The making of a monster. *Playboy*, pp. 41-45.

Normandeau, A. (1968). *Trends and patterns in the crime of robbery.* Unpublished doctoral dissertation, University of Pennsylvania, Philadelphia.

Norris, J. (1988). *Serial killers.* New York: Doubleday.

Norris, J. (1991). *Henry Lee Lucas: The shocking true story of America's most notorious serial killer.* New York: Kensington.

Norris, J. (1992a). *Arthur Shawcross: The Genesee River Killer.* New York: Windsor.

Norris, J. (1992b). *Jeffrey Dahmer.* New York: Windsor.

Norris, J. (1992c). *The killer next door.* London: Random House.

Norris, J. (1992d). *Walking time bombs.* New York: Bantam Books.

O'Brien, D. (1985). *Two of a kind.* New York: New American Library.

O'Donnell, G. (1994). Forensic imaging comes of age. *FBI Law Enforcement Bulletin, 63*(1), 5-10.

O'Neal, C. W., & Wistrand, G. L. (1993, June). NASA offers high-tech support to law enforcement. *The Police Chief,* pp. 50-53.

O'Reilly-Fleming, T. (1992). Serial murder investigation: Prospects for police networking. *Journal of Contemporary Criminal Justice, 8,* 227-234.

O'Reilly-Fleming, T. (Ed.). (1995). *Serial and mass murder: Theory, research and policy.* Toronto: Canadian Scholars' Press.

O'Reilly-Fleming, T. (Ed.). (1996). *Serial and mass murder: Theory, research and policy.* Toronto: Canadian Scholars' Press.

Odland, J. (1988). *Spatial autocorrelation.* Sage university paper series on scientific geography, 9. Newbury Park, CA: Sage.

Ogle, R. S., Maier-Katkin, D., & Bernard, T. J. (1995). A theory of homicidal behavior among women. *Criminology, 33,* 173-193.

Oldfield, D. (1995). *Investigative support for low incidence serious crime.* Unpublished manuscript, Police Research Group, Home Office Police Department, London.

Oliver, T., & Smith, R. (1993). *Lambs to the slaughter.* London: Warner Books.

Olligschlaeger, A. M. (1997). Artificial neural networks and crime mapping. In D. A. Weisburd & J. T. McEwen (Eds.), *Crime mapping and crime prevention: Crime prevention studies, Vol. 8* (pp. 313-347). Monsey, NY: Criminal Justice Press.

Olsen, J. (1983). *"Son": A psychopath and his victims.* New York: Dell.

Olsen, J. (1993). *The misbegotten son.* New York: Dell.

Olson, C. R. (1989). *Profile of a serial killer – The Clifford Olson Case.* Unpublished manuscript.

Olson, C. R. (1992a). *Inside the mind of a serial killer – A profile.* Unpublished manuscript.

Olson, C. R. (1992b). *The phenomena of serial murder – Ten questions.* Unpublished manuscript.

Olson, J. M., & Brewer, C.A. (1997). An evaluation of color selections to accommodate map users with color-vision impairments. *Annals of the Association of American Geographers, 87,* 103-134.

Ostler, T. (1994, July). Making designs on a safer city. *Geographical,* pp. 29-31.

Ouimet, M., & Proulx, J. (1994, November). *Spatial and temporal behaviour of pedophiles: Their clinical usefulness as to the relapse prevention model.* Paper presented at the meeting of the American Society of Criminology, Miami, FL.

Owens, A. M. (1996, March). Living in the shadow. *Canadian Living,* pp. 51-59.

Page, D. W. (1989, July 23). Picking up the trail of serial murderers. *The Victoria Times-Colonist,* pp. A1-A2.

Papa, J. (1995). *Ladykiller.* New York: St. Martin's Press.

Pape, H., & Pedersen, W. (1997, June). *Dangerous victims of violence?: A general population study of violent victimization among young men and women.* Paper presented at the Seminar on Environmental Criminology and Crime Analysis, Oslo, Norway.

Park, R. E. (1936). Human ecology. *American Journal of Sociology, 42,* 1-15.

Park, R. E., Burgess, E. W., & McKenzie, R. D. (Eds.). (1925). *The city.* Chicago: University of Chicago Press.

Patterns of murders committed by one person, in large numbers with no apparent rhyme, reason, or motivation. (1983). Hearings before the Subcommittee on Juvenile Justice of the Committee on the Judiciary, Senate, 98th Congress, 1st Session (Serial No. J-98-52). Washington, DC: U.S. Government Printing Office.

Pearson, P. (1994, June). Murder on her mind. *Saturday Night,* pp. 46-53, 64-68.

Pearson, P. (1995, October). Behind every successful psychopath. *Saturday Night,* pp. 50-63.

Pearson, P. (1997). *When she was bad: Violent women and the myth of innocence.* Toronto: Random House.

Pease, K., & Laycock, G. (1996). *Revictimization: Reducing the heat on hot victims* (NIJ Publication No. NCJ-162951). Washington, DC: U.S. Government Printing Office.

Pemberton, K. (1989b, November 9). Police probe for links among unsolved killings. *The Vancouver Sun,* p. B6.

Pemberton, K. (1992). Serial killers murder close to home, officer's study reports. *Blue Line Magazine, 4*(9), 16.

Petee, T. A., Padgett, K. G., & York, T. S. (1997). Debunking the stereotype: An examination of mass murder in public places. *Homicide Studies, 1,* 317-337.

Peters, W. T. (1990, September). *Psychological profiling.* Lecture presented at Prince Albert Police Training Committee, Prince Albert, SK.

Petit, M. (1990). *A need to kill.* New York: Ivy Books.

Petrucci, S. J. (1997a, February). *A historical, legal, and psychological view of the sexually predator.* Paper presented at the conference of the Western Society of Criminology, Honolulu, HI.

Petrucci, S. J. (1997b). *Victim-Acquisition techniques of serial sexual killers.* Unpublished master's thesis, California State University, Fresno, CA.

Petrucci, S. J. (1998, February). *A victim-acquisition technique typology of serial sexual killers.* Paper presented at the conference of the Western Society of Criminology, Newport Beach, CA.

Pettiway, L. E. (1982). Mobility of robbery and burglary offenders: Ghetto and nonghetto spaces. *Urban Affairs Quarterly, 18,* 255-270.

Pettiway, L. E. (1995). Copping crack: The travel behavior of crack users. *Justice Quarterly, 12,* 499-524.

Pfaffenberger, B. (1988). *Microcomputer applications in qualitative research.* Sage university paper series on qualitative research methods, 14. Newbury Park, CA: Sage.

Phillips, P. (1980). Characteristics and typology of the journey to crime. In D. E. Georges-Abeyie & K. D. Harries (Eds.), *Crime: A spatial perspective* (pp. 167-180). New York: Columbia University Press.

Philpin, J., & Donnelly, J. (1994). *Beyond murder.* New York: Penguin Books.

Pickett, P. O. (1993). Linguistics in the courtroom. *FBI Law Enforcement Bulletin, 62*(10), 6-9.

Pilant, L. (1994, January). Information management. *The Police Chief,* pp. 30-38, 42-47.

Pinizzotto, A. J. (1984). Forensic psychology: Criminal personality profiling. *Journal of Police Science and Administration, 12,* 32-40.

Pinizzotto, A. J., & Finkel, N. J. (1990). Criminal personality profiling: An outcome and process study. *Law and Human Behavior, 14,* 215-233.

Pinto, S., & Wilson, P. R. (1990). *Serial murder* (Trends and Issues in Crime and Criminal Justice No. 25). Canberra: Australian Institute of Criminology.

Ploughman, P. D., & Ould, P. J. (1990, November). *Toward a self-protective, rational calculus: The nexus of routine activities and rape victimization risk.* Paper presented at the meeting of the American Society of Criminology, Baltimore, MD.

Poethig, M. (1989, Fall). Hot spots and isocrimes. *The Compiler,* pp. 11-13.

Pokorny, A. D. (1965). A comparison of homicide in two cities. *Journal of Criminal Law, Criminology and Police Science, 56,* 479-487.

The police were blinded by their own information. (1981, May 24). *The Sunday Times,* pp. 13-15.

Police zero in on serial killers. (1995, June 1). *The Vancouver Sun,* p. A11.

Poole, H., & Jurovics, S. (1993). MUST: A team for unsolved homicides. *FBI Law Enforcement Bulletin, 62*(3), 1-4.

Pope, C. E. (1980). Patterns in burglary: An empirical examination of offense and offender characteristics. *Journal of Criminal Justice, 8*(1), 39-51.

Popkin, J. (1994, September 19). Natural born predators. *U.S. News and World Report,* pp. 64-68, 73.

Porteous, J. D. (1973). The Burnside Teenage Gang: Territoriality, social space, and community planning. In C. N. Forward (Ed.), *Residential and Neighbourhood Studies in Victoria,* (pp. 130-148). Victoria, BC: Western Geographical Series.

Porteous, J. D. (1977). *Environment and behavior: Planning and everyday urban life.* Reading, MA: Addison-Wesley.

Porter, B. (1983, April). Mind hunters. *Psychology Today,* pp. 44-52.

Poythress, N., Otto, R. K., Darkes, J., & Starr, L. (1993, January). APA's expert panel in the Congressional review of the USS *Iowa* incident. *American Psychologist,* 8-15.

Prentky, A. P., Burgess, A. W., Rokous, B. A., Lee, A., Hartman, C., Ressler, R. K., & Douglas, J. E. (1989). The presumptive role of fantasy in serial sexual homicide. *American Journal of Psychiatry, 146,* 887-891.

Prentky, R. A., & Quinsey, V. L. (Eds.). (1988). *Human sexual aggression: Current perspectives.* New York: Annals of the New York Academy of Sciences.

Priest, L. (1992). *Women who killed.* Toronto: McClelland and Stewart.

Prieur, A. (1989, November). *The male role, prostitution and sexual assaults.* Paper presented at the meeting of the American Society of Criminology, Reno, NV.

Project "Green Ribbon." (1992). *RCMP Gazette, 54*(7 & 8), 24-26.

Pron, N. (1995). *Lethal marriage.* Toronto: Seal Books.

Psychology today: An introduction (2nd ed.). (1972). Del Mar, CA: CRM Books.

Pulitzer, L. B., & Swirsky, J. (1994a, February). The confessions of Joel Rifkin. *Penthouse,* pp. 30-35, 42, 68-72, 88.

Pulitzer, L. B., & Swirsky, J. (1994b). *Crossing the line.* New York: Berkley Books.

Pyle, G. F. (1974). *The spatial dynamics of crime* (Research Paper No. 159). Chicago: Department of Geography, University of Chicago.

Pyle, G. F. (1976). Spatial aspects of crime in Cleveland, Ohio. *American Behavioral Scientist, 20,* 175-198.

R. v. Clark (1998), unreported, O.C.J. (General Division).

R. v. Mohan (1994), 89 C.C.C. (3d) 402 (S.C.C.).

Raab, S. (1993, August 1). Serial murder tangle: Where to begin? *The New York Times,* p. 41.

Ramsay, J. (1972, July 29). It is true that nothing is sacred? *The New York Times,* p. 25.

Rand, A. (1986). Mobility triangles. In R. M. Figlio, S. Hakim, & G. F. Rengert (Eds.), *Metropolitan crime patterns* (pp. 117-126). Monsey, NY: Criminal Justice Press.

Rand, M. R. (1987). *Violent crime trends* (BJS Publication No. NCJ-107217). Washington, DC: U.S. Government Printing Office.

Rand, M. R., DeBerry, M., Klaus, P., & Taylor, B. (1986). *The use of weapons in committing crimes* (BJS Publication No. NCJ-99643). Washington, DC: U.S. Government Printing Office.

Rand McNally road atlas. (1994). New York: Rand McNally.

Randall, W. S. (1988). Tom Quick's revenge. *The Quarterly Journal of Military History, 4,* 70-75.

Rappaport, R. G. (1988). The serial and mass murderer: Patterns, differentiation, pathology. *American Journal of Forensic Psychiatry, 9,* 39-48.

Raskin, D. C. (Ed.). (1989). *Psychological methods in criminal investigation and evidence.* New York: Springer.

Read, T., & Oldfield, D. (1995). *Local crime analysis* (Crime Detection and Prevention Series: Paper 65). London: Police Research Group, Home Office Police Department

Reaves, B. A. (1993). *Using NIBRS Data to analyze violent crime* (BJS Publication No. NCJ-144785). Washington, DC: U.S. Government Printing Office.

Reber, A. S. (1985). *The Penguin dictionary of psychology.* Harmondsworth, Middlesex: Penguin.

Reboussin, R., & Cameron, J. (1989). Expert systems for law enforcement. *FBI Law Enforcement Bulletin, 58*(8), 12-16.

Reboussin, R., Warren, J. I., & Hazelwood, R. R. (1993). "Mapless mapping" and the windshield wiper effect in the spatial distribution of serial rapes. In C. R. Block & R. L. Block (Eds.), *Questions and answers in lethal and non-lethal violence: Proceedings of the Second Annual Workshop of the Homicide Research Working Group* (NIJ Publication No. NCJ-147480) (pp. 149-154). Washington, DC: U.S. Government Printing Office.

Reboussin, R., Warren, J. I., & Hazelwood, R. R. (1995). Mapless mapping in analyzing the spatial distribution of serial rapes. In C. R. Block, M. Dabdoub, & S. Fregly (Eds.), *Crime analysis through computer mapping* (pp. 59-64). Washington, DC: Police Executive Research Forum.

Rebscher, E., & Rohrer, F. (1991). Police information retrieval systems and the role of electronic data processing. In E. Kube & H. U. Störzer (Eds.), *Police research in the Federal Republic of Germany: 15 years research within the "Bundeskriminalamt"* (pp. 241-251). Berlin: Springer-Velag.

Reed, P., & Gaucher, R. (1976, November). *Repetitive violence among persons suspected or convicted of homicide in Canada, 1961-74.* Paper presented at the meeting of the American Society of Criminology, Tucson, AZ.

Reese, J. T. (1979). Obsessive compulsive behavior: The nuisance offender. *FBI Law Enforcement Bulletin, 48*(8), 6-12.

Reid, P. (1996, October 13). Fit the profile, pay the price. *The Edmonton Journal,* p. F5.

Reiss, Jr., A. J. (1967). *Place of residence of arrested persons compared with the place where the offence charged in arrest occurred for Part I and II offences.* A Report to the President's Commission on Law Enforcement and Administration of Justice, Washington, DC: U.S. Government Printing Office.

Remesch, K. (1993). Unsolved homicides: No thriller for officers. *Police, 17*(10), 50-52, 55.

Rengert, G. F. (1975). Some effects of being female on criminal spatial behavior. *The Pennsylvania Geographer, 13*(2), 10-18.

Rengert, G. F. (1981). A critique of an opportunity structure model. In P. J. Brantingham & P. L. Brantingham (Eds.), *Environmental criminology* (pp. 189-201). Beverly Hills: Sage.

Rengert, G. F. (1990, November). *Drug purchasing as a routine activity of drug dependent property criminals and the spatial concentration of crime.* Paper presented at the meeting of the American Society of Criminology, Baltimore, MD.

Rengert, G. F. (1991, November). *The spatial clustering of residential burglaries about anchor points of routine activities.* Paper presented at the meeting of the American Society of Criminology, San Francisco, CA.

Rengert, G. F. (1992, November). *The perception of opportunities and risks by residential burglars.* Paper presented at the meeting of the American Society of Criminology, New Orleans, LA.

Rengert, G. F. (1993, October). *Psychological profiles and criminal search processes of residential burglars.* Paper presented at the meeting of the American Society of Criminology, Phoenix, AZ.

Rengert, G. F. (1996). *The geography of illegal drugs.* Boulder, CO: Westview Press.

Rengert, G. F., & Mattson, M. (1998, June). *Using high-definition geographic information systems to track campus crime.* Paper presented at the Seminar on Environmental Criminology and Crime Analysis, Barcelona, Spain.

Rengert, G. F., Piquero, A. R., & Jones, P. R. (1999). Distance decay reexamined. *Criminology, 37,* 427-445.

Rengert, G. F., & Wasilchick, J. (1985). *Suburban burglary.* Springfield, IL: Charles C. Thomas.

Reppetto, T. A. (1974). *Residential crime.* Cambridge, MA: Ballinger.

Reppetto, T. A. (1976). Crime prevention and the displacement phenomenon. *Crime and Delinquency, 22,* 168-169.

Ressler, R. K. (1989, November). *Sexual homicide: Patterns and motives.* Paper presented at the meeting of the American Society of Criminology, Reno, NV.

Ressler, R. K. (1993, March). *Profiling serial killers.* Lecture presented at Mount Royal College, Calgary, AB.

Ressler, R. K., & Burgess, A. W. (1985). Classifying sexual homicide crime scenes: Interrater reliability. *FBI Law Enforcement Bulletin, 54*(8), 12-17.

Ressler, R. K., Burgess, A. W., & Douglas, J. E. (1988). *Sexual homicide: Patterns and motives.* Lexington, MA: Lexington Books.

Ressler, R. K., Burgess, A. W., Douglas, J. E., Hartman, C. R., & D'Agostino, R. B. (1986). Sexual killers and their victims: Identifying patterns through crime scene analysis. *Journal of Interpersonal Violence, 1,* 288-308.

Ressler, R. K., Burgess, A. W., Hartman, C. R., Douglas, J. E., & McCormack, A. (1986). Murderers who rape and mutilate. *Journal of Interpersonal Violence, 1,* 273-287.

Ressler, R. K., Douglas, J. E., Groth, A. N., & Burgess, A. W. (1980). Offender profiles: A multidisciplinary approach. *FBI Law Enforcement Bulletin, 49*(9), 16-20.

Ressler, R. K., & Shachtman, T. (1992). *Whoever fights monsters.* New York: St. Martin's Press.

Ressler, R. K., & Shachtman, T. (1997). *I have lived in the monster.* New York: St. Martin's Press.

Reuland, M. M. (Ed.). (1997). *Information management and crime analysis: Practitioners' recipes for success.* Washington, DC: Police Executive Research Forum.

Review of Navy investigation of U.S.S. Iowa explosion. (1990). Joint hearings before the Investigations Subcommittee and the Defense Policy Panel of the Committee on Armed Services, House of Representatives, 101st Congress, 1st Session (HASC No. 101-41). Washington, DC: U.S. Government Printing Office.

Revitch, E. (1965). Sex murder and the potential sex murderer. *Diseases of the Nervous System, 26,* 640-648.

Reynolds, M. (1991, February). The terror in Gainesville. *Playboy,* pp. 72-73, 130-139.

Reynolds, M. (1992). *Dead ends.* New York: Warner Books.

Rho, Y. (1975). Forensic pathology in crimes of violence. *FBI Law Enforcement Bulletin, 44*(10), 1-3.

Rhodes, D. (1995, April). Taking samples. *Police Review,* pp. 15-17.

Rhodes, W. M., & Conly, C. (1981). Crime and mobility: An empirical study. In P. J. Brantingham & P. L. Brantingham (Eds.), *Environmental criminology* (pp. 167-188). Beverly Hills: Sage.

Rich, T. F. (1995). *The use of computerized mapping in crime control and prevention programs* (NIJ Publication No. NCJ-155182). Washington, DC: U.S. Government Printing Office.

Rich, T. F. (1996). *The Chicago Police Department's Information Collection for Automated Mapping (ICAM) Program* (NIJ Publication No. NCJ-160764). Washington, DC: U.S. Government Printing Office.

Richter, D. (1989). Murder in jest: Serial killing in the post-modern detective story. *The Journal of Narrative Technique, 19,* 106-115.

Rider, A. O. (1994). *The firesetter: A psychological profile* (2nd ed.). Quantico, VA: Federal Bureau of Investigation.

Riedel, M. (1997). Counting stranger homicides: A case study of statistical prestidigitation. *Homicide Studies, 2,* 206-219.

Riedel, M., & Boulahanis, J. (Eds.). (1997). *Lethal violence: Proceedings of the 1995 Meeting of the Homicide Research Working Group* (NIJ Research Report). Washington, DC: U.S. Government Printing Office.

Riedel, M., & Przybylski, R. K. (1993). Stranger murders and assault: A study of a neglected form of stranger violence. In A. V. Wilson (Ed.), *Homicide: The victim/offender connection* (chap. 17). Cincinnati: Anderson.

Riedel, M., & Zahn, M. A. (1985). *The nature and patterns of American homicide* (NIJ Publication). Washington, DC: U.S. Government Printing Office.

Riesenberg, D. (1989). Child molestation and pedophilia: An overview for the physician. *Journal of the American Medical Association, 261,* 602-606.

Robbins, R. (1977). *Mantracking.* Montrose, CA: Search and Rescue Magazine.

Robbins, S. R. (1991). *The spatial typology of serial murder: An exploration of the differences in the methods, motivations, and selected variables between the geographically stable and the geographically transient serial killers.* Unpublished master's thesis, University of Louisville, Louisville, KY.

Roberts, D. (1994, December 20). Number of missing native women alarms police in Western Canada. *The Toronto Globe and Mail,* pp. A1, A5.

Robertson, B., & Vignaux, G. A. (1995). *Interpreting evidence: Evaluating forensic evidence in the courtroom.* Chichester: John Wiley & Sons.

Robinson, P. (1997). ViCLAS, crimes linkage analysis system. *Blue Line Magazine, 9*(7), 14-15.

Rogers, A. (1985). *Regional population projection models.* Sage university paper series on scientific geography, 4. Beverly Hills: Sage.

Rogers, R., Craig, D., & Anderson, D. (1991, March). *Serial murder investigations and geographic information systems.* Paper presented at the conference of the Academy of Criminal Justice Sciences, Nashville, TN.

Rohr, J. (1990). *Violence in America: Opposing viewpoints.* San Diego: Greenhaven Press.

Roncek, D. W., & Maier, P. A. (1991). Bars, blocks, and crimes revisited: Linking the theory of routine activities to the empiricism of "hot spots." *Criminology, 29,* 725-753.

Roncek, D. W., & Montgomery, A. (1984). *Spatial autocorrelation: Diagnoses and remedies for large samples.* Paper presented at the meeting of the Midwest Sociological Society, Des Moines, IA.

Rose, H. M., & McClain, P. D. (1990). *Place, race, and risk: Black homicide in urban America.* Albany, NY: State University of New York Press.

Rosen, J. C., & McReynolds, P. (Eds.). (1992). *Advances in psychological assessment: Vol. 8.* New York: Plenum Press.

Rosenbaum, R. (1990a, May). Travels with Dr. Death. *Vanity Fair,* pp. 141-147, 166-174.

Rosenbaum, R. (1990b, September). Dead reckoning. *Vanity Fair,* pp. 190-197, 274-285.

Rosenbaum, R. (1993, April). The F.B.I.'s agent provocateur. *Vanity Fair,* pp. 122-136.

Rossmo, D. K. (1987). *Fugitive migration patterns.* Unpublished master's thesis, Simon Fraser University, Burnaby, BC.

Rossmo, D. K. (1992, April). *Targeting victims: Serial killers and the urban environment.* Paper presented at the First International Conference on Serial and Mass Murder: Theory, Research and Policy, Windsor, ON.

Rossmo, D. K. (1993a). Geographic profiling: Locating serial killers. In D. Zahm & P. F. Cromwell (Eds.), *Proceedings of the International Seminar on Environmental Criminology and Crime Analysis* (pp. 14-29). Coral Gables, FL: Florida Criminal Justice Executive Institute.

Rossmo, D. K. (1993b). Target patterns of serial murderers: A methodological model. *American Journal of Criminal Justice, 17*(2), 1-21.

Rossmo, D. K. (1994a, Fall). STAC tools: The Crime Site Probability Program. *STAC News,* pp. 9, 14.

Rossmo, D. K. (1994b). A primer on criminal geographic targeting. *IALEIA Journal, 9*(1), 1-12.

Rossmo, D. K. (1995a). *Geographic profiling: Target patterns of serial murderers.* Unpublished doctoral dissertation, Simon Fraser University, Burnaby, BC.

Rossmo, D. K. (1995b). Multivariate spatial profiles as a tool in crime investigation. In C. R. Block, M. Dabdoub, & S. Fregly (Eds.), *Crime analysis through computer mapping* (pp. 65-97). Washington, DC: Police Executive Research Forum.

Rossmo, D. K. (1995c). Place, space, and police investigations: Hunting serial violent criminals. In J. E. Eck & D. A. Weisburd (Eds.), *Crime and place: Crime prevention studies, Vol. 4* (pp. 217-235). Monsey, NY: Criminal Justice Press.

Rossmo, D. K. (1995d). Strategic crime patterning: Problem-Oriented policing and displacement. In C. R. Block, M. Dabdoub, & S. Fregly (Eds.), *Crime analysis through computer mapping* (pp. 1-14). Washington, DC: Police Executive Research Forum.

Rossmo, D. K. (1996). Targeting victims: Serial killers and the urban environment. In T. O'Reilly-Fleming (Ed.), *Serial and mass murder: Theory, research and policy* (pp. 133-153). Toronto: Canadian Scholars' Press.

Rossmo, D. K. (1997). Geographic profiling. In J. L. Jackson & D. A. Bekerian (Eds.), *Offender profiling: Theory, research and practice* (pp. 159-175). Chichester: John Wiley & Sons.

Rossmo, D. K. (1998). Target patterns of serial murderers: A methodological model. In R. M. Holmes & S. T. Holmes (Eds.), *Contemporary perspectives on serial murder* (pp. 199-217). Thousand Oaks, CA: Sage.

Rossmo, D. K., & Baeza, J. J. (1998). *The Upper East Side Rapist: A case study in geographic profiling.* Paper presented at the meeting of the American Society of Criminology, Washington, DC.

Rossmo, D. K., & Routledge, R. (1990). Estimating the size of criminal populations. *Journal of Quantitative Criminology, 6,* 293-314.

Roth, J. A. (1994a). *Firearms and violence* (NIJ Publication No. NCJ-145533). Washington, DC: U.S. Government Printing Office.

Roth, J. A. (1994b). *Psychoactive substances and violence* (NIJ Publication No. NCJ-145534). Washington, DC: U.S. Government Printing Office.

Roth, J. A. (1994c). *Understanding and preventing violence* (NIJ Publication No. NCJ-145645). Washington, DC: U.S. Government Printing Office.

Rule, A. (1980). *The stranger beside me.* New York: Penguin Books.

Rule, A. (1983a). *Lust Killer.* New York: Penguin Books.

Rule, A. (1983b). *The Want-Ad Killer.* New York: Penguin Books.

Rule, A. (1984). *The I-5 Killer.* New York: Penguin Books.

Rumbelow, D. (1977). The Ripper's ladies. In D. Winn (Ed.), *Murder ink* (pp. 200-202). New York: Workman.

Rumbelow, D. (1988). *Jack the Ripper: The complete casebook.* Chicago: Contemporary Books.

Rushton, G., & Lolonis, P. (in press). Exploratory spatial analysis of birth defect rates in an urban population. *Statistics in Medicine.*

Sabljak, M., & Greenberg, M. H. (1990). *Most wanted: A history of the FBI's Ten Most Wanted list.* New York: Bonanza Books.

Sacco, V. F., & Kennedy, L. W. (1996). *The criminal event.* Belmont, CA: Wadsworth.

Sacks, D. (1999). Tracking. *RCMP Gazette,* 61(2/3), 10-12.

Sapp, A. D., Huff, T. G., Gary, G. P., & Icove, D. J. (1994). *A motive-based offender analysis of serial arsonists.* Quantico, VA: National Center for the Analysis of Violent Crime.

Sapp, A. D., Huff, T. G., Gary, G. P., Icove, D. J., & Horbert, P. (1994). *A report of essential findings from a study of serial arsonists.* Quantico, VA: National Center for the Analysis of Violent Crime.

Sargeant, F. (1994, May). Death stalks the hunter. *Sports Afield,* pp. 79-81.

Saville, G. J. (Ed.). (1994). *Crime problems, community solutions.* Port Moody, BC: AAG Inc. Publications.

Saville, G. J., & Murdie, R. (1988). The spatial analysis of motor vehicle theft: A case study of Peel Region, Ontario. *Journal of Police Science and Administration, 16,* 126-135.

Schaller, G. B. (1972). *The Serengeti lion: A study of predator-prey relations.* Chicago: University of Chicago Press.

Schechter, H. (1989). *Deviant.* New York: Simon & Schuster.

Schechter, H. (1990). *Deranged.* New York: Simon & Schuster.

Schechter, H. (1994). *Depraved.* New York: Simon & Schuster.

Schechter, H., & Everitt, D. (1996). *The A to Z encyclopedia of serial killers.* New York: Simon & Schuster.

Schlesinger, L.B., & Revitch, E. (1999). Sexual burglaries and sexual homicide: Clinical, forensic, and investigative considerations. *Journal of the American Academy of Psychiatry and the Law,* 27, 227-238.

Schmitt, J. B. (1992, February). Computerized ID systems. *The Police Chief,* pp. 32-45.

Schreiber, F. R. (1983). *The shoemaker.* New York: Simon & Schuster.

Schutze, J. (1989). *The Matamoros cult killings.* New York: Avon.

Schwarz, T. (1981). *The Hillside Strangler: A murderer's mind.* New York: Penguin Books.

Scott, H. (1992). *The female serial killer: A well kept secret of the 'gentler sex.'* Unpublished master's thesis, University of Guelph, Guelph, ON.

Sears, D. J. (1991). *To kill again: The motivation and development of serial murder.* Wilmington, DE: Scholarly Resources.

The secret identify of Jack the Ripper. (1988, October 26). *KCPQ.* Tacoma, WA.

Segrave, K. (1992). *Women serial and mass murderers: A worldwide reference, 1580 through 1990.* Jefferson, NC: McFarland.

Seltzer, M. (1998). *Serial killers: Death and life in America's wound culture.* New York: Routledge.

Serial killer may still be at work. (1993, March 24). *Winnipeg Free Press,* p. B5.

Serial murderers' trial underway in Ukraine. (1998, November 24). *Comtex Newswire.*

Sessions, W. S. (1989, June). Violent Criminal Apprehension Program: Essential link to joint investigations. *The Police Chief,* pp. 40-44.

Seven, R. (1990, January 1). Green River force cut again. *The Seattle Times,* pp. B1, B3.

Sevilla, C. M. (1990). *Anti-Social personality disorder: Justification for the death penalty?* Unpublished manuscript.

Sex prints. (1991, May 25). *New Scientist.*

Sgarzi, J. M., & Fusfeld, R. T. (1993, October). *The media's influence on behavior and violence.* Paper presented at the meeting of the American Society of Criminology, Phoenix, AZ.

Shargorodsky, S. (1998, November 22). Ukraine – Serial Murders. *Associated Press Newswire.*

Shaw, C. R., & McKay, H. D. (1972). *Juvenile delinquency and urban areas* (rev. ed.). Chicago: University of Chicago Press.

Shaw, S. (1998). *Applying environmental psychology and criminology: The relationship between crime site locations within offences of murder.* Unpublished undergraduate thesis, University of Plymouth, England.

Shedding light on Russian justice. (1992, October 15). *USA Today,* p. 2A.

Sheptycki, J. W. E. (1999). [Review of Contemporary perspectives on serial murder; Serial murder (2nd ed.)]. *British Journal of Criminology, 39,* 323-329.

Sherman, L. W., Gartin, P. R., & Buerger, M. E. (1989). Hotspots of predatory crime: Routine activities and the criminology of place. *Criminology, 27,* 27-55.

Shubik, M. (1982). *Game theory in the social sciences: Concepts and solutions.* Cambridge, MA: MIT Press.

Siegel, L. J. (1992). *Criminology: Theories, patterns, and typologies.* St. Paul, MN: West.

Sikorski, W., Laabs, R. (1998). *Checkpoint Charlie and the Wall* (G. Bailey, Trans.). Berlin: Ullstein. (Original work published 1997).

Silverman, R. A., & Kennedy, L. W. (1993). *Deadly deeds: Murder in Canada.* Scarborough, ON: Nelson Canada.

Silverman, R. A., & Teevan, Jr., J. J. (1975). *Crime in Canadian society.* Toronto: Butterworth.

Simandl, R. J. (1990, January). *Ritual crime investigation.* Lecture presented at the Justice Institute of British Columbia, Police Academy seminar, Vancouver.

Simon, D. (1991). *Homicide: A year on the killing streets.* New York: Ballantine Books.

Simonetti, C. (1984). *Serial murders: 1970-1983.* Unpublished master's thesis, State University of New York at Albany, Albany, NY.

Simons, J. (1994, September 19). Seeking victims in cyberspace. *U.S. News and World Report*, p. 73.

Skiba, K. M. (1994, October). Ex-State resident looked to Gein for inspiration to write 'Psycho.' *The Milwaukee Journal*, pp. 1, 3.

Skinner, M., & Lazenby, R. A. (1983). *Found! Human remains: A field manual for the recovery of the recent human skeleton.* Burnaby, BC: Archaeology Press, Simon Fraser University.

Skogan, W. G., & Atunes, G. E. (1979). Information, apprehension, and deterrence: Exploring the limits of police productivity. *Journal of Criminal Justice, 7*, 217-241.

Smith, C. (1993). *Fatal charm.* New York: Penguin Books.

Smith, C. (1994). *Killing season.* New York: Penguin Books.

Smith, C., & Guillen, T. (1991). *The search for the Green River Killer.* New York: Penguin Books.

Smith, H. E. (1987). Serial killers. *CJ International, 3*(1), 1, 4.

Smith, J. N. M. (1974a). The food searching behaviour of two European thrushes I: Description and analysis of search paths. *Behaviour, 48*, 276-302.

Smith, J. N. M. (1974b). The food searching behaviour of two European thrushes II: The adaptiveness of the search patterns. *Behaviour, 49*, 1-61.

Smith, J. N. M., & Sweatman, H. P. A. (1974). Food-searching behavior of titmice in patchy environments. *Ecology, 55*, 1216-1232.

Smith, S. J. (1986). *Crime, space and society.* Cambridge: Cambridge University Press.

Smith, T. E. (1974). *A choice theory of spatial interaction.* RSRI discussion paper series, 74. Philadelphia: Regional Research Institute.

Smith, W. R., Kühlhorn, E., & Borschos, B.. (1997, June). *Alcohol sales at restaurants/bars and assaults: Geographic data and the prevention of violence.* Paper presented at the Seminar on Environmental Criminology and Crime Analysis, Oslo, Norway.

Snell, T. L. (1996). *Capital punishment 1995* (BJS Publication No. NCJ-162043). Washington, DC: U.S. Government Printing Office.

Snyder, H. N., & Sickmund, M. (1995a). *Juvenile offenders and victims: A focus on violence* (OJJDP Publication No. NCJ 153570). Washington, DC: U.S. Government Printing Office.

Snyder, H. N., & Sickmund, M. (1995b). *Juvenile offenders and victims: A national report* (OJJDP Publication No. NCJ 153569). Washington, DC: U.S. Government Printing Office

Sobol, J. J. (1997). Behavioral characteristics and level of involvement for victims of homicide. *Homicide Studies, 1*, 359-376.

Soley, B. J. (1998). *Looking for love: Dysfunctional attachment in repeat sexual offenders.* Unpublished doctoral dissertation, Brandeis University, Waltham, MA.

Soley, B. J., Knight, R. A., Cerce, D. D., & Holmes, K. (forthcoming). Cultivating prediction of rapist types from crime-scene variables. *Behavioral Sciences and the Law.*

Som, R. K. (1973). *A manual of sampling techniques.* London: Heinemann Educational Books.

Sorensen, S. L. (1997). SMART mapping for law enforcement settings: Integrating GIS and GPS for dynamic, near-real time applications and analyses. In D. A. Weisburd & J. T. McEwen (Eds.), *Crime mapping and crime prevention: Crime prevention studies, Vol. 8* (pp. 349-378). Monsey, NY: Criminal Justice Press.

Sounes, H. (1995). *Fred & Rose.* London: Warner Books.

Sourour, T. Z. (1990). *Rapport d'investigation du Coroner* [Report of the investigation of the Coroner]. Montréal: Gouvernement du Québec, Bureau du Coroner.

Sparrow, M. K. (1994, April). Measuring AFIS matcher accuracy. *The Police Chief,* pp. 147-151.

Spelman, W. G. (1987). *Beyond bean counting: New approaches for managing crime data.* Washington, DC: Police Executive Research Forum.

Spiering, F. (1995). *Who killed Polly?* Monterey, CA: Monterey Press.

Spinks, S. (1985). *Stolen lives.* Toronto: Dell.

The split reality of murder. (1985). *FBI Law Enforcement Bulletin, 54*(8), 7-11.

Spore, C. V. (1994, March). *The antisocial personality disorder as found in serial murderers.* Paper presented at the meeting of the Academy of Criminal Justice Sciences, Chicago, IL.

Springer, P. (1994). *Blood rush.* New York: Windsor.

The Stagg letters. (1994, September 25). *The People,* pp. 2-5.

Stanley, A. (1983, November 14). Catching a new breed of killer. *Time Magazine,* p. 47.

Stark, R. (1987). Deviant places: A theory of the ecology of crime. *Criminology, 25,* 893-909.

Starr, M. (1984, November 26). The random killers. *Newsweek,* pp. 100, 104-106.

Stea, D. (1969). The measurement of mental maps: An experimental model for studying conceptual spaces. In K. R. Cox & R. G. Golledge (Eds.), *Behavioral problems in geography* (pp. 228-253). Evanston, IL: Northwestern University Press.

Stephens, D. W., & Krebs, J. R. (1986). *Foraging theory.* Princeton, NJ: Princeton University Press.

Stephenson, L. K. (1974). Spatial dispersion of intra-urban juvenile delinquency. *Journal of Geography, 73*(3), 20-26.

Stephenson, L. K. (1980). Centrographic analysis of crime. In D. E. Georges-Abeyie & K. D. Harries (Eds.), *Crime: A spatial perspective* (pp. 146-155). New York: Columbia University Press.

Steward, J. R. (1992, January). A kiss for my killer. *Redbook*, pp. 76-83.

Stoufer, A. (1960). Intervening opportunities and competing migrants. *Journal of Regional Science, 1,* 1-20.

Strandberg, K. W. (1994, April). FBI's "Drugfire." *Law Enforcement Technology,* pp. 50-51.

Strean, H., & Freeman, L. (1991). *Our wish to kill: The murder in all our hearts.* New York: Avon Books.

Sullivan, S. (1995, Summer). Just doing it. *Canadian Police Association Express,* pp. 10-12.

Sullivan, T., & Maiken, P. T. (1983). *Killer clown.* New York: Windsor.

Sunde, S. (1993, November 25). Crime computer HITS pay dirt in serial rape case. *Seattle Post-Intelligencer,* pp. B1-B2.

Suttles, G. C. (1968). *The social order of the slum.* Chicago: University of Chicago Press.

Sweet, S. (1996, November). *The effects of a new public transportation stop on nearby crime.* Paper presented at the meeting of the American Society of Criminology, Chicago, IL.

Szakas, J. (1997, November). *Auto thefts, chop shops and GIS.* Paper presented at the meeting of the American Society of Criminology, San Diego, CA.

Szasz, T. S. (1971). *The myth of mental illness.* New York: Harper and Row.

Tanay, E. (1983). The Lindbergh kidnapping – A psychiatric view. *Journal of Forensic Sciences, 28,* 1076-1082.

Taylor, P. J. (1977). *Quantitative methods in geography.* Prospect Heights, IL: Waveland Press.

Taylor, R. B. (1997, July). *Crime and Place: What we know, what we can prevent, and what else we need to know.* Paper presented at the National Institute of Justice Annual Research and Evaluation Conference, Washington, DC.

Taylor, R. B., & Harrell, A. V. (1996). *Physical environment and crime* (NIJ Publication No. NCJ-157311). Washington, DC: U.S. Government Printing Office.

Terry, G., & Malone, M. P. (1987a). The "Bobby Joe" Long serial murder case: A study in cooperation (Part 1). *FBI Law Enforcement Bulletin, 56*(11), 12-18.

Terry, G., & Malone, M. P. (1987b). The "Bobby Joe" Long serial murder case: A study in cooperation (Conclusion). *FBI Law Enforcement Bulletin, 56*(12), 7-13.

Terry, M. (1987). *The ultimate evil.* New York: Bantam Books.

Teten, H. D. (1989). Offender profiling. In W. G. Bailey (Ed.), *The encyclopedia of police science* (pp. 365-367). New York: Garland.

Theodorson, G. A., & Theodorson, A. G. (1969). *A modern dictionary of sociology.* New York: Thomas Y. Crowell.

Thompson, M. (1996). Zeroing in on the serial killer. *RCMP Gazette, 58*(3), 14-15.

Time-Life Books. (1992a). *Mass murderers.* Alexandria, VA: Author.

Time-Life Books. (1992b). *Serial killers.* Alexandria, VA: Author.

Time-Life Books. (1993). *Compulsion to kill.* Alexandria, VA: Author.

Timrots, A. D., & Rand, M. R. (1987). *Violent crime by strangers and nonstrangers* (BJS Publication No. NCJ-103702). Washington, DC: U.S. Government Printing Office.

Tithecott, R. (1997). *Of men and monsters: Jeffrey Dahmer and the construction of the serial killer.* Madison, WI: University of Wisconsin Press.

Tjaden, P., & Thoennes, N. (1998). *Prevalence, incidence, and consequences of violence against women: Findings from the National Violence Against Women Survey* (National Institute of Justice and Centers for Disease Control and Prevention Research in Brief Report, No. NCJ 172837). Washington, DC: U.S. Government Printing Office.

Toch, H. (1992). *Violent men: An inquiry into the psychology of violence* (rev. ed.). Washington, DC: American Psychological Association.

Tomlin, C. D. (1990). *Geographic information systems and cartographic modeling.* Englewood Cliffs, NJ: Prentice Hall.

Topalin, J. (1992). *The journey to rape.* Unpublished master's thesis, University of Surrey, England.

Toufexis, A. (1994, April 4). Dances with werewolves. *Time Magazine,* pp. 50-52.

Trasler, G. (1993). Conscience, opportunity, rational choice, and crime. In R. V. Clarke & M. Felson (Eds.), *Routine activity and rational choice* (pp. 305-322). New Brunswick, NJ: Transaction.

Treen, J. (1993, January 25). The killing field. *People,* pp. 74-80.

Turco, R. N. (1990). Psychological profiling. *International Journal of Offender Therapy and Comparative Criminology, 34,* 147-154.

Turner, S. (1969). Delinquency and distance. In M. E. Wolfgang & T. Sellin (Eds.), *Delinquency: Selected studies* (11-26). New York: John C. Wiley.

Turque, B., & Hammill, R. (1989, December). A string of sixty murders. *Newsweek,* p. 64.

Turvey, B. E. (1999). *Criminal profiling: An introduction to behavioral evidence analysis.* San Diego: Academic Press.

Tversky, A., & Kahneman, D. (1981). The framing of decisions and the psychology of choice. *Science, 211,* 453-458.

Tweedie, N. (1995, August 11). DNA computer nabs burglar. *The London Evening Standard,* pp. 1-2.

Uchida, C. D. (1990). NIJ sponsors system to speed information to police on drug hotspots. *NIJ Reports,* no. 221, 8-9, 36.

Underwood, P. (1987). *Jack the Ripper: One hundred years of mystery.* London: Blandford Press.

Unwin, D. (1981). *Introductory spatial analysis.* London: Methuen.

Upton, G. J. G., & Fingleton, B. (1989). *Spatial data analysis by example: Vol. 2. Categorical and directional data.* Chichester, NY: Wiley.

U.S. Department of Justice. (1988a). *The criminal justice microcomputer guide and software catalogue* (BJS Publication No. NCJ-112178). Washington, DC: U.S. Government Printing Office.

U.S. Department of Justice. (1988b). *Report to the nation on crime and justice* (2nd ed.) (BJS Publication No. NCJ-105506). Washington, DC: U.S. Government Printing Office.

U.S. Department of Justice. (1990a). *Annual report 1990* (National Center for the Analysis of Violent Crime). Washington, DC: U.S. Government Printing Office.

U.S. Department of Justice. (1990b). *Criminal investigative analysis; Sexual homicide* (National Center for the Analysis of Violent Crime). Washington, DC: U.S. Government Printing Office.

U.S. Department of Justice. (1991a). *Serial/Mass murder* (National Institute of Justice topical search TS 011664). Washington, DC: U.S. Government Printing Office.

U.S. Department of Justice. (1991b). *Serial Murder Investigation System Conference* (Federal Bureau of Investigation). Washington, DC: U.S. Government Printing Office.

U.S. Department of Justice. (1991c). *Violent crime in the United States* (BJS Publication No. NCJ-127855). Washington, DC: U.S. Government Printing Office.

U.S. Department of Justice. (1992). *Ted Bundy Multiagency Investigative Team report 1992* (Federal Bureau of Investigation). Washington, DC: U.S. Government Printing Office.

U.S. Department of Justice. (1994a, October 3). *Violent Crime Control and Law Enforcement Act of 1994* (Fact Sheet No. NCJ-FS000067). Washington, DC: U.S. Government Printing Office.

U.S. Department of Justice. (1994b). *Violent crime* (BJS Publication No. NCJ-147486). Washington, DC: U.S. Government Printing Office.

U.S. Department of Justice. (1995). *Certification of DNA and other forensic specialists* (National Institute of Justice Update). Washington, DC: U.S. Government Printing Office.

U.S. Department of Justice. (1996a). *Child Abduction and Serial Killer Unit; Morgan P. Hardiman Task Force on Missing and Exploited Children* (Federal Bureau of Investigation). Washington, DC: U.S. Government Printing Office.

U.S. Department of Justice. (1996b). *Profiling and Behavioral Assessment Unit* (Federal Bureau of Investigation). Washington, DC: U.S. Government Printing Office.

U.S. Department of Justice. (1996c). *Regional seminar series on Developing and Implementing Antistalking Codes* (BJA Monograph No. NCJ-156836). Washington, DC: U.S. Government Printing Office.

U.S. Department of Justice. (1996d). *Suggested guidelines for establishing evidence response teams* (Federal Bureau of Investigation). Washington, DC: U.S. Government Printing Office.

U.S. Department of Justice. (1998). *Regional Information Sharing Systems Program* (BJA Fact Sheet No. FS000037). Washington, DC: U.S. Government Printing Office.

U.S. Department of Justice. (1999). *Proceedings of the Homicide Research Working Group Meetings, 1997 and 1998.* (NIJ Publication No. NCJ-175709). Washington, DC: U.S. Government Printing Office.

U.S.S. Iowa tragedy: An investigative failure. (1990). Report of the Investigations Subcommittee and the Defense Policy Panel of the Committee on Armed Services, House of Representative. 101st Congress, 2nd Session.

van Hoffmann, E. (1990). *A venom in the blood.* New York: Kensington.

van Koppen, P. J., & de Keijser, J. W. (1997). Desisting distance decay: On the aggregation of individual crime trips. *Criminology, 35,* 505-515.

Van Soomeren, P. (1989). The physical urban environment and reduction of urban insecurity: A general introduction. *Local Strategies for the Reduction of Urban Insecurity in Europe* (Urban Renaissance in Europe Study Series, vol. 35, pp. 219-232). Strasbourg: Council of Europe.

Van Zandt, C. R., & Ether, S. E. (1994, April). The real "Silence of the Lambs." *The Police Chief,* pp. 45-52.

Vancouver local areas 1981-1991. (1994). Vancouver: City of Vancouver Planning Department.

Verma, A. (1997). Construction of offender profiles using fuzzy logic. *Policing: An International Journal of Police Strategies and Management, 20,* 408-418.

Vetter, H. (1990). Dissociation, psychopathy, and the serial murderer. In S. A. Egger (Ed.), *Serial murder: An elusive phenomenon* (pp. 73-92). New York: Praeger.

Victim can sue police. (1991). *Blue Line Magazine, 3*(1), 14.

Victims of Violence Society. (1990). *Goodbye Charlie* (Victims of Violence Report, July). Ottawa: Author.

Vogt, W. P. (1993). *Dictionary of statistics and methodology: A nontechnical guide for the social sciences.* Newbury Park, CA: Sage.

Vold, G. B., & Bernard, T. J. (1986). *Theoretical criminology.* New York: Oxford University Press.

Volpe, F. (1994). The Honeymoon Killers. *Gauntlet, 1,* 171-172.

Wagner, D. G. (1984). *The growth of sociological theories.* Beverly Hills: Sage.

Walker, J. T. (1991, March). *Hot spots or concentric rings: Analysis of human ecology in Little Rock, Arkansas.* Paper presented at the conference of the Academy of Criminal Justice Sciences, Nashville, TN.

Wallace, B. (1989, December 18). The making of a mass killer. *Maclean's,* p. 22.

Waller, I., & Okihiro, N. (1978). *Burglary: The victim and the public.* Toronto: University of Toronto Press.

Walmsley, D. J., & Lewis, G. J. (1984). *Human geography: Behavioural approaches.* London: Longman.

Walsh, D. (1986). Victim selection procedures among economic criminals: The rational choice perspective. In D. B. Cornish & R. V. Clarke (Eds.), *The reasoning criminal: Rational choice perspectives on offending* (pp. 39-52). New York: Springer-Verlag.

Walsh, T. (1994, April). Software bits & bytes. *Law Enforcement Technology,* pp. 66-67.

Wambaugh, J. (1989). *The blooding.* New York: Bantam Books.

Ward, J., & Malinowski, S. (1992). Crime database aids multi-agency investigations. *Blue Line Magazine, 4*(3), 26-27.

Warr, M. (1988). Rape, burglary, and opportunity. *Journal of Quantitative Criminology, 4,* 275-288.

Warren, J. I., Reboussin, R., & Hazelwood, R. R. (1991, November). *Geographical dispersion of serial rapes.* Paper presented at the meeting of the American Society of Criminology, San Francisco, CA.

Warren, J. I., Reboussin, R., & Hazelwood, R. R. (1995). *The geographic and temporal sequencing of serial rape* (Federal Bureau of Investigation). Washington, DC: U.S. Government Printing Office.

Warren, J. I., Reboussin, R., Hazelwood, R. R., Cummings, A., Gibbs, N., & Trumbetta, S. (1996, July). *Crime scene and distance correlates of serial rape.* Paper presented at the Third International Conference on Forensic Statistics, Edinburgh, UK.

Warren, J. I., Reboussin, R., Hazelwood, R. R., Cummings, A., Gibbs, N., & Trumbetta, S. (1998). Crime scene and distance correlates of serial rape. *Journal of Quantitative Criminology, 14,* 35-59.

Warren, J. I., Reboussin, R., Hazelwood, R. R., & Wright, J. (1991). Prediction of rape type and violence from verbal, physical, and sexual scales. *Journal of Interpersonal Violence, 6,* 1-23.

Warren, R. L. (1972). *The community in America* (2nd ed.). Chicago: Rand McNally.

Waters, J. K. (1998). The geography of crime. *Mercator's World, 3*(5), 46-51.

Waters, N. (1995a, January). GIS and criminal shadows. *GIS World,* p. 72.

Waters, N. (1995b). The most beautiful formulae in GIS. In J. K. Berry (Ed.), *Spatial reasoning for effective GIS.* (pp. 175-192). Fort Collins, CO: GIS World Books.

Webber, M. J. (1984). *Industrial location.* Sage university paper series on scientific geography, 3. Beverly Hills: Sage.

Weedn, V. W., & Hicks, J. W. (1998). *The unrealized potential of DNA testing* (NIJ Publication No. NCJ-170596). Washington, DC: U.S. Government Printing Office.

Weisburd, D. A., & McEwen, J. T. (Eds.). (1997). *Crime mapping and crime prevention: Crime prevention studies, Vol. 8.* Monsey, NY: Criminal Justice Press.

Welsh, R. M. (1994). *Sex, vice & morality: Tales from a detective's notebook.* Vancouver: Author.

Wendelken, S. (1995a, January). GIS enhances preventive law enforcement. *GIS World,* pp. 58-61.

Wendelken, S. (1995b, January). Vendors capitalize on GIS in policing. *GIS World,* p. 61.

Werner, C. (1985). *Spatial transportation modeling.* Sage university paper series on scientific geography, 5. Beverly Hills: Sage.

Westfall, B. (1992). Westley Allan Dodd. *Police, 16*(7), 58-60, 84.

Whaley, S. (1994). Gerald Gallego. *Police, 18*(3), 63-66.

White, R. C. (1932). The relation of felonies to environmental factors in Indianapolis. *Social Forces, 10,* 498-509.

Widom, C. S. (Ed.). (1984). *Sex roles and psychopathology.* New York: Plenum Press.

Widom, C. S. (1984). Sex roles, criminality, and psychopathology. In C. S. Widom (Ed.), *Sex roles and psychopathology* (pp. 183-217). New York: Plenum Press.

Widom, C. S. (1992). *The cycle of violence* (BJS Publication No. NCJ-136607). Washington, DC: U.S. Government Printing Office.

Widom, C. S. (1995). *Victims of childhood sexual abuse – Later criminal consequences* (BJS Publication No. NCJ-151525). Washington, DC: U.S. Government Printing Office.

Wiggers, D. (1990, February 8). Hunting humans. *York University Excalibur,* pp. 10-12.

Wilcox, S. (1973). *The geography of robbery* [The prevention and control of robbery, vol. 3]. Davis, CA: The Center of Administration of Criminal Justice, University of California at Davis.

Williams, E. (1967). *Beyond belief.* London: World Books.

Williams, F. P., & McShane, M. D. (1988). *Criminological theory.* Englewood Cliffs, NJ: Prentice Hall.

Williams, S. (1996). *Invisible darkness: The strange case of Paul Bernardo and Karla Homolka.* Toronto: Little, Brown and Company.

Wilson, A. (Ed.). (1983). *The portable Dickens.* New York: Viking Penguin.

Wilson, A. G. (1967). A statistical theory of spatial distribution models. *Transportation Research, 1,* 253-269.

Wilson, A. V. (Ed.). (1993). *Homicide: The victim/offender connection.* Cincinnati: Anderson.

Wilson, C. (1960). My search for Jack the Ripper. In R. G. Jones (Ed.), *Unsolved! Classic true murder cases* (pp. 13-32). New York: Peter Bedrick Books.

Wilson, C. (1984). *A criminal history of mankind.* London: Grafton Books.

Wilson, C. (1988). *The mammoth book of true crime.* London: Robinson.

Wilson, C., & Odell, R. (1987). *Jack the Ripper: Summing up and verdict.* London: Corgi Books.

Wilson, C., & Pitman, P. (1961). *Encyclopaedia of murder.* London: Pan Books.

Wilson, C., & Seaman, D. (1989). *Encyclopaedia of modern murder.* London: Pan Books.

Wilson, C., & Seaman, D. (1990). *The serial killers: A study in the psychology of violence.* London: W. H. Allen.

Wilson, C., & Wilson, D. (1995). *A plague of murder: The rise and rise of serial killing in the modern age.* London: Robinson Publishing.

Wilson, J. B. (1993). *Criminal investigations: A behavioral approach.* Prospect Heights, IL: Waveland Press.

Wilson, J. Q., & Herrnstein, R. J. (1985). *Crime and human nature.* New York: Simon & Schuster.

Wilson, M., & Daly, M. (1993). A lifespan perspective on homicidal violence: The young male syndrome. In C. R. Block & R. L. Block (Eds.), *Questions and answers in lethal and non-lethal violence: Proceedings of the Second Annual Workshop of the Homicide Research Working Group* (NIJ Publication No. NCJ-147480) (pp. 29-38). Washington, DC: U.S. Government Printing Office.

Wilson, P., Lincoln, R., & Kocsis, R. N. (1997). Validity, utility and ethics of profiling for serial violent and sexual offenders. *Psychiatry, Psychology and Law, 4,* 1-11.

Wilson, P., & Soothill, K. (1996, January). Psychological profiling: Red, green or amber? *The Police Journal,* pp. 12-20.

Wilson, T. F., & Woodward, P. L.. (1987). *Automated fingerprint identification systems: Technology and policy issues* (BJS Publication No. NCJ-104342). Washington, DC: U.S. Government Printing Office.

Winn, D. (Ed.). (1977). *Murder ink.* New York: Workman.

Winn, S., & Merrill, D. (1979). *Ted Bundy: The killer next door.* New York: Bantam Books.

Wolf, M. J., & Mader, K. (1986). *Fallen angels.* New York: Ballantine Books.

Wolfe, R. I. (1963). *Transportation and politics.* Princeton: D. Van Norstrand.

Wolff, L., & Geissel, D. (1993). *Street prostitution in Canada* (Juristat Service Bulletin vol. 13, no. 4). Ottawa: Statistics Canada.

Wolfgang, M. E. (1958). *Patterns of criminal homicide.* Philadelphia: University of Pennsylvania Press.

Wolfgang, M. E., & Ferracuti, F. (1967). *The subculture of violence.* London: Tavistock.

Wolfgang, M. E., & Sellin, T. (Eds.). (1969). *Delinquency: Selected studies.* New York: John C. Wiley.

Wolfgang, M. E., & Weiner, N. A. (Eds.). (1982). *Criminal violence.* Beverly Hills: Sage.

Wood, D. (1991, February). *An ecological analysis of violent and other crime in the four cultural regions of western North America.* Paper presented at the conference of the Western Society of Criminology, Berkeley, CA.

Wood, D. R. (1998). Geospatial analysis of rural burglaries. In N. G. La Vigne & J. Wartell (Eds.), *Crime mapping case studies: Successes in the field* (pp. 117-121). Washington, DC: Police Executive Research Forum.

Wood, P. B., Gove, W. R., Wilson, J. A., & Cochran, J. K. (1997). Nonsocial reinforcement and habitual criminal conduct: An extension of learning theory. *Criminology, 35,* 335-366.

Wood, W. P. (1994). *The bone garden.* New York: Simon & Schuster.

Woodhull, T. (1992). Lawrence Bittaker. *Police, 16*(11), 51-54.

Worthington, P. (1993, July). The journalist and the killer. *Saturday Night,* pp. 30-35, 50-55.

Wright, C., & Gary, G. (1995, February-March). Paul Kenneth Keller: A profile comparison with typical serial arsonists. *International Association of Arson Investigators Newsletter,* pp. 10-19.

Wright, R. T., & Decker, S. H. (1996). Choosing the target. In P. F. Cromwell (Ed.), *In their own words: Criminals on crime* (pp. 34-46). Los Angeles: Roxbury Publishing.

Wyre, R., & Tate, T. (1995). *The murder of childhood.* London: Penguin Books.

Yager, R. R., & Zadeh, L. A. (1994). *Fuzzy sets, neural networks, and soft computing.* New York: Van Nostrand Reinhold.

Yuille, J. C. (Ed.). (1986). *Police selection and training: The role of psychology.* Dordrecht: Martinus Nijhoff.

Zagare, F. C. (1984). *Game theory: Concepts and applications.* Sage university paper series on quantitative applications in the social sciences, 41. Beverly Hills: Sage.

Zahm, D., & Cromwell, P. F. (Eds.). (1993). *Proceedings of the International Seminar on Environmental Criminology and Crime Analysis.* Coral Gables, FL: Florida Criminal Justice Executive Institute.

Zip code finder. (1993). New York: Rand McNally.

Zipf, G. (1950). *The principle of least effort.* Reading, MA: Addison Wesley.

Zytaruk, T. (1994, March 12). Fifth woman falls victim to tag team rapists. *Surrey/North Delta Now,* p. A3.

Index

A

Abbotsford Killer, 215
Abduction, 138
Abduction murders, children, 31, 32, 61, *see also* Murder; Serial murder
Abuse, 21, 41
Accessibility, victims, 150
Accomplices, 46, *see also* Arson
ACIU, *see* Analytical Criminal Intelligence Unit
ACPO, *see* Association of Chief Police Officers
Activity space, 44, 90–91, 120, 195
AFIS, *see* Automated fingerprint identification system
African Americans, 9–10, 101
Age, 101
Aggression, 40
Aggressiveness, 22–23
Akratic behaviour, 115
Alcohol, 22, 41, 48, 146
Ambusher, 140, 141, 144, 165
American Psychological Association (APA), 75–76
Analytical Criminal Intelligence Unit (ACIU), 81
Anchor point
    behavioural geography, 91
    geographic profiling, 215
    offender residence prediction, 200, 209
    predator patterns, 161, 167
Anger–excitation, 8, 38, 39, 43
Anger–retaliation motive, 38, 39
Animal movement, 131–132
Antisocial personality disorder (APSD), 19, 21, 48, 167
APA, *see* American Psychological Association
Applications, criminal profiling, 73–74

Apprehension, offender, 148, 211
APSD, *see* Antisocial personality disorder
ARPI, *see* Arson Risk Prediction index
Arson, 127, 132–133, 196
    typology, 45
Arson Risk Prediction Index (ARPI), 187
Artificial neural networks, 187
Association of Chief Police Officers (ACPO), 80
Atlanta Child Murders, 116–117, 132, 191, 230
Atlanta Olympics pipe bombing, 84
Attack, 29, 42, 138, 148
Attention motive, 46
Attention space, 146
Attractors, crime, 125
Attribution error, 68
Aura phase, 17
Automated fingerprint identification system (AFIS), 55
Automated recognition systems, 56
Availability, victim, 28, 29
Awareness space, 90–91, 119

B

Babb, Adrian, 194, *see also* Tower Block Rapist
Background noise, 58, *see also* Noise
Backtracking, 180
Bank robbery, 180, 189–190
Bayesian belief networks, 70
Bayesian probability methods, 83–84
Behavioural geography
    awareness and activity spaces, 90–91
    centrography, 91–94
    mental maps, 89–90